Fresh Verdicts
on Joan of Arc

THE NEW MIDDLE AGES
VOLUME 2
GARLAND REFERENCE LIBRARY OF THE HUMANITIES
VOLUME 1976

THE NEW MIDDLE AGES

BONNIE WHEELER
Series Editor

The New Middle Ages presents transdisciplinary studies of medieval cultures, with particular emphasis on women's history and feminist and gender analyses. The series includes both scholarly monographs and essay collections.

Clothes Make the Man: Female Cross Dressing in Medieval Europe
by Valerie R. Hotchkiss

Medieval Mothering
edited by John Carmi Parsons and Bonnie Wheeler

Fresh Verdicts on Joan of Arc
edited by Bonnie Wheeler and Charles T. Wood

Fresh Verdicts on Joan of Arc

EDITED BY
BONNIE WHEELER
CHARLES T. WOOD

GARLAND PUBLISHING, INC.
NEW YORK AND LONDON
1996

First paperback edition published in 1999 by
Garland Publishing Inc.
A Member of the Taylor & Francis Group
19 Union Square West
New York, NY 10003

10   9   8   7   6   5   4   3   2   1

Library of Congress Cataloging-in-Publication Data

Wheeler, Bonnie and Charles T. Wood.
     Fresh verdicts on Joan of Arc / Edited by Bonnie Wheeler and Charles T.
Wood.
        p.   cm. — (The new Middle Ages ; vol. 2. Garland reference li-
brary of the humanities ; vol. 1976)
     Includes bibliographical references.
     ISBN 0-8153-3664-0/paperback {alk. paper}
     1.   Joan, of Arc, Saint, 1412-1431. 2.   Joan, of Arc, Saint, 1412-
1431—Military leadership. 3. Christian women saints—France—Biography. 4. France—History—Charles VII, 1422-1461. I. Wheeler, Bonnie.
II. Wood, Charles T. III. Series: Garland reference library of the
humanities ; vol. 1976. IV. Series: Garland reference library of the humanities. The new Middle Ages ; vol 2.
DC103.F75   1996
944'.026'092—dc20   95-53140
                                                                             CIP

Printed on acid-free, 250-year-life paper
Manufactured in the United States of America

For

Régine Pernoud

CONTENTS

PREFACE

In 1970, when I first touched on the topic of this book, I could only wonder at the challenges involved. "No one can hope to explain Joan of Arc," I wrote, "and possibly we should not try: in mystery lies the secret of her appeal."[1] A quarter century later, however, I would stress a different point, the extent to which that very mystery spurs new explorations and the kind of fresh verdicts to be found in the essays that follow. For in them readers will discover evidence explaining why, even after the passage of more than twenty years, reminiscing veterans of her military campaigns still found Joan to have been a remarkably gifted commander; why so many of her contemporaries or near-contemporaries, churchmen and poets alike, found it possible to accept the validity of her mission and voices; why modern politicians and artists both literary and cinematic have been so quick to adopt her as the symbolic vehicle for their own visions; and why, on the very eve of her twentieth-century canonization, Devil's Advocates were still worrying whether chance male glimpses of what the duke of Alençon had solemnly testified were her beautiful breasts should deny her all hope of formal sanctification. Indeed, one of the editors of the so-called "new Quicherat" will even make clear how more accurate manuscript transcriptions, minor though the changes often are, open the door to new insights.

Nevertheless, Régine Pernoud is undoubtedly correct in her concluding essay when she claims that, for all our new insights, the fundamentals of Joan's story remain remarkably unchanged. She is, after all, still the maid whose mission proved the salvation of her people, the maid whose love of chivalry ended the age of chivalry even as it ushered in a new age, the outcome of which is not yet known. If Mlle. Pernoud is right (and she has wrestled with Joan's story far longer than I), what that means, in turn, is that even though much of the mystery I saw in 1970 stays mysterious no longer, all of the wonder remains.

Charles T. Wood

1. Charles T. Wood, *The Age of Chivalry* (London, 1970), p. 150.

Jean-Auguste-Dominique Ingres, Joan of Arc at the Coronation of
Charles VII, *1854. Courtesy of The Musée du Louvre, Paris.*

JOAN OF ARC'S SWORD IN THE STONE

Soo in the grettest chirch of London—whether it were Powlis or not the Frensshe booke maketh no mencyon—alle the estates were longe or day in the chirche for to praye. And whan matyns and the first masse was done there was sene in the chircheyard ayenst the hyhe aulter a grete stone four square, lyke unto a marbel stone, and in myddes therof was lyke an anvylde of stele a foot on hyghe, and theryn stack a fayre swerd naked by the poynt, and letters there were wryten in gold about the swerd that saiden thus: "WHOSO PULLETH OUTE THIS SWERD OF THIS STONE AND ANYVLD IS RIGHTWYS KYNGE BORNE OF ALL EN[G]LOND."[1]

In early March of 1429, between the time that she was validated by her dauphin, later Charles VII, but before she started her battle march to Orleans, Joan of Arc sent a man, an unnamed armorer of Tours, to collect a sword that she said would be found buried below or behind the altar of the church of Sainte-Catherine-de-Fierbois. The sword was located immediately and brought to her swiftly. Almost exactly two years later, on February 27, 1431, the judges at her condemnation trial asked her how she knew there was a sword to be found there. She answered:

That sword was in the earth, rusted, bearing five engraved crosses; she knew that the sword was there by her voices and she had never before seen the man who went to look for the aforesaid sword and she wrote to the men of the church of that place asking if it might please them that she might have this sword and they sent it to her. That sword was not deeply buried in the earth and the men of the church, rubbing it on the spot, made the rust fall off.

Swords identify, authorize, and authenticate medieval warriors in fact and in legend. Roland's sword Durendal contained relics: St. Peter's tooth, St. Basil's blood, St. Denis's hair, and even a bit of the Virgin's cloth[2]: that sword was so crucial to Roland's Christian identity that the poet of the *Chanson de Roland* tells us the dying hero whacked it against a stone in a vain attempt to destroy it so that it would not fall into the hands of pagan scavengers. Charlemagne with his sword Joyeuse returned to wreak vengeance for Roland's death against the

Saracen Baligant, who had absorbed the strategic uses of identity-bearing swords from Charlemagne: "Par sun orgoill li ad un num truvet/Par la Carlun dunt il oït parler" ("In his perversity, he found a name for it:/After Charles's sword, which he has heard about").[3] In the *Poema de Mio Cid*, the hero Ruy Diaz, Mio Cid de Vivar, gained the famous swords Tizon and Colada as battle booty; he flattered his sons-in-law by including these swords in his daughters' dower, but the Heirs of Carrion proved themselves cowards unequal to the honor of their weapons. The young Arthur in Malory's late fifteenth-century version of the Arthurian story (quoted above) is legitimized by his capacity to remove the sword magically secured in the stone that appears in a London churchyard backing up to the high altar. This is only one of King Arthur's three notable swords, the most famous of which was his gift-sword Excalibur, whose scabbard magically protected its bearer.

Like the King Arthur and Cid of legends, Joan of Arc had several swords, each of which marked a particular aspect of her identity. First, she had a gift-sword from her early sponsor Robert de Baudricourt, received when she was on the road to Chinon to meet the dauphin. This was her craft-sword, identifying her as a warrior by profession. Later, she took a "good sword of war, made for giving and taking good blows,"[4] as a prize from a Burgundian, and she may have had at least one additional war sword. These are her prowess-swords, identifying her as champion. But for her contemporaries, the sword from Sainte-Catherine-de-Fierbois must have had special resonance, as it does for us, since it so neatly yokes Joan's spirituality and bellicosity.

Fierbois itself replicates that yoking of war and religion in another famous sword. When she passed through Fierbois on the final stage of her journey to Chinon, Joan may well have heard the famous story of Charles Martel's sword, which he left there in the chapel of Sainte-Catherine to commemorate his victory nearby over the Saracens in the autumn of 732. Is it more than happy coincidence that swords of these famous champions, each of whom exercised profound claims on the French imagination as saviors of the country's core identity and ideologies, were allegedly housed in one country chapel? Legend later identifies Joan's sword as that of Charles Martel. In *La Pucelle ou la France delivrée*, Jean Chapelain claims that the great Carolingian *chef de guerre* buried the sword behind the altar so that it would be found in time of need by another liberator of his people. Neither Joan nor her supporters allege that her sword from Sainte-Catherine-de-Fierbois was the sword of Charles Martel, but all were fully aware of the connection of Fierbois with another renowned champion, Maréchal Boucicaut, that model of Christian chivalry at the end of the age of chivalry, who became a benefactor of the chapel when it was rediscovered in the late fourteenth century.

The sword of Roland contained relics, but it was not a mystic object. The swords of Charlemagne and Mio Cid conveyed the quality of these champions' superb military prowess, but not their religiosity. Remarkably, it is King Arthur's mythic sword in the stone that most closely approximates Joan's actual sword from Fierbois: both swords are connected with a church, even an altar, and each is mysterious in origin, mysterious in appearance. These liminal objects map the juncture of the material and spiritual worlds. The sword of Sainte-Catherine-de-Fierbois authorizes Joan's mission as French captain and champion just as the sword of the London churchyard authenticates Arthur's mission as king. The London townspeople, according to Malory, accepted the authority of the sword in the stone (whether its appearance was due to miracle, magic, or a mirage created by Merlin), and after a year of patient waiting for the nobility to agree, they demanded finally that Arthur be named king. No such patient procrastination marked the people of Fierbois, who, according to Joan and the trial witnesses, validated Joan's mission when they sent her not only the sword but a precious sheath to hold it: "For their part, the men of the church of Saint-Catherine-de-Fierbois gave her a sheath, as did the people of Tours; she had therefore two sheaths, one of vermeil velvet and the other of cloth-of-gold, and she herself had one made in heavy leather, very strong."[5] Joan's basic disposition is practical; for her, strong leather replaces richly decorated velvet and lavish gold. Joan's basic disposition is seen also in the paratactic simplicity of her recorded language ("That sword was in the earth, rusted, bearing five engraved crosses; she knew that the sword was there by her voices"); for her, saintly voices lead to her material sword as cause leads to effect: this is logical, practical, and unassailable.

The trial judges poke continually into Joan's body, clothing, and possessions. They investigate and reinvestigate her body to see if a nonvirgin, therefore necessarily an impure liar or heretic, can be found lurking there. They are endlessly curious about her things, including her personal war equipage, especially her design for her standard and banner, whose symbolism the judges find potentially subversive. They require full details about her suit of armor, and, of course, no subject fascinates or repels them more than her choice of wardrobe and her cross dressing. The trial records show the interrogation spiraling around these matters, obsessively returning to them in attempts to locate and demonstrate Joan's purported deviance. It is therefore especially notable that these judges query Joan about acquiring the remarkable sword from Sainte-Catherine-de-Fierbois only once.

Why do they not pursue the story of Joan's vision-sword? Why do they not look more deeply into the potential sacrilege of disturbing the sacred space of the church and altar of Sainte-Catherine-de-Fierbois? Why do they not argue that only witchcraft could have caused the sword's encrusted rust to fall off with one mere rubbing? Why do they not inquire more deeply into the sword's current whereabouts? Why do they not probe more deeply its connection to Fierbois, to the gift-sword of Charles Martel?

The answer, I think, is that judges intent on condemning Joan could gain nothing by this exchange. The judges had plotted a line of questioning—from the rituals of the fairy tree in Domrémy to the voices to the sword and then to the standard; clearly, they were trying to provoke Joan into some admission or slip that would indicate witchcraft practices. Instead Joan stated simply that she knew of the sword's existence only "per voces."[6] Since the judges shared with Joan a belief in the liminal world whose barriers heavenly saints could transgress, the judges could not in theory deny the possibility that Joan's "voices" were those of God's saints. Furthermore, the judges could not suggest that the sword itself was polluted without suggesting that it had polluted the very orthodoxy of the church in which it was found. Joan especially loved that sword because it was found in the church dedicated to St. Catherine, the saint who was one of her "voices": "Item dicit quod bene diligebat illum ensem, quia repertus erat in ecclesia beatæ Katharinæ quam bene diligebat."[7] The *Journal du Siège d'Orléans* provides a different version of the story, a variation in which Charles VII interrogates Joan about the sword.

Le roy luy voulant doner une belle espée, elle luy pria qu'il luy pleust luy en envoyer querir une, qui avoit en la lemelle (2) cinq croix emprez la croisée, et estoit à Saincte-Katerine du Fierboys. Dont le roy fut fort esmerveillé, et luy demanda s'elle l'avoit oncques veue. A quoy elle respondit que non; mais toutesfois savoit qu'elle y estoit. Le roy y envoya, et fut trouvée celle espée avecques autres, qui là avoient esté données le temps passé, et fut aportée au roy, qui la fesit habiller et garnir honnestement.

[The king wishing to give her a fine sword, she asked that it might please him to send for one which had five crosses close to the hilt on the blade, and was at Sainte-Catherine-de-Fierbois. Whereat the king marvelled greatly amazed, and asked her if she had ever seen it, to which she answered no: but nonetheless she knew that it was there. The king sent there, and that sword was found, along with others which had been given there in time past. And it was brought to the king, who had it honorably dressed and furnished.][8]

There are additional early versions of the story, such as that told by Greffier de la Rochelle, in which Joan asked the dauphin to send to Fierbois for the ancient sword from a coffer in front of the high altar. Such variations enhance the sword's spiritual and cultural associations.

Had Joan's trial judges pursued their original queries about the sword, they might well have provoked or enhanced associations dangerous to their own cause. If they had pressed her any harder on this point, they ran the risk of converting that identity-sword into a sign far more potent than its physical self: from being a blade with antiquarian interest, it might easily be turned into a talisman of the delivery of Christian France, a "relic" of Charles Martel and of the Hundred Years War, or an object like the Holy Grail, with mystic as well as historic associations.

Readers of this story are always impressed by the flat factuality with which Joan speaks of her sword. She is accustomed to receiving information through her voices, just as she is accustomed to bearing arms. She therefore evinces no surprise about the discovery of the sword: it was where it should have been. What delights her and spurs her to confide for a moment in her judges is not any connection the sword might bear to a grand past, but the connection of the sword to St. Catherine and the promise of an everlasting future. In the face of that innocent serenity, the judges fell silent.

The studies in this volume touch among other things on that blending of bellicosity and spirituality in Joan of Arc, on her keen, compelling simplicity of speech, on her mythic reception. The essays are arranged chronologically from investigations of Joan in her own time to Joan in our time. They interrogate the accuracy of Johannine texts and provide fresh views of such especially contested sites and issues as Joan's body, her voices, her tranvestism. Though the essays represent widely differing views of Joan and her mission, they produce a collective image of a Joan whose identity—her understanding of her own past—is transformed by her verbal interactions with her judges as much as by her experience of childhood, war, prison, or a faithless dauphin. These studies suggest that the volatile perception of Joan by her contemporaries is matched by the volatile and hyper-charged reception of Joan in subsequent centuries. Joan of Arc remains raw in our cultural imaginations.

No historian in our century has done more to return us to the Joan of documentary history than has Régine Pernoud, *chartiste,* to whom we dedicate this volume. Her Joan of Arc glows through the documents then and analysis now as a figure of resistance and a resistant figure: the "mystic, wonderful" Joan who proves that self-confidence and independent judgment are qualities so rare and suspect, especially in women, that they are sure to be punished, sometimes by death.

Bonnie Wheeler

1. Thomas Malory, *Works,* ed. Eugène Vinaver (Oxford, 1971), p. 7.

2. Pierre Tisset, ed. with Yvonne Lanhers, *Procès de condamnation de Jeanne d'Arc,* 3 vols. (Paris, 1960–71), vol. 2, p. 76.

3. *La Chanson de Roland,* ed. Gerard Brault (University Park, 1984), ll. 2345–48.

4. Ibid., ll. 3144–45.

5. Tisset, 2.76.

6. Jules Quicherat, ed., *Procès de condamnation et de réhabilitation de Jeanne d'Arc dite La Pucelle,* 5 vols. (Paris, 1841–49), vol. 1, p. 76.

7. Ibid., 1.77.

8. Ibid., 4.129. My translation.

Fresh Verdicts
on Joan of Arc

A WOMAN AS LEADER OF MEN:
JOAN OF ARC'S MILITARY CAREER

Kelly DeVries

> *Joan did not offer her soldiers terrestrial possessions; she offered them religious possibilities, even salvation. Though she was radically different from other contemporary military leaders, her troops followed her with a loyalty unsurpassed by any other late-medieval captain.*

No person of the Middle Ages, male or female, has been the subject of more study than Joan of Arc. She has been portrayed as saint, heretic, religious zealot, seer, demented teenager, protofeminist, aristocratic wanna-be, savior of France, "turner-of-the-tide" of the Hundred Years War, and even Marxist liberator.[1] And yet in all of these analyses, few words have been devoted to her capabilities as a military leader, despite this being the central reason for her fame or infamy.[2]

Born in Domrémy, in Lorraine, on January 6, 1412, of comparatively wealthy peasant parents, she led a normal life until the fall of 1428, when she approached the castle of Vaucouleurs with her now famous tale of having heard heavenly voices. Their message, spoken to her in the wind and in the village church bells since childhood, was that she was to seek out the dauphin of France, Charles, and that he would give her an army with which she would deliver France from its English occupiers. Why Robert de Baudricourt, the castellan at Vaucouleurs, did not turn her away or place her in the "insanity wing" of the local hospital is one of the great mysteries of history, surpassed only by the mystery of why later at Chinon the dauphin, having been introduced to Joan by Robert de Baudricourt, actually provided her with the desired army.[3]

It is not my purpose here to dwell on these questions. There is another less frequently asked question that is more crucial to Joan's military accomplishments in the Hundred Years War than either her success with the castellan of Vaucouleurs or with the dauphin: why did the soldiers of France follow Joan? No troops of the Hundred Years War had ever followed a woman into battle, for whatever reason, and those few occasions in earlier medieval history of women leading soldiers were not well known, were thought to be mythological, or were, at best, a distant historical memory.[4] Often, too, the rumor of a woman leading an opposing army had been used by leaders to incite their troops against the obvious heresy, sorcery and immorality of their opponents. Indeed, in this instance it was so used by the English army: the anonymous bourgeois diarist of Paris writes that one English soldier referred to Joan as a "bloody tart."[5] And Joan's page, Louis de Coutes, recalled at the retrial of his mistress that as Joan addressed the English defenders of Orleans, one opposing soldier, identified as the Bastard of Granville, asked Joan "whether she expected them to surrender to a woman" or to her soldiers, who were, in his words, "unbelieving pimps."[6]

Such incidents, and many more like them, did not, however, deter the French soldiers from following Joan. Why? If one locates the military history of Joan of Arc amid the history of other military leaders during the Middle Ages, one is struck by the absence of military qualities shared by her and the noble generals. Instead, one notes Joan's greater similarity to the leaders of the Free Companies, those mercenary captains who were then quite numerous. One finds such men as John Hawkwood, Robert Knolles, Albergio da Barbiano, Werner of Urslingen, Albert Sterz, Ettore Manfredi, John Fastolf, Conrad of Landau, Jacques de Lalaing, Castruccio Castracane, Hannekin Bongarten, Bertrand de la Salle, and Ambrogio Visconti leading armies of mercenaries. Skilled warriors fought loyally and often successfully for these captains, who rewarded their services with booty and other payments. Finally, all these captains were well remembered, even made into myths, by their soldiers long after their death.[7]

Joan fulfilled the first and third parts of this description; her warriors seemed to have been the best, most skilled soldiers of France, and they rewarded her with frequent victories, at least in comparison with victories achieved by the French army before her arrival. These troops, too, fondly remembered her and her martial talents long after her death. This latter point refers directly to Joan's rehabilitation trials of the 1450s and the testimony of so many of her military colleagues there. Most modern authors have discounted these testimonies of events in Joan's life owing to the distance of time and to the fact that France had by the 1450s almost completely driven the English from their lands. This study does not seek to describe what happened to Joan *historically* but only why soldiers followed her—in other words, what emotions they felt that tied them to her leadership—thus the testimony of these recollections, whether or not the events to which they testify occurred, provides a basic source of crucial information about responses to Joan in her own time.

What of the second part of the description of a late-medieval mercenary captain? What did Joan offer her troops when, despite the Bourgeois of Paris's belief to the contrary, she refused to allow them to loot or pillage captured lands or towns?[8] Joan did not offer her troops terrestrial possessions; she offered them religious possessions, in particular salvation. And in the fifteenth century, in an age of flourishing popular religion, personal devotion, mysticism, and adherence to several living saints, especially to *mulieres sanctae*, Joan's gift to her troops was sufficient to entice them to follow her with a loyalty unknown to any French noble leader of the time, or even to the dauphin himself.[9]

Before establishing this thesis, let me outline Joan's military career.[10] After Joan approached the dauphin in the spring of 1429, and passed examinations of her virginity by the queen and other ladies in the court and of her "divine mission" by court officials, Charles gave her some troops and assigned her to the army then attempting, without much success, to relieve the English siege of Orleans. Joan joined this army in April 1429. It was a demoralized force, led by Count Dunois, the Bastard of Orleans, who had led his troops only two weeks before to an embarrassing defeat at the battle of the Herrings. Dunois was reluctant to attack the English in their well-fortified siegeworks; instead, he wanted to retreat from Orleans, leaving it to the English. Joan would have none of this, for her voices had told her that a victory at Orleans must precede the crowning of the dauphin. A new strategy was undertaken, with the French attacking several of the forts surrounding the town that were held by the besiegers. Finally, on May 6, Joan herself led her soldiers against the best-fortified and best-armed fortress held by the English, the Tourelles, which guarded the bridge and main gate leading into the town. Despite a formidable English defending force and an unusually large number of gunpowder weapons guarding this boulevard, Joan prevailed, with little loss of life. With the fall of Tourelles, the siege was raised. The first dictate of Joan's voices had been accomplished.

From Orleans, Joan's troops moved against the towns of Jargeau, Meung, and Beaugency, all of which stood in the way of a coronation at Reims and all of which she took with relative ease. The English were not accustomed to such defeats, and their army, led by the capable captains John Fastolf and John Lord Talbot, was determined not to let this trend continue. They decided to face the French in open battle, outside of the town of Patay. On June 17, 1429, this battle was fought, and the French again were victorious; Joan again was present.[11] This defeat was as embarrassing to the English as the prior defeat of the battle of Herrings was to the French; Talbot was captured, and Fastolf, believing it unsafe to go against the French with his depleted force, retreated to the safety of Paris's walls. On July 17, 1429, the dauphin was crowned King Charles VII of France at Reims. Joan was by his side, accomplishing the second charge of her voices.

Joan's mission was technically over, but Paris was still in enemy hands, and Joan's voices now added a new charge to her duties: she must recapture the French capital, at that time under the control of a sizable English army, led by John, duke of Bedford. Before the year was out, and after fending off a few relatively minor and bloodless skirmishes with Bedford's force, Joan attacked the Parisian suburb of St. Denis. Here, she met her first defeat, for she was unable to capture St. Denis and was wounded in the leg with a crossbow bolt. But she returned the next spring, attacking north of Paris at the towns of Senlis and Melun.

Once more, she met with less success than she wished, for these towns did not fall; but her persistence was enough to irritate the duke of Bedford and to drag Philip the Good, duke of Burgundy, into the fray. In April 1430, the Burgundians attacked the French-controlled town of Compiègne, north of Paris, driving Joan to move her troops there to defend against a Burgundian takeover of the town. On May 23, leading a sortie out of Compiègne, Joan was captured by the Burgundians, sold to the English, and on May 30, 1431, burned as a heretic.

Jean Chartier, writing between 1440 and 1450, remarks on the history of Joan of Arc: "It was a very strange thing to see a woman fight in such an army."[12] Yet there seems to have been no wavering on the part of the soldiers she led, all of whom, again it seems, followed her without hesitation. The anonymous English author of *The Brut* believes that this was because Joan kept her troops in line by her "crafte of sorcerie,"[13] while the Bourgeois of Paris claims that "all who disobeyed her should be killed without mercy."[14]

But these were enemy commentators, trying in vain to rationalize the losses their side suffered against her. No French witnesses agree with their assessments of her ability to gain loyal military adherents. "Everyone followed her," exclaimed one of the king's squires, Gobert Thibault, at the trial of Joan's rehabilitation.[15] The anonymous author of the *Journal du siège d'Orléans* agrees: "All regarded her with much affection, men and women, as well as small children. And there was a very extraordinary rush to touch her, or even to touch the horse on which she sat."[16]

Even before she arrived at Orleans, news of her appearance at the king's court and the promise of leadership had reached her troops. But instead of dreading her advent, the troops seemed to have been pleased. As Jean de Mâcon, an eyewitness of the siege of Orleans, writes: "Only one derision was made ... they all had great confidence in God and in the good justice of their king and their lord."[17] The *Chronique de Lorraine* adds: "All the army promised always to obey her."[18] Many even sought to copy her standard.[19] Joan in turn promised them victory;[20] each victory motivated more loyalty and further victory.[21]

Though the soldiers loyally accepted Joan's leadership, other leaders of the French forces seemed less willing. The Dean of the Collegiate Church of Saint Thibaud of Metz writes that some of the French captains met the announcement of Joan's military role with "derision and mockery ... murmuring against the king and his counselors," and saying sarcastically, "Here is a valiant champion and captain to recover the realm of France."[22]

But like any successful nonnoble "mercenary captain" of the late Middle Ages, Joan ignored the comments of those she displaced in leadership and favor. She thought nothing of going against these proven inept captains. According to the retrial testimony of one of their number, Jean II, duc d'Alençon, she reassured her recalcitrant colleagues that "they would have no difficulty in attacking the English, for God was conducting their campaign...if she were not sure that God was conducting their campaign, she would rather keep her sheep than expose herself to dangers like these."[23]

At times, she harshly rebuked the French captains, especially the Bastard of Orleans. Dunois himself testified that when he defended a near-disastrous strategy for Orleans to Joan, which "he and others, wiser on this matter…believed the best and surest," she replied,

> … in the name of God, the counsel of our Lord God is surer and wiser than yours. You thought to deceive me but it is you who are more deceived, for I am bringing you better help than ever came from any soldier or any city, because it is the help of the king of heaven. It does not come through love for me, but from God himself who, on the petition of St. Louis and St. Charlemagne, has had pity on the town of Orleans and has refused to suffer the enemy to have both the body of the lord of Orleans and his city.[24]

On another occasion, she even threatened the count. At the retrial, Joan's squire, Jean d'Aulon, recalled these words from the later saint to Dunois: "Bastard, Bastard, in the name of God I command you that as soon as you hear of Fastolf's coming you will let me know. For if he gets through without my knowing it, I swear to you that I will have your head cut off." To this, the count "answered that he did not doubt that, and that he would certainly let her know."[25]

When none of these tactics worked, she simply disobeyed the orders of her noble superiors. Simon Charles, the president of the Chamber of Accounts, testified at the retrial that when the French captains felt, after capturing a few bastilles at Orleans, that they should not make further attacks against the English, even ordering a guard, under the command of the Sire de Gaucourt, placed at the gates "so that no one would go out from the camp," Joan opposed this decision: "And against the will of this de Gaucourt, the soldiers left to make an assault on the Bastille des Augustins, which they captured with strength and violence."[26]

None of this bickering among leaders seems to have influenced the French soldiers to forsake their loyalty to Joan. In some cases, it may well have helped her, for in their eyes she brought action and victory, while older, noble generals had achieved nothing but inaction and defeat. Before long, the French captains began to agree with and even admire her; by the end of the siege of Orleans, the French leaders included her in their strategy sessions. Some, like the ever-faithful duc d'Alençon, frequently sought her martial advice.[27] Her acceptance by these leaders strengthened her favor among the troops.

Most witnesses claim that Joan was without dispute herself a good soldier. "Joan was very simple in all her actions, except in the conduct of war, in which she was altogether an expert," testified Simon Charles.[28] Marguerite la Touroulde, Joan's hostess at Chinon, agreed: "Joan was very simple and ignorant and knew absolutely nothing, it seemed to me, except the art of war."[29] Thibault d'Armagnac or de Termes, a knight and captain of Chartres, added:

> Except in matters of war, she was simple and innocent. But in leading and drawing up armies and in waging war, in ordering an army for battle and motivating the soldiers, she behaved like the most experienced captain in all the world, one who had been educated in warfare for an entire lifetime.[30]

"She could ride a horse wielding a lance as well as a more experienced soldier could," witnessed Marguerite la Touroulde,[31] with the duc d'Alençon claiming that she was a skilled tilter.[32] She seemed to have been especially adept at sighting the relatively new gunpowder weaponry that the French used in their sieges, something agreed to by both the Bastard of Orleans and the duc d'Alençon. As the duke testified:

> … everyone marveled at this, that she acted so wisely and clearly in waging war, as if she was a captain who had the experience of twenty or thirty years; and especially in the setting up of artillery, for in that she held herself magnificently.[33]

In battle, there was no equal to her. No less an important figure than Pope Pius II was impressed by her battlefield capabilities. He writes:

> The woman was made the leader of war. Arms were brought to her, horses led; the girl mounted with defiance, and burning in her armor, her lance quivering, she compelled her horse to dance, to run, and in no way to turn from its course.[34]

Yet others remember that, although Joan may have been adept in the military arts, she refused to use her sword in battle or to shed blood, preferring to carry her standard instead.[35] According to Jean d'Aulon, the latter is true, for Joan, he says, was unable to suffer the sight of spilled blood.[36]

But this is not the legacy of Joan of Arc. Our impression of Joan is not one of her military skills; it is instead one of her religious devotion. Why should we think that the fifteenth-century impression of her would be different, even among her soldiers? The evidence certifies that Joan during her life and especially at the time of her retrial was remembered for her spiritual devotion. She was considered by those who knew her to be a *mulier sancta*, sent by God to perform duties that no one else could: to lead the French army to victory and to ensure that the crown of France was placed on the head of its rightful heir. Her spiritual sanctity would rub off, and her soldiers would be able to participate in the salvation that was obviously hers.

"Many people believed that she had come from God," writes Jean Chartier, "because her works and leadership demonstrated so."[37] Almost all of Joan's French contemporaries say the same thing; and most of her enemies, principally Burgundian and English witnesses, claim the opposite, that she was from the devil.[38] This is both the most essential and—perhaps especially for modern historians—the least understandable aspect of Joan's attraction for her soldiers. But her time was one of mystical devotion to religion, where men and especially women of high sanctity, good morals, and honest Christian character testified to a special consciousness of God, and they gathered legions of adherents with their spiritual skills. They also frequently crossed the line of heresy, at least to some observers.[39]

Joan was one of these. In his retrial testimony, Jean Luillier, a citizen of Orleans, averred

> ... that he and all the people of the city believed that, if the Maid had not come from God to help them, the inhabitants and the city would in a short time have been at the mercy and in the power of the enemy besieging them.[40]

To many, she was like Deborah, Esther, or Judith from the Old Testament—spiritual women who brought their people relief because they followed their messages from God.[41] To others she was the fulfiller of prophecy, from Merlin, Sibyl, and even Bede.[42] Perhaps there is no more eloquent a witness than Christine de Pizan, who writes a message to the enemies of France before Joan's death:

> Oh, all you blind people, can't you detect God's hand in this? If you can't, you are truly stupid for how else could the Maid who strikes you down dead have been sent to us?—And you don't have sufficient strength! Do you want to fight against God?[43]

Joan was striking in her display of morality and devotion. This especially impressed her soldiers, as testified to by Jean Barbin, doctor of law and advocate to the Court of Parlement: "The soldiers considered her a saint, for she behaved in such a godly way when with the army, both in words and deeds, that no one could have uttered a reproach against her."[44]

In particular, at her retrial Joan was remembered for her religious devotion and service. She attended confession often, devoted herself "assiduously" to her prayers, heard mass every day, and "frequently" took the eucharistic sacrament. She was especially devout to the Blessed Virgin. She also refused to fight on Ascension Day. As Seguin de Seguin, a Dominican friar and professor of theology, summarized: "She was never found lazy in her religious duties."[45]

Joan was also remembered as being charitable to all, but especially to the poor and destitute.[46] She was even merciful to her enemies; on one occasion, testified Louis de Coutes, when she encountered an English prisoner who had been "hit ... on the head" and left for dead by a Frenchman, "she dismounted and received the Englishman's confession, holding his head and comforting him as much as she could."[47]

Joan set an elevated moral tone for her soldiers. Witnesses at the retrial recalled that she would not allow blasphemy[48] or gambling.[49] She would also not allow looting, even for food, and she refused herself to eat anything that might have been plundered.[50] Joan especially abhorred prostitutes, those "immoral women" who generally followed the armies of the Hundred Years War, offering their services to the soldiers. On one occasion near the town of Château Thierry, recalled Louis de Coutes,

> when she saw the mistress of one of the soldiers, who was a knight, she chased her with a naked sword. She did not strike the woman, but she warned her gently and kindly that she must never appear in soldier's company again, or she, Joan, would do something to her that she would dislike.[51]

Joan frequently, exhorted her soldiers to "confess their sins and give thanks to God" for their victories, and she thought nothing of scolding her troops "harshly" when she saw them doing what she thought "ought not to be done."[52] The threat was always present. If her troops would not follow her religious example, Joan told her confessor, Jean Pasquerel, "she would not stay among them longer, but would leave their company."[53]

She was also remembered for her "military" miracles. Joan had passed through almost all of enemy-held Burgundy on her route to the king, seemingly without hindrance.[54] She had raised the siege of the town of Orleans and had conveyed the king to his coronation at Reims, precisely as she said she would.[55] When the winds needed to change to allow the ships carrying provisions to the town of Orleans to deliver their cargo, as Joan said they would, they changed.[56] When the town of Troyes needed to fall in three days, because Joan predicted that it would, it fell.[57]

Perhaps the most impressive of Joan's "miracles" and evidence of her sanctity was her virginity, and the fact that they, as soldiers in the field, felt no sexual arousal when around her.[58] Even her nudity did not inspire arousal. This was recalled at the retrial by Jean d'Aulon, Joan's squire:

> Although she was a young girl, beautiful and shapely, and many times when helping to arm her or otherwise he had seen her breasts, and other times when he was dressing her wounds he had seen her legs quite bare, and he had gone close to her many times—and he said that he was strong, young, and vigorous in those days—never, despite any sight or contact I had with the Maid, was my body moved to carnal desire for her, nor did any of her soldiers or squires, as he had heard them say and tell many times.[59]

Did her own qualities and the restrictions she placed on normal soldierly activities divert the attention of her soldiers from Joan? Did this discourage her soldiers' adherence to her? In no way. They seemed to have welcomed the holiness that she represented, and in fact some marveled and even relished the spirituality of their own existence when with her. They seemed to draw nearer to her when fighting by her side, and after her death, they remembered her military activities with a legend-building fealty.

The fifteenth century was an age of change, "the prospect of Europe," in the words of Margaret Aston.[60] Joan was at the junction of two such changes. She was a *mulier sancta*, a holy woman who sought for her own spiritual and mystical experiences at the end of the Middle Ages. She was also the nonnoble leader of a "modern" army, similar in so many ways to the image of other late-medieval captains of mercenary bands. Unlike all others, however, she rewarded her soldiers not with booty, but with spiritual riches. For this, they followed her unfailingly. Simon Beaucroix in his testimony at her retrial summed up nicely the feeling of these soldiers, of whom he was one, that "he well remembered that when he conversed with her he never had a desire to sin."[61]

This essay is dedicated to Professor John Gilchrist, who was tragically killed in an auto accident during the Christmas break, 1992. He was not only a superb scholar and the outside examiner of my dissertation at the Centre for Medieval Studies but also a generous friend to all young scholars with whom he came in contact. Requiescit in pacem.

NOTES

1. An indispensable bibliography of original and secondary sources for the study of Joan of Arc is Nadia Margolis, *Joan of Arc in History, Literature, and Film: A Select, Annotated Bibliography* (New York, 1990), which is complete to 1988. As evidenced by the additions found in the bibliographies of the *International Medieval Bibliography* and the *Annales de Bourgogne*, much continues to be written about this fifteenth-century French military leader.

2. Far more was written about Joan's military career during the nineteenth century than has been written about it during the twentieth. See Margolis, pp. 174–92.

3. Almost all of the numerous biographies of Joan contain a history of her life before meeting with the dauphin. The most accessible currently, although far from the best, is Marina Warner, *Joan of Arc: The Image of Female Heroism* (Harmondsworth, 1981).

4. Little has been written about women warriors in the Middle Ages. See Megan McLaughlin, "The Woman Warrior: Gender, Warfare and Society in Medieval Europe," *Women's Studies* 17 (1990), 193–209. I have found no evidence of late-medieval women warriors other than Joan.

5. *Journal d'un bourgeois of Paris*, in *Procès de condamnation et de réhabilitation de Jeanne d'Arc dite La Pucelle*, 5 vols., ed. Jules Quicherat (Paris, 1841–49) [hereafter Quicherat], 4:465: "Paillard! Ribaude!" The translation of this French expletive as "bloody tart" comes from Janet Shirley's translation of the Bourgeois of Paris's writings (*A Parisian Journal, 1405–1449* [Oxford, 1968], p. 240).

N.B.: In the final two volumes of Jules Quicherat's edition can be found a collection of all contemporary sources for Joan of Arc known to him. While there are in many instances better editions of these sources, I have used Quicherat's edition for its accessibility to readers.

6. In Quicherat, 3.68:

> Cui Johannae quidam vocatus le *Bastard de Granville* dixit plures injurias, quaerendo ab eadem Johanna si vellet quod se redderent uni mulieri, vocando Gallicos cum eadem Johanna exsistentes "*maquereaulx mescréans.*"

(The translation of "maquereaulx mescréans" as "unbelieving pimps" is by Régine Pernoud, *The Retrial of Joan of Arc: The Evidence at the Trial for Her Rehabilitation*, trans. J.M. Cohen [London, 1955], p. 136.) See also the retrial testimony of Jean Pasquerel, in Quicherat, 3.108, 110; Mathieu

Thomassin, *Registre delphinale*, in Quicherat, 4.311–12; Dean of the Collegiate Church of St. Thibaud of Metz, *Chroniques de la noble ville et cité de Metz*, in Quicherat, 4.327; Thomas Basin, *Histoire de Charles VII*, in Quicherat, 4.353; Letter from John, duke of Bedford, in Quicherat, 5.136–37; and *Proceedings and Ordinances of the Privy Council of England*, ed. H. Nicolas (London, 1835), vol. 4, p.223.

7. On late-medieval mercenaries, see Michael Mallett, *Mercenaries and Their Masters: Warfare in Renaissance Italy* (Totowa, 1974), especially pp. 25–106; Philippe Contamine, *War in the Middle Ages*, trans. M. Jones (Oxford, 1984), pp. 99–101, 150–65; Malcolm Vale, *War and Chivalry: Warfare and Aristocratic Culture in England, France and Burgundy at the End of the Middle Ages* (London, 1981), pp. 151–57; Christopher Allmand, *The Hundred Years War: England and France at War, c.1300–c.1450* (Cambridge, 1988), pp. 73–76; and Fritz Gaupp, "The Condottiere John Hawkwood," *History* n.s. 23 (1938–39), 305–21.

8. See, for example, Simon Beaucroix's retrial testimony, in Quicherat, 3.81.

9. On the religious devotion of the age, see Francis Oakley, *The Western Church in the Later Middle Ages* (Ithaca, 1979), pp. 80–130; Steven Ozment, *The Age of Reform, 1250–1550: An Intellectual and Religious History of Late Medieval and Reformation Europe* (New Haven, 1980), pp. 73–135; Johan Huizinga, *The Waning of the Middle Ages: A Study in the Forms of Life, Thought and Art in France and the Netherlands in the XIVth and XVth Centuries* (Garden City, 1949), pp. 151–200; Margaret Aston, *The Fifteenth Century: The Prospect of Europe* (London, 1968), pp. 149–73; Denys Hay, *Europe in the Fourteenth and Fifteenth Centuries*, 2nd ed. (London, 1989), pp. 320–57; Richard Kieckhefer, "Major Currents in Late Medieval Devotion," in *Christian Spirituality: High Middle Ages and Reformation*, ed. Jill Raitt (New York, 1987), pp. 75–108; and Alois Maria Haas, "Schools of Late Medieval Mysticism," in *Christian Spirituality: High Middle Ages and Reformation*, ed. Jill Raitt (New York, 1987), pp. 140–75.

On the late-medieval *mulieres sanctae*, see Caroline Walker Bynum, "Religious Women in the Later Middle Ages," in Raitt, pp. 121–39; Brenda M. Bolton, "Mulieres Sanctae," in *Women in Medieval Society*, ed. S.M. Stuard (Philadelphia, 1976), pp. 141–58; Valerie M. Lagorio, "The Continental Women Mystics of the Middle Ages: An Assessment," in *The Spirituality of Western Christendom, II: The Roots of the Modern Christian Tradition*, ed. E.R. Elder (Kalamazoo, 1984), pp. 71–90, 309–12; Michael Goodich, "The Contours of Female Piety in Later Medieval Hagiography," *Church History* 50 (1981), 20–32; Susan Dickman, "Margery Kempe and the Continental Tradition of the Pious Woman," in *The Medieval Mystical Tradition in England: Exeter Symposium III*, ed. M. Glasscoe (Woodbridge, 1984), pp. 150–68. For Joan of Arc as a *mulier sancta*, see Anne Llewellyn Barstow, *Joan of Arc: Heretic, Mystic, Shaman* (Lewiston, 1986), pp. 1–20.

10. On Joan's military career, see Régine Pernoud, *Joan of Arc by Herself and Her Witnesses*, trans. Edward Hyams (New York, 1964), pp. 70–164; W.S. Scott, *Jeanne d'Arc* (New York, 1974), pp. 46–99; Alfred H. Burne, *The Agincourt War: A Military History of the Latter Part of the Hundred Years War from 1369 to 1453* (London, 1956), pp. 225–71; Robin Neillands, *The Hundred Years War* (London, 1990), pp. 252–65; Desmond Seward, *The Hundred Years War: The English in France, 1337–1453* (New York, 1978), pp. 213–32; Jim Bradbury, *The Medieval Siege* (Woodbridge, 1992), pp. 172–75; Hugh Talbot, *The English Achilles: An Account of the Life and Campaigns of John Talbot, 1st Earl of Shrewsbury (1383–1453)* (London, 1981), pp. 91–102; and Pierre Duparc, "La délivrance d'Orléans et la mission de Jeanne d'Arc," in *Jeanne d'Arc: une époque, un rayonnement* (Paris, 1982), pp. 153–58.

11. Joan's influence at the battle of Patay is a matter of dispute. See Enguerran de Monstrelet, *Chronique*, in Quicherat, 4.372–74.

12. Jean Chartier, *Chronique de Charles VII*, in Quicherat, 4.70.

13. *The Brut or The Chronicles of England*, ed. F.W.D. Brie (London, 1908), vol. 2, p. 439.

14. Bourgeois of Paris, in Quicherat, 4.469: "… qu'il fust ordonné que trestous ceulx qui lui desobéiroient, fussent occis sans mercy." This quotation is included in Joan's initial comments made to the dauphin, as noted by the Bourgeois of Paris, who was nowhere near the event at the time. For the complete speech of Joan to the dauphin, see pp. 467–74.

15. In Quicherat, 3.76. See also *Journal du siége d'Orléans et du voyage de Reims*, in Quicherat, 4.135.

16. In Quicherat, 4.153.

17. Jean de Mâcon, *Chronique du siège d'Orléans et de l'établissement de al fête du 8 mai 1429*, ed. André Simon, in *Bibliothèque de l'Ecole des Chartes* 8 (1847), 503. See also *Chronique de la Pucelle*, in Quicherat, 4.213–14.

18. In Quicherat, 4.336–37. See also Jean Barbin's testimony at the retrial, in Quicherat, 3.84.

19. See Joan's testimony at her trial, in Quicherat, 1.97.

20. See Seguin de Seguin's testimony at retrial, in Quicherat, 3.204.

21. See Jean d'Aulon's deposition, in Quicherat, 3.213.

22. In Quicherat, 4.327. Most historians believe that Joan had little impact on command decisions at Orleans and was far·from being "in command of the French army" there. As Marina Warner writes (p. 79):

> There is no evidence at all, contrary to the popular story, that she was in command of the troops at Orleans in any official capacity. That she roused their loyalty and fighting spirit is refutable; but the king had not given her the command.

See also Warner, pp. 79–84; Pernoud, especially pp. 74–84, 107; Seward, pp. 218–19; and Neillands, pp. 259–60. Only Burne differs with this view, implying that "official" command is insufficient to define Joan's leadership role at Orleans or elsewhere (pp. 236–71). In agreement with Burne, in a future publication, I shall seek to substantiate this implication.

23. In Quicherat, 3.95. See also Jean Chartier, in Quicherat, 4.59–60.

24. In Quicherat, 3.5–6.

25. In Quicherat, 3.212. See also *Chronique de la Pucelle*, in Quicherat, 4.218–19.

26. In Quicherat, 3.116–17.

27. See the retrial testimony of Dunois, in Quicherat, 3.10–11; the deposition of Jean d'Aulon, in Quicherat, 3.211; the *Journal du siège d'Orléans*, in Quicherat, 4.182–83; and Guillaume Gruel, *Chronique d'Arthur de Richemont*, in Quicherat, 4.317.

28. In Quicherat, 3.116.

29. In Quicherat, 3.87.

30. In Quicherat, 3.120. See also Perceval de Cagny, *Chronique des ducs d'Alençon*, in Quicherat, 4.30–31 and Mathieu Thomassin, in Quicherat, 4.309–10. According to the retrial testimony of Dunois, Joan also knew her military limits, in Quicherat, 3.16.

31. In Quicherat, 3.88.

32. In Quicherat, 3.92. See also the duke's testimony in 3.100.

33. In Quicherat, 3.100. See also Dunois's testimony, in Quicherat, 3.13.

34. *Commentarii rerum memorabilium quae temporibus suis contingerunt*, in Quicherat, 4.510. See also duc d'Alençon, in Quicherat, 3.95; Jean d'Aulon, in Quicherat, 3.214; Mathieu Thomassin, in Quicherat, 4.306; the Dean of the Collegiate Church of St. Thibaud of Metz, in Quicherat, 4.322; Jacobus Philippus Foresti Bergomensis, *De plurimis claris sceletisque mulieribus*, in Quicherat, 4.523; and Edmond de Dynther, *Chronica nobilissimorum ducum Lotharingiae et Brabantiae ac regum Francorum*, in Quicherat, 4.426.

35. See the retrial testimony of Seguin de Seguin, in Quicherat, 3.205.

36. In Quicherat, 3.213. See also the retrial testimony of Louis de Coutes, in Quicherat, 3.68–69.

37. In Quicherat, 4.66.

38. See, for example, the account of Joan's exploits found in the *Journal* of the Bourgeois of Paris, in Quicherat, 4.461–74.

39. See above, note 10.

40. In Quicherat, 3.5–26. See also Dunois's testimony, in Quicherat, 3.3; Jean Chartier, in Quicherat, 4.69–70; Robert Blondel, *De reductione Normanniae*, in Quicherat, 4.347–49; and Martin Le Franc, *Champion des dames*, in Quicherat, 5.45.

41. See Thomas Basin, in Quicherat, 4.356–57; Christine de Pizan, *Ditié de Jehanne d'Arc*, ed. Angus J. Kennedy and Kenneth Varty (Oxford, 1977), p. 33; and an anonymous Latin poet of France, in Quicherat, 5.35.

42. See Christine de Pizan, p. 34; Catherine Le Royer, in Quicherat, 2.446–47; Jean Barbin, in Quicherat, 3.82–83; the Dean of the Collegiate Church of St. Thibaud of Metz, in Quicherat, 4.323; Mathieu Thomassin, in Quicherat, 4.305; and Walter Bower, *Scotichronicon*, in Quicherat, 4.480–81.

43. Christine de Pizan, p. 37:

> N'appercevez–vous, gent avugle,
> Que Dieu a icy la main mise?
> Et qui ne le voit est bien bugle,
> Car comment seroit en tel guise
> Ceste Pucelle ça tramise
> Qui tous mors vous fait jus abatre?
> —Ne force [n']avez qui souffise!
> Voulez–vous contre Dieu combatre?

(The translation is by the editors and on p. 48.) See also pp. 36–39; Dunois' s retrial testimony, in Quicherat, 3.45; *Journal d'un siège d'Orléans*, in Quicherat, 4.127, 129; Mathieu Thomassin, in Quicherat, 4.309–10; Jean de Mâcon, p. 503; Guillaume Girault, *Note dur la levée du siège d'Orléans*, in Quicherat, 4.282; and a letter from Alain Chartier to a foreign prince, in Quicherat, 5.135.

44. In Quicherat, 3.84: "Dicit insuper quod armati eam reputabant quasi sanctam, quia ita se habebat in exercitu, in dictis et factis, secundum Deum, quod a nullo reprehendi poterat." See also the retrial testimonies of Raoul de Gaucourt, in Quicherat, 3.18–19 and Louis de Coutes, in Quicherat, 3.67.

45. In Quicherat, 3.205. See also the testimonies of Bertrand de Poulengy, in Quicherat, 2.458; Gobert Thibault, in Quicherat, 3.76; Simon Beaucroix, in Quicherat, 3.81; Pierre Vaillant, in Quicherat, 3.14; Raoul de Gaucourt, in Quicherat, 3.219; Louis de Coutes, in Quicherat, 3.66; Jean Pasquerel, in Quicherat, 3.101–02; the duc d'Alençon, in Quicherat, 3.124; and Dunois; and the chronicle accounts of Thomas Basin, in Quicherat, 4.354, the Dean of the Collegiate Church of St. Thibaud of Metz, in Quicherat, 4.322; and Jean de Mâcon, p. 505.

46. See, for one, Marguerite la Touroulde, in Quicherat, 3.87–88.

47. In Quicherat, 3.71–72:

> Dicit insuper quod ipsa Johanna erat multum pia, et habebat magnam pietatem de tanta occisione, quia, cum quadam vice unus Gallicus duceret certos Anglicos captivos, ipse qui eos ducebat percussit unum aliorum Anglicorum in capite, in tantam quod ipsum reddidit quasi mortuum. Ipsa Johanna hoc videns descendit de equo, et fecit eumdem Anglicum confiteri, tenendo eum per caput, et consolando eum pro posse.

48. See the testimonies of Seguin de Seguin, in Quicherat, 3.205–06, Reginalda, widow of Jean Huré, in Quicherat, 3.34–35, Simon

Beaucroix, in Quicherat, 3.81, Raoul Gaucourt, in Quicherat, 3.19, and Louis de Coutes, in Quicherat, 3.72–73.

49. See the testimony of Marguerite la Touroulde, in Quicherat, 3.87.

50. See the testimony of Simon Beaucroix, in Quicherat, 3.81.

51. In Quicherat, 3.73. See also the retrial testimonies of Simon Beaucroix, in Quicherat, 3.81, and the duc d'Alençon, in Quicherat, 3.99.

52. See the testimonies of Jean Pasquerel, in Quicherat, 3.106, and Simon Charles, in Quicherat, 3.116.

53. In Quicherat, 3.106.

54. See Gobert Thibault's retrial testimony, in Quicherat, 3.75. The one group of soldiers who "laid an ambush to capture her, and rob her and her company ... had found themselves unable to move from their positions; and so Joan and her company had escaped without difficulty," testified Seguin de Seguin, in Quicherat, 3.203.

55. See the retrial testimonies of Seguin de Seguin, in Quicherat, 3.205, Louis de Coutes, in Quicherat, 3.70–71, and Jean Pasquerel, in Quicherat, 3.104–06, as well as the narrative accounts of Jean Chartier, in Quicherat, 4.69, and Perceval de Cagny, in Quicherat, 4.30–31, and the *Ditié* of Christine de Pizan (p. 46).

56. See Dunois's retrial testimony, in Quicherat, 3.6.

57. Ibid., 3.13.

58. See the *Miroir des femmes vertueuses*, in Quicherat, 4.268, and the testimonies of Maguerite la Touroulde, in Quicherat, 3.87 and Jean Pasquerel, in Quicherat, 3.102. Jean Pasquerel also claimed that Joan would curse anyone who called her a whore (in Quicherat, 3.110). On the importance of virginity to early Christian spirituality see Peter Brown, "The Notion of Virginity in the Early Church," in *Christian Spirituality: Origins to the Twelfth Century*, ed. B. McGinn and J. Meyendorff (New York, 1986), pp. 427–43.

59. In Quicherat, 3.219. See also the retrial testimonies of the duc d'Alençon, in Quicherat, 3.100; Dunois, in Quicherat, 3.15; Gobert Thibault, in Quicherat, 3.76–77; and Bertrand de Poulengy, in Quicherat, 2.457.

60. Aston's excellent book on fifteenth-century history is subtitled "The Prospect of Europe."

61. In Quicherat, 3.81.

JOAN OF ARC'S MISSION
AND THE LOST RECORD OF HER
INTERROGATION AT POITIERS

Charles T. Wood

At Poitiers Joan limited her mission to the relief of Orleans, but her nullification trial reaffirmed Charles VII's legitimacy.

Joan of Arc is that rare medieval figure, one for whom we have adequate biographical data. Even though some of the evidence, notably that involving her voices, tends to raise issues not easily addressed within the rules of historical explanation, most of the twists and turns of her life are remarkably well documented, the one obvious exception being the short period during which Charles VII had her examined at Poitiers before putting her in charge of the relief of Orleans. Still, nice though it would be to have the record of this interrogation, its loss is less than grievous. Indeed, we may be fortunate in not having it, insofar as its disappearance forces us to ask just why it should have gone missing. In turn, that question leads to answers that shed considerable new light not just on the original scope of Joan's mission but on the evolution of her own thinking at Rouen, as well as on the multiplicity of purposes underlying the nullification trial that was finally to restore her good name in the 1450s.

That Charles VII should have wanted Joan thoroughly investigated seems unremarkable. After all, even in the Middle Ages it was a bit unusual for a cross-dressed teenager of uncertain origin to descend uninvited on the royal court, all the while insisting that God had sent her to restore king and realm alike. When Joan arrived at Chinon, she soon found herself being sent to Poitiers, in March 1429, for an ecclesiastical examination of some two weeks' duration. Because Charles decided to have his judges' findings distributed widely at the time, they have survived as the full record has not. It must be said, though, that these Poitiers conclusions, so called, seem far from expressing the kind of total support for Joan and her mission that is often assumed:

> The king ... ought not to ... reject the maid who says that God has sent her to bring him aid even though those promises may be nothing but the works of man. Neither ought he lightly or hastily to believe in her. But ... he must try her in two ways: to wit, with human wisdom by inquiring of her life, morals, and motive; ... and by earnest prayer asking for a sign ... by which to tell whether it is by God's will that she is come. ... Since the coming of the said maid, the king has observed her in the two manners aforesaid ... for the space of six weeks, ... but no evil has been found in her, only good, humility, virginity, and devoutness, honesty, and simplicity. As for the second ordeal, the king asked her for a sign, to which she replied that she would give it before Orleans, ... for thus it is ordained of God.
>
> Now, seeing that the king ... finds no evil in her, and ... seeing her urgent request that she be sent to Orleans to show there that the aid she brings is divine, the king should not hinder her from going to Orleans with men-at-arms. Rather, he should send her there in due state, trusting God. For to fear or reject her would be to rebel against the Holy Ghost and to render oneself unworthy of divine aid. . . .'

As Deborah Fraioli will demonstrate in her book on the theology of Joan, what the judges were here attempting to show is that they had tried to follow the best contemporary advice, notably Gerson's, on the ways in which fallible human beings could best distinguish between the diabolical and the divine. The authorities held, in brief, that a person claiming divine inspiration had to exhibit both purity of life and a sign, the miraculous nature of which would then confirm God's sanction of person and mission alike. These experts assumed, however, that judgment in such a matter would take place only with the sign already in existence, whereas in Joan's case the miracle of Orleans had yet to occur.

This troubling difference helps to bring into focus an important aspect of this document that has hitherto escaped much notice: the extent to which Joan's judges at Poitiers arrived at conclusions that were cunningly evasive, not to say hopelessly mealy-mouthed. Note how they avoid all personal responsibility for their decision by repeatedly emphasizing that it was the king, not they themselves, who had found no impurity in Joan. When they gravely add that he alone will bear the consequences if he fails to send her to Orleans, their unstated premise is that he will also bear the full responsibility, should she there fail to produce the needed sign. Nice judges, these! No more her supporters than those whom she was later to face at Rouen.

One more point needs stress. Whenever these judges sought to know Joan's sign, she appears to have limited her response to a discussion of Orleans and of the success she expected to achieve there. Nowhere is any broader mission mentioned, in particular one that would culminate in Charles's triumphant coronation at Reims. Yet this omission should not in itself be surprising, since, as Joan was later to testify at Rouen, when St. Michael first informed her of the need to go to France, his sole explanation lay in his insistence that speed was necessary if she was to "raise the siege of Orleans."[2] Since she then further testified that at Vaucouleurs she had told Robert de Baudricourt only that "she must come to France,"[3] it looks as though she had initially thought of her mission as being confined solely to Orleans. Because the Poitiers conclusions are silent on Reims, there are strong grounds for believing that in late March 1429 the coronation had yet to become one of her goals. As Dunois was later to testify in the 1450s, the crowning of Charles became part of her mission only in the course of the lengthy debates on strategy that took place between the princes of the blood and the king's military commanders in the aftermath of Orleans.[4]

Dunois contradicts the testimony of all of the other witnesses at the nullification trial. In confirming the statement given by Durand Laxart, the uncle who had taken Joan to Vaucouleurs, Michel Lebuin swore that at that point her one purpose in going to France had been to get the dauphin "anointed at Reims."[5] Another witness insisted that when her Poitiers judges asked her why she always called Charles dauphin rather than king, she had replied: "I will not call him king until he has been anointed and crowned at Reims. To that city I intend to take him."[6] Joan's own confessor, Jean Pasquerel, solemnly swore that she herself had told him that at her first interview with Charles she had assured him that God "sends me to lead you to Reims so that you may receive your crowning and your consecration."[7]

It is within the context of all this insistence on Reims that the reasons for the disappearance of Joan's interrogation at Poitiers become intriguing. It is possible no such record ever existed, but that seems unlikely. Joan herself thought that such documents existed, at several points early in her Rouen trial asking that they be sent for and produced.[8] Even more tellingly, it is hard to imagine her Poitiers judges, all of them *parlementaires*, being willing to proceed in the absence of all that scribal support that was the necessary companion of their normal judicial routines.

Everything suggests that a full record of Joan's interrogation at Poitiers once existed. Given that record's potentially capital importance, it was something to be preserved with care. Yet neither it nor the surviving Poitiers conclusions were ever introduced at the nullification trial, and this in spite of the fact that Joan herself had once confidently believed that this evidence would help her to win at Rouen. Why, then, had it seemingly vanished only a quarter-century later?

Although it is difficult to prove a negative, it seems unlikely in the extreme that Charles or his judges had simply lost or misplaced what Joan called "the register at Poitiers." Even if that were the case the problem would remain: though the Poitiers conclusions had themselves survived, they, too, were never introduced into evidence. In conjunction, these two facts suggest that Charles and his advisers did not want the Poitiers interrogation to play a role in the nullification trial and hence that they themselves in all probability had had the register destroyed. If so, it may be worth asking when this event might most logically have occurred. There are at least two possibilities, both of them not without significance.

The first occasion on which those of Charles's party might have wanted to eliminate all vestige of Poitiers came over an extended period of time, one that started with Joan's capture at Compiègne and that culminated with her burning at Rouen. That is, if Orleans and all the triumphs that followed it had initially been taken as the signs needed to confirm the divine origin of Joan's mission, then her subsequent capture, imprisonment, and condemnation could well have been taken as earth-shattering proofs either that God had changed His mind or that the preliminary human judgment had been mistaken. Better by far, then, neither to attempt the rescue that Joan so fondly anticipated, at least at the beginning,[9] nor to preserve any damning evidence that would show that there had once been a time when the king had found "no evil" in this relapsed heretic, "only good, humility, virginity, devoutness, honesty, and simplicity."

Even though such reasoning explains how the record of Joan's interrogation could have been destroyed as early as 1430–31, in no way can it speak to why the Poitiers conclusions, themselves very much in existence, were not introduced at the nullification trial. The failure to do so suggests that even in the victorious days of the 1450s, days for which Joan herself had fought and longed, there must still have remained aspects of the Poitiers findings that Charles VII preferred to keep hidden from this new investigation. What that means, in turn, is that if the record had not in fact been suppressed earlier, it surely was suppressed now, as a logical by-product of all the planning and scheming that went into Joan's rehabilitation.

Vindication of the Maid was far from being the only goal pursued in the nullification trial. Of far greater immediate importance was the reaffirmation and validation of the divine legitimacy undergirding Charles's own kingship. No ruler would want his chief supporter at a critical moment to remain condemned as a relapsed heretic. But what was really at stake is suggested by the testimony of all those witnesses at the nullification trial who insisted that Charles's coronation had been the crucial component of Joan's mission from the very beginning. That testimony was false, as we have seen, but possibly its most striking feature is the frequency with which it insisted that, just as Joan's Poitiers judges had stressed that Orleans was to be her sign, the ordeal she needed to undergo successfully in order to demonstrate the divine origins of her mission, so, too, did these later witnesses hold that the coronation was a kind of sign or ordeal, and hence that Reims had made Charles truly king for reasons that transcended his simple right to wear the crown. In this reading, because Charles had received the holy chrism without incident, the ease with which he had become God's anointed confirmed the legitimacy of his kingship by proving that he was indeed the legitimate son of his father Charles VI—and hence his equally worthy successor on the throne of France. If Pasquerel's testimony had Joan assuring her gentle dauphin at Chinon that God had sent her to lead him to Reims, he has her introduce that promise with the explanation: "On the part of my Lord, I tell thee thou art true heir of France and son of the king."[10] Strikingly, too, even Charles VII in his later years claimed that he had known from the beginning that Joan's was a divinely inspired mission precisely because she had so decisively answered his secret prayer in which he had asked God to end his own doubts about the legitimacy of his birth.[11]

All this testimony is demonstrably nonsense. If there had been doubts in 1429 about Charles's right to rule, they were a result of his disinheritance by Parlement and the treaty of Troyes because of his complicity in the murder of John of Burgundy ten years earlier, at Montereau. When Philip the Good returned to French allegiance in 1435, it was that issue, and that issue alone, he sought to dispel when he prevailed upon Luigi *de Gariis*, a Bolognese jurist, to write an opinion demonstrating that neither Charles VI nor any of those acting on his behalf had sufficient authority to deny what was, after all, his son's God-given right to succeed him.[12] In so arguing, the duke of Burgundy's jurist added little to the case already presented in 1429 by Jacques Gélu, archbishop of Embrun, in his *De puella aurelianensi dissertatio*. For in that work, probably written before Reims, he, too, argued not the legitimacy of Charles's birth, but only the fact that his parents had been properly married, a reality that demonstrated the injustice of his disinheritance under all law, whether divine, human, or natural.[13] All the evidence given by Charles's partisans before the time of the nullification trial proves that the legitimacy of his birth was not then at issue. The sole issue was the lawfulness of his disinheritance, which they all denied by insisting that mere mortals lacked the authority needed to quash the inheritance rights of one whom God, not man, had chosen to succeed in the very act of conception. As I have argued elsewhere, it was that truth alone that Joan of Arc was seeking to confirm through her sponsorship of the king at his quasi-sacramental coronation at Reims.[14]

By the 1450s, however, Charles VII faced a profoundly different challenge. Burgundy and Paris had long since returned to his allegiance, but his successes had also led the supporters of Henry VI to mount a different kind of attack on the legitimacy of his kingship. From the time that Isabeau of Bavaria lay on her deathbed, unable to respond, dark rumors began to circulate that, far from being Charles VI's true son, Charles the Victorious was no more than the chance byproduct of his mother's "notorious" adulteries, in this instance probably with Louis of Orleans.[15] Even though that rumored paternity would have kept it all in the family, so to speak, this was an allegation that had to be convincingly countered because French dynastic thinking had long held that kingship had to be directly and seminally transmitted.[16] For delicacy's sake, however, the response had to avoid raising too many specifics of the variety that bedevil today's merry wives of Windsor.

In all probability, that is why Joan of Arc found her mission so profoundly enlarged and transformed in the testimony presented at the nullification trial. The coronation of Charles VII now became its centerpiece, and if that rite remained a quasi-confirmation in the sacramental sense, what it now confirmed was the legitimacy of the king's conception and birth, not the legal impossibility of his disinheritance through human agency. Still, if that was a principal aim of those sponsoring Joan's rehabilitation, that meant in turn that they had to turn a blind eye toward all evidence that might undercut the validity of these higher royal truths they were so unobtrusively seeking to disseminate. Even though both documents were still in existence, neither the Poitiers conclusions nor Jacques Gélu's endorsement of Joan and her mission could be safely introduced into evidence insofar as their 1429 specifics were at variance with the dynastic ones now being celebrated. Similarly, if the full record of Joan's interrogation at Poitiers had not already gone missing in 1430–31, it surely did so now, the point being that her complete testimony about the nature and purpose of her mission before its first success at Orleans would have been much more destructive of the legitimizing royal cause than were the mere assertions of Gélu's *dissertatio* or the brief and evasive findings of Charles's own judges. Had either of these documents surfaced unexpectedly at the nullification trial, with any luck the royal lawyers could have managed the ensuing problems. But Joan's own words *in extenso* would have posed an insurmountable difficulty. Little wonder, then, that we no longer have them.

Although unprovable, this reconstruction does force us to see at least two aspects of Joan's documented career with greater clarity. First, that her mission would culminate in the coronation at Reims, not the relief of Orleans, was initially a reality well hidden from Maid and king alike. That mission and its objectives were clearly shaped in response to events as they unpredictably unfolded, and they were given their final, near-mythic form only long after Joan's death and for reasons that had little to do with her own experience. Second, if the record of Joan's rehabilitation has long been deemed even more fraudulent than that compiled for her condemnation, we now have grounds for suspecting that the worst frauds resulted less from pious attempts to restore Joan's good name than from a concerted effort to remove the stain of alleged bastardy from the authority and good name of the one for whom Joan had fought.

If the lost Poitiers record forces a rethinking of the nature and objectives of the nullification trial, it also suggests new ways of understanding the evolution of Joan's responses at Rouen. Early in that trial, on February 27, 1431, she evaded queries about the dress of her saints by responding: "I have not leave to reveal it. If you do not believe me, send to Poitiers!"[17] She then parried a repeat of the question by insisting that "if I had leave I would gladly tell you. It is written down in the register at Poitiers."[18] With a bold front, she thus attempted to face down the bishop of Beauvais by appealing to the record and findings of another ecclesiastical court that she clearly thought had wholeheartedly supported her. As she put it later on the same day: "The clergy of her party held that there was nothing but good in her mission."[19]

Four days later, however, she was forced to admit that she did not really know "whether her own party firmly believed her to be sent from God,"[20] and a week after that, on March 10, she revealed the grounds for her uncertainty when she testified that upon showing the king her sign, "she thanked Our Lord for her delivrance from the trouble arising from the opposition of the clergy of her party ... [which] ceased opposing her when they had recognized the sign."[21]

Although this was doubtless a truthful answer, for Joan it must have had troubling aspects not unrelated to the long-remarked evasiveness she always employed when trying to convince Cauchon's court of the God-given reality of her sign. That is, the Poitiers conclusions demonstrate that Charles's judges believed that she lacked a sign other than the one she promised to display at Orleans, but her undoubted success there was surely an uncertain reed on which to base any proof of a divine mission in 1431. For if she had met the test at Orleans—and later at Reims—after that her mission had become little more than a series of failed ordeals and unmet challenges: Paris still in enemy hands; Burgundy still the ally of England; she herself ignominiously captured at Compiègne and long a prisoner; and, worst of all, Charles VII seemingly no closer to being the accepted ruler of all of France.

In spite of that record, Joan herself might continue to insist that God had truly sent her, but the dismal nature of this more recent evidence appears to have forced her to recognize that her present judges were unlikely to accept Orleans as a sign that was in any way persuasive. As a result, she tried to avoid all discussion of it in this context. On February 27, for example, when the court sought to know "what revelations the king had," while she stressed that he had "had a sign touching of her mission before he believed in her," her real response was: "You will not learn them from me this year."[22] Since the judges refused to let the matter drop, by March 10 she was attempting to end their curiosity by assuring them that her sign, the specifics of which she still refused to reveal, was nevertheless "most credible," an object that was "the richest in the world," and one that "will last for a thousand years and more" within "the king's treasure."[23] Only on March 13 did a seemingly terrified and worn-down woman, "too much pressed to tell it," testify confusedly in prison "that the sign was that an angel assured her king by bringing him the crown and saying that he should possess the whole and entire kingdom of France by the help of God and the labors of the said Joan."[24]

Although this evolution in Joan's responses demonstrates yet again the brutality of the ordeal to which she was subjected, another point also deserves noting. If Joan's refusal to claim Orleans as her sign demonstrates her belief that those confronting her at Rouen were unlikely to accept it, she must also have begun to see that this attitude was apt to be widely shared, even by the partisans of France. By the end of the trial, everything suggests that she had arrived at the dismaying conclusion that even one-time supporters would take the seemingly bad end to her mission as having necessarily undercut the likelihood of its divine origins.

Although proof of the point seems to lurk in the obvious despondency with which she gave up hope of rescue and made her initial recantation,[25] it shows up much more concretely in her response of May 2 when, during her Public Admonition, she was asked "whether she would refer herself and submit to the church at Poitiers where she was examined."[26] On the face of it, Joan should have leapt at this seeming offer of a return to that town where, as her testimony of February 27 had naively put it, "[t]he clergy ... held that there was nothing but good in her mission." Yet this was a leap she refused to make. Instead, she ended the charade with a curtly dismissive: "Do you think you will catch me in that way and hence draw me to you?"[27]

The woman who made that response still did not fully grasp the cunning evasiveness with which her Poitiers judges had framed their conclusions. Nevertheless, in so answering she revealed a level of insight far beyond anything she had ever possessed before setting off for France. Venturing forth into a world of sin, she had learned that men—even French churchmen—were not to be trusted, and that lesson continues to have value even at a time when the descendants of those who burned her are as one in condemning their ancestors' action. Historical regrets about the disappearance of Joan's interrogation at Poitiers may seem of little moment, but insofar as investigation of that loss has led to a fuller understanding of Joan's evolving outlook and of the ways in which her life was given seemingly historical shape by the dynastic needs of the man she made king, it may well be that these regrets, too, are just another proof of human fallibility.

NOTES

1. Jules Quicherat, ed., *Procès de condamnation et de réhabilitation de Jeanne d'Arc, dite La Pucelle*, 5 vols. (Paris, 1841–49), 3.391-92. Hereafter cited as Quicherat. Translations are my own unless otherwise indicated.

2. W.P. Barrett, ed. and trans., *The Trial of Jeanne d'Arc* (London, 1931), p. 44, as translated from Quicherat, 1.52–53. Hereafter cited as Barrett.

3. Barrett, p. 45, from Quicherat, 1.53.

4. Quicherat, 3.11–13.

5. Quicherat, 2.440. In further testimony, it was claimed not just that Reims had been central from the beginning but that Joan had learned about the plight of Orleans only after her arrival at Chinon!

6. Quicherat, 3.20.

7. Quicherat, 3.103.

8. Barrett, pp. 59, 60, from Quicherat, 1.71–72.

9. Barrett, pp. 73–4, from Quicherat, 1.87–78.

10. Quicherat, 3.103. Note, however, that while I doubt Pasquerel's claim that Joan had directly assured Charles that he was the true *filz du roy*, elsewhere in this volume Jean Fraikin argues that he must have so testified even though these words do not appear in London, British Library, MS Stowe 84, a manuscript unknown to Quicherat but preferred by Pierre Duparc in his new edition of the nullification trial. Fraikin may well be

right, but it should also be noted that Stowe 84's emphasis solely on Charles as *vray héritier* is much more consistent with Joan's known views, ones that spoke not to the legitimacy of his birth but only to the inability of mere mortals to disinherit him because of his supposed crimes. That being the case, what intrigues me is the real issue underlying the problematic reliability of Stowe 84. That is, did Pasquerel in fact testify about Joan's knowledge of Charles's legitimacy, or was this a claim put into his mouth only after the event by those anxious to restore the good names of the king and his mother? J. Fraikin and I believe that this is an issue best left to the judgment of the reader.

11. Régine Pernoud, *The Retrial of Joan of Arc: The Evidence at the Trial for Her Rehabilitation,* trans. J.M. Cohen (London, 1955), p. 125, n. 1.

12. Charles T. Wood, *Joan of Arc and Richard III: Sex, Saints, and Government in the Middle Ages* (New York, 1988), pp. 145–7.

13. Quicherat, 3.401.

14. Wood, pp. 140–41.

15. Richard C. Famiglietti, *Royal Intrigue: Crisis at the Court of Charles VI, 1392–1420* (New York, 1986), pp. 41–45, demonstrates conclusively that Isabeau of Bavaria's sluttish reputation, almost universally accepted, was entirely the product of deathbed rumors as popularized only by much later writers like Brantôme.

16. Wood, chap. 1 and especially pp. 20–22.

17. Barrett, p. 59, from Quicherat, 1.71.

18. Barrett, p. 60, from Quicherat, 1.72.

19. Barrett, p. 62, from Quicherat, 1.75.

20. Barrett, p. 82, from Quicherat, 1.101.

21. Barrett, p. 93, from Quicherat, 1.121.

22. Barrett, p. 62, from Quicherat, 1.75.

23. Barrett, p. 92, from Quicherat, 1.120.

24. Barrett, pp. 106–07, from Quicherat, 1.139.

25. Barrett, pp. 73–74, 342–45, from Quicherat, 1.87–88, 442–50.

26. Barrett, p. 301, from Quicherat, 1.397.

27. Barrett, p. 301 as slightly modified, more accurately to translate Quicherat, 1.397.

TRUE LIES: TRANSVESTISM AND IDOLATRY IN THE TRIAL OF JOAN OF ARC

Susan Schibanoff

The ecclesiastical case against Joan of Arc gradually narrowed to the central charge of idolatry. Joan was condemned for worshipping false gods, the saints of her visions, and for making herself into an idol of masculinity—a "false lie"— by wearing male attire.

According to the scribe who annotated the final interrogation of Joan of Arc that occurred on May 28, 1431, what ultimately sent her to the stake as a relapsed heretic was her "fatal reply"[1] that she had again heard her divine voices. Not only had St. Catherine and St. Margaret spoken to her, but, Joan reported, they declared that her earlier recantation was evil and treasonous, her accusers false. Joan's return to a belief in the validity of her voices was probably sufficient to convict her of the charges written on her cap when she was subsequently burned by the English on May 30: *Heretica, Relapsa, Apostata, Idolater.*[2] Yet all of these characterizations—heresy, relapse, apostasy, and idolatry—applied equally well to Joan's other "fatal" action shortly before, or on, May 28: her resumption of male attire. On that Monday, the judges began by interrogating Joan's overt marks of relapse, her return to male dress, and only then moved on to ferret out what to them were the invisible, inaudible signs, the recurrence of her private voices. Joan's male attire and voices are inextricably linked in the transcript of her final condemnation; her transvestism serves to introduce and manifest her suspect revelations. As Beverly Boyd phrases it, "The issue was, of course, [Joan's] voices, ... but the emblem of her heresy was her wearing of men's clothing."[3]

Jeffrey Burton Russell observes that "most of the charges levelled against Joan were complete falsifications," for hers was at best a "lurid political trial."[4] Régine Pernoud finds the original case a "tissue of trickery and falsification," and she argues that Joan's so-called relapse was based on a forged document.[5] Johannine scholars largely agree with these characterizations of the accusations made against Joan. Indeed, Boyd comments, Joan's "trial [was] so unjust that the evidence eventually canonized the accused."[6] Trumped up as the accusations may be, I nevertheless wish to examine them carefully here. Although the charges themselves are lies—"mendacious propositions," Pernoud calls them[7]—I believe they can yield certain "truths" about sexuality, gender, and gender construction in the late Middle Ages. In particular, I shall analyze why Joan's cross dressing was coupled with her voices, that is, explore in what sense both were regarded as evidence of heresy, specifically idolatry.

Here, too, one might question the wisdom of taking the charges literally or precisely, for both heresy and idolatry were fluid concepts, often circular in definition, hence vulnerable to political manipulation. Late-medieval heresy, Russell remarks, was any belief the pope found heretical;[8] similarly, idolatry might be any form of devotion deemed improper, as Carlos M.N. Eire observes. "'Idolatry,'" Eire continues, "is a fighting word": it "presupposes a definition of what is true and false in religion, for an idol cannot be universally recognized as such.... One man's devotion was another man's idolatry."[9] Idolatry was also an all-encompassing vice throughout the Middle Ages. Tertullian named it "the chief crime of mankind, the supreme guilt of the world, the entire case put before judgment," for every sin "is committed within idolatry."[10] Centuries later, Aquinas still viewed idolatry as "the cause, beginning and goal of every sin because there is no kind of wickedness which idolatry does not produce at some time...."[11] Despite the elastic nature of medieval idolatry, I shall argue that there is a calculated and precise, albeit perverse, rationale that underlies Joan's condemnation, and my ultimate aim is to identify what cultural work the censure of her overt idolatry, transvestism, performed.

TEXT AS PRETEXT: FRAMING JOAN'S CASE

The denouement of Joan's judicial ordeal, her execution as a relapsed heretic, an idolater, was neither abrupt nor arbitrary; the final act was in the making for months as the trial passed through its various phases. During this period, from February to the end of May 1431,

Joan's transvestment was relentlessly scrutinized. Valerie R. Hotchkiss counts more than thirty appearances of the charge in the trial text's preliminary lists of accusations and admonishments.[12] At the retrial that began posthumously in 1455 and soon exonerated or "rehabilitated" Joan, her lay compatriots clearly perceived the centrality of her transvestment in her earlier condemnation first by ecclesiastical and then by university officials. One witness singled out Joan's transvestism as the exclusive cause of her execution: Pierre Cusquel, a mason of Rouen evidently employed at the castle where Joan was held prisoner, testified that "people said that the sole cause of her condemnation was that she had resumed male clothes...."[13] Although not literally true, Cusquel's statement was not far off the mark, for as Joan's prosecutors honed and polished their case against her, they gradually narrowed it in effect to a single overarching charge of idolatry, articulated into two varieties or manifestations, one of which was Joan's resumption of male attire. The effort Joan's judges expended to frame the charge of idolatry gives it an import beyond mere political expediency or a convenient excuse to get rid of her.

The text of the proceedings against Joan is a complex and unwieldy document, albeit typical of trials before the Inquisition, yet it does reveal a pattern of selectivity that ends with an exclusive focus on idolatry.[14] First recorded in French during the trial of 1431, only a portion of this putatively verbatim transcript survives. The Latin translation of the full French minutes of the trial was not made until sometime after 1435, and into it were inserted letters and other ancillary material, including narrative accounts of the events that resulted in Joan's abandonment to the secular powers and subsequent execution. The accuracy of this later official text is as difficult to assess as is that of the fragmentary French one, but exactitude was not necessarily the main objective in compiling either document. Legitimizing, even rationalizing, Joan's death was surely on the minds of the editors of the post-1435 trial text. To this end, the Latin text searches for, and eventually finds, a dominant theme, a consistent set of accusations against Joan. Judicially (and charitably) speaking, the official text records the efforts of Joan's judges to cull out bogus charges against her; literarily speaking, it reveals the labors of its authors to construct a coherent and credible narrative of her crimes. Inexorably, the narrative edges Joan closer to the fire.[15]

The first stage of Joan's judicial ordeal, the initial interrogation or preparatory trial, lasted for over three months. During this phase, Joan was asked hundreds of questions, all potential accusations.[16] The queries ranged from the seemingly mundane—what was Joan doing yesterday morning when her voice came to her? did her king have a crown when at Reims?—to the profound—would Joan submit herself to the judgment of the Church Militant? From the myriad questions and answers of the preparatory trial, the authorities drew up a list of seventy charges, which were read aloud to Joan over the course of a week. The Latin text records both the accusations and Joan's responses to them.[17] Following this second interrogation, known as the ordinary trial, Joan's ecclesiastical judges digested the seventy accusations into twelve articles.[18] The digest not only streamlined the case against Joan, but focused it and began to develop the major themes that would eventually constrict into the central charge of idolatry. The digest also omitted Joan's responses, for at this point the proceedings clearly dropped whatever pretense of adjudication they had had and began to prove their case against her.

The twelve-article digest eliminated trivial and fanciful accusations of witchcraft and sorcery from the ordinary trial, such as Article VII, that Joan had carried a magical mandrake in her bosom for the purpose of gaining good fortune, and Article XX, that she had put a spell on her ring and standard to the same end. The digest also discarded charges that Joan was first a resident prostitute, then a camp-follower. Articles VIII, IX, and X of the earlier ordinary trial place Joan in a house of prostitution in Neufchateau before she began having her visions, and Article XI specifies that she had intimate relations with Robert de Baudricourt, captain of Vaucouleurs, to whom she boasted that she would bear three sons, one to become a pope, one an emperor, and one a king. Although Voltaire, most notably, would later exploit this image of Joan's carnality in his mock epic, *La Pucelle d'Orléans*,[19] the ecclesiastical authors of the digest in fact dismissed all suggestions of her sexual misconduct with men, for reasons I shall examine below. Instead, the Rouen judges shaped their case around Joan's saints and visions and her male attire; they also cited her leap from the tower of Beaurevoir castle (a supposed suicide attempt or proof of Joan's presumptuous belief that her saints would save her), her departure from her paternal home in Domrémy without parental consent, her dictation of letters signed "Jhesus

Maria," and, in the final article, her alleged refusal to submit to the Church Militant if its dictates conflicted with her sense of God's commands or with her revelations.

The bulk of the articles in the digest, I, II, III, IV, IX, X, and XI, focus on Joan's admission that the saints Gabriel, Michael, Catherine, and Margaret appeared to her, spoke to her, revealed a knowledge of the future and of secret things to her, and convinced the dauphin to allow her to lead his troops against the Burgundian–English alliance. The most damning of these charges concerns Joan's response to the "voices and spirits whom she calls St. Michael, St. Gabriel, St. Catherine, and St. Margaret," for specification of her reaction to them opens the digest and recurs in the penultimate article. To these "spirits," the digest implies, Joan "made reverence" as if they were divinities:

> St. Catherine and St. Margaret have appeared to the said woman who saw them in the flesh. And every day she sees them and hears their speech; and, when she embraces and kisses them, she touches them and feels them physically. She has seen, not only the heads of the said angels and the saints, but other parts of their bodies, whereof she has not chosen to speak. [20]
> [Joan] has uncovered, knelt, and kissed the ground where they walked, and has consecrated her virginity to St. Catherine and to St. Margaret, when she embraced and saluted them. And she has touched them bodily and felt them....(232–33; 1. 295)

Next in importance of the digest's charges is Joan's male attire, a subject also raised in Article I and then elaborated in two subsequent articles. Article I interconnects Joan's saints with her transvestism, claiming that Joan confessed that St. Catherine and St. Margaret instructed her, "in the name of God, to take and wear a man's clothes" (227; 1. 290) when she approached the dauphin, and that Joan stubbornly continues to obey their command even though doing so bars her from hearing Mass and receiving the sacrament of communion. Articles V and VII escalate the accusation in that they personalize it, placing the onus on Joan herself for deciding to wear men's clothes and for actually obtaining them. Eliminating the intermediary saints, Article V quotes Joan as claiming that God directly commanded her to dress as a man, and VII asserts that a captain (Robert de Baudricourt) "lent this woman a man's clothes and a sword *at her own request*" (231, italics mine; 1. 293).

The digest *per se* refrains from analyzing Joan's trespasses. That task was reserved for the subsequent faculty body at the University of Paris that deliberated over the accusations the digest presented. But the joint opening opinion of the Rouen court, which had authored the digest, sets the stage for later developments: tentatively and briefly, it classifies one of Joan's sins as "idolatry, or at least misleading fiction" (236; *ydolatrium aut, ad minus, conficcionem mendosam,* 1. 299), but says no more. The Rouen judges also subscribed individual opinions to the digest, and one of these clerics, Raoul Le Sauvage, elaborated upon the charge of idolatry:

> In respect of Article XI, that she embraced and kissed bodily and with her senses St. Catherine and St. Margaret, I see in this nothing but imagination and fictitious lies [*fictum mendacium*], or the deception of demons: and if she had adored them, simply and unconditionally, she would not have rashly exposed herself to the charge of idolatry [*forte discrimini cuiusdam ydolatrie temerarie se submisit*]. (263; 1. 326)

For Le Sauvage, then, Joan's vulnerability to the charge of idolatry centers on her visions, specifically, her "fictitious lie" that her saints possessed a *material* existence to which she did reverence. When the Rouen judges later rephrased the charges of the digest and read them to Joan on May 2 for her response, they widened the scope of idolatry beyond her "fictitious lie" to the inherent danger of this sin in Joan's presumption to decide for herself whether or not her apparitions were true:

> She said also that she had adored these novel things which appeared to her, although she had concerning them no sufficient proof for her to believe that they were good spirits; that she had not taken the counsel of priest or any other ecclesiastic on this point, but presumed too much upon herself, in a matter wherein the danger of idolatry [*periculum idolatrie*] is ever imminent. (275; 1. 341)

Joan's "case"—the rewritten twelve-article digest minus her responses of May 2—was next sent to the theological faculty of the University of Paris, which deliberated and rendered judgment upon it twice, rewording it several times in the process. If the Rouen judges stopped a hair short of declaring Joan an idolater, the Paris academics convicted her forthwith on the grounds of her apparitions, which they declared to be "false lies" (*ficta mendacia,* 1. 361). Regarding Article I, the nature of Joan's visions, on May 19 the Paris faculty stated outright that Joan had concocted fictitious, pernicious, and seductive lies (*ficta mendacia, seductoria, et perniciosa,* 1. 361) and therefore was an idolater (*est ydolatra,* 1. 362). At the same time, the Paris faculty extended the concept of idolatry into Article V, which regards Joan's attire, a connection the Rouen judges had failed to make:

> Regarding article the fifth, the said woman is blasphemous towards God, contemptuous of God in his sacraments, unmindful of divine and sacred law and the ecclesiastical sanctions, evil thinking and erring in the faith, foolishly boastful, and must be suspected of idolatry, and of the execration of herself and her garments; she has imitated the rites of the heathen [*et habenda et suspecta de ydolatria et exsecracione sui ac vestium suarum demonibus, ritum gentilium imitando*]. (290; 1.361)

Finally, the text of the trial had found its focus; both Joan's visions and attire evidenced her sin of idolatry, a sin grave enough to justify her excommunication as a heretic if she did not recant her errors. With what would soon become a fatal symmetry, Joan's visible idolatry, her attire, had been synchronized with her invisible idolatry, her visions.

On May 23, the Rouen court read aloud a memorandum of Joan's many "faults, crimes, and errors" to her, and she was allowed the opportunity to "correct and reform herself" (301; 1. 375) and to repudiate her mistaken beliefs, which the trial text records Joan did on May 24. In the document of her abjuration, transcribed first in French and signed in the accused's own hand, Joan confessed to idolatry in "adoring and calling up evil spirits" (313; *et ydolatrant par aourer mauvais esperis,* 1. 390) and to "breaking the divine law, Holy Scriptures, and the canon laws" in wearing immodest male attire "against the decency of nature" (313; 1. 389). (To give Joan's words the required gravity, the trial document immediately translates them into Latin, so that her confession is not merely doubled but, in effect, bilingual [1. 390–91].) On the afternoon of the same day, Joan also reformed her most visible erroneous action: she was given woman's dress (*vestes muliebres,* 1. 394), which she put on immediately after she took off her male costume. She also allowed her hair to be "shaved off and removed" (317; 1. 394) as a correction of her short (masculine) hairstyle. In sum, Joan renounced both her external and internal idolatry, as well as a raft of other crimes and trespasses, thus saving her soul from perdition. Nevertheless, quite to her surprise, she was condemned to perpetual imprisonment.

The text of the proceedings does not end at this point, however. Indeed, the denouement it has been preparing for has yet to come. The penultimate act that the text anticipates throughout occurred when, of all the many sins Joan confessed and abjured, she relapsed into one alone: idolatry. On May 28, she was observed to have resumed male attire in her prison cell. Once again, in the "manner of the heathen," Joan had visibly performed her idolatry. As her inquisitors probed more deeply the extent of her relapse, they soon uncovered evidence of the invisible partner of Joan's idolatrous transvestism, her claim that the voices of St. Catherine and St. Margaret had spoken to her again, among other things telling her that she had made a mistake in recanting in order to save her life. Joan's voices also instructed her to resume male attire. Predictably enough, in the final "trial" for relapse conducted on May 29, only two interlocking pieces of evidence against Joan were presented:

> … obeying the orders of the Church, Jeanne [had] put off male costume and wore woman's dress. But … led on by the Devil she had once more before many witnesses declared that the voices and spirits which were wont to visit her had returned to her and told her many things; and Jeanne … once more rejected woman's dress in favour of male costume. (321; 1. 402)

To a man, the Rouen judges found Joan's idolatry sufficient to convict her of a return to heresy. Their only point of disagreement was whether or not to recommend that the secular arm to which they would soon turn her over treat her with mercy. Such deliberation mattered not at all: immediately following the act of excommunication on May 30, Joan was released to the secular authorities and burned at the stake. In this near-final act of the drama that the trial document records, the reading of the sentence, all manner of epithets were hurled at her (330–31; 1. 414), although when she went to the stake Joan was given a cap to wear that bore but four epithets. Three of them described her status in relationship to the church—*heretica, relapsa,* and *apostata.* The fourth epithet singled out the crime that had pitted Joan in this fatal opposition to authority: *idolater.*

PASSING IN THE MONASTERY: HOLY TRANSVESTISM

The ponderous caution with which Joan's judicial opponents moved—in particular, their obvious effort to link her transvestment with her visions—is perhaps typical of Inquisition politics, yet it also suggests that the "case" against her was not an open-and-shut affair. Medieval attitudes to female transvestism reveal the stumbling block Joan's judges encountered: transvestism *per se* was regarded but not necessarily treated as transgressive. Indeed, despite the scriptural prohibition on wearing the apparel of the other sex (Deut. 22:5) and Paul's prohibition of women cutting their hair (1 Cor. 11:6), there were well-established exceptions to these biblical sanctions. To be sure, as Vern L. and Bonnie Bullough observe, one might search the church fathers in vain for overt and unconditional approbation of transvestism, and specific canons against it are easy to find.[21] Nevertheless, even when condemned, transvestism often excited no comment at all or only "passing attention" from the canonists.[22] And one version of transvestism appears to have been both admired and encouraged, albeit indirectly, in the legends of female saints who disguised themselves as men in order to live as monks. Essential to understanding both the medieval anxiety about transvestism that surfaced in Joan's trial and the specific way in which her judges labored to frame her case is first to analyze those instances in which transvestment did not evoke alarm and was evidently valorized, as is the case of the "holy transvestites" of hagiographical tradition.[23]

Although, as James Anson argues, the motif of the transvestite female saint may have had baptismal implications in its earliest uses— signifying and effecting the birth of a new physical as well as spiritual self in Christ—the lives of the later transvestite virgins "move in a world of pure erotic romance."[24] One such "romance," the life of St. Margaret, is recorded in Jacobus de Voragine's thirteenth-century *Legenda aurea*. Fearing for her virginity on her wedding night, Margaret cut off her hair, donned male attire, stole away from her new husband, and went to a monastery, where she successfully passed herself off as Brother Pelagius. Pelagius led an exemplary life as a monk but was soon put to the test by the devil, who wished to "hinder her prosperous career and bring her into disrepute."[25] Believed to be male, and thus the only man in the convent, (s)he was blamed for the pregnancy of one of the nuns, the portress, and driven into exile in a mountain cave. Pelagius endured both the calumny and the harsh living conditions of banishment silently. Only at the moment of death did (s)he reveal in a letter to the abbot her sexual identity—and her innocence.

For Anson, the inner logic and justification, of such erotic romances, in which the female monk is accused of seduction, turns on the concept of woman as ritual sacrifice. These narratives were written largely by (male) monks for (male) monks, and their apparent purpose is to discharge or exorcise the female sexuality so threatening in this masculine milieu. Typically, the disguised female monk becomes the victim of another woman's seduction and false accusation; predatory female sexuality is thus diverted from men and displaced onto ritual female victims, who neutralize its effects. The "holy transvestite" recuperates her own sex: "It is as if she undoes the guilt of her whole sex by becoming the victim of its designs against men," Anson argues.[26]

While Anson would explain the "valorization" of the female transvestite monk as a function of this figure's crucial role in creating yet containing the fantasy of monastic heterosexual desire, the Bulloughs and other scholars explain the positive cultural reaction to holy transvestment from a sociological rather than psychoanalytical perspective. Noting that women transvestites can be celebrated, even sanctified, in medieval culture, whereas male transvestites are never worthy of admiration, the Bulloughs credit such asymmetry to the enduring status differential between men and women in western culture: "female cross dressers have not only been tolerated but even encouraged, if only indirectly, through much of western history, since it was assumed they wanted to become more like men and, therefore, were striving to 'better' themselves."[27]

Yet another medieval rationale for condoning female transvestment resides within the narrative motif of the holy transvestite. Structurally, it comprises the first and second of the three sections that Anson finds in these legends: flight from the world, and disguise and seclusion.[28] The women who dress as men typically do so in order to retain and protect their virginity, even against their spouses, as in the example of Margaret/Pelagius, who flees from the world—her marital bed—on her wedding night. No less an authority than Thomas Aquinas was adduced to validate transvestment under such circumstances, for Aquinas had opined that although expressly forbidden in the law, wearing the clothes of the opposite sex may be done "without sin in case of necessity [*ex necessitatis causa*], for instance, in order to hide from enemies, or because there are no other clothes, or for some such good reason."[29] As Hotchkiss notes, defenders of Joan of Arc's wearing of male attire seize upon Aquinas's endorsement of protective transvestment and specifically link both with the actions of the female monks.[30] For example, in exonerating Joan, the anonymous author of the *Sibylla Francica* (1429) quotes Aquinas's rationale of necessary disguise—*ex necessitatis causa*—and offers the example of St. Marina, whose father wishes to enter a monastery and can protect his daughter only by disguising her as male and taking her to the monastery with him (where, as Marinus, she is subsequently accused of seducing a young woman and ostracized for it).[31]

Both the psychoanalytical and sociological explications of why the Middle Ages sanctioned certain types of female transvestism make valid observations, yet each fails to articulate precisely enough the paradigm of transvestment it seeks to illuminate. Medieval transvestism was by no means a monolithic phenomenon, and the utilitarian justification advanced by Aquinas and others can help recapture some of its nuances.[32] Aquinas specifically validates transvestism as disguise, as a means of hiding oneself from enemies (*se occultandi ab hostibus*). In modern terms, what Aquinas refers to, then, is not merely *cross dressing*, partial or episodic transvestment in which the subject's biological sexual identity remains apparent or known, but *crossover*, or *passing*, the complete and continuous impersonation of the opposite sex, including whatever changes in hair style, clothing, voice, behavior, and attitude may have been necessary to achieve total masquerade in the Middle Ages.[33] The holy transvestites fall into this latter category, for they "pass" as men and monks until the moment of discovery, usually after their deaths. Their choice of profession as monks enables their crossover, for monastic attire conveniently masks women's distinctive anatomical features, and monastic cells afford a degree of physical privacy that delays discovery of their sexual identity until after death. And when Vern and Bonnie Bullough cite medieval acceptance of women transvestites who wish to "better" themselves by becoming male, they have in mind women, like the female saints, who pass, not women who cross-dress, who "wear the breeches" or, as does Chaucer's Wife of Bath, put on the spurs, but otherwise remain recognizably female. One common denominator among medieval female transvestites who were culturally sanctioned, then, is that they achieve complete disguise, total effacement of their female sex, and I am arguing here that medieval women who passed as men were the ones eligible for sanctification, the so-called "holy transvestites." Those who cross-dressed or retained some aspect of their female identity, however, were censured or even, as in the case of Joan of Arc, condemned to the fire.

"SAVE NATURE'S OWN DISTINCTIVE MARKS"

Because of the medieval distinction between cross dressing and passing, Joan's accusers were careful to specify and record the precise nature of her transvestment. Article XII of the preparatory trial, which tends not to draw conclusions about Joan's behavior, first offers a detailed description of the way in which she "put off and entirely abandoned woman's clothes":

> ... with her hair cropped short and round like a young fop's [*ad modum mangonum*], she wore shirt, breeches, doublet, with hose joined together and fastened to the said doublet by 20 points, long leggings laced on the outside, a short mantle reaching to the knees, or thereabouts, a close-cut cap, tight-fitting boots and buskins, long spurs, sword, dagger, breastplate, lance and other arms in the style of a man-at-arms [*more hominum armorum*]. .... (152; 1. 205)

In addition to wearing male costume and bearing masculine "weapons of offense," which, Aquinas's exceptions notwithstanding, the Rouen judges stated was contrary to divine law and prohibited by ecclesiastical decree, the preparatory trial also accused Joan of wearing "rich and sumptuous habits," clothes of gold and fur (154; 1. 207).

When the judges prepared their digest, they narrowed the charge to wearing male attire, eliminating the accusations concerning Joan's arms and sumptuous attire. At the same time, however, the Rouen officials introduced a crucial detail that altogether ruled out the most likely medieval defense of Joan's transvestism: she wore man's clothes, cut her hair short, and retained "nothing about her to display and announce her sex, *save Nature's own distinctive marks*" (230, italics mine; *preter ea que natura eidem femine contulit ad feminei sexus discrecionem*, 1. 293). The Paris faculty took its cue from Rouen, for in its memorandum of Joan's crimes, it repeats the all-important exception: Joan had kept nothing about her to denote her sex "*save what nature ha[d] given [her]*" (303, italics mine; *excepto eo quod tibi natura contulit*, 1. 377). That is, unlike the holy transvestites, who totally disguised their sex, Joan had not concealed her anatomy or other "marks" of her biological femininity. Intentionally or not, she had cross-dressed.

Fifteenth-century visual images of Joan depict her transvestment variously, yet they typically reveal her as a woman who wears men's clothing or armor. In the only extant pictorial representation of Joan made during her lifetime, a cartoon by the scribe Clement de Fauquembergue in the margin of a manuscript on the siege of Orleans, her left hand rests on the sword she wears, and her right hand holds a staff and pennon.[34] Otherwise, though, Joan is depicted as female: she has on a dress, which is cut to emphasize her full breasts, made even more obvious by her position in profile, and her long hair trails down over her shoulders. In the oldest extant miniature of Joan, from 1451, she holds a lance and shield and wears armed leggings and a breastplate. Yet here, too, Joan is shown in a skirt, her hair is long, and her body armor outlines a female anatomy.[35] A fifteenth-century bronze statuette of Joan on horseback encases her entirely in armor but clearly indicates the female structure of her waist and torso.[36]

In practical terms, Joan's cross dressing was strategically useful to her opponents, for it crippled the most obvious defense of her wearing male costume. Aquinas's vindication of transvestism as a means of hiding from enemies, or, as Raoul Le Sauvage phrased it, to "escape violence and keep [one's] virginity" (262; 1. 325–26), was predicated on total disguise, on passing, and no one in the trial ever suggested that Joan "passed" as a man. At least one legend to that effect exists, but it was not cited during the judicial proceedings.[37] And although her defenders, such as the anonymous author of the *Sibylla Francica*, argued that Joan wore men's clothes to escape harm, their rationale was undercut by the ecclesiastical pronouncement that women protected themselves by total, not partial, sex masquerade and the general perception that Joan had taken little if any care to disguise her biological identity. Rather than buttress Joan's case, the ecclesiastical justification *ex causa necessitatis* cut the ground out from under it.[38]

TRUE AND FALSE LIES: IMAGE AND IDOL

The nature of Joan's transvestment, cross dressing, not only barred the traditional medieval defense of it but enabled her judges to make an eventually fatal association between her attire and her visions, classifying both as idolatry, hence heresy. The connection between cross dressing and idolatry was not invented by Joan's judges. Early in the Middle Ages, Tertullian's *De spectaculis* had linked the two,[39] and echoes of this coupling reverberated throughout the later medieval period, as in the anonymous fifteenth-century *Miroir aux dames,* which rewords the prohibition in Deuteronomy 22:5 to indict the female cross dresser of this religious sin:

> It is forbidden in the Bible
> That a woman be so bold
> On pain of terrible torment,
> To commit the idolatry
> Of wearing on a single day of her life
> The dress that belongs to a man.[40]

Unlike such popular poems as the *Miroir,* however, Joan's judges were more careful and precise, albeit complex, in the nexus they created among Joan's cross dressing, her visions and voices, and idolatry.

The diction these authorities employ in the various condemnations of Joan's idolatry—such phrases as "lying fiction" (*conficcionem mendosam,* 1. 299) and "false lie" (*fictum mendacium,* 1. 326, 1. 361)—may strike modern ears as tautological and hyperbolic, yet it evidences a technical rather than merely popular conception of idolatry. To the layperson, idolatry consisted of the worship of false gods, or idols, but to the ecclesiast, idolatry carried with it profounder metaphysical implications as well. In his *Etymologiae,* Isidore of Seville derived the word "idol" from *dolus,* or fraud,[41] and the idol, typically a human statue, was not merely a false god, but a counterfeit or false *representation* of the true god, the Christian God. By implication, there had to be true or valid representations of God, and to distinguish the bogus from the legitimate another word was employed; the latter was called an "image." Neither idol nor image was the thing itself, the *res* or signified, but a simulacrum or likeness of it. Both were fictions, then, or "lies," but idols were "false" fictions, whereas images were "true" fictions. What determined the mendacity or veracity of the figuration was its effect on the perceiver. The true fiction diverted attention from itself, from its own materiality, and pointed the viewer to its transcendental meaning; it directed the perceiver from an apprehension *corporaliter* to one *spiritualiter*. As Aquinas phrased it, the true lie caused the mind to move toward it in so far as it is the "image of something else."[42] The true lie performed a disappearing act, so to speak:

> The efficacy of images ... resided in their ability to rouse the mind to spiritual intentions, and the sooner the accidents or externals of the representations were left behind the better, since "dallying in imagery conceals the poison of idolatry." And this poison—the adoration of the man-made object, instead of what this stood for— was to be avoided at all costs.[43]

The false fiction, however, had no such outward or upward referentiality; the perceiver's apprehension of it became an end in itself. In early Christian eras, the cross was an image, a true fiction, for it referred the viewer to what it signified, Christ; it was a "true" lie in the sense that it sacrificed itself and became a means of pointing to a higher reality. The idol, on the other hand, was a "false" lie, for it demanded that the viewer pay it reverence by attending to its corporeality, its accidents and externals, rather than use it as a means, to transcend this materiality and gain access to a higher spiritual significance. The idol was regarded as using sensuous means— typically, the physical representation of corporeality in the three-dimensional statue—to seduce the perceiver.

The later Middle Ages experienced a blurring of the distinctions between idol and image;[44] in particular, "the image and the prototype often became indistinguishable" to the layperson.[45] Increasingly material, indeed three-dimensional, representations of saints and other religious figures appeared, which the church itself had begun to defend against iconoclastic heresies, such as Lollardy.[46] Yet the traditional discourse of idolatry persisted and was ready to hand when, for instance, Joan's judges at Rouen and the University of Paris deliberated her case. Their recurring queries about the actual nature of Joan's apparitions probed for idolatry: if Joan had experienced a corporeal, physical apprehension of her saints, she was suspect, for the "false lie," the idol, seduced by such material, sensuous means.

With what at times seems prurient obsession, Joan was from the very first, in the preparatory trial, quizzed about how she physically apprehended her saints. Was St. Michael naked? Did he have any hair? Did he have scales? How did she know whether her apparitions were male or female? What bodily parts of them did she see? Did she see anything of her saints other than their faces? What did their voices sound like? Did they speak in English? The trial transcript records that Joan often parried these inquisitions with witty counter-questions. Why should St. Michael be naked?, Joan retorted; did her judges think God lacked the wherewithal to clothe him? Why should St. Margaret speak English when she is not on the English side? Although George Bernard Shaw later celebrated these humorous remarks and made them the hallmark of his *Saint Joan,* Joan's answers in fact edged her closer to the fire, for they offered her enemies confirmation that her visions were "false gods," idols who had seduced her by corporeal means.

Proof positive of this seduction soon materialized, for Joan was shown to have misdirected her reverence to these idols. She had bowed to them, kissed the ground they walked upon, and embraced their feet. Once raised, these accusations plagued Joan until her death. As early as the second phase of the proceedings against her, the ordinary trial, Joan's physical apprehension of her visions (Article XLII) and her corporeal veneration of them—"embracing and kissing them ... and entering into familiarity with them" (Article XLIX)—had led her judges to the conclusion that such actions "seem to partake of idolatry" (191; *videntur ad ydolatriam pertinere,* 1. 249). And every subsequent part of the proceedings against Joan repeated the charge that her apparitions were "false lies" that had seduced her into idolatrous reverence of them.

Implicated in the charge of idolatry was not merely the idol itself but the idolizer as well, for the latter also participated in a kind of arrogant self-referentiality. Joan's judges argued more than once that she, too, had made herself into a false god by inviting the veneration of the people and that her idolatry was thus presumptuous and blasphemous.[47] In yet another fashion as well, the judges charged, Joan had made herself into an idol, for she had dressed as a man. Joan's transvestism was literally linked with idolatry in the sense that wearing the clothes of the opposite sex "imitated the rites of the heathen" (290; 1. 361), an argument that dated back to at least Tertullian. But Joan's cross dressing did more than mimic heathen customs; it transformed her into the "false lie" that constituted the idol. By retaining visible aspects of her female anatomy, "what Nature had given her," Joan made herself into an idol of the male sex, a counterfeit or false representation of it. Had Joan "passed," in the mode of the holy transvestites, she would have correctly figured or imaged the male gender, presenting the "true lie" that diverted attention from itself and directed the viewer toward a higher reality, in this case, the traditionally superior male sex. But Joan's attire occasioned no such transcendental perception; her partial male attire did not mask but drew attention to her materiality, her female body, and thus "seduced" its viewers. Like the idolatrous heathens Tertullian so despised, Joan had made a spectacle of herself; the all too obvious "accidents" of her biological sexual identity diverted the attention of her viewers from what she might represent to her corporeal substance. Like the bodies of the saints she embraced, the cross-dressed Joan had turned her own body into an idol, a "false lie."

ROTTING AWAY IDLY IN BED

Idolatry was a much-castigated religious offense throughout the Middle Ages, especially in the earlier eras, for it embodied the power of nascent Christianity's rivals. In the later Middle Ages, however, Camille argues, the idol came to stand more widely for the Other—past and present, foreign and domestic—as western Europeans sought to define themselves; the discourse of idolatry provided a "propaganda of fear and prejudice" against the pagan, the Muslim, the Jew, and the homosexual.[48] As it applies to transvestism, this discourse also reveals deep-seated anxieties about western Europe's "oldest Other"—woman. In the alarm raised by cross dressing in Joan's trial, there is an implicit but powerful suspicion about the "false lie" of male attire clothing female anatomy. This disquieting concern is not that the "false lie" is in some way true but that it has the power to become so: the woman who openly wears man's clothes destabilizes *his* sexual identity, not her own, for her action effeminates him. Ultimately, the female cross dresser threatens to "adulterate" man, to mix in the (female) other and turn him into woman.[49]

Such dread about sex/gender instability surfaces in medieval narratives of transvestment both within and outside the hagiographical tradition. An example of the latter is Boccaccio's biography of the Assyrian queen Semiramis, in *De claris mulieribus* (ca. 1355–59).[50] Drawing on Justinus, Valerius Maximus, and other classical authors, Boccaccio shapes his rendition of the life of Semiramis into a two-part fable of transvestism that contrasts passing and cross dressing and unmasks the threat of the latter. To suggest Semiramis's notoriety, Boccaccio positions her life-story second in his work, immediately following Eve's. Yet Boccaccio begins his narrative with an altogether positive affirmation of one incident in Semiramis's life: her passing as her son in order to rule the realm when her husband, King Ninus, is slain in battle. The valiant King Ninus, Boccaccio explains, had subjugated all Asia, which he ruled by force. After his death, Semiramis was reluctant to entrust command of this great empire to so young a child as their son, also named Ninus, and therefore she conceived a "great stratagem" to deceive her late husband's army into believing that she was the heir to the throne, the boy Ninus.[51] Boccaccio emphasizes that Semiramis's "stratagem" is crossover, complete masquerade. She was "still quite young" (4) enough herself to pass as a boy, bore physical resemblance to her son, and went to extreme lengths to effect a total disguise:

> Semiramis's face looked very much like her son's; both were beardless; her woman's voice sounded no different from her young son's; and she was just a trifle taller, if at all. Taking advantage of this resemblance, she always wore a turban and kept her arms and legs covered so that in future nothing might disclose her deceit. At that time it was not the custom of the Assyrians to dress in this guise. Lest the novelty of her garb shock her countrymen, Semiramis decreed that everyone should dress in this fashion. And so this woman, who had been Ninus' wife, masqueraded as a man and pretended to be her own son. (5)

For Semiramis's "marvelous subterfuge" of passing, Boccaccio has nothing but praise: "By pretending *very carefully* to be a man," Boccaccio observes, "she achieved many things which would have been great and noble even for the strongest of men" (5; italics mine). Eventually, however, Semiramis revealed her sexual identity, though she continued to rule the realm and to take up arms "with manly spirit" (5). As queen, Semiramis exerted her power successfully, subduing Ethiopia and India and rebuilding the city of Babylon. But in this second part of the narrative, Boccaccio's attitude to Semiramis begins to shift from celebration to censure, and the pivotal point occurs during a scene of vestment. One day while Queen Semiramis was having maids comb her hair "with feminine care into braids" (6), news came that the city of Babylon had rebelled. Although her hair was only half-braided, Semiramis was so angered that she "immediately abandoned her womanly pursuits"(6), put on her armor, and rode out to subdue the revolt. A huge bronze statue of Semiramis—with her hair braided on one side, loose on the other—was erected to testify to her brave deed, yet for Boccaccio the statue becomes an emblem of Semiramis's evil, not her virtue, for he employs it to introduce a cautionary motif about female cross dressing and its effects on men. As a cross-dressed woman, a queen in arms, Semiramis commits a sin "more beastly than human" (6), Boccaccio confides to his audience in horror. She gives herself as a lover to her own son, Ninus. This act confounds Ninus's identity, an observation Boccaccio couples with an image, or idol, of female cross dressing, the queen in arms: "As if he had changed sex with his mother, Ninus rotted away idly in bed, while [Semiramis] sweated in arms against her enemies" (6). Although Semiramis's male attire correlates to her "manly" spirit, Ninus's gender identity, and possibly his sexual identity, is transformed from masculine to feminine, and this, Boccaccio implies, is the threat of female cross dressing: it effeminates men.[52] The woman who passes, however, as had Semiramis earlier, and the holy transvestites, poses no danger to men; if anything, the female passer enhances masculinity.

Like cross dressers, medieval women who experience a partial transsexualism also affect men's sexuality, or so the legends of the bearded female saints suggest. The most famous of these legendary women is Wilgefortis, also known as Uncumber. The daughter of a pagan father and Christian mother, Wilgefortis determined early to follow her mother's religion and to remain a virgin. When her father insisted upon her marriage to the King of Sicily, Wilgefortis prayed to Christ to rescue her. Her relief soon arrived in the form of the mustache and beard she grew. Wilgefortis's father demanded that she veil her hirsutism, but she let this cover slip in the presence of her husband-to-be. Her appearance had a chilling effect upon his ardor. Seeing Wilgefortis's beard and mustache, the king of Sicily gave up all interest in the marriage. Crucified by her father, Wilgefortis, alternatively named "Uncumber," became the patron saint of women who wanted to rid—disencumber—themselves of their husbands. Like the effect of the cross-dressed woman on such men as Ninus, the cross-sexed or hirsute woman also registers an impact on male sexuality. Nominally celebrated as saints, the bearded women nevertheless suffer scorn and ostracism in their narratives, even if they find such disparagement preferable to marriage.

These fables and legends suggest that the medieval female transvestite who passed did not evoke the cultural anxiety that the cross dresser did. It may be, as Vern and Bonnie Bullough explain it, that the woman cross dresser "threatened the male establishment by taking too overtly masculine a role," whereas the female passer did not carry the matter so far, or as Hotchkiss claims, that "a corollary exists between historicity, perceived or actual, and critical views of cross dressing. Transvestism can be sanctioned or even lauded, if the woman does not challenge male authority, or if she disguises herself only temporarily."[53] Yet I would argue that what threatened the patriarchal establishment about cross dressing was more complex than female usurpation of conventionally male power.[54] Boccaccio's narrative suggests that women cross dressers do not merely make themselves into men but make men into something else, that is, into something less—into women–men, the effeminated Ninuses who "rot away idly in bed" or the male suitors who lose interest in their brides. Women cause this change in men indirectly. Although they do not alter men themselves, the thing or *res*, women cross dressers affect the sign or image of maleness by their admixture of visible female elements, thereby debasing, or adulterating, and hence effeminating the masculine image. In an era that often saw little or no distinction between *res* and sign, however, tampering with the latter was tantamount to an assault on the former. Semiramis's partial disguise, then, is not so much dressing up, a woman arrogating male power, as dressing down, for her visible femininity degrades the male image, adulterates it, and the actual male in the narrative, Ninus, experiences a mimetic degradation into woman–man. In contrast, the woman who passes, who disguises the "accidents" of her gender, as did Semiramis early on in Boccaccio's narrative and the female monks, effaces her femininity and therefore does not corrupt the sign of maleness—or, more significantly, the *res*. In the first part of Boccaccio's legend of Semiramis, her crossover registers no impact on her son. Indeed, if Anson's interpretation is taken, male monks become even more "manly," or less "womanish," through the female passers who enable their heterosexual desires.

MAKING DESIRE IMPOSSIBLE

Late medieval patriarchal culture did not experience the degree of gender anxiety that Levine detects in its early-modern successor,[55] although its sensitivity to Joan's cross-dressing suggests that her transvestment involved something more threatening than simple female arrogation of male power or abrogation of scriptural command. The deeper nature of her affront is perhaps best illustrated in the posthumous retrial or rehabilitation proceedings of 1455. Ironically, to reverse Boyd's formulation of the matter, the evidence voiced in the retrial to exonerate Joan may well have served as the silent subtext that earlier convicted her, for her male colleagues-in-arms repeatedly testified to the fact that they never felt carnal desire for the cross-dressed Joan, even when they slept in the same room with her and saw her unclad body.

Jean de Metz, who stated that Joan slept beside him each night "without taking off her doublet and breeches," swore on oath that he "never had any desire or carnal feelings for her."[56] Jean II, duc d'Alençon, experienced the same phenomenon even though he caught a glimpse of Joan's breasts: "Sometimes, when we were in the field, I slept with Joan and the soldiers 'on the straw,' and sometimes I saw Joan get ready for the night, and sometimes I looked at her breasts, which were beautiful. Nevertheless I never had any carnal desire for her" (123–24). Joan's squire, Jean d'Aulon, had occasion to see even more of her body, yet neither he nor, he asserts, any other man physically desired her:

> Although she was a young girl, beautiful and shapely, and when helping to arm her or otherwise I have often seen her breasts, and although sometimes when I was dressing her wounds I have seen her legs quite bare, and I have gone close to her many times—and I was strong, young, and vigorous in those days—never, despite any contact I had with the Maid, was my body moved to any carnal desire for her, nor were any of her soldiers or squires moved in this way, as I have heard them say and tell many times....(134)

One of Charles's squires, Bertrand de Poulegny, also recalls his own virility in those days with Joan, "but all the same [he] had no desire or carnal urge to touch her as a woman" (79). Another royal squire, Gobert Thibault, testified that the soldiers in the field with Joan "believed that it was impossible to desire her." And if they were even "talking among themselves about the sins of the flesh," when "they *saw* her and drew near to her, they could not speak like this any more. Suddenly, their sexual feelings were checked" (51–52; italics mine). The mere sight of Joan, the cross-dressed idol, the "false lie," nullified their desire. And Jean Dunois generalized the "impossible" effect Joan had upon male desire to include all women: "…when we were in [Joan's] company we had no wish or desire to approach or have intercourse with women" (111).

In such testimonies at the retrial, these witnesses inadvertently reveal the underlying threat that Joan's cross dressing posed to masculine authority, if not to ecclesiastical powers. Doubtless, Joan's male comrades meant to brighten her tarnished image as the "whore of the Armagnacs," to suggest her madonnalike purity. But such a defense was technically unnecessary, for Joan's judges had dropped their accusations about her sexual immorality and conceded her virginity. Tellingly, Joan's male defenders appear more concerned— at times, like Jean d'Aulon, puzzled and surprised—about their own (hetero)sexuality, or apparent lack of it, than about Joan's. What hovers just beneath the surface of their admiration for the cross-dressed Joan is the fear that the idol of masculinity she constitutes has rendered them effeminate, sexless, with respect both to her and to other women.

So powerful, albeit subtle, in the retrial, Joan's threat to masculinity lives on in representations of one central figure in her drama: the dauphin. Both early and postcanonization playwrights shape Charles into the effeminate foil of a masculinized Joan. In the chronicle histories that served as Shakespeare's source for *1 Henry VI*, Holinshed had noted that Joan "counterfeit[ed] mankind" in her attire, and Shakespeare's dauphin registers the effects of her cross dressing. Charles's "womanly" nature initially takes the form of his servile devotion to Joan; in Act I, scene ii, after she defeats him in a mock sword fight, the dauphin fawns upon her as the "bright star of Venus" (l. 144). At the end of the play (Act V, scene iv), when Joan claims she is pregnant in a desperate attempt to avoid the fire and first names the dauphin as the father of her unborn child, the jest (and proof of Joan's mendacity) is that such an ineffectual fop as Charles could never achieve paternity. Shaw, who discusses Joan's "abnormal" manliness in the preface to his *Saint Joan* and outright labels her an "unwomanly wom[a]n," molds Charles into her mirror opposite, the "gentle little Dauphin" who does not want to be either a father or a son, especially a son of St. Louis (Scene II). And in the preface to *The Lark*, Jean Anouilh admits to the knowledge that Joan was a "big, healthy girl" and goes on to create a dauphin who confesses to being frightened by virgins even though Charles knows his disclosure invites his wife to tell him one more time that he is "not virile enough."

To Joan, her cross dressing was, she insisted, "but a little thing, the least of all" (153; 1. 206), yet to her opponents, and even to her defenders, it became all important. For some, it caused confusion concerning her sexual or gender identity; the judges at Rouen opined that "in all things [Joan] behaves more like a man than a woman" (158; *in omnibus virum magis se gerens quam mulierum*, 1. 212). Others went farther and wondered whether she was human or monster: "What it was, God only knows," the anonymous author of the *Parisian Journal* exclaimed.[57] As I have argued here, however, the most disturbing question Joan's cross dressing posed to her cohorts and judges alike was not who she was, or what her gender was, but what gender itself was, specifically the male gender—what constituted it, what menaced it, what preserved it, and what relationship it bore to biological sex. To contemporary churchman and layperson alike, to both her nominal friends and her enemies, Joan was a "false lie," an idolater and an idol who threatened to come true, to adulterate masculinity itself. For that reason, if Englishmen had not burned Joan of Arc, Frenchmen probably would have. As Shaw observes in the preface to *Saint Joan*, when Joan was captured, her Armagnac military colleagues were close by and probably could have saved her. But these soldiers were as glad to be rid of her as were the churchmen, for what was "at stake" was not merely God, king, and nation but the traditional constituent of all three, manhood.

JOAN AND THE TAILOR: RE-HABILITATION

Joan's retrial and exoneration were prompted by political changes in France. Once Charles VII was on the throne, it was in his own best interests to clear the name of the woman who had put him there, especially since a new assault on his legitimacy, his actual paternity, was being raised by the English in the 1450s.[58] To reclaim Joan, to deny her visible sign of idolatry, she had to be literally re-dressed— re-habilitated—as a woman. While the retrial gave voice to the fears that had animated opposition to the cross-dressed Joan, it also laid the groundwork of vestmentary purification that culminated in her canonization in 1920. Once Joan's clothes were burned in the fire, according to the testimony of the author of the *Parisian Journal*, the executioner exposed her body for all to see; then he stoked up the fire again and burned her "poor carcass" to ashes, which were scattered in the Seine.[59] Other legends had it, though, that Joan's body was irreducible in the fire, that her heart would not burn, and the inevitable rumors circulated that Joan had been sighted alive.[60] Purged of her former attire in the fire, this reborn naked Joan was available for reclothing, a process that began in the retrial records. Several male witnesses testified that the first time they saw Joan, she was wearing women's clothing, specifically, a red dress, of poor condition befitting her social status.[61] On their prompting or direct suggestion, they rationalized, Joan exchanged this garb for riding clothes to make her way to the dauphin. Mentioned almost incidentally, this travel wear is male costume of a colorless nature. Far more memorable, as well as prophetic, is the image of the peasant Joan in the red dress.

Joan also acquired a tailor in her re-habilitation. Jean Marcel stated that when the duchess of Bedford conducted an examination to determine whether Joan was a virgin, she ordered the tailor, Jeannotin Simon, to make a woman's tunic for Joan.[62] As Simon tried the garment on Joan, he was moved to "softly put his hand on her breast," an advance Joan repelled by slapping his face. Unlike Joan's cross dressing, which checked male desire for her, her female attire now encouraged such ardor, and this new image of Joan in woman's garb anticipates what would develop over the next several centuries. Joan's re-habilitation made her increasingly attractive to the men around her; poets, dramatists, and librettists lost little opportunity to cast her in amorous roles, with both male friends and enemies alike.[63] Civic officials thought she looked best in female peasant garb, as Chapu had sculpted Joan in 1872.[64] By the early twentieth century, Joan had been rescripted and reclad to serve the interests of God, king, country, and, finally, masculinity—male heterosexual desire—itself. In this new garb, Joan was canonized in 1920. The "Most Blessed Father," Pope Benedict XV, declared her to be an "object of veneration, of imitation."[65] In the eyes of the church, Joan of Arc had become an image of holiness, a "true lie," forever.

NOTES

1. Pierre Tisset and Yvonne Lanhers, eds., *Procès de condamnation de Jeanne d'Arc*, 3 vols. (Paris, 1960–71), vol. 1, p. 397.

2. Marina Warner, *Joan of Arc: The Image of Female Heroism* (New York, 1981), p. 117.

3. Beverly Boyd, "Wyclif, Joan of Arc, and Margery Kempe," *Mystics Quarterly* 12 (1986), 117.

4. Jeffrey Burton Russell, *Witchcraft in the Middle Ages* (Ithaca, 1972), p. 261. Russell notes that Joan's judges toyed with accusations of witchcraft but withdrew them altogether, as I explore below.

5. Régine Pernoud, *The Retrial of Joan of Arc: The Evidence at the Trial for Her Rehabilitation*, trans. J.M. Cohen (London, 1955), pp. 51–52.

6. Boyd, p.116. Boyd sees Joan's trial as an extension of English concern over heresy, Lollardy, at home. In 1401, England enacted laws against heresy, including state execution by burning, and on February 23 the first such execution (of William Sawtre) took place. Anne Llewellyn Barstow, *Joan of Arc: Heretic, Mystic, Shaman* (Lewiston, 1986), p. 85, holds a similar view, noting that in 1428, the year Joan began her mission, "an apparent recurrence of Lollard belief in eastern England had led to the arrest of sixty suspects, three of whom were burned to death by the Bishop of Norwich, who later became an observer at Joan's trial. The remains of John Wyclif … were dug up and burned [in 1428]." Both Boyd and Barstow further note the association between female mystics and heresy.

7. Pernoud, p. 47.

8. Jeffrey Burton Russell, *Dissent and Reform in the Early Middle Ages* (Berkeley, 1965), p. 5.

9. Carlos M.N. Eire, *War against the Idols: The Reformation of Worship from Erasmus to Calvin* (Cambridge, 1986), p. 5.

10. J.H. Waszink and J.C.M. Van Winden, eds. and trans., *Tertullianus, De idolatria: Critical Text, Translation and Commentary* (Leiden, 1987), vol. 1.1, p. 23.

11. *Summa theologiae*, 2a2ae, 94, 4. trans. Blackfriars (New York, 1964), vol. 40, p. 35.

12. Valerie R. Hotchkiss *Clothes Make the Man: Female Cross Dresing in Medieval Religion, Literature, and History* (New York, 1996), ch. 4 ("Transvestism on Trial: The Case of Jeanne d'Arc"). I am indebted to Hotchkiss's wide-ranging study, which the author generously shared with me early on in the preparation of this article.

13. Pernoud, p. 183.

14. Pierre Duparc, ed., *Procès en nullité de la condamnation de Jeanne d'Arc*, 5 vols. (Paris, 1977–1988), vol. 5, pp. 118–19, instances numerous appearances of the accusation of idolatry in the proceedings and final condemnation, although he does not make a case for the eventual exclusive focus on this charge in the so-called trial for relapse.

15. Elsewhere in this volume, Steven Weiskopf argues that Joan gains control over the text by *becoming* the text, which she alone can interpret, whereas I read Joan as largely constructed by the trial text. In part, our different readings turn upon the question of whether medieval judicial transcripts, secular or ecclesiastical, constitute life-writing. Whose "voice(s)" do we hear in these documents?

16. Tisset, 1. 40–179.

17. Tisset, 1. 184–286.

18. Tisset, 1. 290–97. J. van Kan, "Bernard Shaw's *Saint Joan*: An Historical Point of View," in *"Saint Joan": Fifty Years After, 1923/24–1973/74*, ed. Stanley Weintraub (Baton Rouge, 1973), pp. 44–53, discusses the relationship between the initial seventy points of accusation and the subsequent twelve points.

19. See Ingvald Raknem, *Joan of Arc in History, Legend, and Literature* (Oslo, 1971), pp. 70–77.

20. W.P. Barrett, ed. and trans., *The Trial of Jeanne d'Arc* (London, 1931), p. 227. The original Latin text occurs in Tisset, 1. 290. All subsequent quotations of Barrett's translation are indicated parenthetically by page number in my text, followed by the volume and page number of the original text in Tisset. I include the original text from Tisset parenthetically in cases where the actual wording is important to my argument.

21. Vern L. and Bonnie Bullough, *Cross Dressing, Sex, and Gender* (Philadelphia, 1993), p. 51. The Bulloughs cite the Council of Gangra (ca. 345), which condemns women who disguise themselves as monks. As I note below, this same activity was later valorized in a different medieval discourse, the saint's legend. The Theodosian Code (435) also prohibited female tonsure.

22. James A. Brundage, *Law, Sex, and Christian Society in Medieval Europe* (Chicago, 1987), pp. 213, 251.

23. Bullough and Bullough, p.51, note exceptions to the cultural sanction of holy transvestism; for example, the Council of Gangra had condemned pious women who posed as male in order to join monasteries. Marie Delcourt, *Hermaphrodite: Myths and Rites of the Bisexual Figure in Classical Antiquity*, trans. Jennifer Nicholson (London, 1958), pp. 84–101, surveys medieval legends of female saints in masculine clothing. See also Rudolf M. Dekker and Lotte C. van de Pol, *The Tradition of Female Transvestism in Early Modern Europe*, trans. Judy Marcure and Lotte Van de Pol (London, 1989), pp. 44–46; Vern L. Bullough, "Transvestism in the Middle Ages," *American Journal of Sociology* 79 (1974), 1381–94; and Hotchkiss, ch. 2 ("Female Men of God").

24. James Anson, "The Female Transvestite in Early Monasticism: The Origin and Development of a Motif," *Viator* 5 (1974), 11. There is considerable controversy over the origin of the motif. Delcourt, *Hermaphrodite*, pp. 84–102, finds in the motif evidence of female aspiration

to bisexuality, which amounts to the asexuality so prominent in early Christian asceticism. Earlier scholars saw in the motif a survival of the cult of the bisexual Aphrodite of Cyprus. My concern here is not to identify the source of holy transvestism but to understand its significance to the later Middle Ages.

25. *The Golden Legend of Jacobus de Voragine*, trans. Granger Ryan and Helmut Ripperger (1941; rpt. New York, 1969), p. 613.

26. Anson, p. 19. Ultimately, however, Anson concludes, the legend of the transvested female monk enables rather than cancels monastic heterosexual desire, for it makes the woman disguised as man "appear guilty of the very temptation to which the monks are most subject."

27. Bullough and Bullough, *Cross Dressing*, p. 46.

28. Anson, p. 13.

29. *Summa theologiae*, 2a2ae. 169, 2, vol. 44, p. 239.

30. Hotchkiss, ch. 4. Hotchkiss surveys other medieval defenses of Joan's transvestism, including the "practical argument that male clothing is more appropriate for waging war."

31. Jules Quicherat, ed., *Procès de condamnation et de réhabilitation de Jeanne d'Arc dite La Pucelle*, 5 vols. (Paris, 1841–49)), 3. 440–41. As I argue below, however, Joan's judges took care to invalidate this defense.

32. Medieval transvestism, especially male transvestism, is an understudied phenomenon. New documents on the latter are coming to light, such as David Lorenzo Boyd and Ruth Mazo Karras, "The Interrogation of a Male Transvestite Prostitute in Fourteenth-Century London," *GLQ: A Journal of Lesbian and Gay Studies* 1 (1995), 459–65. As the various medieval fables and legends of castration and eunuchry suggest, transsexualism also warrants investigation; see my discussion below.

33. From here on, I use the terms "transvestment" and "transvestism" generically to indicate any degree of disguising one's sexual identity and/ or assuming the identity of the other sex, whereas "cross dressing" refers to partial masquerade and "passing" or "crossover" to complete, even if episodic, assumption of the appearance of the opposite sex. On the use of these terms, see Marjorie Garber, *Vested Interests: Cross-Dressing and Cultural Anxiety* (New York, 1992).

34. Pernoud, *Joan of Arc by Herself and Her Witnesses*, trans. Edward Hyams (New York, 1964) plate 4 (following p. 128). Also reproduced in Warner, plate 15 (following p. 228).

35. Pernoud, *Joan*, plate 3a.

36. Pernoud, *Joan*, plate 1. Sixteenth-century depictions of Joan increasingly feminize her costume, as does the 1581 painting commissioned by the aldermen of Orleans (plate 7), in which Joan wears a plumed hat and bodiced dress. The only vestige of male attire is the rather diminutive sword Joan displays. Pernoud remarks that the "Aldermen's Painting" influenced iconography for the next two centuries.

37. In his chronicle, Jean Germain, bishop of Nevers and Châlons, reported that Joan tried to "pass herself off as a man" in order to evade capture. See Charles Wayland Lightbody, *The Judgements of Joan: Joan of Arc, A Study in Cultural History* (Cambridge, Mass., 1961), p. 83.

38. When Joan herself chose to defend her cross dressing, she sometimes implied it was intended to ward off sexual assault when, for instance, she was imprisoned by male guards. What she must have meant was that cross dressing in some way dissuaded her would-be ravishers from attacking her, frightening them off. She could not have believed that male attire literally thwarted sexual attack; at best, pants provide a short-lived obstacle to such violence. As I shall examine below, Joan's male friends remarked upon the antilibidinal effect her cross dressing had upon them. Ecclesiastical authorities, to be sure, did not sanction female cross dressing as a charm against male sexual aggression or attraction; to do so would perhaps empower women too much and countenance demonry. Only the more passive and orthodox "passing" was culturally acceptable.

39. Tertullian condemns the stage because everything about it, including actors who "counterfeit" sex through transvestment, involves idolatry; see *De spectaculis* xxiii, trans. T. R. Glover, (New York, 1931), p. 287.

40. *"Le miroir aux dames": poème inédit du XVe siècle* (Neuchâtel, 1908), ll. 505–10; translation quoted from Warner, p. 148.

41. Cited by Michael Camille, *The Gothic Idol: Ideology and Image-making in Medieval Art* (1989; repr. Cambridge, 1992), p. 50. I am generally indebted to Camille's Chapter 5, "Idols in the Church," which traces the backgrounds of Christian attitudes to images and idols.

42. Camille, p. 207.

43. Margaret Aston, *Lollards and Reformers: Images and Literacy in Late Medieval Religion* (London, 1984), p. 139.

44. Camille, p. 207. As Camille remarks earlier (p. xxvii), "The Christian Church was never in doubt that idolatry should always be condemned; the perennial debate was how to define and separate 'correct' visual representations from incorrect idols and how to operate within that definition."

45. Eire, p. 5.

46. On the ecclesiastical defense of images in late-medieval England, see Margaret Aston, *England's Iconoclasts* (Oxford, 1988), pp. 143–54.

47. Of particular interest to the judges was whether Joan had "seen or had made any images or pictures of herself or in her likeness" (87; 1. 98). Although Joan denied both actions, she was later held responsible for misleading people and encouraging them to "set up her images on the altars of saints, wear medals of lead or other metal in her likeness, like those made for the anniversaries of saints canonized by the Church" (202; 1. 261).

48. Camille, p. xxix.

49. Adultery and idolatry were traditionally linked, for both were seen as producing false or counterfeit images. See Aston, *Iconoclasts,* pp. 466–79. In patriarchal thinking, men who wear women's clothing do not "adulterate" the female sex or threaten to turn women into men, for adultery (from *ad + alter*) implies the mixing in of an inferior or foreign element, the "other." On the increasing fear of effeminization during the Renaissance, see Laura Levine's provocative study, *Men in Women's Clothing: Anti-Theatricality and Effeminization, 1579–1642* (Cambridge, 1994).

50. On Chaucer's use of this episode, see my "Worlds Apart: Orientalism, Antifeminism and Heresy in Chaucer's *Man of Law's Tale,*" *Exemplaria: A Journal of Theory in Medieval and Renaissance Studies* 8 (1996), 59–96.

51. Guido A. Guarino, trans., *"Concerning Famous Women" by Giovanni Boccaccio* (New Brunswick, 1963), p. 4. Subsequent quotations of this translation are cited parenthetically by page number in my text.

52. Nancy F. Partner, "No Sex, No Gender," in *Studying Medieval Women: Sex, Gender, Feminism* (Cambridge, Mass, 1993) pp. 117–42, distinguishes between biological sexual identity (male or female) and gender identity (living socially as man or woman) and raises interesting and important questions about the relationships between the two identities in the Middle Ages. Boccaccio seems to imply that Ninus trades both identities with his mother. (Partner also discusses the relationship between transsexualism and transvestism.)

53. Bullough and Bullough, p. 68; Hotchkiss, ch. 8.

54. The predominating view of the nature of the transgression involved in female transvestism is that "it attacked men by aping their appearance in order to usurp their function" (Warner, *Joan,* p. 155); that is, women try to make themselves into men. At the same time, Warner notes, female transvestism also flattered men and affirmed their supremacy, for men "remain the touchstone and equality a process of imitation." Hotchkiss, ch. 4, agrees that Joan's wearing of male attire reaffirmed the sexual hierarchy but argues that her "clear presentation of herself in female terms as a virgin and innocent vessel for a divine plan" created a "hero clearly defined by her female sex, yet unconfined by gender constructs for women." My point here is somewhat different, for I interpret female cross dressing in terms of its effect on male sexual and gender identity.

55. Levine concludes that the profoundest fear driving Renaissance antitheatricalism and antitransvestism is that "there is no real masculinity, no masculine self" or, worse yet, that "locked away within the man—tucked away somewhere inside his own body—is a woman herself" (*Men in Women's Clothing,* p. 23). See also Peter Stallybrass, "Transvestism and the 'Body Beneath': Speculating on the Boy Actor," in *Erotic Politics: Desire on the Renaissance Stage,* ed. Susan Zimmerman (New York, 1992), p. 76; R. Valerie Lucas, *"Hic Mulier:* The Female Transvestite in Early Modern

England," *Renaissance and Reformation* 24 (1988), 68–69; and Jean E. Howard, "Cross Dressing, the Theater, and Gender Struggle in Early Modern England," in *Crossing the Stage: Controversies on Cross Dressing*, ed. Lesley Ferris (New York, 1992), pp. 20–46.

56. Pernoud, *Retrial*, p. 75. Subsequent quotations of retrial testimony are from this translation and cited parenthetically by page number in my text.

57. Janet Shirley, ed., *A Parisian Journal, 1405–1449* (Oxford, 1968) p. 240.

58. Charles T. Wood, *Joan of Arc and Richard III: Sex, Saints, and Government in the Middle Ages* (New York, 1988), pp. 147–50, analyzes the rehabilitation trial in light of Charles's need to confirm the legitimacy of his birth. See also Wood's article in this volume.

59. Shirley, p. 264.

60. For instance, in the *Chroniques de la noble ville et cite de Metz* of 1445, printed in Quicherat, *Procès*, vol. 5.

61. Pernoud, *Retrial*, pp. 73, 76, 78.

62. Pernoud, *Retrial*, p. 177.

63. For instance, in his *Die Jungfrau von Orleans*, Friedrich Schiller has Joan fall in love with an English officer, Lionel.

64. *Joan of Arc Loan Exhibition Catalogue* (New York: Joan of Arc Statue Committee, 1913), p. 41.

65. Text of the official pronouncement of canonization is reprinted in Wilfred T. Jewkes and Jerome B. Landfield, eds., *Joan of Arc: Fact, Legend, and Literature* (New York, 1964), p. 165. Elsewhere in this volume, H.A. Kelly describes the proceedings that led to the canonization.

WAS JOAN OF ARC A "SIGN" OF CHARLES VII'S INNOCENCE?

Jean Fraikin

An analysis of the liturgical contexts, textual evidence, and current misinterpretations of Joan's first meeting with Charles VII.

About five o' clock on the afternoon of Tuesday, February 22, 1429, Joan of Arc and an escort of six men left Vaucouleurs by the Porte de France. Eleven days later, having crossed unhindered a territory filled with potential ambushes, they arrived at Chinon almost as the noon Angelus was ringing.[1] On that Friday, March 4, they found lodging at an inn.[2] Everyone could breathe again, for Joan had kept her word to Baudricourt: "I must be with the king before Mid-Lent even if it means wearing my feet off to the knees."[3] Lunch over, they climbed to the castle where her traveling companions presented her to a royal entourage[4] that displayed no enthusiasm.[5] At first glance, her youth, peasant look, and manners could only engender mistrust among people more used to meeting this type of woman in the countryside than at court.[6] Asked about her reasons for coming, she obstinately refused to furnish explanations to anyone but the dauphin. Since the counselors were divided, this response did not receive a unanimous welcome: some thought that the king should give her no heed; others, less hostile, thought that he could at least hear what she had to say to him.[7]

At Charles's command, priests assembled and tried to interrogate her, and the favorable responses they received from Joan clashed with the opinion of the nobles whose influence reinforced the king's own hesitation about receiving her. Perhaps the physical examination of Joan's virginity[8] was the determining factor.[9] In any event, she was at last allowed to see Charles face to face.[10] On March 6, "the Maid came to the king."[11] When she entered the royal chamber, "she

61

recognized him among the others through the advice of her voice, who revealed him to her."[12] In a letter addressed to Charles VII, she had indicated that she was confident in her ability to identify people,[13] something she had already demonstrated in the case of Robert de Baudricourt at Vaucouleurs.[14] According to Jean Pasquerel, Joan's confessor, she had confided to him that she had been shown in by the count of Vendôme.[15] The testimony of two witnesses heard at the rehabilitation trial, Simon Charles,[16] president of the Chamber of Accounts, and Jean Moreau,[17] a bourgeois of Rouen and originally a countryman of Joan's, establishes that a hoax had been contrived. Jean Chartier[18] and other chroniclers are filled with this story,[19] among them a clerk from La Rochelle, a contemporary, who adds a nice touch to the first interview between Joan of Arc and Charles VII.[20] He reports that when Joan asked to speak with the king, she was first shown Charles de Bourbon pretending that he was the king; but she soon said that he was not the king and that she would recognize him easily, if she saw him, even though she had never seen him. After that, they brought in a squire[21] pretending to be the king, but she well knew that he was not; and soon thereafter the king came out of another room, and as soon as she saw him she said that that was he, and she told him that she had come on behalf of the King of heaven and wanted to speak with him.[22]

The reality of these masquerades has been denied,[23] but the evidence for such a scene is multiple, and an overlooked clue allows us to prove its credibility, for no doubt now exists about the date of this encounter. In 1429, Laetare Sunday fell on March 6. According to traditions going back to the Renaissance, in France and Belgium Mid-Lent falls on the Thursday preceding the fourth Sunday of Lent. In the Middle Ages, however, the universal understanding was that Mid-Lent was Laetare Sunday.[24]

The festivities organized for this occasion on the banks of the Meuse, at Domrémy, are evoked in their naive freshness by the witnesses who experienced and reported on them at the rehabilitation trial. On Fountains Sunday, the lords and ladies of the village went to relax under the "fairy tree," bringing with them girls and boys who sang, danced, and happily ate rolls baked by their mothers.[25] Likewise, at the castle of Chinon that winter, people did not just cool their heels in attendance, for they, too, took part in the merrymaking. In his youth, Charles had himself showed a propensity "both night and day, and more than was useful, to get caught up in banquets, dances, and pleasures."[26]

When Joan entered the great hall of the castle, she believed "that there were at least three hundred knights and fifty torches."[27] Her arrival, minutely regulated, unexpectedly took place theatrically in front of a crowd of spectators. Dressed in men's habit—"black doublet, attached hose, short coat of coarse gray-black color, hair short and black, and a black hat on her head"[28]— she was introducing herself into a masquerade without suspecting that hers was to be the role of the fool. Divided minds, prejudice, and fear of ridicule[29] had led to the cruel ordeal, one that would cause no harm to the king if it failed. This farce, put on to test Joan's gifts of divination, became instead a source of confusion for its initiators, though they were still far from having lost the game.

This "mise en scène designed to fool Joan" is not just a "hypothesis," and one cannot maintain with Claude Desama that this reconstruction "must be avoided as lacking in all foundation."[30] Moreover, to draw a veil of silence over the witnesses who saw it and argue that Simon Charles and Jean Moreau "were not at Chinon and were repeating hearsay in the course of a sharply focused trial" in no way reduces the likelihood of the episode.[31] Simon Charles, an important personage, would have no reason to invent a fable. He was content to make himself the interpreter of what he had heard told, in the month of March, upon his return from an embassy to Venice. Jean Moreau was relating a public rumor, rather more suspect and smacking of the miraculous: two copperware merchants, Nicolas Saussart and Jean Chando, had informed him at Rouen of the news about Joan, a girl from his native parts, news that was spreading throughout the royal domain. In the solemn context of the rehabilitation trial, must we imagine that this bourgeois of Rouen had believed it necessary to propagate a fictitious rumor? The allusion was much too hesitant to have led to consequences. What is more, to sweep aside the chroniclers in whom the incident is echoed because they wrote late and in distant provinces, or because they copied Alain Chartier, who may have drawn his information from the rehabilitation trial is to rest one's case on a conjecture even more hazardous: the clerk from La Rochelle, another contemporary chronicler, has simply been overlooked in the evidence drawn up in order to refute them.

The riddles put to Joan have nothing to do with a "legendary version."[32] Rather, one should see in them a diverting game whose meaning has been obscured by texts that give only a glimpse of the fact that the welcome given to the liberator of Orleans took place within Mid-Lent's atmosphere of burlesque gaiety.

CERTAIN THINGS SAID TO THE KING IN SECRET

Ever since 1429, people have asked about the sign Joan brought to the king so that he would no longer doubt the mission of the ambassador from heaven. Going beyond earlier assumptions, Guenée's recent thesis has opened new vistas.[33] This thesis maintains that after the murder of John the Fearless, duke of Burgundy, at the bridge of Montereau on September 10, 1419, Charles, tormented by remorse, had asked himself whether his father, Charles VI, and his mother, Isabeau of Bavaria, were not right to disinherit him in the Treaty of Troyes of May 21, 1420. In his confusion, "he asked God to prove to him that he was true heir of the kingdom."[34]

Guenée uncovers the answer in Joan's trials: "Why not just believe Brother Pasquerel, Joan's confessor," he writes, "when he declares that Joan, speaking in God's name, has said to the dauphin: 'Thou art the true heir of France'? And why not believe Joan herself when she says that 'the king had a sign concerning his deeds' (Habuit rex suus signum de factis suis)? It was not his birth that Charles doubted; it was his deeds. And Joan's mission was to convince him that God had forgiven him for Montereau, first through her words at Chinon in February 1429, then through her victory at Orleans in May 1429."[35]

Without getting into the whole issue of the "sign" and of the diverse interpretations it inspired, we shall limit ourselves here to faulting some of the materials on which this still revolutionary opinion is based.

The scholarly editor to whom the Société de l'Histoire de France[36] assigned the monumental task of preparing the nullification trial for publication prefers a manuscript that is preserved in England and that was unknown to the original editor of the rehabilitation trial. In his eyes, Ms Stowe 84 of the British Library is possibly the copy that was deposited in the Trésor des Chartes and is probably the authentic version that came into the hands of Charles du Lys, a lawyer at the Cour des Aides. In all likelihood, Charles du Lys consulted it in the course of genealogical research designed to make himself a member of Joan of Arc's family. Finally, Duparc favors the London manuscript "because of its source, and because it has never been used."[37] That is why it serves as "the base text" for his edition.[38] Duparc is at pains to add, however, that he has utilized MS Latin 5970 of the Bibliothèque Nationale at Paris "in the case of lacunae" whenever the scribe of Stowe 84 "through carelessness omits words or parts of sentences."[39] He uses the same approach with MS Latin 8838 (Urfé).[40] In spite of the esteem due Duparc for all his labor on the nullification trial, his predilection for the London manuscript rests on fragile foundations, as is shown by the treatment its copyist reserved for Jean Pasquerel's deposition.[41]

This Augustinian hermit was the sole witness who mentioned, at the jubilee of Le Puy in 1429, the presence of Isabelle Romée, Joan's mother, and a few members of the escort that had led her daughter to Chinon.[42] In that year, the Annunciation (March 25) coincided with Good Friday.[43] The Stowe manuscript has the inadmissable reading "in villa Anciensi," one that scholars have tried to identify with Anche en Touraine.[44] The occasion was really a pilgrimage to the Black Virgin of Le Puy, and that was what allowed Joan's companions to talk Pasquerel into following them: "And he came with them to Tours, the city where he was a lector in a convent" ("Et cum eisdem venit usque ad villam Turonensem, in cujus conventu ville Turonensis ipse loquens erat lector"), one reads in Stowe, which omits seven words.[45] The other two manuscripts are more precise: "Et cum eisdem venit ad villam de 'Chinon' et dehinc usque ad villam Turonensem."[46] They came back through Chinon before continuing on their way to Tours.

Some people, among them Duparc, claim that the date of Joan's first physical examination remains unknown.[47] Yet we know that before her arrival brought her close to the king at Chinon, she was notably visited by Jeanne de Preuilly, the wife of Raoul de Gaucourt, governor of Orleans, and by Jeanne de Mortemer, the wife of Robert le Maçon, chancellor of France.[48] So there was not just one physical examination, but two, the one directed by madame de Gaucourt and the other by madame de Trèves. Again, the manuscripts charged with inferiority counter the claim of ignorance about this date by giving, apropos of these examinations, a fuller version of Pasquerel's deposition: "And he heard it said that Joan, when she came to the king, was twice visited by women in order to know her state, both whether she was a man or a woman and whether she was deflowered or a virgin; and she was found a woman, still a virgin not yet in puberty" ("Et audivit dici quod ipsa Johana, dum venit versus regem, fuit visitata bine vice per mulieres quid erat de ea, et si esset vir vel mulier, et an esset corrupta vel virgo; et inventa fuit mulier, virgo tamen et puella").[49] Stowe leaves out the fact that Joan was twice visited by matrons and midwives—per mulieres—and that the examination had the goal of first determining whether she was not a man disguised as a woman and then whether her conduct was beyond reproach: et si esset vir vel mulier, et an esset corrupta vel virgo.[50]

The unreliability of the Stowe scribe also becomes clear from a short phrase in French in the text: "Esse pas là 'la Pucelle?"[51] The other two manuscripts put the following words into the mouth of the knight who insulted Joan by claiming behind her back that if he were to spend a night with her, he would not return her a maid: "Est-ce pas là 'la Pucelle' ?"[52]

My last comment about the testimony of Joan's confessor relates to the words she addressed to the king. The manuscripts that Duparc claims are less admissible cite them this way: "On my Lord's part I say to thee that thou art true heir and son of the king" ("Ego dico tibi ex parte /de Messire, que tu es vray heritier et filz du roy").[53] These last four words are omitted from Stowe,[54] which, as we have seen, Duparc has preferred to MSS Latin 5970 and 8838 of the Bibliothèque Nationale. Without discrediting this version entirely, the carelessness of its copyist surely marks it as inferior to the two others. We must reject the first argument advanced for this new thesis, since it sets aside complete documents in favor of a work filled with holes.[55]

The second argument of the new thesis also rests on an interpretation of Duparc, who advances a bold translation of a passage from the condemnation trial. "It appears nevertheless probable," he writes, that the true sign given only to the dauphin—one carefully concealed by Joan even though the inquisitors attempted to lead her astray about its nature—concerned what has been called the dauphin's secret. On February 27, having declared to the judges that she had seen nothing at the time of that interview, Joan added that "the king had a sign about his deeds before he believed her" : "habuit rex suus signum de factis suis."[56] The deeds in question seem to be those of the king, if the Latin is correct."[57]

It is unusual to expect so much of a Latin that, in the condemnation trial, is filled with solecisms. In this case the "correct" text should have read: "habuit rex eius signum de factis suis."[58] Relying on grammatical anachronism, scholars will soon be able to rewrite Joan's history. What kind of reading will they give to her words of March 10: "rex suus dedit fratribus suis arma, videlicet unum scutum …"?[59] If the Latin is correct, those are the king's own brothers, not Joan's, to whom he is giving arms—an azure shield bearing two golden lilies and a sword in the middle. In the same way, when Joan stated on March 12 that "pater suus dicebat fratribus suis …,"[60] she meant to say that her father charged his own brothers, Joan's uncles, with drowning her if she left home in the company of soldiers.

Reading the question asked of Joan on February 27 provides a context for the sign that presumably lets us see the source of this error:

> "Interrogata qualiter rex suus adhibuit fidem dictis eius: Respondit quod ipse habebat bona intersignia et per clerum. Interrogata quales revelaciones rex suus habuit: Respondit: Vos non habebitis eas adhuc a me de isto anno. Item dixit quod per tres ebdomadas fuit interrogata per clerum, apud villam de 'Chinon' et Pictavis; et habuit rex suus signum de factis suis, priusquam vellet ei credere. Et clerici de parte sua fuerunt huius opinionis quod videbatur eis in facto suo non esse nisi bonum."[61]

> [Asked how the king gave credence to her words, she answered that he had good signs, and through the clergy. Asked what revelations the king had, she answered: "You will not learn them from me this year." She said that for three weeks she was examined by the clergy, at Chinon and Poitiers; and the king had a sign about her deeds before he was willing to believe in her. And the clergy of her party were of this opinion, that it appeared to them that there was nothing but good in her mission.[62]]

The words "dictis eius" in the first sentence have naturally caused another meaning to be attributed to "factis suis," which has been retained rather than "factis eius," the correct reading. A little farther down in the text, the words "facto suo"[63]—that is, the mission of the clergy, if the Latin is correct—have caught no one's attention. It is true, however, that they were emended to "facto eius" in the promoter's address to the court.[64]

Under Article 51 of the charges, Jean d'Estivet's presentation reviewed only a part of the interrogation of February 27 concerning the sign; he passed in silence over the sentence containing "factis suis," and it appears nowhere else.[65] But people have inadequately

noted that this sentence involves Joan's second interrogation at
Chinon as well as that at Poitiers—and that the rest involves the
first meeting between Joan of Arc and Charles VII.

In conclusion, Joan arrived at Chinon on March 4, 1429. Two
days later, Laetare Sunday, she was brought into the king's presence.
Coinciding with the merriment of Mid-Lent as it did, the occasion
provided too ripe an opportunity not to involve her. Disturbed by
her personality, the king agreed to give her a private interview in
which Joan revealed some secret matters to him. Some texts,
incomplete and wrongly interpreted, have favored a historical
reconstruction of these events that compare badly with earlier
versions.

NOTES

1. Maurice Vachon, *La topographie, auxiliaire de l'histoire: études
d'itinéraires, dans Jeanne d'Arc: une époque, un rayonnement: colloque
d'histoire médiévale,* Orleans, October 1979 (Paris, 1982), pp. 237–41; and
idem, *La topographie au service de l'histoire: essai pour une recherche
méthodologique des applications aux itinéraires de Jehanne la Pucelle,*
unpublished Doctorat d'Etat thesis, UER Lettres et Sciences Humaines de
l'Université de Reims, 1985, pp. 271–309, cited by Georges Peyronnet,
"Gerson, Charles VII et Jeanne d'Arc," in *Revue d'histoire ecclésiastique,* 84
(March–June 1989).

2. Pierre Tisset, ed. with Yvonne Lanhers, *Procès de condamnation
de Jeanne d'Arc,* 3 vols.(Paris, 1960–71), 1.51, 215 : Joan had arrived at Chinon
"about midday and took lodging at a hostelry. After dinner, she went to
the king who was in the castle." But, as Dunois makes clear (Pierre Duparc,
ed., *Procès en nullité de la condamnation de Jeanne d'Arc,* 5 vols.[Paris, 1977–
88], p. 317), she had to wait two days before meeting him. In good faith,
Joan thought she would quickly be brought before Charles VII; she could
not have imagined the distrust and reservations she inspired, which she tried
to cover up during her trial (on February 22, before Jean Beaupère).

3. Duparc, 1.230, 1.290, deposition of Jean de Metz; ibid., 1.305,
deposition of Bertrand de Poulengy: "[Charles VII], her lord, would bring
her aid before Mid–Lent."

4. Duparc, 1.291, deposition of Jean de Metz.

5. Hermann Korner, *Chronica novella usque ad annum 1435 deducta,*
in *Corpus historicum medii aevi sive scriptores rerum in urbe universo praecipue
in Germania,* ed. Johann-Georg von Eckhart, (Frankfurt, 1743), vol. 2, cols.
1292–93; Jean-Baptist Joseph Ayroles, *La vierge-guerrière* (Paris, 1898),p.
280. Edmond Richer, *Histoire de la Pucelle d'Orléans,* ed. Philippe-Hector
Dunand, (Paris, 1911), vol. 1, p. 77.

6. "Quae quanquam pro primo ob puerilem aetatem, incomtam rusticanamque personam a vasallis Principis despiceretur"; cf. Korner, cols. 1292–93.

7. Duparc, 1.399–400, deposition of Simon Charles.

8. Ibid., 1.389, deposition of Jean Pasquerel.

9. The matrons (women with formal medical expertise) concluded, after they had visited Joan, that she was not a man but a woman, still a virgin, and not yet fully formed. As such, she did not meet the conditions necessary to qualify as a sorceress, and so the king did not have to fear any sorcery from this "shepherdess."

10. The investigation required as a preliminary to their meeting was shortened from three days to two, if one believes Perceval de Boulainvilliers: "The King's Council required that she not see the king's face nor be presented to him before three days. But suddenly the feelings of those men were transformed. The Maid was sent for." Cf. Jules Quicherat, ed., *Procès de condamnation et de réhabilitation de Jeanne d'Arc dite La Pucelle,* 5 vols. (Paris, 1841–49), 5.118–19; Jean–Baptist Joseph Ayroles, *La paysanne et l'inspirée* (Paris, 1894), pp. 244, 541.

11. *Chronique du Mont-Saint-Michel*: cf. Ayroles, *La libératrice* (Paris, 1897), p. 272; Quicherat, 4.313: "Environ miech careme […] ven al rey de Fransa […] une piusela"; cf. *Registres consulaires de Cahors,* in Ayroles, *La vierge-guerrière,* p. 396 and n. 1; *Chronique d'Antonio Morosini,* ed. Germain Lefèvre-Pontalis and Léon Dorez, (Paris, 1901), vol. 3, p. 45, n. 2.

12. Tisset, 1.51–52, 215.

13. Ibid., 1.76, 228.

14. Ibid., 1.49 (MS d'Orléans): "Son oncle la mena audit Robert de Baudricourt, lequel elle congneut bien, et si ne le avoit jamais veu. Et dit qu'elle le congneust par la voix qui luy avoit dist que c'estoit il." Joan's recognition of Baudricourt was referred to in the session of February 22 (Tisset, 1.215) and twice later, in almost the same words, in the promoter's brief, under articles 10 (ibid., 1.202–03) and 17 (ibid., 1.215). The charge contained in the latter article had as its aim to discredit Joan with magical practices. The seventh of the twelve articles submitted to the faculties of theology and canon law at the University of Paris makes only a faint allusion thereto (ibid., 1.249: art. VII). Siméon Luce, strikingly enough, has striven to explain this act of recognition as a purely natural phenomenon. One year before Joan approached the captain of Vaucouleurs, her father, Jacques d'Arc, had met him in the aftermath of a pecuniary dispute between the inhabitants of Greux and of Domrémy on the one hand and the damoiseau of Commercy, who was supposed to guarantee their safety, on the other: "The natural perspicacity of this young visionary, fully alert to what she had heard Jacques d'Arc report, would be adequate to explain this event; when subject to accusation, she nonetheless attributed it, with a mystical humility equal to her sincerity, to a divine revelation." Cf. Siméon Luce, *Jeanne d'Arc à Domrémy,* 2nd ed. (Paris, 1887), pp. 58–162, 171–72.

15. Duparc, 1.389.

16. Ibid., 1.400.

17. Ibid., 1.462.

18. Quicherat, 4.52–53. The historian Jean Chartier did not derive his information from the rehabilitation trial, as Claude Desama has averred in "La première entrevue de Jeanne d'Arc et de Charles VII à Chinon (mars 1429),"*Analecta Bollandiana* 84 (1966), 121. His narrative account of Joan of Arc is dependent on the *Chronique de La Pucelle*. These texts are earlier than 1450. Cf. Ayroles, *La libératrice*, pp. 61–66; Quicherat, 4.51, 203–04, 207; *Chronique de La Pucelle,* ed. Auguste Vallet de Viriville (Paris, 1849), pp. 4, 61–63, 273.

19. Of these chroniclers, Claude Desama (p. 121) crudely maintains that some "copied Jean Chartier pure and simple" and that others "isolated in their distant provinces … wrote more than thirty years after the events." He is referring to the Clerk of Court of Albi and the Dean of Saint-Thibaud of Metz, who could not have heard more than "an echo confused by propaganda."

20. This chronicler has been forgotten by Claude Desama (pp. 120–21), whose vision is clouded by a feverish desire to refute the "legendary version" or the "fable according to which Joan, thanks to her voices, outwitted a farce designed to make her mistake a gentleman of the court for the king himself." It is more likely that Desama has confused the clerk of La Rochelle with the dean of Saint-Thibaud of Metz, whose chronicle is silent on this subject. On the other hand, the reference to it by the clerk of Court of the city hall of Albi is explicit (Quicherat, 4.300–01). Dom Calmet nevertheless wrote (*Histoire de Lorraine* [Nancy, 1745], vol. 3, col. 551) that "the Maid recognized him among all his courtiers, although that day he was wearing on purpose a very simple outfit."

21. A double would not have been unlikely.

22. Ayroles, *La libératrice*, pp. 202–03. Jules Quicherat, "Relation inédite sur Jeanne d'Arc," *Revue historique* 4 (1877), 336–37. The fifteenth-century register of the Hôtel de Ville of La Rochelle has been destroyed. Some extracts were copied in the sixteenth century.

23. One might ask why Claude Desama, who declares that he will not "let himself be blinded by a philosophical or religious premise," has spent so much energy in vain and has had recourse to hypotheses devoid of any foundation in order to deny a perfectly plausible and realistic explanation that does not require recourse to heavenly voices. Claude Desama, "Jeanne d'Arc et Charles VII: l'entrevue du signe," *Revue de l'histoire des religions* 196 (1966), p. 29. This fusillade repeats, almost word for word, a footnote of Jacques Cordier (*Jeanne d'Arc, sa personnalité, son rôle* [Paris, 1948], pp. 106–07, n. 50).

24. Waldemar Liungman, *Traditionswanderungen Euphrat-Rhein: Studien zur Geschichte der Volksbrauche* (Helsinki, 1938), p. 980.

25. Jean Fraikin, "Regard sur l'au-delà de Jeanne d'Arc," *Tradition wallonne* (Brussels, 1993), vol. 10, pp. 50–51. Laetare Sunday was also called

Fountains Sunday in Joan's *pays*. It was also called *dominica Rosae*, or *de Rosa*, or *rosata*, the Sunday of the Five Breads, etc. Cf. *L'art de vérifier les dates* (Paris, 1818), vol. 2, *Glossaire des dates passim*.

26. Thomas Basin, *Histoire de Charles VII*, ed. Charles Samaran, (Paris, 1964), vol. 1, pp. 102–03. The charge that the dauphin was dissolute in his youth has been refuted: cf. Georges du Fresne de Beaucourt, *Histoire de Charles VII* (Paris, 1882), vol. 2, p. 190. But this unrealistic position has been rejected by a demonstration from literary sources of the sincerity of the bishop of Lisieux: cf. Pierre Champion, *Histoire poétique du quinzième siècle* (Paris, 1923), vol. 1, pp. 60–61.

27. Tisset, 1.76, 256.

28. These original details derive from the La Rochelle redactor: cf. Quicherat, "Relation," p. 336; Ayroles, *La libératrice*, p. 202.

29. "Her arrival surprised everyone, and everyone explained it in his own fashion. The king, who was afraid that he might be taken for an excessively credulous spirit, had her examined by cunning men from every profession." Calmet, *Histoire*, vol. 3, col. 551.

30. Desama, "La première entrevue," pp. 120–21.

31. Ibid.

32. See n. 20, above.

33. Bernard Guenée, *Un meurtre, une société: l'assassinat du duc d'Orléans, 23 novembre 1407* (Paris, 1992). See especially the *Épilogue*, pp. 283–89.

34. Guenée, p. 287: a paraphrase of the silent prayer that Charles VII had made in a moment of distress, "asking God among other things to protect him if he were the true heir of the kingdom. It was the exact detail of that prayer, the dauphin's secret, that Joan was supposed to have known by divine inspiration and of which she reminded him." Cf. Duparc 5.192.

35. Guenée, pp. 287–88.

36. The commissioner responsible for the appointment was the regrettable Pierre Marot.

37. Duparc, 1.xii–xiii.

38. Ibid., 5.192.

39. Ibid., 1.xx.

40. Paul Doncoeur and Yvonne Lanhers, eds. *La rédaction épiscopale ou procès de 1455–1456* (Paris, 1961), B.N. MS Lat. 8838.

41. BM MS Stowe 84, f° 78v°–79v°.

42. Duparc, 1.388.

43. A sign of marvelous things and of extraordinary events, according to Nicolas of Savigny (died 1427), who was dean of Lisieux, a canon of Paris, and lawyer for the most famous men of his generation; cf. Luce, *Jeanne d'Arc*, pp. 319–320.

44. Quicherat, 3.101, n. 1–2; Duparc, 5.138.

45. Duparc, 1.388, n. 2.

46. Ibid., 1.388.

47. Ibid., 5.185.

48. Ibid., 1.389.

49. Ibid.

50. Ibid., n. 1–2.

51. Ibid., n. 4.

52. Ibid., 1.389.

53. Ibid., 1.390.

54. Ibid., n. 1.

55. Guenée, seeking certainty rather than probability, places absolute confidence in Duparc's remark about Pasquerel's testimony that "Joan, speaking in the name of God, would have told the dauphin, 'You are the true heir of France.' The claim that she added 'and king's son' seems to be a later addition, not found in the base manuscript [Stowe 84], and hardly likely.... " Cf. Duparc, 5.192.

56. Tisset, 1.76.

57. Duparc, 1.190.

58. In the transcript of Joan's interrogation, we find forty-seven "incorrect" occurrences of "rex suus" and three "correct" occurrences of "rex eius."

59. Tisset, 1.114, 269.

60. Ibid., 1.127.

61. Ibid., 1.76.

62. If the Latin were "correct," the translation of the last sentence should be as follows: "And the clergy, for their part, were of this opinion, that it appeared to them there was nothing but good in their behavior."

63. Tisset, 1.76.

64. Ibid., 1.256. The defective use of "suus" for "eius" gave Lorenzo Valla an occasion to dilate at length on that subject: Lorenzo Valla, *De reciprocacione sui et suus, libellus plurimum utilis*, published as a supplement to his *De linguae latinae elegantia libri sex* (Lyon, 1538), pp. 465–91.

65. Ibid., 1.256. Insufficient attention has been given to Pasquerel's deposition about Joan's arrival at court and Charles VII's response:

> Et pluries audivit dicere dicte Johanne quod de facto suo erat quoddam ministerium; et cum sibi diceretur: 'Nunquam talia fuerunt visa sicut videntur de facto vestro; in nullo libro legitur de talibus factis, ipsa respondebat:': "Dominus meus habet unum librum in quo unquam nullus clericus legit, tantum sit perfectus in clericatura."

> [And quite often he heard people say to the aforesaid Joan that there was something like a divine ministry in her mission, and when someone said to her, 'Never were such things seen as are seen in your mission; in no book can one read of such deeds,' she used to reply, 'My Lord has a book that no clergyman has ever read, no matter how perfect his (*clergie*) learning.']

> Cf. Duparc, 1.396.

TRANSCRIPTION ERRORS IN TEXTS OF JOAN OF ARC'S HISTORY

Olivier Bouzy

An analysis of several transcription mistakes in texts concerning Joan of Arc show that her history, trapped as it is between continued respect for traditional views and simple reading mistakes, is still susceptible to new interpretations.

Under the direction of Académie Française member Philippe Contamine, the Centre Jeanne d'Arc in Orleans is preparing a reedition of volumes 4 and 5 of Jules Quicherat's *Procès de Jeanne d'Arc*. This huge task was initiated in 1960 by Pierre Tisset, who reedited Quicherat's first volume into three volumes. After 1977, it was continued by Pierre Duparc, who published five volumes containing Quicherat's volumes 2 and 3. Quicherat's volumes 4 and 5 will be published in at least five volumes by the Centre Jeanne d'Arc—the first volume covering the period from Joan's first appearance at Charles VII's court to the king's coronation on July 17, 1429.

No entirely reliable edition of these texts exists. This article presents several transcription errors we found, some of which have never before been noticed and have misled even the most recent historians of Joan of Arc and editors of texts. Some mistakes are less important than others: most will not considerably influence our conception of Joan of Arc's history, but they will serve to draw our attention to the importance of choosing the right edition. We have eliminated the mistakes cited below in our edition of Quicherat. Most examples in this article concern the period before the king's coronation and they reflect conclusions from our new edition.

In addition to ordinary transcription mistakes, editors and scholars face at least two deep-rooted but erroneous beliefs about Joan of Arc. The most widespread of these concludes that Joan was a shepherdess, something she herself declared to be incorrect. Another concerns Joan's first meeting with Charles VII. Following the account by Raoul de Gaucourt and the king's doctor, Regnault Thierry, both of whom witnessed the scene, Wladimir Raytses proposed a radical reconstruction of this crucial event: Charles VII was not in fact hidden among his courtiers, few of whom were present. Furthermore, the conversation between him and Joan was short and formal.[1] Such new interpretations are likely to modify our conception of her history, and reliable editions of these texts is the first precondition for elaborating new interpretations.

Philippe Contamine has described the first modest steps of Joan's historiography at the end of the fifteenth century,[2] and Georges Goyau has shown the ambiguous attitude Joan of Arc inspired in later authors who either despised or admired her but were in general incompletely informed about her.[3] In addition to the scientific history embodied in the Urfé, Saint-Victor, and Orleans manuscripts, the more reliable historians included such figures as Richer, L'Averdy, Buchon, Le Brun de Charmette, and Guido Görres, but even their knowledge of Joan of Arc was limited. Guido Görres wrote a biography of three hundred fourteen pages, for example, in which he quotes but does not edit texts concerning Joan.

Finally, between 1841 and 1849, Quicherat published the first collection of texts on the history of Joan of Arc. Philippe Contamine has explained why the Société d'Histoire de France appointed the young historian to do this work at a time when to almost everyone in France "La Pucelle" was best known as the title of Voltaire's erotic poem.[4] *Die Jungfrau von Orleans* was to the German reader the title of Schiller's play, and the figure of Joan of Arc symbolized resistance to foreign invaders. Of course, Quicherat worked without cameras or microfilms, cars, or even trains. His research was limited to the Paris archives; he went only once to Tours, where he apparently stayed just a short while. He published only one of the two versions of the city's accounts—the draft version discarded by Quicherat contained one insignificant sentence more than the version he published. He also asked correspondents to send him transcriptions of manuscripts to which they might have access. This is where the trouble began: Quicherat's correspondents made several mistakes reading these manuscripts. Moreover, Quicherat, hampered by limits of time and quality of tools, simply did not find all the relevant documents, many of which were hidden in public and private archives. This is why, one hundred thirty-nine years later, the same Société de l'Histoire de France made the Centre Jeanne d'Arc responsible for producing a new edition of the Joan of Arc manuscripts.

What follows are examples of the types of errors we have thus far identified. The cases of Chandos's banner, Gélu's treatise, and Joan's letters exemplify typical transcription errors and their consequences. Other cases, such as that of Guy de Cailly's ennoblement or La Piuzela d'Orlhienx, are shown to be forgeries, and still others ("the Good Tidings" and the case of Cauchon's ashes) are utter inventions.

CHANDOS'S BANNER

The most striking example of a reading mistake is Charles VII's letter to Narbonne, in which he mentions the presence of Captain Chandos's banner at the head of the English troops under siege in the fortress of Les Tourelles.[5] This English captain's death in combat in 1370 is described by Froissart.[6] The name Chandos is replaced by the name Glacidas (Glasdale) if one sees either the original or a photograph of the letter. Anxious to thank the man who did the precious transcription for him, Jules Quicherat indicated his name: a Mr. Tournal, then secretary of the Archaeological Commission of Narbonne, who is now exposed to the historians' condemnation. His transcription of this letter is typically replicated without verification.[7] Colonel de Liocourt recently described and commented on this reference to Chandos's banner, although he published a photograph of the king's letter on which one can clearly read the name of Glacidas.[8]

JACQUES GÉLU'S TREATISE

When it came to publishing the theological treatises ordered by Charles VII at Joan's examination in Poitiers and on the occasion of her rehabilitation trial, Quicherat was hindered by his political and philosophical opinions. The treatise by Jacques Gélu (died 1431), archbishop of Embrun, provides a case in point, as I discovered when editing the text.[9] Quicherat severely criticized the text:

> Gélu's treatise is quite an uninstructive hodgepodge. I made it considerably shorter, taking out parts of the passages where points of religious dogma are discussed. The reader may be assured that no passage of any historical interest was eliminated. Wherever there was any word of importance to the historian, I preferred to reproduce

whole passages even when they were obviously useless and tiringly obscure, rather than losing one word.[10]

Quicherat therefore did not publish all these theological treatises justifying the beginning of Joan's adventure and her rehabilitation. Later, others did. Jacques Gélu's Latin treatise was edited in 1889 by Pierre Lanéry-d'Arc, then summarized in French by Ayroles,[11] and finally transcribed but not published in 1960 by Jean Ventach.[12] These versions contain many mistakes and do not clearly identify relevant manuscripts.[13] Moreover, Ayroles's summary is strongly tinted by the author's patriotic preoccupations: Charles VII is invited to grow from virtue to virtue, "so that in this blissful vision you say grace [to God] in your fatherland" (*in patria visione beatifica dotatus*).[14] Translating "patria visione" by "vision of the Father," rather than "in the fatherland," better reflects the mentality of a pious archbishop like Gélu. This text has hardly ever been consulted by historians, although it provides interesting evidence for the way the fifteenth-century church perceived Joan. The text stresses the problem of Joan's cross dressing—this shows that in 1429, even the prelates who supported Charles VII were reluctant to accept a young girl dressed as a man. Apparently, Charles VII decided in favor of Joan only because his confessor, Gérard Machet, was convinced that Joan was the girl whose coming had been announced in a prophecy by Marie Robine, a hermit from Avignon; and even then, Charles required that she be thoroughly examined. Several other treatises that have never been translated (apart from Gerson's tract) are likely to hold surprises for us as well.

JOAN OF ARC'S LETTERS

In 1860, Henri Wallon published two volumes on Joan of Arc that were reedited in 1876 in one volume with illustrations. To my knowledge, this book contains the first facsimile reproduction of two letters by Joan: the first written to the people of Riom on November 9, 1429, and the other written on March 16, 1430. The reproduction is almost accurate. The placement of her signature on the second letter is altered and placed under the phrase "met je doubte que" at the end of the second to last line, probably because there was not enough room at the bottom of the page. The "J" in this signature was crossed by a short stroke, most probably caused by a drop of humidity on the original, a detail that has importance for what is to follow.

In the fourth edition of Wallon's work (1883), the signature on the letter to Reims of March 16 is identical to the one on the letter to Riom. This facsimile was reproduced with the mistake by Jadart in 1887[15] and Debout in 1906 in his first two editions.[16] Seeing a striking similarity between the two signatures, the historians at the time concluded that Joan had a fixed handwriting style and therefore that she could write. In 1909, however, Count Maleyssie-Melun published a booklet on Joan of Arc's letters,[17] illustrated with photographs of letters, including those to Riom and Reims, with their respective signatures reproduced correctly and at the right place. As a result, in 1913, Bishop Debout reproduced without comment, in the third edition of his work, only the signature of the letter to Riom.[18]

Jadart unfotunately took no notice of Maleyssie-Melun's publication; the addition he makes to his book in 1910 contains without correction the reproduction of Wallon's incorrect facsimile of the letter to Reims of March 16, 1430.[19]In 1921, Baron de Terline was struck by the likeness between the signature of the letter to Riom and the one on the letter to Reims as it appeared in Wallon's fourth edition, from which he concluded that the letter to Reims was probably a forgery.[20] The matter was decided in 1929 by the learned archivist Jules de la Martinière, who found that the confusion went back to a printing mistake in Wallon's fourth and fifth editions.[21] Even as late as 1989, however, a renowned professor, lecturing to a well-known French historical society, fell into the trap set one hundred six years earlier by the neglectful typographer of the Editions Didot, as he argued that the copy of the Riom signature made in 1877 was the actual signature of the letter to Reims.[22]As we have seen, this copied signature has a particularity: the initial "J" is crossed on its lower end by a small stroke, which clearly identifies the signature and proves the mistake.

JOAN'S HOUSE IN ORLEANS

In 1876, head archivist Doinel of the Archives du Loiret wrote a short note on a house Joan of Arc purportedly owned in Orleans.[23] This error began in the misreading of a document kept in the Archives Départementales du Loiret (série G, fonds de Sainte-Croix, reg. in 4°, 1418–50). This document concerns the sale of a house lease in

Orleans by Guillot de Guyenne to Jehan Feu, in which Guillot acts
on behalf of a woman called "la Pinelle." Patriotic zeal caused Doinel
to read "la Pucelle" instead of "la Pinelle," and to speculate about
when Joan might have rented this house and why the lease was sold
so late, several months after her death. Bishop Henri Debout
depended upon Doinel's article for his *Histoire de la bienheureuse
Jeanne d'Arc.*[24] In 1908, Eugène Jarry, the new head archivist, read
the text and proved Doinel's theory to be false,[25] and in 1913, in the
third edition of his history of Joan of Arc, Canon Debout elegantly
and honestly admitted the mistake this time (third and fourth
editions, 1913 and 1922, p. 156, n.1).

GUY DE CAILLY'S ENNOBLEMENT

Charles du Lys, the sixteenth-century lawyer from Orleans at the
Cour des Aides, forged several documents in order to establish his
descent from one of Joan's brothers, and Quicherat published one
that claimed a prestigious ancestry for du Lys's wife.[26] On the basis
of this forgery, the manor of Reuilly near Chécy was for long assumed
to be one of the places where Joan of Arc stayed. This text claims
that, in the company of Guy de Cailly, she spent the night of April
28–29, 1429, in this house, where angels appeared to her. This manor
is in the middle of a region then entirely controlled by the English.
If held then by the French, Reuilly must have been an impregnable
fortress, but it was nothing of the kind. Eugène Jarry, head archivist
of the Archives Départementales du Loiret, has shown that in Joan's
time there was only a small holding owned by a squire called Pierre
de la Motte. There was also no Guy de Cailly, for Charles du Lys's
wife's grandfather was not noble, nor lord of Cailly, nor lord of
Reuilly.[27]

Quicherat is not responsible for this forgery, since he had not
seen the original documents in the Orleans archives, where he could
have uncovered the fraud. Even though he reproduced this text,
which he had been told was authentic, he stressed his suspicions
about its authenticity. Still, on most of the maps representing Joan's
itinerary, Reuilly is even today identified as one of the places she
stayed.

LA PIUZELA D'ORLHIENX

In 1890, Pierre Lanéry-d'Arc and Charles Grellet-Balguérie edited the text of the register of Albi. Their edition contains many errors and one entirely invented title: "la piuzela d'Orlhienx."[28] Many analyses based on this fraudulent title try to prove that Joan had a title and thus that she may have been related to Charles VII. This hypothesis, bred only in the fertile imaginations of nineteenth-century historians, was dismantled by Grandeau, who found some irony in the idea that a girl descended from Isabeau of Bavaria would use her own illegitimate origins as an argument to reassure Charles VII about his own legitimacy.[29] Unfortunately, some still continue to use this "proof" to advance a belief in Joan's noble origin.

THE GOOD NEWS

In the complete absence of any source, "history" is sometimes based entirely on romantic imagination. No trace of that will be found in the new Quicherat. But in 1885, for example, Bishop de Cabrières of Montpellier wrote in the magazine *L'univers* that the chapel Notre Dame de Bonne Nouvelle (Our Lady of Good News) of Montpellier took its name from the announcement of Joan of Arc's victory. The story states that a messenger sent by Charles VII was sent to Montpellier to announce raising of the siege of Orleans.[30] Arriving after sunset, the messenger found the gates of the city closed, and he spent the night in an inn outside the city walls. Later, on the site of the inn, a chapel was built and called "la bonne nouvelle." Not one reference is made to any text that might document this legend. Why should the Parisians, who were opposed to Charles VII, build a chapel called "bonne nouvelle"? How is it that the people of Orleans called a chapel "bonne nouvelle," although they needed nobody to bring them the good news that the siege of their city had been raised? The "good news" here (in Greek, *Euvangelion*) refers not to Joan of Arc's victory but to what had been announced to another woman in a far more ancient time. The bishop of Montpellier might have been more biblical or more skeptical. His story of the "good news" was spread by local scholars[31] as well as by Debout[32] and Ayroles.[33] The story still has its believers; it has been reproduced even in a recent biography of Joan of Arc.[34]

THE SCATTERING OF CAUCHON'S REMAINS

Bishop Cauchon was the ideal scapegoat for Joan's rehabilitation trial since he died in 1456. By accusing the dead Cauchon of all the wrongs against Joan of Arc, one could render guiltless the other two hundred thirty judges, assessors, and clerks who had taken part in the trial of condemnation—some of whom subsequently made brilliant careers in Charles VII's service, after the reconquest of Paris and Normandy. When historians became interested once again in Joan of Arc, and especially after 1890, Cauchon became the despised symbol of all human failings: a defector, traitor, and executioner of a saint, he had the qualities needed to make him hateful. The idea that he died peacefully, without either remorse or punishment, was unacceptable to some, who imagined a posthumuous punishment for him: on the orders of Louis XI, his corpse was said either to have been exhumed and thrown to the dogs, or to have been dumped on a rubbish heap by the revolutionaries in 1793.

Reality is more prosaic. Cauchon was buried in the cathedral of Lisieux, where his tombstone was moved, most likely in 1783, to make room for Bishop de Condorcet's burial place. The tombstone was used to block a window in the transept, where it was rediscovered in 1869.[35] However, Cauchon's coffin remained unmoved. Opened in May 1931, it was found still to contain the bishop's corpse, crozier and ring.[36]

CONCLUSION

The figure of Joan of Arc has been celebrated, studied, and analyzed for so long that it might seem unthinkable that the slightest details concerning her could remain unknown. So many books have been written on this subject that their titles have been collected in specialized bibliographies by Lanéry d'Arc[37] and Nadia Margolis,[38] not to mention another now assembled by the Centre Jeanne d'Arc. Few publications, however, are text editions. In Margolis's bibliography, they are a mere 264 items out of 1516 (17%), only 3% in the bibliography of the Centre Jeanne d'Arc, and 2.4% of Lanéry d'Arc's listing. Moreover, more than half of the text editions listed in Margolis's work concern the trials; editions of sources other than the trials therefore represent only 7% of all publications.

This small number of edited documents would not be problematic if the editions were reliable. In my work on the trials, for example, I find the thirteen volumes edited by Duparc, Tisset, and Doncoeur almost always sufficient. But are existing editions of the other manuscripts complete and correct? The few examples cited here may give us cause for modest concern. One asks whether the editions of texts other than the trials have been correctly transcribed, and, if not, whether reliable editions of the trials are sufficient for Joan of Arc's history. If not, is our view of Joan correct? Since we know now that editions of texts other than the trials have not been correctly transcribed, then it seems obvious that reliable editions of the trials are not sufficient for a study of Joan of Arc's entire history. Merely in order to interpret obscure passages in the trial manuscripts, we need to understand more perfectly fifteenth-century mentalities, and the information from chronicles, letters, and other documents mentioning Joan will significantly enhance our understanding of the fifteenth century.

The way we see Joan of Arc is necessarily incomplete if we interpret her only in the light of her trials, and it must be distorted if we use unreliable editions. We should not anticipate any drastic changes as a result of new manuscript analyses, but better comprehension of fifteenth-century religious and political mentalities will surely lead to reconceptions of Joan and her environment between 1429 and 1431.

NOTES

1. Wladimir Raytses, "La première entrevue de Jeanne d'Arc et de Charles VII à Chinon. Essai de reconstitution d'un fait historique," *Bulletin de l'Association des Amis du Centre Jeanne d'Arc* 13 (1989), 7–18. For an opposing view, see Jean Fraikin's essay in this volume.

2. Philippe Contamine, "Naissance d'une historiographie. Le souvenir de Jeanne d'Arc, en France et hors de France, depuis le 'procès de son innocence' (1455–1456) jusqu'au début du XVIe siècle," *Francia* 15 (1987), 233–256.

3. Georges Goyau, *Sainte Jeanne d'Arc* (Paris, 1920).

4. Philippe Contamine, "Jules Quicherat historien de Jeanne d'Arc," *Bulletin de l'Association des Amis du Centre Jeanne d'Arc* 14 (1990), 7–19.

5. Jules Quicherat, *Procès de condamnation et de réhabilitation de Jeanne d'Arc dite La Pucelle,* 5 vols. (Paris, 1841–1849), vol. 5, pp. 100–04.

6. Kervyn de Lettenhove, ed., *Oeuvres de Froissart* (Brussels, 1869), vol. 7, pp. 444–50.

7. Régine Pernoud, *La libération d'Orléans* (Paris, 1969), p. 242.

8. Colonel F. de Liocourt, *La mission de Jeanne d'Arc*, vol. 2, *L'exécution* (Paris, 1981), p. 111. See plate 35, line 28, word 8. Colonel de Liocourt died before volume II of his work was published and probably had no occasion to compare the transcription with the manuscript.

9. Olivier Bouzy, "Le traité de Jacques Gélu, De Adventu Johanne," *Bulletin de l'Association des Amis du Centre Jeanne d'Arc*, 16 (1992), 29–39.

10. Quicherat, *Procès*, vol. V, p. 474.

11. Jean-Baptiste Joseph Ayroles, *La vraie Jeanne d'Arc*, vol.1, *La Pucelle devant l'Eglise de son temps* (Paris, 1890), pp. 39–52.

12. Whom by mistake I cited as *Pierre* Ventach in my article on Jacques Gélu; which shows again that one should not see the mote in one's neighbor's eye without thinking about the beam in one's own.

13. The manuscript edited by Pierre Lanéry d'Arc is the Latin MS 6199 of the Bibliothèque Nationale; the one transcribed by Jean Ventach is the MS B 3139 of the Archives Départementales de l'Isère (at Grenoble). The manuscript collection Dupuy 639 (fol. 100–126) of the Bibliothèque Nationale is an eighteenth-century copy of the Grenoble manuscript.

14. Ayroles, p. 39.

15. Henri Jadart, *Jeanne d'Arc à Reims, ses relations avec Reims, ses lettres aux Rémois* (Reims, 1887), pl. II, facing p. 58.

16. Henri Debout, *Histoire de la bienheureuse Jeanne d'Arc, 1412–1431*, 2 vols. (Paris, 1906), vol. 2, p. 945.

17. Comte Charles de Maleissye, *Les reliques de Jeanne d'Arc, ses lettres* (Paris, 1909).

18. Debout, 2.683.

19. Henri Jadart, *Jeanne d'Arc à Reims, ses relations avec Reims, ses lettres aux Rémois, notes additionnelles* (Reims, 1910), pl. II, facing p. 32.

20. Baron de Terline, "Une signature suspecte de Jeanne d'Arc," *Revue d'histoire de l'Eglise de France* 35 (1921).

21. Jules de la Martinière, "A propos d'une signature de Jeanne d'Arc, ou les suites fâcheuses de la distraction d'un metteur en pages," *Bulletin de la Société archéologique et historique de l'Orléanais* 36(1929), 180–182.

22. Pierre Duparc, "A propos des lettres de Jeanne d'Arc," *Bulletin de la Société Nationale des Antiquaires de France* (1989), 71–80.

23. Jules Doinel, "Note sur une maison de Jeanne d'Arc," *Mémoires de la société archéologique et historique de l'Orléanais*, vol. XV, 1875.

24. Debout, 2.202.

25. Eugène Jarry, "Une fausse maison de Jeanne d'Arc, correction au tome XV de nos Mémoires," *Bull. de la société archéologique et historique de l'Orléanais* (1908), 191.

26. Quicherat *Procès*, 5.342–346 .

27. Eugène Jarry, "La prétendue réception de Jeanne d'Arc à Reuilly," *Bulletin de la Société Archéologique et Historique de l'Orléanais* 21 (1908), p. 257–277. A summary of this article is found in Henri Labrosse, *Congrès*

historique du Ve centenaire de Jeanne d'Arc à Rouen (Rouen, 1932), pp. 30–31.

28. Pierre Lanéry-d'Arc et Charles Grellet-Balguerie, *La piuzela d'Orlhienx, récit contemporain en langue romane de la mission de Jeanne d'Arc* (Paris, 1890).

29. Yann Grandeau, *Jeanne insultée, procès en diffamation* (Paris, 1973), p. 146.

30. Abbot Granger, *Jeanne d'Arc et le Périgord* (Périgueux, 1894), p. 12.

31. Canon d'Aigrefeuille, *Histoire de la ville de Montpellier* (without place nor date of publication), p. 316, may have been the first to spread this legend.

32. Debout, *Histoire,* vol. 1, 1st ed. (1906), p. 514, 3rd ed. (1913), p. 389.

33. Ayroles, p. 8; ibid., *Les diocèses de la Bienheureuse Jeanne d'Arc* (Orleans, 1909), p. 23.

34. Liocourt, p. 119.

35. V. Lahaye, *La chapelle Notre-Dame dans la cathédrale de Lisieux* (Lisieux, 1914), p.12.

36. *L'Illustration,* n° 4602 (16 mai 1931), 93.

37. Pierre Lanéry-d'Arc, *Le livre d'or de Jeanne d'Arc* (Paris, 1894).

38. Nadia Margolis, *Joan of Arc in History, Literature, and Film* (New York, 1990).

"I DO NOT NAME TO YOU THE VOICE OF ST. MICHAEL": THE IDENTIFICATION OF JOAN OF ARC'S VOICES

Karen Sullivan

Readers of the transcripts of Joan's Rouen heresy trial have traditionally concentrated on their content rather than form and on Joan's answers rather than on the questions that provoked her answers. The interplay between the clerics' questions about Joan's "voices from God" and Joan's answers lead one to conclude that the "truth" about these voices is not so much represented as it is produced in the course of the trial.

In Jules Bastien-Lepage's painting, Joan of Arc stands in an orchard outside her father's house in Domrémy.[1] Her spinning lies unattended behind her, the stool from which she has presumably just arisen, overturned. In her roughly laced jerkin and thick brown skirt, she seems the young village girl that she was before her departure for France, yet her gaze is directed on an object beyond the trees and foliage of her immediate, empirical surroundings. With her face uplifted and her eyes transfixed beyond the view of the painting, she seems calmly and intently focused on that which she is witnessing. The masculine viewer of this painting cannot help but be aware that she is hearing voices that he cannot hear and seeing visions that he cannot see. As he beholds the outer signs of Joan's inner sensations, he cannot help but wonder what it is that she perceives and that he is barred from perceiving. Yet Bastien-Lepage does not fail to suggest to his frustrated viewer, at least in part, what Joan must have apprehended in this orchard. Though Joan's gaze is fixed outside the limits of the painting, inside the painting, behind her, hover three translucent figures, one a knight in golden armor, holding out a sword, another a lady, swathed in a filmy veil, with her hands clasped in prayer, the third another female figure with her face buried in her hands. With these images, the artist gives the viewer at least partial access to Joan's inner experiences of her voices.

In the transcripts of Joan's trial for heresy in Rouen in 1431, the clerics examining her, like Bastien-Lepage, seek access to the inner experience of her voices, yet they strive to attain it not through imaginative depictions, but through interrogations that compel her to share with them her experiences of these voices and, in particular, her perception of these voices' identity. Who are the voices from God that she hears? they demand of Joan. Are they those of angels, saints, or God Himself? To modern readers of the trial transcripts, these questions might appear innocuous. In asking Joan to identify her voices, the clerics rely upon a Christian theological framework within which the only voices capable of conveying the word of God to a mortal would be those of angels, saints, or God. They seem to reason that, if voices from God have indeed spoken to Joan, as she claims that they have, then these voices must belong to one of these three parties. They presuppose that, when Joan claims to have heard "voices from God," the vagueness of her phrase reflects neither the phenomena themselves nor her perception of these phenomena but her expression of her perception, so that it is fair to push her to depict this inner experience more precisely. Given such a rationale, the clerics' demand for the specific identity of her voices might appear logically justifiable.

When the clerics respond to Joan's allegation to have heard "voices from God" by asking who exactly these voices are, their intellectual movement mirrors a movement typical of scholastic literature. When Thomas Aquinas takes on a topic—"angels," for example—he breaks it down into *quaestiones,* such as the movement of the angels, the knowledge of the angels, and the hierarchy of the angels, and then breaks these *quaestiones* down into *articuli,* such as whether angels move through intermediate space on their way to a destination, whether angels know singulars or just universal's, and whether angels belong to particular orders because of their different natures.[2] By responding to the questions that he has posed, Aquinas aims to move beyond a general understanding of angels as servants and messengers of God and attain a highly specific understanding of angels in virtually all of their aspects. For scholastics, like the *doctor angelicus* and the clerics at Rouen, reality exists with a high degree of definition. Angels are not just vague messengers of God but beings whose movement, knowledge, and hierarchy, in addition to their creation, substance, speech, capacity for sin, and numerous other attributes, are all distinct and distinguishable. Joan's voices from God are, similarly, not just vague messengers from God but beings whose individual identities are specific and specifiable. It is the task of the scholastic, whether participating in a speculative or a judicial investigation, to ask questions that will uncover the essential definition of the reality at hand.

Despite the seemingly firm foundation of their questions about Joan's voices, the clerics seem to have been the only ones who asked them during the fifteenth century. Dozens of Joan's contemporaries at the rehabilitation, scores of chroniclers, and several poets allude to the voices during her lifetime and shortly thereafter, yet virtually none of them exhibits an interest in the precise identity of her voices or, more generally, in her inner experience of the voices comparable to the interest which the clerics exhibit in their interrogations. It is not that these other parties are not skeptical, as the clerics are skeptical, of Joan's claim to hear voices from God instructing her to save France. These contemporaries and authors, too, seek to ascertain the truth of Joan's allegations, yet they try to do so through other avenues than interrogations of her interior perceptions. The guards who escorted Joan from her village to the king, the soldiers who fought alongside her on the battlefield, and the burghers who lodged her in their houses during her campaigns cite her personal attributes and actions as evidence that her voices were authentic. Sir Jean de Nouillompont, who went with her to the king, asserts at the rehabilitation that he was inflamed by her words and by her love of God and that "he believes that she was sent by God, for she never swore, she liked to hear mass, and in taking an oath she crossed herself."[3] The chronicler Perceval de Cagny points to Joan's seemingly miraculous success at subjugating seven cities and several fortified towns and castles in four months, at leading the king to his coronation at Reims, and at inspiring knights, squires, and other men-at-arms to continue fighting despite their low pay as proof of the divine origin of her mission. The poet Christine de Pizan, whose *Ditié de Jehanne d'Arc* is one of the first two literary works devoted to the

Maid, likewise emphasizes Joan's piety and virtue and her astonishing military achievements, as well as the prophecies foretelling her advent, as indications that she is divinely inspired. While the clerics at Rouen consider the evidence of character, miracles, and prophecies, in addition to her responses to their interrogations, when they evaluate Joan's claims to hear voices from God, it does not seem to have occurred to these lay contemporaries to consider Joan's inner experience of her voices, in addition to these other criteria, when performing their own evaluations. For these laypersons, Joan's allegations to divine inspiration are to be judged not by an in-depth analysis of her experience of this inspiration but by an examination of these allegations within the surrounding context of her life.

Because lay culture seems to have lacked both an interest in and, hence, the tools for the study of Joan's inner experience of her voices, the conflict between the clerics and Joan during her interrogations about the depiction of her voices can be read as a conflict between two modes of thought—one that presupposes that reality is precise and that the beholder of reality must therefore perceive and be able to express that precision and one that does not make such an assumption. The one mode of thought may be identified with a clerical culture, the other with a popular culture. When the clerics demand, in their questions, that Joan convey the identities of her voices, they demand, I shall argue, that Joan depict her experience of the voices with a degree of detail that she does not appear to have perceived and that she thus translate her vague, vernacular perception of her voices into a precise, learned discourse. When Joan resists this demand in her responses, deferring her answer to their questions, complaining that she does not know this answer, that she forgot it, that she does not have permission to give it, that she has given it before, she resists reconfiguring her inner experience of the voices so that it makes sense within a scholastic episteme.

Since the birth of modern scholarship on Joan in the mid-nineteenth century, it has generally been agreed that Joan identified the voices that inspired her to lead the French to victory over the English in the Hundred Years War with St. Catherine of Alexandria, St. Margaret of Antioch, and St. Michael the Archangel. The founding fathers of what would later become known as Johannic studies, Jules Michelet and Jules-Etienne-Joseph Quicherat, though radically different in their approaches to Joan, both asserted that

Joan identified her voices with these three saints. In 1841, Michelet published a narrative account of Joan's life in which he declared that Joan saw the voices who spoke to her and that "one of them had wings and seemed to be a wise and worthy man" and that "the worthy man was none other than St. Michael."[4] Michelet goes on to state that, soon after his first appearance to Joan, St. Michael informed her that St. Catherine and St. Margaret would come to her and that "then came the white figures of the saints."[5] In 1850, Quicherat noted, in his critical volume on Joan, that Joan perceived different intonations among her voices, that she attributed these intonations to different speakers, and that "she named, in particular, St. Michael, St. Catherine, and St. Margaret."[6] Subsequent scholars, whether because they have accepted Michelet and Quicherat's authority or because they have imitated their reading of the original documents, have followed these two historians' identification of Joan's voices with these saints. In 1903, Philippe-Hector Dunand, in his two-volume study of Joan's voices, declared, "The superior beings that appeared to [Joan] and that she named her 'voices,' because the sound of their voices usually announced their presence, were no others, she asserted, than the archangel St. Michael and the two saints Catherine and Margaret."[7] The Catholics, who argued that Joan's voices were of divine origin, the rationalists, who diagnosed her voices as the symptoms of physical or psychological disorders, and the spiritualists, who connected her voices with mysterious forces permeating the universe, all agreed, despite their differing interpretations of these voices, that Joan perceived these voices to be these three figures.[8]

At first glance, the unanimous identification of Joan's voices with these three saints appears to be the result of a sound reading of the original documents. When Michelet speaks of St. Michael appearing to Joan and announcing to her the advent of St. Catherine and St. Margaret, he echoes Joan's own words in the transcripts of her trial for heresy in Rouen in 1431.[9] When Quicherat speaks of Joan naming these three saints, he provides a note referring the reader to three passages in the interrogation transcripts where Joan names her voices in this manner. Not only do the interrogation transcripts record Joan as having identified her voices with these saints on numerous occasions, but the faithfulness of these transcripts in recording Joan's actual words appears unassailable. Twenty-five years after Joan's death, when Joan's condemnation for heresy was being reviewed, several participants in the earlier trial, including the principal notary himself, testified that the transcripts accurately reflect that which Joan said during her interrogations. Given that Joan identifies these voices with these three saints on several occasions in the principal record of her depiction of her voices and given that the accuracy of this record has been verified, it might appear incontestable that Joan actually perceived her voices as these figures.

It is only upon a second consideration of Joan's interrogation transcripts that this traditional identification of her voices with these saints becomes problematic. Michelet, Quicherat, and later historians assumed that Joan's responses about her voices during her interrogations represent her experience of these voices. They have assumed, too, that Joan's experience of her voices is fixed and defined prior to her representation of this experience, that this experience remains unchanged by the representation, and that this representation thus serves as a vehicle providing direct access to this experience. They have assumed, in brief, that signs signify not through their interplay with other signs but through their indication of a referent. In their assertions that Joan perceived her voices as these three saints, historians have thus made presuppositions about language that have by now been discredited in linguistics, philosophy, and literary studies for decades, though the consequences of this discrediting have rarely affected the reading of historical documents, like the transcripts of Joan's interrogations.[10] It is these assumptions that I mean to call into question here through a reexamination of Joan's identification of her voices with these saints, first in the chronicles and the testimony of her companions from her military campaigns and then in the transcripts of her interrogations at Rouen. I intend to demonstrate not only that Joan's identification of her voices with these three saints is far more complex than Michelet, Quicherat, and their successors have acknowledged but that this identity of these voices is not so much represented in as constituted by these trial transcripts.

Neither the chronicles, many of which are based on first-hand contact with Joan, nor the testimony of her contemporaries after her death make many references to St. Catherine, St. Margaret, or St. Michael. The overwhelming majority of these texts depict Joan as claiming to be guided not by saints but by God himself. The duc d'Alençon, one of Joan's closest comrades-in-arms, remembers an attendant having fetched him while he was hunting and informed him that a maid had arrived "who declared herself sent by God to put the English to flight and to lift the siege they had set before the city of Orleans." An anonymous chronicler associated with Alençon records Joan as asserting that "she was sent to [King Charles] on the part of God to help him conquer his kingdom possessed by the said English."[11] Another knight, Raoul de Gaucourt, who was present when Joan first appeared before the court, relates that she told the king, "'I have come and am sent by God to bring help to you and to the kingdom.'"[12] Marguerite la Tourolde, the widow of one of the king's counselors, echoes these words when she relates that Joan "came on the part of God, sent by him to strengthen the king and the subjects obedient to him."[13] While the largest number of speakers remember Joan referring to God as God, others remember her indicating Him through other names. Some report Joan alluding to God as "her Lord." Jean de Nouillompont, who escorted Joan from her native district to the king, claims that Joan told him that "it is necessary that I act thus because my Lord wishes it" and that, when he asked who her lord was, she replied that this Lord was God. Bertrand de Poulengy, another companion on this voyage to the king, portrays himself similarly confusing Joan's Lord with a mere temporal potentate.[14] Numerous sources, including Henri LeRoyer, in whose house Joan lodged on the way to the king, Dunois, the Bastard of Orleans and another of Joan's closest companions on the field, and Jean Pasquerel, her confessor, recall Joan speaking of "God, my Lord." Others remember Joan referring to God as "the king of heaven." Gobert Thibaut, a squire in the king's stables, reports having heard Joan say, "'I come on the part of the king of heaven to lift the siege of Orleans.'"[15] Master François Garivel, a counselor to the king, likewise relates having heard her claim that "she was sent by the king of heaven to the help of our noble dauphin to reestablish him in his kingdom, to lift the siege of Orleans and to conduct the dauphin to Reims."[16] Simon Charles, the president of the *Chambre de Comptes,* Pasquerel and LeRoyer similarly testify having heard Joan indicate God in this manner. Some, finally, remember Joan referring to God as "messire," a term of respect for socially elevated personages that derived from "monseigneur" and that would later become "monsieur." Colette Milet, who went to see Joan when she was in Orleans, recalls Joan telling her that "'Messire sent me to help the good city of Orleans.'"[17] Colette's husband, Pierre, and the anonymous authors of the *Chronique de la Pucelle* and the *Journal d'un Siege d' Orleans* also cite Joan as referring to God in this manner. If one puts together these references to God as God with those to God as Joan's lord, the king of heaven, or "messire," the gist of approximately four out of five medieval references to Joan's divine contact outside the interrogation transcripts can be reduced to one sentence: Joan was sent by God to help France.

What is remarkable about these references to Joan's divine communications is not only their allusion to God rather than to the saints Catherine, Margaret, and Michael but also their brevity. When the chronicles turn to Joan, they typically relate that during the season of Lent in 1429 there arrived in the king's court a young maid from a village named Domrémy, near Vaucouleurs, in the duchy of Bar; that this maid was from eighteen to twenty years of age and had previously spent her time guarding sheep; and that she claimed to have been sent by God to help the king regain his kingdom. The chronicles, in general, do not go on to explain how she learned that she was sent by God, whether she learned of this mission from God directly or through intermediaries, or in what form these intermediaries appeared to her. Though it is clear, from the chronicles' depiction of Joan's references to God as her lord, the king of heaven, and "messire," that Joan conceptualized God along the lines of a feudal seigneur, there is no investigation into the relation, in Joan's thinking, between the heavenly king who sent her and the terrestrial king to whom she was sent. Instead of elaborating upon the nature of Joan's contact with God, the chronicles go on to recount one or more of her marvelous accomplishments at court, such as her immediate recognition of the king despite never having seen him before, her discovery of a mysterious sword buried near a church's altar, or her brilliant responses to the clerics who examined her. After devoting one line to Joan's divine inspiration, the chronicles proceed to devote many pages to a description of her relief of the siege of Orleans, often commenting on how Joan's success at this or that feat proved that she was sent by God. This disproportion between the chroniclers' attention to Joan's divine encounters and to her actions suggests that they are interested in Joan's voices not so much insofar as she experiences them but insofar as they affect the war, that they are interested in the divine, not so much insofar as it touches one individual, but insofar as it appears in the world. The syntax of Joan's own speech in these texts indicates that the chroniclers were not alone in their concerns. According to countless chronicles and witnesses, Joan did not merely claim to have had mystical experiences, as many medieval woman claimed to have had: she claimed to have been sent by God to accomplish a particular goal, such as the relief of the siege of Orleans, the coronation of her king at Reims, or the expulsion of the English from France. The fact that the stress of this sentence falls not on Joan's communication with God but upon the political purpose for which God communicated with her suggests that it was not only the chroniclers, but Joan herself who viewed her contact with God as less important than the effect of that contact, the fact that God spoke with her as less important than that which God told her to do.

While the vast majority of documents depict Joan referring to God alone, whether as God, my lord, the king of heaven, or "messire," as the origin of her mission in France, a few documents provide additional information about her divine communications. Certain sources employ the vocabulary of "voice" and "voices" that has come to be most associated with Joan's divine contact. Seguin de Seguin, a cleric who examined Joan before she was allowed to lead French troops, recalls Joan speaking of "a voice" that came to her when she was guarding animals and that told her that God had great pity for the people of France and that it would be necessary for her to go to France.[18] Dunois relates that, when Joan was discouraged by people who did not believe her, she would withdraw and pray to God, complaining about them, and that, when her prayer was finished, "she would hear a voice saying to her, 'Daughter of God, go, go, go. I will be helping you. Go.'"[19] When she heard this voice, Dunois continues, "she rejoiced greatly and wanted always to stay in the same state, and, what is even more striking, in repeating the words of her voices she had amazing transports of joy, lifting her eyes toward heaven."[20] These depictions of Joan hearing "a voice" differ from the depictions of Joan being sent by God in that they introduce an intermediary between God and Joan, an as yet unnamed voice that informs her of God's pity for the people of France and of the need for her to go to France, that at once urges her to go forth and promises her help if she does so, and that brings her such joy that she wants to remain forever in the state that she is in when she hears it. While the depictions of Joan's being sent by God were brief, mere notices of the divine origin of her endeavors preceding their recounting, these depictions of Joan hearing voices are longer and more involved. The documents concerned with God's will, as it is expressed through Joan's activity, move quickly to an account of how this will is revealed in the world, but the documents concerned with Joan's apprehension of God's will through the voice turn, instead, to an elaboration of this apprehension. When the text turns from speaking of God to speaking of the voice, the focus shifts from France to Joan, from the public to the private, from the political effects of this contact with God to the personal sensation of this contact. Other documents employ the vocabulary not of "a voice" and "voices" but of "revelations" and "counsel," a vocabulary that will also reappear in the trial transcripts, though to a far more limited extent. The *Chronique de La Pucelle* refers to "some revelations" that Joan had, while Dunois recalls Joan speaking of "the counsel of God" that she received and Alençon remembers her speaking of "voices and a counsel that counseled her what she had to do."[21] These references to "revelations" and "counsel," like the references to "a voice" and "voices," accentuate not the public, political side of Joan's divine communications but her own private, personal apprehension, whether of the future events that are revealed to her or of the counsel that is given to her. With these allusions, as with the allusions to "a voice" or "voices," the texts turn from France's outer circumstances to Joan's inner experience.

In addition to the documents that identify Joan's divine contact with God, "a voice" or "voices," "revelations" and "counsel," a few isolated documents identify this contact with individuals. Dunois cites Joan claiming to have had visions of St. Louis and St. Charlemagne, though his testimony is not substantially supported by other texts. The *Miroir des femmes vertueuses* portrays Joan receiving her mission from the Virgin Mary, St. Catherine, and St. Agnes, though no other document links the Virgin or Agnes with Joan. Included in this category of rare depictions of Joan's voices are two texts that identify Joan's voices as the saints Michael, Catherine, and Margaret. The first, the journal of the so-called Bourgeois of Paris, an anonymous Burgundian, contains two separate depictions of Joan, one written before her capture and trial for heresy and one written after. In his first depiction of Joan, in 1429, the Bourgeois states simply that she called herself a prophet; that, when she was young, birds were said to come and eat bread from her lap when she called them; and, in a more negative tone, that she was a creature "in the form of a woman."²² Though the Bourgeois refers to Joan's allegedly supernatural powers, he makes no allusion to any contact between Joan and divine beings. It is only in his second depiction of Joan, in 1431, that the Bourgeois relates that Joan led people to believe that "the glorious archangel St. Michael, St. Catherine, and St. Margaret and several other saints appeared to her often."²³ In this second depiction, however, the Bourgeois paraphrases in such detail the transcripts of the trial, and, in particular, the crimes with which the clerics charged Joan and the sentences with which they condemned her, that he makes clear his exposure either to the materials of the trial themselves or to the conversation of clerics who had participated in the trial. This exposure would not be surprising given that many of the most active participants were clerics from the University of Paris and that the faculties both of theology and of canon law at the university approved Joan's condemnation— given that the Bourgeois of Paris is himself now believed to have been not a bourgeois after all but a cleric. The Bourgeois cites, in fact, the sermon of the Dominican inquisitor Jean Graverent about Joan at St.-Martin des Champs on August 9, 1431, in such detail that he appears to have been present at this event. The second text that identifies Joan's voices with St. Michael and St. Catherine, though not with St. Margaret, the chronicle of the anonymous dean of the Collegiate Church of St. Thibaut in Metz, is not as easily accounted for. This document, unlike that of the Bourgeois of Paris, is pro-French and written by an inhabitant of Joan's native region, yet it relates that Joan told her king that "if he wanted to believe her and have faith in God, in monsieur St. Michael and madame St. Catherine and in her, she would lead him to be crowned at Reims and would restore him in peace in his kingdom" and that she attacked the English outside Orleans "crying out the names of God, St. Michael, and St. Catherine."²⁴ While textual and circumstantial evidence cannot establish this chronicler's familiarity with Joan's trial at Rouen, as they can establish the Bourgeois of Paris's familiarity with these proceedings, this chronicle is presumed to have been written in 1445, fourteen years after the trial, and thus could have undergone such an influence. In sum, the two brief references to St. Michael and St. Catherine in this chronicle from St. Thibaut of Metz constitute the only references to these saints independent of the trial transcripts in the thirty-nine medieval chronicles that address the Maid and in the fifty or so depositions that companions from her military campaigns gave after her death, and these references could themselves be due to the influence of these trial transcripts.[25]

If one looks to the transcripts of the first few days of Joan's interrogations during her trial at Rouen, one finds a similar dearth of allusions to St. Catherine, St. Margaret, or St. Michael. During these initial days of the proceedings, Joan continues to claim that she has been sent by God, as she was continually said to have claimed in the chronicles and the depositions of her contemporaries. On the third day of the trial, she asserts "that she has come on the part of God and that she does not have any business here, asking that she be sent back to God, from whom she has come."[26] At the beginning of the fourth day of the trial, she warns her judges to take care with what they do because, as she puts it, "I am sent on the part of God and you put yourself in great danger."[27] These declarations echo the claim Joan is recorded to have made in the chronicles and in the depositions of her contemporaries, yet she does not finish them. While these other texts invariably record her claiming to have come or to have been sent on the part of God in order to accomplish a particular goal, such as the relief of Orleans or the expulsion of the English, here she refrains from expressing the purpose for which she was sent. For the first time, Joan speaks of her contact with God without placing the stress on the political purpose of that contact, perhaps because she is now speaking to persons of the opposite camp who would be opposed to that purpose. This shift from the public to the private, from the external to the internal, from the political purpose of the mystical experience to the mystical experience itself, is reflected by the shift from references to God to references to the voices. For whereas four out of five allusions to Joan's divine communications outside these transcripts are to God, now, in the first three days of the trial, only one out of twelve of such allusions is to God, and, with the exception of lone references to Joan's "revelations" and "counsel," all the rest are to her voices. On the second day of the trial and the first day when she is seriously interrogated, Joan relates that "when she was thirteen years old, she had a voice coming from God to help her govern herself," that this voice came to her at noon in her father's garden from the direction of the church, and that a light accompanied this voice.[28] From this very opening interrogation, the focus is on not the public effect of this divine contact but the private experience of it, in accordance with the clerics' alleged interest in political accomplishments rather than in the state of her soul.

It is as a part of this shift from the public to the private, from the external to the internal, that the clerics ask Joan repeatedly for further identification of her voice. On the second day of the trial, though the transcripts do not convey the interrogator's question, they relate that "Joan added that her interrogator would not obtain from her, at this time, under what form this voice appeared to her."[29] On the third day of the trial, the transcripts report that Joan is "interrogated if the voice that she says to appear to her is an angel or if it comes from God immediately or if it is the voice of a saint."[30] Joan responds, "The voice comes on the part of God, and I believe that I do not tell you perfectly all that I know, and I have greater fear of failing these voices by saying something that displeases them than I have in responding to you. And, as for this question, I ask for a delay."[31] For two days, therefore, the clerics press Joan for further specification of her voice, whether for the form under which the voice appeared to her or for the identity of the voice as an angel, a saint, or God Himself. For two days, Joan refuses to satisfy these demands for a greater specification, deferring her response to a later date.

It is only on the fourth day of the trial that Joan performs the identification of her voice which the clerics have repeatedly sought. On this day, the transcripts record: "interrogated if it was the voice of an angel that spoke to her, or if it was the voice of a saint or of God without intermediary, she responded that it was the voice of St. Catherine and St. Margaret, and their faces are crowned with beautiful crowns, very opulent and very precious."[32] The transcripts continue,

Interrogated which appeared to her first, she responded, "I did not recognize them so quickly, and I knew well once, but have forgotten, and if I had permission I would say willingly, and it is in the register at Poitiers." Item she also said that she had comfort from St. Michael. Interrogated which of the aforesaid apparitions came to her first, she responded that St. Michael came first. Interrogated if much time elapsed after she first had the voice of St. Michael, she responded, "I do not name to you the voice of St. Michael, but I speak of a great comfort." Interrogated which was the first voice coming to her, when she was thirteen years old or around that age, she responded that it was St. Michael whom she saw before her eyes, and he was not alone but was accompanied by angels from heaven. She said also that she did not come to France except by the command of God.[33]

It is in this passage from the trial transcripts that the conventional identification of Joan's voices with St. Catherine, St. Margaret and St. Michael has its root.

By asking repeatedly, first, whether Joan's voice was that of an angel, a saint, or God Himself and, then, whether St. Catherine or St. Margaret appeared to her first, the clerics betray the assumptions that underlie their interrogation. They assume that a voice from God, like that which Joan claims to hear, must be that of an angel, a saint, or God Himself and that, if Joan has heard this voice from the time that she was thirteen years old, as she claims to have done, she must know into which category this voice falls. Indeed, if one considers the experiences of other medieval visionaries, such as St. Catherine of Siena, St. Bridget of Sweden, or the numerous minor figures examined in Elizabeth Petroff and William Christian's studies of medieval visionaries, it is true that most do identify the divine beings which they behold with angels, saints, or God Himself.[34] The fourteenth-century Dominican tertiary Catherine of Siena, has apparitions of Jesus Christ, the twelfth-century Benedictine nun Elisabeth of Schönau perceives angels, and the vast majority of the late-medieval and Renaissance Spanish visionaries examined by Christian see the Virgin Mary.[35] Pierre Duparc has hypothesized that Joan's judges pressured Joan to identify her voices as saints or angels because they "probably found themselves disconcerted in front of a mysticism, inspired by God, without a handle on it. The intervention of angels or saints would permit them to operate in a more familiar world."[36] The clerics assume, in addition, when Joan has told them that she has heard the voices of St. Catherine and St. Margaret, that she must have heard one of these voices before the other and that she must know which of the two she first heard. Again, this assumption appears to be not a reckless conjecture, destined to distort the nature of Joan's response, but a reasoned inference from the premises they are given. The clerics assume, finally, that their questions about the identity of Joan's voices and about the voice that first appeared to her merely push Joan to share with them information that she already possesses and that, if she does not answer these questions, it is because, out of her obstinacy, she refuses to share that information with them.

If the clerics' assumptions are fair, it is true that, in these responses, Joan makes remarkable efforts to avoid sharing her knowledge of her voices with them. When the clerics ask whether her voice is that of an angel, a saint, or God Himself, she twice defers answering this question before she provides the answer. When they ask whether St. Catherine or St. Margaret appeared to her first, she replies with a series of contradictory statements. She claims that she did not recognize her voices so as to be able to tell which came to her first, but then she states that she once knew which came first but has now forgotten. She claims that she has forgotten which voice came first, but then she asserts that she would give them this information if she had permission to do so. She claims that she does not have permission to reveal this information, but then she states that she revealed it to the clerics who questioned her earlier at Poitiers. Finally, after protesting that she cannot tell them which voice came to her first because she never knew, because she had once known but has now forgotten, because she does not have permission to tell them and because she had previously told other clerics, Joan utters the name of St. Michael and thus seems to name the voice that first appeared to her. When the clerics ask which voice appeared to her first, she responds ambiguously. She does not reply in the terms of their question, stating that "St. Michael appeared to her first," but rather alters these terms, maintaining that "she had comfort from St. Michael." It is not clear from her response whether St. Michael appeared to her first or, indeed, given that she claims only to have had comfort from him, whether he ever appeared to her. A moment later, she increases this ambiguity, asserting that she speaks not of the voice of St. Michael, but of a great comfort. Having affirmed, in response to the previous question, that St. Michael appeared to her first, she now withdraws this identification and insists, instead, upon the emotion that she experienced at that time. While the clerics ask her to focus upon the objective identity of the being who appeared to her, she focuses, instead, upon her subjective sensation. Finally, when the clerics attempt to direct her speech through their questions, Joan provides information extraneous to their inquiries. Though the clerics ask Joan, on the fourth day, merely if her voice is the voice of an angel, a saint, or God Himself, Joan does not limit her answer to the identification of this voice with St. Catherine and St. Margaret but adds that these voices "are crowned with beautiful crowns, very opulent and very precious," as if she is dissatisfied with the mere naming of these saints and feels it necessary to insist upon their worthiness. Though the clerics ask her merely if St. Michael was the first voice to appear to her, she does not limit her answer to affirming this question but adds that he was accompanied by angels and, even more irrelevantly, that she did not come to France except by God's command. When Joan does not respond to the clerics' questions with too little information, she responds with too much; whether by restraint or by excess, she refuses to provide the neat answer that the clerics seek. In brief, through her deferrals, her contradictory protests, her ambiguities, or her interjections, Joan refuses to tailor her responses to the clerics' questions.

The transcripts show the lack of importance the clerics attach to Joan's resistance to their questions. In the course of these interrogations about the voices, the clerics ask Joan three times about the specific identity of her voice and three times about the identity of the voice that first appeared to her, thus attempting, through their repetitions, to cut through her obfuscations and to force her to respond to their question. In the course of their first set of accusations about Joan, the clerics quote this discussion of the voices in the interrogations and summarize it by saying that "Joan says to have had and to have continually for five years visions and apparitions of St. Michael, St. Catherine, and St. Margaret," thus dismissing all of her utterances except those that respond directly to their question.[37] By repeatedly asking the same questions despite her resistance to them and by reducing her responses to that which corresponds to their questions, the clerics distinguish between Joan's speech when it satisfies their questions and her speech when it either resists or exceeds their expectations. As the clerics see it, when Joan identifies her voices as St. Catherine, St. Margaret, and St. Michael or when she identifies St. Michael as the voice who first spoke to her, her speech is full, substantial, communicative, while when she resists answering these questions or provides information outside these questions' aim, her speech is empty, insubstantial, noncommunicative, a purely negative attempt to avoid answering the question. When she states that St. Michael came to her first, her speech is recognizable to the clerics, and thus valuable, while when she states that she does not speak of St. Michael but of a great comfort, her speech is unrecognizable and therefore to be ignored.

If Joan's resistance to the clerics' questions is read, however, not as a mere willful rejection of the clerics' demands but as the marker of a deeper opposition to the assumptions of their questions, this distinction between what the clerics interpret as substantial and insubstantial speech takes on a new meaning. When Joan stays within the limits of the clerics' questions, as she does when she identifies her voices as St. Catherine and St. Margaret or when she names St. Michael as the first voice that came to her, her speech exhibits certain characteristics. She provides this information only after having been asked several times about the identity of her voices and about the first voice that spoke to her, only after having deferred answering these questions to a later day and only after having explained, in numerous and contradictory ways, why she cannot respond to these questions. By furnishing the clerics with these answers, she has gained relief from a further repetition of these questions but has done so only by ceasing to depict her voices as she depicted them in the early days of the trial and in the documents outside these transcripts. When Joan exceeds the limits of the clerics' questions, however, as she does when she asserts that the voice comes on the part of God, or that she speaks of a great comfort, or that she did not come to France except by the command of God, her speech displays radically different characteristics. She offers these declarations not only without any delay or protest but without any request by the clerics that she offer them. She speaks with apparent spontaneity. By interjecting such remarks into the interrogations, Joan rebels against the strictures of the interrogation, which dictate that she speak only in response to questions, and against the strictures of the assumptions embedded within the clerics' questions, which dictate that she express her experience in terms of these assumptions. By interjecting such remarks, Joan fails to satisfy the clerics' demand for answers to their questions and thus gains no relief from the repeated interrogations, yet she expresses her experience in terms consonant with expressions earlier in the trial and in other documents.

It might appear at this point that the distinction between Joan's utterances in the trial that appear manufactured by the pressures of the interrogation and her utterances in the trial that appear free of such pressures might correspond to a distinction between a true expression of her experience and a false expression of her experience. In his reading of the transcripts of early modern witch trials, Carlo Ginzburg has suggested that the confessions of accused witches are composed both of elements that reflect the suggestive interrogations of the inquisitors, such as the depictions of the black mass, and of elements that do reflect the actual experience of those accused, such as the depictions of night-riding.[38] It might appear that Joan's final admission to have heard the voices of St. Catherine, St. Margaret, and St. Michael resembles these witches' confession to have participated in the Sabbath in that it results more from the clerics' demand that she identify her voices than from her own initiative. As we have seen, virtually no documents outside the trial transcripts depict Joan as identifying her voices with these saints. The trial transcripts themselves, during the first three and a half days of interrogation, depict Joan calling her voices "her voices" and resisting a more specific nomenclature. As we have seen, it is only when the clerics ask Joan repeatedly, first, whether her voice is that of an angel, a saint, or God Himself, only when they dismiss her attempts to describe the voice outside such terms, only when they disregard her hesitations, her retractions, and her ambiguities of expression, that she identifies her voices with these saints. It might appear, in addition, that Joan's depiction of her voices as anonymous beings who brought her comfort when she was distressed, who urged her on and assured her of their help, and who brought her a joy that she wanted to retain forever resembles the witches' depiction of their night-riding in that it results from her own free, spontaneous avowal. It might appear, we can conclude, that Joan did not experience her voices as St. Catherine, St. Margaret and St. Michael but was merely forced to claim to do so by the pressures of the trial. Yet this is precisely the conclusion that the transcripts prevent us from making.

If one cannot dismiss Joan's identification of her voices with these saints, despite the pressure that the clerics impose in order to bring about this identification, it is because, first, though it is the clerics who demand that Joan identify her voices with an angel, a saint, or God Himself, it is Joan who decides to identify her voices with St. Catherine, St. Margaret, and St. Michael. While it is the clerics who demand that she locate her voices within these three categories, it is Joan who selects the categories and the individual members within them. Joan never refers in the transcripts to the particular legends of these saints but, as has often been pointed out, these legends are not without relevance to her own life. Catherine of Alexandria and Margaret of Antioch resemble Joan in that they were also virgins who emerged in public life out of obedience to the Christian God and who, despite their youth, their sex, and their lack of familial or social support, became powerful in their societies.[39] When fifty philosophers attempted to convert St. Catherine to paganism, she defeated them with arguments so convincing that she became the patron saint of the University of Paris; it was to St. Catherine that several chroniclers compared Joan after she responded brilliantly to the clerics who examined her at Poitiers. When the devil attempted to subdue St. Margaret in the form of a dragon, she crushed him under her foot; it was because virgins were reputed to be powerful in repelling the devil that Joan was, on more than one occasion, physically examined in order to verify her claims to virginity. These virgin saints resemble Joan, not only in their wisdom and their virtue, but also in their capacity to endure great suffering as a result of their fidelity to the Christian God. Though the sufferings of which Joan complains in prison cannot be compared to the multiple tortures to which these virgin martyrs are submitted, when Joan recalls the voices telling her that she must accept her suffering or *martyre* willingly and that she will ultimately come to the kingdom of heaven, it is to this model of heroic martyrdom that she alludes. Andrea Dworkin, comparing Joan's voices to role models, explains that Joan "learned from them the way a genius learns: she did not repeat them in form or content; she invented new form, new content, a revolutionary resistance" to male power.[40] While St. Catherine and St. Margaret evoke Joan in their virginity, their powerfulness, and their suffering, St. Michael resembles Joan in his angelic status and in his association, in the fifteenth century, with the royal family of France. Like St. Michael, Joan appeared to bypass the corporeal distinctions of masculinity and femininity by dressing in men's clothes and performing men's deeds.[41] Like St. Michael, Joan mediated between God and humans, conveying to her countrymen God's will in the Hundred Years War and undertaking military feats on his behalf. Like St. Michael, whose stronghold on Mont-Saint-Michel remained an island of French soil in English-occupied territory throughout the war, Joan remained faithful to the Valois dynasty.[42] It is to an angel that many of the chroniclers compare her and to an angel that, at one point in the trial transcripts, Joan compares herself. While the clerics compel her to identify her voices with specific individuals, the individuals whom Joan chooses reflect her own curious situation as a virgin warrior sent by God.

In addition, however reluctantly Joan first identifies her voices with St. Catherine, St. Margaret and St. Michael during the fourth day of her trial, as the trial proceeds her reluctance to identify her voices disappears and is replaced by an apparent eagerness and spontaneity. By the sixth day of interrogation, four days after she had first pronounced their names, the transcripts relate that Joan said of these saints "I saw them with my eyes and I believe that they exist as firmly as God exists" and that "she saw so well the said St. Michael and the female saints that she knows well that they are saints in paradise."[43] Though, on the second day of interrogation, Joan had stated that a mere "voice" came to her when she was thirteen and taught her to govern herself and to frequent the Church, by the eleventh day of the trial she confidently maintains that it was St. Michael who had instructed her at that time. By the end of the interrogations, the transcripts relate that Joan "believes, as firmly as she believes that Our Lord Jesus Christ suffered death for us in redeeming us from the torments of hell, that these are St. Michael and St. Gabriel, St. Catherine and St. Margaret, whom Our Lord sent to her to comfort and counsel her."[44] It is as if once Joan has been obliged to identify her voices as St. Catherine, St. Margaret and St. Michael, the voices begin to reveal themselves to her to be St. Catherine, St. Margaret, and St. Michael. It is as if once Joan had been compelled to identify her voices with these three saints, she began to perceive them to be the individuals with whom she had identified them.

If, as I have attempted to show here, Joan not only begins to name her voices as the Saints Catherine, Margaret, and Michael in the course of her interrogations but begins to experience her voices as these saints, the consequences of this development are apparent. While the clerics and the subsequent readers of these transcripts have presupposed that truth exists prior to the representation of this truth, these trial transcripts demonstrate the contrary possibility. They show the potential of an interrogation to create the very truth that it is purporting to represent. This power of interrogation to end not in the revelation of the suspect's understanding but in the transformation of the suspect's understanding so that it reflects that which the interrogators seek to reveal, can help explain the prevalence of false confessions today even in societies where the traditional causes of such confessions, such as torture, lengthy incommunicado detentions, and the deprivation of legal counsel, have been eradicated. The transformation that Joan underwent when identifying her voices during her trial at Rouen is best articulated by Christian Ranucci. A young man who confessed, under interrogation, to having murdered a child, Ranucci, largely on the basis of his confession, was guillotined in France in 1976 but his guilt has been contested since that execution. Describing how he came to confess to a crime that he later claimed not to have committed, Ranucci explains his thought process when confronted with the interrogators' assumption of his guilt. He relates, "In the beginning [of the interrogation], I told myself, 'It's impossible.' But after being in this hole for several hours, there began to be room for this drama, and then it stuck, and they seemed so sure of themselves and of the proof that they showed me. And then I ended by saying, 'it's possible,' then 'it's probable,' and then, 'it's me.'"[45] It is this capacity of interrogation to introduce a possibility, in the form of a question, and to transform this possibility into a probability and then into a certainty, to lead a respondent to believe that her voices are those of three saints, which Joan's case, as well as Ranucci's, demonstrates.

NOTES

1. Jules Bastien-Lepage, *Joan of Arc.* Oil on canvas, 1879, Metropolitan Museum of Art.

2. See Thomas Aquinas, *Summa theologiae,* vol. 9 (Angels, 1a. 50–64), ed. Kenelm Foster O. P., Blackfriars (Cambridge, 1968).

3. "credit quod ipsa erat ex Deo missa, quia ipsa nunquam jurabat, libenter missas audiebat, et jurando crucis signo se signabat," *Procès de condamnation et de réhabilitation de Jeanne d'Arc,* ed. Jules Quicherat (Paris, 1847), vol. 4, p. 291. All translations are my own unless otherwise indicated.

4. Jules Michelet, *Jeanne d'Arc et d'autres textes,* ed. Paul Viallaneix (Paris, 1974), p. 52.

5. Ibid.

6. Jules Quicherat, *Aperçus nouveaux sur l'histoire de Jeanne d'Arc* (Paris, 1850), p. 48.

7. Philippe-Hector Dunand, *Etude historique sur les voix et visions de Jeanne d'Arc,* 2 vols. (Paris, 1903), p. 6.

8. The studies offering explanations for Joan of Arc's voices fall, in general, into three categories. First, a large number of critics, including Monsignor Félix Dupanloup, the bishop of Orleans instrumental in Joan's canonization, and Régine Pernoud, the author of numerous popular works on Joan and founder of the Centre Jeanne d'Arc in Orleans, maintain that Joan's voices did derive from God. Dunand's *Etude historique* provides the most exhaustive exposition of this thesis. In the first part of this work, Dunand argues, as a self-proclaimed follower of the critical–historical school, that Joan's knowledge of a secret the dauphin had shared only with God, her retrieval of a mysterious sword buried in the church of Saint-Catherine de Fierbois, and her predictions of the relief of Orleans, the victory at Patay, the king's coronation, the conquest of Paris, and the expulsion of the English from France are as well documented as are any events of the late Middle Ages, and to doubt the occurrence of these miracles is to doubt the very existence of Joan of Arc. In the second part of this work, Dunand demonstrates, as a Catholic, that Joan satisfies the criteria of *persona, modus,* and *effectus* through which the church approves revelations. While the problems that such a mystical interpretation of Joan's voices pose for non-Christans are self-evident, such a reading is also complicated by the church's recognition of St. Catherine and St. Margaret, the figures with whom Joan eventually identifies her voices, as apocryphal and its removal of these saints from the calendar. Indeed, when the Office for the Congregation of Saints finally approved Joan's canonization in 1920, it refrained from pronouncing judgment on her voices and recommended her canonization not as a martyr who died in defense of her divine mission but as a virgin of exemplary life. Six years after the appearance of Dunand's work, Anatole France produced his own two-volume *Vie de Jeanne d'Arc* (Paris, 1909), which soon became the manifesto of a rationalist approach to the Maid. France dismisses Joan's voices as hallucinations and includes, as an appendix to his work, a letter by a Sorbonne neuropathologist, Georges Dumas, which attributes these hallucinations to hysteria. Endless specialists in medicine and psychology have joined Dumas in diagnosing the illnesses that caused Joan's revelations. While the physicians base their interpretations largely upon the observation of Joan's page that she did not suffer from "the secret illness of women," the psychiatrists ground their verdicts upon Joan's recollection of her father, foreseeing her departure with soldiers in a dream, declaring that he would prefer to see her drowned than become a camp-follower. Spiritualists provide the third branch of interpretation of Joan's voices. Andrew Laing , the spirtualist best known for his writings on Joan, wavers between depicting the voices as objective and subjective phenomena. See Laing, *The Maid of France, Being the Study of the Life and Death of Jeanne d'Arc* (London, 1908), especially Appendix D, "The Voices and Visions of Jeanne d'Arc," pp. 327–30, and "The Voices of Jeanne d'Arc" in *The Valet's Tragedy and Other Studies* (London, 1903),

pp. 193–227. Léon Denis provides a more coherent spiritualist reading of Joan's voices in his *Jeanne d'Arc Médium* (Paris, 1910), where he asserts that Joan, like other sensitive souls throughout history, detected the occult forces that pervade the universe and identified them according to the religious idiom available to her. All of these authors, whether Catholic, rationalist, or spiritualist, perceive the trial transcripts as a means to gain access to a reality external to the text and thus differ from that which I am attempting to achieve here.

9. Michelet worked from manuscript sources when composing his text on Joan of Arc. While scholars had hoped for a published edition of the documents from as early as the mid-seventeenth century, it was only with Jules Quicherat's *Procès de condamnation et de réhabilitation de Jeanne d'Arc dite La Pucelle,* 5 vols. (Paris, 1841–49) that this hope was realized. In his history of Joan's trial transcripts in his preface to the *Procès de condamnation de Jeanne d'Arc,* ed.Pierre Tisset with Yvonne Lanhers, 3 vols. (Paris, 1960–71), vol. 1, ix–xvii, Pierre Marot relates how the Société de l'Histoire de France commissioned Quicherat, a recent graduate of the Ecole des Chartes, to edit the transcripts in order that a French edition might supersede that of the German Guido von Goerres then in progress.

10. Hayden White's work is an important exception. See, in particular, White's important essay on medieval annals in *The Content of the Form: Narrative Discourse and Historical Representation* (Baltimore, 1987).

11. "Asserens se missam ex parte Dei, ad fugandum Anglicos et levandum obsidionem positam per eosdem Anglicos ante villam Aurelianensem," *Procès en nullité de la condamnation de Jeanne d'Arc,* ed. Pierre Duparc, 5 vols. (Paris, 1977–88), vol. 1, p. 381. "envoyée à luy de par Dieu, luy aider à conquérir son royaume possédé par lesdictz Anglois," Quicherat, 1.38.

12. "ego veni et sum missa ex parte Dei, ad prebendum adjutorium vobis et regno," Duparc, 1.326.

13. "a Deo venit, et missa extitit ad relevandum regem et incolas sibi obedientes," ibid., 377. It should be observed, in addition, that all of the letters that were sent in Joan's name during her military campaigns refer to her as being sent by God. See, for example, Joan's letter to the duke of Bedford, where Joan speaks of herself as "venue de par Dieu." Quicherat, 4.139.

14. "Et hoc faciam, quia Dominus meus vult ut ita faciam," ibid., p. 290.

15. "Ego venio ex parte Regis celorum, ad levandum obsidionem Aurelianensem," ibid., p. 368.

16. "Erat missa ex parte Dei celi in favorem nobilis dalphini, pro reponendo eum in suo regno, pro levando obsidionem Aurelianensem, ed conducendo ipsum Remis ad consecrandum," ibid., p. 328.

17. "Messire m'a envoyée pour secourir la bonne ville d'Orléans," ibid., p. 407.

18. "Quedam vox sibi apparuit, que sibi dixit quod Deus habebat magnam pietatem de popolo Francie, et quod oportebat quod ipsa Johanna veniret ad Franciam," ibid., p. 471–72.

19. "Audiebat unam vocem dicentem sibi: 'Fille De, va, va, va, je serai à ton aide, va,'" ibid., p. 323.

20. "Multum gaudebat, ymo desiderabta semper esse in illo statu; et, quod fortius est, recitando hujusmodi verba suarum vocum, ipsa miro modo exultabat, levando suos oculos ad celum," ibid.

21. "aucunes révélations," Quicherat, 1.213; "consilium Dei," Duparc, 1.318; "voces et consilium que sibi consulebant quid haberet agere," ibid., p. 382.

22. "en forme de femme," *Procès de condamnation,* Quicherat, 1. 464.

23. "Le glorieux archange saint Michel, sainte Katerine et sainte Marguerite, et plusieurs autres sains et saintes se apparoient à ly souvent," ibid., p. 478.

24. "s'il la vouloit croire et avoir [foy] en Dieu, en monsieur sainct Michet et madame saincte Catherine, et en elle, qu'elle le moinroit corroner à Reims et le remectroit paisible en son royaume," ibid., p. 326; "en reclamant Dieu, sainct Michiel et saincte Catherine," ibid., p. 327.

25. It could be argued that these sources fail to identify Joan's voices with Sts. Catherine, Margaret, and Michael not because Joan did not identify her voices with these figures at this time but because she resisted informing those around her of her voices. From her opening words in the trial transcripts, Joan asserts, "As for the revelations that had been made to her on the part of God, she had never revealed them to anyone, if it was not to Charles alone, whom she says to be her king, and that she would not reveal them even if they had to cut off her head, for she held from her visions or her secret counsel that she should reveal them to no one" [*de revelacionibus eidem factis ex parte Dei, nunquam alicui dixerat seu revelerat, nisi soli Karolo quem dicit regem suum, nec eciam revelaret si deberet eidem caput amputari; quia hoc habebat per visiones sive consilium suum secretum ne alicui revelaret*]," Tisset, 1.38. While it is obviously impossible to argue how Joan "really" perceived her voices at any moment, it should be observed that here it is not "her visions or her secret counsel," but, rather, the "revelations which had been made to her on the part of God" which she insists that she has kept secret and must continue to keep secret. It is not about her voices who speak to her, but, rather about the information which has been made known to her that she has been and must be silent. As the interrogations progress, Joan's "secret" will be identified not with the identity of her voices but with the sign through which she persuaded her king that she had been sent by God.

26. "venit ex parte Dei et non habet hic negociari quicquam, petens ut remictereretur ad Deum a quo venerat," ibid., p. 57.

27. "ego sum missa ex parte Dei, et ponitis vos ipsum in magno periculo, gallice, en grat dangier," ibid., p. 59.

28. "dum esset etatis XIII annorum, ipsa habuit vocem a Deo pro se iuvando ad gubernandum," ibid., p. 47.

29. "Addiditque prefata Iohanna quod interrogans non haberet, pro illa vice, ab ipsa in qua specie vox illa sibi apparuerat," ibid., p. 48.

30. "utrum illa vox quam dixit sibi apparere, sit unus angelus, vel utrum sit a Deo immediate, vel an sit vox unius sancti vel sancte," ibid., p. 60.

31. "Illa vox venit ex parte Dei; et credo quod ego non dico vobis plane illud quod ego scio; et habeo maiorem metum deficiendi, dicendo aliquid quod displiceat illis vocibus, quam ego habeam de respondendo vobis. Et quantum ad istud interrogatorium, rogo vos ut habeam dilacionem," ibid.

32. "Interrogata an erat vox angeli que loquebatur ei, vel an erat vox sancti aut sancte aut Dei sine medio: Respondit quod illa vox erat sancte Katharine et sancte Margarete. Et figure earum sunt coronate pulchris coronis multum opulenter et multum preciose," ibid., p. 71.

33. "Interrogata que illarum sibi primo apparuit, respondit: Ego non cognovi eas ita cito; et illud bene scivi aliquando, sed oblita sum; et si habeam licenciam, ego diacam hoc libenter; et est positum in registro apud Pictavis. Item dixit eciam quod habuerat confortacionem a sancto Michaele. Interrogata que predictarum sibi apparencium venit primo ad ipsam, respondit quod sanctus Michael primo venit. Interrogata an sit multum tempus elapsum postquam primo habuit vocem sancti Michaelis, respondit: Ego non nomino vobis vocum de sancto Michaele, sed loquor de magna confortacione. Interrogata que fuit prima vox veniens ad eam, dum esset etatis xiii annorum vel circiter, respondit quod fuit sanctus Michael quem vidit ante oculos suos; et non erat solu, sed erat bene associatus angelis de celo. Dixit eciam quod non venit in Franciam nisi ex precepto Dei," ibid., p. 73.

34. See William A. Christian, *Apparitions in Late Medieval and Renaissance Spain* (Princeton, 1981) and Elizabeth Alvilda Petroff, *Medieval Women's Visionary Literature* (Oxford, 1986).

35. The twelfth-century nun Hildegard of Bingen also had visions of Jesus Christ for which she was venerated rather than persecuted, as was argued by Anita Obermeier and Rebecca Kennison in their paper, delivered to the Joan of Arc Symposium in Honor of Régine Pernoud at the 30th International Congress of Medieval Studies at Western Michigan University in May, 1995, who compared Hildegard and Joan's visions in "The Word Made Flesh: *Visio* vs. *Vox* in the Mystical Experiences of Hildegard of Bingen and Joan of Arc."

36. Duparc, 5.167. Duparc writes, "The visions seem only bit by bit to have become concrete apparitions of saints .... It is the judges who contributed to the personification of the voices, that of St. Michael and the others, pressuring Joan to give a concrete appearance to her visions," pp. 166–67.

37. "Iohanna, dicens se habuisse et habere continuo a quinque annis visiones et appariciones sancti Michaelis et sanctarum Katherine et Margarete," Tisset, 1.201.

38. Carlo Ginzburg, *Ecstasies: Decoding the Witches' Sabbath* (Berkeley, 1991). See also Ginzburg's *The Night Battles: Witchcraft and Agrarian Cults in the Sixteenth and Seventeenth Centuries,* trans. John and Anne C. Tedeschi (Baltimore, 1983), for a discussion of ways in which interrogators influence the responses of the suspects they are questioning.

39. Catherine and Margaret were among the most popular saints of the Middle Ages and were often paired. Of St. Catherine, Pierre Duparc points out that she was considered, as of the fourteenth century, the most powerful intercessor before God after the Virgin Mary and, along with St. John the Baptist, one of the most popular subjects of religious statues. Joan's connections with this saint, from her village life, have often been observed. There was a church dedicated to St. Catherine in Maxey, across the river from Joan's native village of Domrémy. Anatole France writes of St. Catherine, "On lui faisait dans la vallée de la Meuse des oraisons en rimes, comme celle-ci: 'Ave, très sainte Catherine, / Vièrge pucelle nette et fine," *Vie de Jeanne d'Arc,* in *Oeuvres complètes* (Paris, 1928), vol. 15, p. 111. Joan's older sister, the wife of a certain Colin de Greux, a deponent at the rehabilitation, was named Catherine; she is known to have died before 1429 and to have remained dear to Joan, so that Joan asked her pregnant aunt Aveline, if her child was a girl, to name her after her late sister. Of St. Margaret, is has often been noted that a statue of the saint, extant today, was most likely in the church in Domrémy during Joan's lifetime. According to France, "Madame sainte Marguerite était grandement honorée dans le royaume de France et elle y faisait beaucoup de grâces. Elle assistait les femmes en couches et protégeait les paysans au labour. Elle était la patronne des liniers, des recommanderesses, des mégissiers et des blanchisseurs de laine. On lui était dévot en Champagne et en Lorraine autant qu'en aucun pays chrétien," p. 108. According to one version of St. Margaret's legend (here also known as Pelagia), she disguises herself as a man in order to enter a monastary, a detail that has been connected to Joan's own preference for men's clothes. Charles T. Wood has suggested as well that Joan may have identified her voices with these saints because their feast days fell between September and November, during the time when the siege of Orleans was beginning. See his *Joan of Arc and Richard III: Sex, Saints, and Government in the Middle Ages* (New York, 1988), p. 133.

40. Andrea Dworkin, *Intercourse* (New York, 1987), p. 95.

41. On the relation between angels and gender, see Stuart Schneiderman, *An Angel Passes: How the Sexes Became Undivided* (New York, 1988).

42. For the importance of St. Michael to Joan and to France at this time, see Etienne Delaruelle, "L'archange saint Michel dans la spiritualité de Jeanne d'Arc," in *La piété populaire au poyen âge* (Turin, 1975), pp. 389–400; François-Marie Lethel, "Jeanne d'Arc et l'ange," in *Colloque sur l'ange,* Centre Européen d'Art Sacré, Pont à Maison, Meurthe-et-Moselle, 26–28 juin 1981, Abbaye des Prémontrés (Pont à Maison, 1982), 55–70, and Colette Beaune, *Naissance de la France* (Paris, 1982). Pierre Duparc has suggested that it was no accident that Joan named as one of her voices the archangel who expelled the wicked angels from paradise and conducted worthy human souls to heaven after their deaths. Duparc proposes that "in 1429 the idea of a just war led against the invader, of a struggle against wicked persons, as well as help to departed combatants, could coalesce to make St. Michael the indirect inspirer of Joan, the symbol of the resistance to the enemy," *Procès en nullité,* vol. 5, p. 169. It has been observed, in addition, that Joan was no doubt familiar with Saint-Mihiel, the capital of the duchy of Bar, and Saint-Michel-sur-Meurthe in the canton of Saint-Dié.

43. "Ego vidi ipsos oculis meis, et credo quod ipsi sunt eque firmiter sicut Deus est," Tisset, 1.92. "ipsum sanctum Michaelem et illas sanctas ita bene vidit quod bene scit eas esse sanctos et sanctas in paradiso," ibid., p. 91.

44. "dixit quod ipsa credit eque firmiter sicut credit quod Dominus noster Ihesus Christus passus est mortem pro nobis, redimendo de penis inferni, quod sunt sancti Michael, Gabriel, sancte Katharina et Margareta quod Dominus noster misit ei pro eam confortando et consulendo," ibid., p. 248.

45. Gilles Perrault, *Le pull-over rouge* (Paris, 1984).

READERS OF THE LOST ARC: SECRECY, SPECULARITY, AND SPECULATION IN THE TRIAL OF JOAN OF ARC

Steven Weiskopf

This essay explores the unstable and potentially shifting relationships between bodies and texts, and their relation to institutional and counter-institutional claims to interpretive authority in the trial of Joan of Arc.

> To you has been given the secret of the kingdom of God, but for those outside everything is in parables; they may indeed see but not perceive, and may indeed hear but not understand, lest they should turn and be forgiven.
> —Mark 4:11–12

> The scholarship on Joan is extremely abundant, but upon surveying the catalogues devoted to it, this seeming abundance hides only emptiness.   —Auguste Moliner

> I do not know what you wish to examine me on. Perhaps you might ask such things that I would not tell.   —Joan of Arc

In an entry dated May 1431, the Bourgeois of Paris, anonymous author of the *Parisian Journal*, records the chilling and curious execution of one of France's most enigmatic figures:

She was at once unanimously condemned to death and was tied to a stake on the platform (which was built of plaster) and the fire lit under her. She was soon dead and all her clothes were burned. Then the fire was raked back and her naked body shown to all the people *and all the secrets that could or should belong to a woman*, to take away any doubts from people's minds. When they had stared long enough at her dead body bound to the stake, the executioner got a big fire going again round her poor carcass, which was soon burned up, both flesh and bone reduced to ashes [my emphasis].[1]

In order that her ashes were not used for maleficium, they were scattered in the Seine.[2]

What "doubt" haunts the crowd in the Bourgeois's description? And what secrets in this quasi-pornographic account are the spectators hoping to discover, or more to the point, uncover? What are they hoping to see? Anne Llewellyn Barstow offers the most literal explanation, linking the Bourgeois's morbid description to the crowd's fascination with and confusion over Joan's sexual identity. Troubled by the notion that a woman could be "a powerful war leader," both friend and foe "thirsted to know whether she was a man or a woman."[3]

Barstow's reading of the crowd's confusion over Joan's sexuality is strengthened by another passage from the *Parisian Journal*. Using neither the feminine nor the masculine pronoun, the Bourgeois writes quizzically of Joan, "What *it* was, God only knows."[4] Linked solely to her sexual identity or not, much of this uncertainty about how to interpret Joan remains. To cite only two of the most recent studies, she must have been a mystic, shaman, prophet, harlot, androgyne, knight, amazon, saint, patriot, witch, and heretic.[5] Perhaps most fascinating of all is the fact that no one contributes more to this enigmatic identity than Joan herself, who from the opening lines of her trial defies fixed definition. Commanded to eschew all "subterfuge and shift that hinder truthful confession," Joan is "to take proper oath, with her hands on the holy gospels, to speak the truth in answer to such questions put to her." To this formal exhortation, Joan evasively replies, "I do not know what you wish to examine me on. Perhaps you might ask such things that I would not tell."[6] The court presses, "Will you swear to speak the truth concerning matters of faith, which you know?" Joan responds that she will speak of her mother and father or of why she took the road to France, but she boldly insists that much of what she knows is none of the court's business:

concerning the revelations from God, these she had never told or revealed to anyone, save only to Charles, whom she called king; nor

would she reveal them to save her head; for she had them in visions
in her secret counsel; and within a week she would know whether
she might reveal them.[7]

Adding to this bold and defiant proclamation of secrecy, Joan
compounds the court's frustration by threatening to lie when she
sees fit: "You may well ask me such things, that to some I shall answer
truly, and to others I shall not. . . If you were well informed about
me, you would wish me out of your hands. I have done nothing
except by revelation."[8] With such teasing and menacing responses,
Joan becomes for her judges, and for centuries of would-be
interpreters, nothing less than a hermeneutic nightmare: a
dangerously enigmatic text embodying the mysterious relationship
between divine revelation and kingship. She represents the "secret of
the kingdom," to return to the Gospel of Mark, standing in as a
clear and present sign of salvation to the chosen and as an ominous
"riddle" or "parable" for those outside the kingdom of God "who
may indeed see but not perceive, and may indeed hear but not
understand, lest they should turn and be forgiven." For the
ecclesiastical court, the "readers" in whom Joan acknowledges no
hermeneutic mastery, her true meaning is lost.

What do we make of a revelatory text that refuses to be revealed?
Recent feminist scholarship has brought to our attention the ways
in which texts, according to the logic of their male readers, could,
like women, be undressed to reveal truths previously hidden.[9] If we
reverse the terms of this unfortunate analogy, we can explore the
process by which Joan's judges try to reveal her previously hidden
truths, and how Joan effectively upsets such a strategy of reading.
What we find is that Joan's learned, ecclesiastical readers are presented
not with a text figuratively construed as female but with a female
who, with tactical brilliance, construes herself as a living and breathing
text; a text fraught with willful exclusions, brash eruptions, and
recalcitrant disregard for the interpretive efficacy of her clerical
readership.

This standoff between the female as text and the male as reader
indeed suggests that the Bourgeois's entry entails more than a mere
physical inventory of Joan's anatomy. For Joan's secrets go far beyond
questions of whether or not she was a woman; they are also
symptomatic of the frenzied clamoring for religiopolitical legitimacy
and the very authority to affirm that legitimacy in the turbulent

decade of the 1420s. The fixation on Joan's secrets and what they *might* mean reveals more about male secular and ecclesiastical anxieties displaced onto Joan than it ever could about Joan herself; and these male fears are charged with notions of reading, interpreting, and writing.

In terms of textual interpretation, the Bourgeois's grisly account of Joan's execution points to a fantasy of reading Joan not possible in her lifetime. In this fantasy, the raking back of the fire is analogous to the opening of a now silent and, its readers believe, potentially decipherable text. Joan's corpse is, we learn, burned *within* rather than *beyond* recognition: "She was soon dead and all her clothes were burned." The clothes removed and the body in view, Joan's physical secrets are made manifest. Her captors have literally undressed this troublesome text, and onlookers are invited to participate in the fantasy of reading a text that they believe contains a truth previously veiled by obscurity. But what do her readers gain from this fantasy? What "truth" if any can they expect to discover?

In her recent study of the ways in which women of medieval London were displayed in processions as a form of punishment and humiliation, Sheila Lindenbaum links the male fantasy of sight-as-knowledge in medieval processions to viewing hardcore pornography, demonstrating how both play out fantasies of male mastery:

> The image of the woman on display thus responded to the same masculine desire to see, to know and control. . . . When the unwanted part of the male self, its weakened or castrated condition, was projected into the external realm of vision where it could be mastered in the captive woman's form, the projection allowed the viewer to investigate her interior state, to probe her body sadistically for the kind of secrets that were best revealed when she was not in control.[10]

Might we be able to say the same about Joan's captors? Did her lifeless body lend itself to the type of sadistic probing that would satisfy her viewers' thirst to unlock her secrets, to project onto her captive form that weakened condition in themselves for which they believed her responsible? The answer may be yes and no: yes, in that the crowd, at least according to the Bourgeois, was able to discern that she had the anatomy of a woman; no, in that surveying her female anatomy at their leisure did little if anything to foreclose a fixed meaning on her prior military victories. She was a woman, but there was still no tangible explanation for her success. So while the body of Joan is made manifest to the crowd, her secrets, not fully contained in the body, become the latent text of which the crowd has no real comprehension. The speculation surrounding Joan's secrets, fueled rather than extinguished by the sight of this undressed text, becomes an exercise of hopeless indeterminacy. This lifeless text, *by virtue* of its being undressed, seals the fate of its readers, banishing them to a realm of infinite deferral where no one or fixed answer can ever be revealed.

The endless quest to understand and therefore to control Joan's secrets, the secrets that loom teasingly beyond vision as knowledge, is not a dilemma presented only by a corpse. The troubling distinction between the latent and the manifest Joan is one that she herself actively exploits during the trial as well. Joan's tactics illustrate what Diane Elam has recently referred to as the "*mise en abyme* of women"—or what she punningly terms the "ms. en abyme." Critiquing notions about a singular truth of woman, Elam explains that the "series of images in the *mise en abyme* is without end; each additional image changes all the others in the series without ever completely filling up the abyss, which gets deeper with each additional determination."[11] Elam's explanation of the "ms. en abyme" opens up the possibility of considering the unstable relationship between male readers and their female texts in this paradigm of abyssal indeterminacy:

> …the infinitely receding object in the *mise en abyme* closes down the possibility of a stable subject/object relation. On the one hand, the object cannot be grasped by the subject; it slips away into infinity. On the other hand, this produces a parallel regression in the subject or viewer of the *mise en abyme*. As the object recedes into itself, the subject is destabilized; it loses not merely its capacity to grasp the object, but also its grasp on itself. The subject is thus faced with its inability to know what it knows, to see what it sees.[12]

Receding into the private and mysterious realm of her secret counsel of saints, baiting her inquisitors to discern truth from fiction in her testimony—to demonstrate to her and to themselves that they really *know* what they claim they are sanctioned by God to know—Joan becomes the receding object that is always just out of the court's grasp. Her inquisitors, conversely, find themselves in the role of receding subjects. Trapped in a kind of parallel regression, they are effectively destabilized by their object of study and are faced with the troubling question of whether they fully comprehend the meaning of what they see. The relationship finally forces these subjects to say of their object—and here I return to the Bourgeois's words—"What it was, God only knows," and of itself as a subject, "I'm not so sure anymore who or what I am either." The ultimate indeterminacy of Joan of Arc, in both life and death, points then to just such an instability of subject/object relationships, raising questions about ecclesiastical and secular authority's ability to interpret texts and thereby to constitute itself and its ever-tenuous claims to power through knowledge.

Although the religiopolitical connections in the trial of Joan of Arc are impossible to ignore, we can go back as far as the year of Joan's execution to find evidence that the Lancastrians wanted to downplay such a connection. Shortly after Joan's death, a letter was sent on behalf of the boy king Henry VI to the "emperor, the kings, and other princes of all of Christendom," informing them that her secular captors, although fully justified in trying her themselves, had submitted her case to the "mature consideration" of the ecclesiastical court.[13] A closer look at this ecclesiastical court, however, effaces the distinction between the secular and the ecclesiastical that the letter sets out to make. The collusive relationship of the Lancastrians and the trial's ecclesiastical judge, Pierre Cauchon, bishop of Beauvais, is well known.[14] And such collusion makes sense considering the combined threat that Joan posed to the interpretive efficacy of ecclesiastical and secular institutions. In the *Genesis of Secrecy*, Frank Kermode writes that "interpreters usually belong to an institution....As members of the institution they possess the right to affirm, and the authority to accept, the superiority of the latent over the manifest."[15] And it is Joan's unconventional claim of interpretive power of the latent over the manifest, her claim, in fact, to embody literally the latent *in* the manifest, to which we will now turn.

> —Asked whether, when she saw the voice coming to her, there was a light, she answered that there was a great deal of light on all sides, as was most fitting. She added to the examiner that not all the light came to him alone! (Barrett, p. 70)

The greatest concern, if not fear, of Joan's inquisitors was the existence and nature of her secret voices. The source of this fear was the way in which Joan and her secret counsel appeared to supplant the church's role as intermediary between God and humanity. When Joan snaps at her inquisitor "that not all the light came to him alone," she metaphorizes the actual light, which she claims always accompanied her voices, into a divine knowledge, the "latent," which is supposedly accessed only by the chosen few of the ecclesiastical court. The trial records the objection to Joan's metaphor:

> …in respect of her revelations and visions she professed to have, that she would not submit to the Church Militant or any living man, but intended to refer herself to God alone in respect of her acts and sayings. He expounded to her on this point the nature of the Church Militant, the authority it derives from God, in Whom its power resides; how every Christian is bound to believe that the Holy Church is one and Catholic, that the Holy Spirit governs it, and it never falls into error … that none, whatever his apparitions or revelations, must on their account withdraw from the judgment of the Church. [16]

The problem with Joan's metaphor is clear: the "light" should be coming to the Church Militant, but Joan, constructing herself as a revelatory text, insinuates herself into the privileged roles of intermediary and interpreter.

But how is this accomplished? How does Joan access and then become a repository for this metaphorical light, this secret of divine knowledge that contains veiled truth, especially when such truth is supposedly reserved for sacred texts and their institutional readers? Recent studies of medieval and Renaissance mysticism provide one way to approach this question. They describe how the uninitiated, that is, those not officially affiliated or sanctioned by institutions like the church or the university, attain divine knowledge. Denied access to authorized statements of the written word, such as church doctrine, biblical commentaries, or patristic writings, and barred from the institutional space of authority from which to interpret any such writings, mystics construct their bodies as the place of the sacred text itself: a place to which, in which, and from which divine knowledge could be delivered, mediated, and revealed.[17] While some of Joan's supporters championed her mission in writing, either by virtue of their position within an institution, by their learning, or both, Joan, who relied on voices and visions, had comparatively less recourse to the written word. Whether Joan was literate or not, and the point is a contended one, it was her voices and visions, existing outside of institutional boundaries, that presented the more powerful threat.[18] Rejecting the institutional approach that privileges the written word, Joan experiences her visions through an alternative text, that of her own body, while making claims to the same God, totally unmediated by the clergy. She not only interprets the text; she is the text. Joan represents for some the sacred repository "into whom" Christine de Pizan tells us, "the Holy Spirit poured his great grace."[19]

The way in which Joan figures herself as a text is characteristic of the strategies of other female mystics. In order to make her body a place for divine revelation, the mystic must go through a process of self-alienation. She must create a void in herself; she must empty out her ego. Having achieved this, the mystic must completely tie her desire to the will of God. "Through a kind of exile," Karma Lochrie explains, "the mystic subject establishes her subjectivity on the basis of desire and this lack. The 'I,' then, is the empty space from which the Other speaks."[20]

We see a similar process underway when Joan recalls one of her initial meetings with St. Michael. The preparatory interrogation, dated March 17, records the following:

> Asked how she knew it was St. Michael, she replied: By the speech and language of angels. And she firmly believes that they were angels. Asked how she knew it was the language of angels, she answered that *she believed it immediately; and desired to believe it.* She also said that St. Michael, when he came to her, told her that St. Catherine and St. Margaret would come to her, and that she should follow their counsel; for they were ordered to lead and counsel her as to what she should do; and that she should believe what they told her, *for it was by Our Lord's command* [my emphases]. [21]

Rather than placing herself in the hands of the Church Militant, to whose judgment she should defer her own, Joan, without one thought of ecclesiastical judgment or mediation in this instance, immediately embraces her counsel for no other reason than that she simply *desires* to believe in them. Worse yet, from the court's perspective, ecclesiastical presence is effectively erased from the equation as St. Catherine and St. Margaret, at least in this passage, supplant the clerical machinery to which Joan is required to submit herself. Affirmed and legitimized by "our Lord's command," Joan and her secret counsel, tied solely to the will of God, assume the speaking position in divine revelation, while the ecclesiastical court is relegated to the place of listener. And by the time we finish this game of mystical chairs, the traditional formulation of the church as intermediary between God and humanity is reversed. Joan comes to resemble what is said about her in George Bernard Shaw's play: "She acts as if she herself were the church."[22]

Having established herself as a revelatory text, Joan then attempts to control her revelation through tactics of deferral and secrecy. One such tactic, employed with a slightly different twist throughout each session of the trial, is a refusal to take an oath according to the terms set by her inquisitors. The opening of the third session of the trial is particularly striking. Asked to swear the oath, Joan responds, "Perhaps I shall not answer you truly in many things you ask me, concerning the revelations; for perhaps you would constrain me to tell things I have sworn not to utter, and so I should be perjured, and you would not want that."[23] After several exhortations and a stern admonition, she replies, "I am ready to swear to speak the truth of what I know concerning the trial."[24] She frequently refuses to swear the whole truth because of previously sworn oaths to her voices, just as she asserts her will to decide what does and does not pertain to the trial. In making such moves, Joan defers to her own counterinstitutional apparatus with its own set of laws and oaths. These oaths, sworn to her voices, and therefore to God, supersede the importance and even draw into question the basic legitimacy of any oath she might take with Cauchon's court. Consequently, any information concerning her voices or the nature of her mission is not, at least at this point, within the institutional claims of her inquisitors. If and when Joan's divine counsel deems that information suitable for public consumption, then, and only then, will she discuss everything concerning her revelations. It is abundantly clear where she places her allegiance: "I am more afraid of failing the voices by saying what is displeasing to them, than of answering you."[25]

After acquiring permission from her voices, Joan finally identifies them as the archangel Michael, St. Catherine, and St. Margaret. Although Michael, as we have seen, is the first voice ever to come to her, it is clear that her female voices, Catherine and Margaret, who visit her at least once a day, serve as her primary counselors and comfort. The frequency of her secret counselors' visits, occurring at any time of the day or in any place, including the trial itself, and sometimes for no particular reason, suggests that Joan not only remains in constant touch with her voices but has a type of casual relationship with them. She claims even to embrace them and to speak with them as she would anyone else. Reporting on this informal and conversational tone, the Bourgeois writes that Michael, Margaret, and Catherine appeared to her frequently and talked to her "as one friend does to another; *not by revelation*, as God has sometimes spoken to those he loves, but bodily, by mouth, as a friend speaks to a friend"[26] (my emphasis). The Bourgeois's entry exemplifies not only the confusion and discomfort about the existence but also the very form of Joan's revelations. These are bodily revelations, a materialized discourse so alien in form that the Bourgeois cannot even bring himself to recognize them as divine revelations at all. Even more alarming is the notion that these revelations are written on the body of the only one who claims she can interpret it.

How can a text be its sole interpreter? This concern, although certainly one for the ecclesiastical court, is a secular one as well. Joan's initial description of her partners in revelation, Catherine and Margaret, bears a secular relation to the court's repeated questions about Joan's affiliation with Charles VII, French claimant to the monarchy in France, and to the religiopolitical sign that she claims to have revealed to him. She describes Margaret and Catherine: "Their heads were crowned in a rich and precious fashion with beautiful crowns," but concerning the rest of their dress, "I will not tell you more now; I have not leave to reveal it."[27] The principal anxiety over Joan's voices has much to do with crowns, kingship, and the message she relays from her saints to Charles VII. For as much as Cauchon's ecclesiastical court has an investment in debunking the legitimacy of her voices to maintain its own monopoly in matters of divine mediation, Lancastrian England, haunted by doubts of its own dynastic legitimacy, is equally obsessed with doing so. And in that secret sign to Charles VII is believed to lie the answer to the question of who can rightfully claim the throne in France.

Like much of the information in the trial, unveiling Joan's secret sign proves frustrating for her inquisitors. Throughout the interrogation, she defiantly claims that all of her secret counsel concerning Charles VII is not an issue in the trial. Her voices and the sign she brought to the king, and therefore the king himself, are not under the jurisdiction of this ecclesiastical court financed by the

English: "Do you want me to tell what concerns the king of France? There are many things that are not on trial."[28] Joan taunts the court at times with her religiopolitical secret "sign." When the court again asks for the full revelations of her voices, she barks "that is not your case at all"[29] but later assures the court that she told Charles VII absolutely everything about her secrets.[30] There are many such instances of willful exclusion: "I have revelations concerning the king I shall not tell you."[31] "My voices told me to say certain things to the king and not to you."[32] "I have already said that I will not tell you what touches or concerns our king; and what touches our king, I shall not tell you."[33] Her position is clear: her inquisitors lie far "outside of the kingdom," a kingdom that is now at once ecclesiastical and secular. Such examples represent only a few of the many times that Joan refuses to reveal her "secret counsel" about her meeting with Charles VII, and it is precisely the claims of Charles VII that *are* on trial. Increasingly uncontainable in the eyes of the English, these claims must be embodied and punished in someone. And in the absence of a king, another body will have to do.

On May 24, 1431, one of Joan's inquisitors, Collaume Erard, chastises her for her king's heretical ways: "I'm talking to you, Joan, and I tell you that your king is a heretic and schismatic."[34] Perhaps no single phrase in the documents concerning Joan's trial highlights better the crucial confluence between the political and religious as does this one. At this point, the Anglo-Burgundian court implies the charge of "heretic" and "schismatic" toward the one they perceive to be the symbolic embodiment of the illegitimate king of France. And by a substitution in which Joan's body becomes the locus of this illegitimacy, Charles VII's dynastic body is now on trial. For the Lancastrians, haunted by their own questionable claims of legitimacy, and perhaps anxious about the fact that their king, Henry VI, was a small child, capturing and fixing a potentially controllable body facilitated their tactic of projecting a perceived weakened self onto another body. Perceptions of a weakened or castrated English monarchy were current indeed.

The way in which Charles VII and Joan become "heretics" against the English throne directly relates to the religiopolitical sign Charles VII receives from Joan at their first meeting in Chinon. Following another barrage of questions concerning the "sign" she gave the king, Joan finally, with the permission of her counsel, discloses on March

13, 1431, her long concealed secret sign and its significance for Charles VII and the English. In the last week of February 1429, Joan travels to Chinon and gives the yet uncrowned Charles a sign. Within a month, Joan participates in a military campaign against Anglo-Burgundian forces. Spirited in part by Joan's presence, the French army quashes in less than six months the English military campaign in France. The legendary relief of Orleans by the French, which Joan had predicted at that initial meeting with Charles, culminates on May 8, 1429. In the "relief," the English lose Salisbury, a celebrated veteran commander, and historians, then and now, mark the event as a turning point in favor of the French.

English as well as French sources roughly contemporaneous with Joan's success ascribe more importance to her presence than appears to be accurate. No compelling evidence suggests that Joan was at all in charge at the legendary relief of Orleans, and yet one English chronicler chooses to record the event in the following manner: "In the monythe of May, was the sege of Orlyance i-broke with the Pusylle, Bastarde of Burbon and other Armynackys."[35] Another chronicle also records the longstanding effects of the English defeat in Orleans and the death of Salisbury: "This same yere, the gode Erle of Salesbury . . . leyd Seiege unto Orlyaunce; at which segie he was slayn. . . . And sith for that he was slayn, English men neuer gat ne preuailed in Fraunce, bot euer after began to lefe, bi litel and lytel, til al was lost."[36] While Joan is not directly linked with the siege of Orleans in this entry, her formidable powers are duly noted only a few paragraphs later. Of those who aid the "Dolphin" in making "destres upon Englissh men," there was "especial A maid" who "rode like a man, & was A valyant Capitayn Among thame, & take vpon hir many gret enterpryses, in so much that thei [the French] had A byleve to have recouered al ther losses by hir."[37] So as the English begin to leave "by litel and lytel," their presence progressively diminished, the French conversely recover all their losses through Joan. Both of these chronicles betray a fear of incapacitation at the hands of this mysterious woman: a fear that the powerful body of the English monarchy, once represented by Henry V, is being unmanned "bi litel and lytel."

If the English chroniclers are not as forthright as they could be about stressing the troubling gender implications of one woman running out an entire army of English men, Christine de Pizan, with characteristic candor, has no trouble spelling it out for them:

> Oh, how clear this was at this siege of Orleans where her power was first made manifest! It is my belief that no miracle was ever more evident, for God so came to the help of His people that our enemies were unable to help each other any more than would dead dogs. It was there that they were captured and put to death. Oh! What honour for the female sex! It is perfectly obvious that God has special regard to it when all these wretched people who destroyed the whole kingdom—now recovered and made safe by a woman, something that five thousand men could not have done—and the traitors have been exterminated. Before the event, they would scarcely have believed this possible. [38]

With no lack of partisan fervor, Christine throughout the poem underscores the fact that English domination of the French, once secured by England's male army, has been dismantled. The success of the English, especially during Henry V's reign, had made France appear to be a comparatively weak and penetrable body. The legendary victory of the English at Agincourt in 1415 and the treaty of Troyes in 1420, which effectively disinherited Charles VII, both reinforced English claims to the throne in France. But English fortunes had begun to wane after Henry V's death in 1422, and both sides progressively found themselves in a deadlock, with no clear sign about who was to take power, or indeed had the power of God's affirmation.

With such uncertainty in the ranks, Joan's secret sign to Charles had to be all the more enervating for the Lancastrians and their sympathetic ecclesiastical court. The meeting at Chinon between Joan and Charles went something like this. An angel came to Joan, accompanied her to the king's chamber at the castle of Chinon, and presented before the eyes of Joan a crown of gold "so rich and precious [the same adjectives used to describe the crowns of Catherine and Margaret] that she did not know how to count or appreciate its riches; and it signified that her king would gain the kingdom of France." [39] Along with the angel was an entire retinue of angels and the saints Catherine and Margaret. Joan claims that Charles and the archbishop of Reims, as well as other churchmen, saw the crown. It would be fitting that Charles VII and the archbishop, the King's ecclesiastical supporter, would share in this vision of the crown. For in these two figures Joan marries French religious and political leadership. The crown, according to Joan, rightfully belongs to Charles, and Reims, the city over which the archbishop presided, was the traditional location for the coronation of French kings. The archbishop of Reims was traditionally endowed with the responsibility of placing the crown on the king's head during a coronation.

Joan recounts that the crown was given by the angel "to the archbishop of Reims, so it seemed to her, in the presence of her king; and the archbishop received it and gave it to her king."[40] Although, as some have suggested, there are contradictions and disavowals in Joan's testimony about her visionary ceremony at the castle of Chinon, the coronation it portends is clear enough.[41] Clearer yet were the results following their meeting. Within six months, French forces would cut into Anglo-Burgundian–held Reims, and Charles, with all the traditional pomp and circumstance of his French predecessors, would be crowned and anointed Charles VII, king of France.

Joan's vision of Charles VII's coronation was similar to the visual display England had hoped to carry out in France on behalf of Henry VI, England's child claimant to the French throne. Bedford, Henry's regent, shaken by the results of Joan's perceived power, had a vision of his own. He was hopeful that a coronation at Reims would serve as a spectacular visual display, demonstrating England's right to the throne in France, and that such a demonstration would, as R.A. Griffiths writes, "counter the impact of the Maid and the proposed crowning of Charles VII in Rheims Cathedral."[42] But Joan and Charles would beat Bedford and the boy-king to the punch. By the time of Charles VII's coronation, the English had not even succeeded in giving young Henry VI a coronation in England. He was, after all, only eight years old. Finally, on November 5, 1429, the English would, in a game of dynastic "catch-up," rush this child through a magnificent and sumptuous coronation and proclaim him king of England. They then whisked him off to France in the hopes of a second coronation. In short, a program was underway to restore belatedly the masculine presence and legitimacy of the departed Henry V to the English throne after its perceived emasculation at the hands of the Pucelle and her forces.

Bedford's impulse for visual display, while not always on the scale of spectacular coronations, was nothing new; he had also long subscribed to the visual power of texts. He had attempted to solidify young Henry's legitimacy in France through a combination of verbal and visual media. In 1423, years before the appearance of Joan at Chinon, Henry commissioned an Anglo-Burgundian notary and royal secretary, Lawrence Calot, to write a poem in French to accompany a pictorial representation tracing both Henry VI's paternal and maternal descent to Louis IX. The poem and picture were hung side by side in Notre Dame Cathedral and other churches in France.[43] "This pictorial genealogy and poem," writes Bertram Wolffe, "both represent the fact of the dual monarchy, first realized in the person of Henry VI."[44] Another form of visual presentation was a new coinage circulated in France that represented Henry VI as the coming savior of the French kingdom.[45] Such were the attempts of the English to make their king into a text. But had not Joan's secret vision and her success undone such representations "bi litel and lytel"? Had not the Maid, defended and lauded as France's new savior by Christine de Pizan and others, thrown a religiopolitical monkey wrench of enormous proportions into the Lancastrian propaganda machine? Had the enigmatic powers of the *Pucelle* from the tiny village of Domrémy, a recognized savior of the French kingdom in her own right, actually forged a spiritual coin of the realm worth more in symbolic capital than all the real coins that the English had circulated in France?

The fate of Joan of Arc is inextricably linked to the legitimacy of voices and visions, whether we interpret these as bearing on political or religious spheres or, as I have argued, a religiopolitical one that stresses their innate connectedness. Neither Joan's enemies nor her supporters ever doubted or wanted to doubt the existence of her voices and visions. And by May 1431, the month of Joan's execution, Joan's enemies had perhaps more invested in the verity of their existence, if not in their legitimacy. The materiality of saints— their ability to be embraced, for example—and Joan's indefatigable insistence on their existence, all ran counter to church doctrine. The court determined that Joan's invisible friends, by virtue of the "material" nature that she attributed to them, were demons. It would not have been enough to dismiss them or Joan's accomplishments as chimerical; English and French perceptions of the damage inflicted at Orleans were too strong for that. As Christine writes of Joan's accomplishments, "Her achievement is no illusion . . . in short, a thing is proved by its effect."[46] Given the circumstances, the Lancastrian-funded court had to produce some *thing* that it could recuperate or destroy or, considered in other terms, something onto which it could project its weakened and castrated condition. The court initially believed recuperation to be a better alternative, as it would affirm both its authority and its mercy to those, like Joan, who had gone astray:

> All the assessors were ecclesiastical and learned men, experienced in canon and civil law, who wished and intended to proceed with her in all piety and meekness, as they had always been disposed, seeking not vengeance or corporal punishment, but her instruction and her return to the ways of truth and salvation. [47]

Joan is thankful but initially assures the court that she has "no intention of departing from the counsel of Our Lord."[48] She refuses to submit to the written word and the clerical learning it represents and maintains the interpretive efficacy of her own voices. The importance of Joan's abjuration would not only secure the institutional authority of the ecclesiastical court, valorizing the written over the spoken, but it would by extension also delegitimize if not demonize Charles VII. If the voices were false, and Joan as a heretical text was corrupt, so would be the errant reader, Charles VII, who followed her revelations.

When Joan, under great duress, finally does make her public recantation and abjuration of May 24, 1431, she is temporarily brought back under church control and is given a life sentence in prison. We read that her abjuration is written according to the "formula" of the church. Her sentence is life imprisonment. Made to conform to the written formula of the church and chained to the wall of the prison, Joan briefly becomes the symbolic capital which the English and their judges had worked to produce. The powerful force that threatened to emasculate the authority of the English king now comes to represent the feminine illegitimacy of Charles VII. But before the English even have a chance to don their party hats, the party is over. Joan relapses three days later. The written text of the court and the English claims to dynastic supremacy are once again put into peril by the random and uncontainable power of vision and speech. Joan reports that "God had sent her word through St. Margaret and St.

Catherine of the great pity of this treason by which she consented to abjure and recant in order to save her life; that she had damned herself to save her life."[49]

Her inquisitors feared the fire as well, for Joan's death promised a potential for martyrdom in the minds of the many who would continue to believe her—and many would. The later charges, that she had committed "treason against God," that she had "usurped His office," smacked of a political language that belied a religiopolitical anxiety surrounding her death. But she anticipates those charges. For as we see in the above passage, it is precisely at the moment of her abjuration to the ecclesiastical court that God, through Joan's secret counsel, charges her with treason. Treason, then, is equated with abjuring those revelations that validated Charles VII as king.

Although the English had succeeded in revealing and destroying the manifest Joan, her dead body bound to the stake for all to see, the latent Joan, the Joan of secret voices, remained a formidable phantom for them. Paradoxically full of determinations and yet always empty, always just beyond comprehension, Joan of Arc as a revelatory text would ultimately never be fixed in meaning. Three years after Joan's death, in a letter to Henry VI, Bedford is still compelled to demonize her achievements against the English as "false enchantment and sorcery," suggesting that the anxieties they had displaced onto her had not found a new home.[50] Joan would not quite die across the Channel either. In 1445, the *Chroniques de la noble ville et cité de Metz* reports that its author spotted Joan in 1436, five years after her execution, as he sojourned overnight in Metz, perhaps suggesting the author's own nostalgia about her place as a resurrected savior of France.[51] What do we bring away from Bedford's attacks on Joan or the chronicler's insistence that she never died? That ideas outlive their authors and that interpreters bring their own set of desires and anxieties to those ideas. And those anxieties demonstrate the continual doubts about authority's own ability to fully convince itself, not to mention anyone else, of its legitimate claims to knowledge and power.

NOTES

1. Janet Shirley, ed., *A Parisian Journal, 1405–1449* (Oxford, 1968), pp. 263–64. The anonymous author is referred to by scholars simply as "the Bourgeois."

2. T. Douglas Murray, ed., *Jeanne d'Arc* (New York, Phillips, 1902), pp. 301, 302, 305.

3. Anne Llewellyn Barstow, *Joan of Arc: Heretic, Mystic, Shaman* (Lewiston, 1986), p. 109. Barstow bases her reading on the way that medieval thought and, more specifically, church doctrine, upheld dichotomies, including gender. She contends that the church authorities "did not want these categories blurred" and that Joan challenged these categories by living as a single lay woman who dressed in men's clothing, associated with men, enjoyed success "in a man's world," and asserted an "overwhelming independence of mind and action."

4. Shirley, p. 240.

5. I refer here to Barstow and to Marina Warner, *Joan of Arc: Image of Female Heroism* (New York, 1981).

6. W.P. Barrett, ed. and trans., *The Trial of Jeanne d'Arc* (London, 1931), p. 50.

7. Ibid., p. 50.

8. Ibid., p. 54.

9. Carolyn Dinshaw, *Chaucer's Sexual Poetics* (Madison, 1989), p. 21.

10. Sheila Lindenbaum, "London Women on Display: The Case of Eleanor Cobham" unpublished, pp. 12–13. As a case study, Lindenbaum uses the case of Eleanor Cobham, who in 1441 was charged with plotting the death of Henry VI through witchcraft so that she and her husband could ascend the throne of England. Her discussion of pornography is based on Linda Williams, *Hard Core: Power, Pleasure, and the Frenzy of the Visible* (Berkeley, 1989), p. 51. For the major accounts of Eleanor's punishment, see Friedrich W.D. Brie, ed., *The Brut.* (London, 1908), p. 481; Nicholas Harris Nicholas, ed., *A Chronicle of London* (London, 1827), p. 129; John Sylvester Davies, ed., *An English Chronicle* Camden Society 64 (London, 1856), p. 59; and John Allen Giles, ed., *Incerti scriptoris Chronicon Angliae De regnis trium regum Lancastrensium* (London, 1848), p. 31. I am indebted to Professor Lindenbaum for her characteristic generosity in allowing me to see a version of her paper and for reading earlier drafts of this essay.

11. Diane Elam, *Feminism and Deconstruction: Ms. en abyme* (New York, 1994), p. 30.

12. Ibid., p. 28.

13. Barrett, p. 344.

14. Warner, p. 47. She writes that Cauchon "earned a handsome stipend, and his niece Guillemette, the daughter of his sister Joan, married King Henry VI's French Secretary, Jean de Rinel, whose letter penned full

amnesty to all who had taken part in the trial of Joan of Arc." Cauchon was also responsible for buying Joan from the Burgundian John of Luxembourg for approximately 8,000 livres and in turn received 756 livres for working to compile the evidence against her. For a fuller discussion of Cauchon's connections with the English, see Daniel Rankin and Claire Quintal, eds., *The Biography of Joan of Arc* (Pittsburgh, 1964), pp. 54–64.

15. Frank Kermode, *The Genesis of Secrecy: On the Interpretation of Narrative* (Cambridge, Mass., 1979), p. 2.

16. Barrett, p. 271.

17. Michel de Certeau, *The Mystic Fable* (Chicago, 1992), p. 178. Certeau's study deals more with the Renaissance mystic. For female medieval mystics, see Karma Lochrie, *Margery Kempe and the Translation of the Flesh* (Philadelphia, 1991).

18. See Christine de Pizan, *Ditié de Jehanne d'Arc*, ed. and trans. Angus J. Kennedy and Kenneth Varty (Oxford, 1977). For a more comprehensive study of texts written about Joan in the period, see Deborah Fraioli, "The Literary Image of Joan of Arc: Prior Influences," *Speculum* 56 (1981), 812–30. I realize that "literacy" means many things to many people. Here, I refer simply to the debate over whether she could read and/ or write.

19. Christine de Pizan, p. 44.

20. Karma Lochrie, *Margery Kempe and the Translation of the Flesh* p. 62. Lochrie's fascinating and useful discussion is indebted to Certeau's work. See Michel de Certeau, *Heterologies: Discourses on the Other* (Minneapolis, 1986), pp. 80–100.

21. W.S. Scott, ed. and trans., *The Trial of Joan of Arc* (London, 1956), p. 120.

22. George Bernard Shaw, *St. Joan* (New York, 1983), p. 102. I am not suggesting that Joan simply refuses to acknowledge in all instances the apparatus of the church. As several readers of this essay have kindly pointed out to me, Joan indicates on more than one occasion that she would gladly be transferred to the care and judgment of the pope. It seems in this instance, however, that Joan attributes no significant connection between her judges and the papacy.

23. Barrett, p. 59.

24. Ibid.,p. 60.

25. Ibid., p. 62.

26. Shirley, p. 261.

27. Barrett, p. 68.

28. Ibid., p. 80.

29. Ibid., p. 79.

30. Ibid., p. 101.

31. Ibid., p. 61.

32. Ibid., p. 62.

33. Ibid., p. 81.

34. M.G.A. Vale, *Charles VII* (Berkeley, 1974), p. 47.

35. James Gairdner, ed., *The Historical Collection of a London Citizen in the 15th Century* (London, 1876), p. 164.

36. Brie, p. 500.

37. Ibid., p. 501.

38. Christine de Pizan, p. 46. English and French sources linked the weakening of the English forces to Orleans, but according to a deposition given by Dunois in 1455: "The Maid was always of the opinion that it was necessary to go to Reims, that the king should be consecrated, giving a reason that, if once the king were consecrated and crowned, the power of his adversaries would decline, and that in the end they would be past the power of doing any injury, either to him or to his kingdom." See Murray, p. 239. As the frenzied race to get Henry VI to France for his own coronation suggests, the English concurred with Joan.

39. Barrett, p. 108.

40. Ibid., p. 108.

41. Warner, p. 126. Charles Wood also remarks on Joan's often "vague, ambiguous, and contradictory" testimony. (*Joan of Arc and Richard III: Sex, Saints, and Government in the Middle Ages* [New York, 1988], p. 143.)

42. R.A. Griffiths, *The Reign of Henry VI: The Exercise of Royal Authority, 1422–1461* (Berkeley, 1981), p. 188. Griffiths also argues that the haste with which Henry was sent to France "was dictated almost solely by the need for a striking English response to the revival of French fortunes under the Maid's inspiration." (p. 189). Bertram Wolffe (*Henry VI* [London, 1981]) also argues that the coronation had not taken place "for any reasons of state, but specifically to facilitate and hasten his arrival in France, to take possession of the French Kingdom."

43. Griffiths, p. 52. For more on this, see J.H. Rowe, "King Henry VI's Claim to France in Picture and Poem," *The Library* 4th ser. 13 (1933), 77–88. For an English translation of Calot's poem and other poems dedicated to Henry VI, see Henry Noble MacCracken, ed., *The Minor Poems of John Lydgate* (Oxford, 1961).

44. Griffiths, p. 52. On coinage, see J.W. McKenna, "Henry VI of England and the Dual Monarchy: Aspects of Royal Political Propaganda," *Journal of Warburg and Courtauld Institutes* 38 (1965), 145–51.

45. Griffiths, p. 53.

46. Christine de Pizan, p. 45.

47. Barrett, p. 138.

48. Ibid., p. 138.

49. Ibid., p. 319.

50. Griffiths, p. 55.

51. The chronicle is found in vol. 5 of Quicherat, ed., *Procès de condamnation et de réhabilitation de Jeanne d'Arc dite La Pucelle*. 5 vols, (Paris, 1841–49).

JOAN OF ARC AND CHRISTINE DE PIZAN:
THE SYMBIOSIS OF TWO WARRIORS IN
THE *Ditié de Jehanne d'Arc*

Christine McWebb

In the Ditié de Jehanne d'Arc, *the autobiographical subject of authorial enunciation becomes female as Christine de Pizan steps out of the androgynous framework of most of her previous work. At the same time, Christine canonizes Joan's myth as an emblem of female heroism.*

Joan of Arc, the most celebrated woman in French history, provides a perfect emblem to enhance French patriotism that is still exploited today. Even during her lifetime, her courage and strength were subjects of praise. Christine de Pizan composed the first written account of Joan of Arc's deeds in 1429, in her final work the *Ditié de Jehanne d'Arc.*[1]

The poem commemorates the heroic victory of the French army and the defeat of the English at Orleans and praises the crowning of the dauphin in Reims. These events were to a large extent due to Joan of Arc, a maiden who accomplished more than any warrior before her: "Mais, toute somme,/Une femme—simple bergiere—/ Plus preux qu'onc homs ne fut à Romme!" (197–99) (But, after all, a *woman*— a simple shepherdess—braver than any man ever was in Rome).

Christine de Pizan was fascinated by this young woman whose existence helped Christine overcome the life of self-imprisonment that she had led for eleven years. Toward the end of her life and her career as a writer, Christine took up the pen one last time to illustrate the miraculous deeds performed by La Pucelle.

Christine's decision to resume her public career as a writer in order to praise a female contemporary also situates her continued position

in the contemporary debate about women and misogyny.[2] Christine
herself was forced to assume a marginalized position as a writer in
an antifemale literary community dominated by clerics. As Kevin
Brownlee describes it, "The clerkly voice was by definition male,
linked to Latin as father-language and to the dominant association
of Latin learning with exclusively male social institutions."[3] Christine
de Pizan was a stranger within her own profession.[4]

The attempt to situate herself within a patriarchal setting can be
traced directly in some of Christine's writings. In the *Epistre au Dieu
d'Amours*,[5] the poem that initiated the *querelle* about the *Roman de
la rose* by Guillaume de Lorris and Jean de Meung, Christine profits
from established masculine authority. She casts herself as narrator in
the role of Cupid's secretary and thus attains the position of courtly
cleric at his court:

> Savoir faisons en generalité
> Qu'a nostre Court sont venues complaintes
> Par devant nous et moult piteuses plaintes
> De par toutes dames et damoiselles
>
> Nostre secours requerans humblement,
> Ou, se ce non, du tout desheritées
> De leur honneur seront et ahontées.[6]
>
> [To one and all about we make it known
> That here, before our court, complaints have come
> To us, and plaints so very piteous,
> From women, both the young and older ones,
>
> Most humbly asking us to intervene.
> Failing our help, they'll be completely shorn
> Of every dignity, and shamed.][7]

The first person plural "nous" includes Christine in the circle of
clerics at Cupid's court and elevates her status to that of her male
counterparts. From this position, she can exploit the authority
attached to it.[8]

In the *Livre de la mutacion de Fortune*,[9] an almost epic
autobiographical poem, Christine adopts the male gender. She
metamorphoses into a man required to navigate a ship in distress,
since no one else is there to help her:

> Or fus je vrays homs, n'est pas fable,
> De nefs mener entremettable,
> Fortune ce mestier m'apprist

Et ainsi de ce fait me prist.
Com vous ouëz, encor suis homme
Et ay esté ja bien la somme
De plus de XIII. ans tous entiers....[10]

[...Now see,
Like a real man; I have to be.
Fortune kindly taught me the way
To do manly deeds, to this day.
As you can tell, men are my peers
As they have been for thirteen years.][11]

Christine's struggle to find her own literary authority within a male profession is echoed in this sexual transformation. Christine's recognition that her gender represents an enormous obstacle in her career surfaces in her attempt to "man" an almost-capsized ship. As a writer and a poet, Christine cannot escape from assuming an androgynous identity.

In the *Livre de la cité des dames*,[12] Christine laments that she had not been born a man. Lynne Huffer sees in this expression of despair Christine's struggle between body and spirit: "[she] is at the same time defending and denying her femininity by rejecting her body. In fact, Christine defends 'woman' by presenting herself as an essentially masculine being."[13] Huffer concludes: "The feminine voice is in constant tension with its phallic inscription in a masculine order precisely because the feminine voice cannot speak itself."[14]

Joan of Arc, dressed as a soldier, fighting in the French army, likewise adopts a masculine role. Yet Joan does not arbitrarily choose a man's attire but rather selects one that represents "positive virtue, maleness and knighthood," as described by Marina Warner.[15] A central accusation brought against Joan was her transvestism and her repeated refusal to wear woman's clothes. As Valerie Hotchkiss expresses it, it was not Joan but "female individuality" that was on trial.[16] The pen and the sword are allied instruments as Christine shares her fate with her heroine in the *Ditié de Jehanne d'Arc*. Both women remain exceptional for their time: Christine as a female writer and defender of her sex with her pen and Joan as a female fighter and defender of her sex and her country with her sword. Maureen Quilligan emphasizes the importance of the connection between the two women. Christine, as a well-known writer and poet at court, might have used Joan of Arc's extraordinary achievements to "prepare them [the court] to accept a woman's authority."[17]

The *Ditié* marks a progression in Christine de Pizan's endeavor to establish her own literary authority as a feminine one. This stands in contrast to certain of her previous works that remain ambiguous with regard to the identity of the autobiographical subject of enunciation. In the *Ditié*, the "I, Christine" signature that is emblematic of her style, undergoes a transformation: it steps out of its androgynous framework by becoming a female subject of enunciation.[18] The *Ditié* can thus be seen as a final effort by Christine to confirm her own narrative "I" as a female subject and, at the same time, to present her hero as a female hero, not yet contaminated by masculinist mythification.

Although Julia Walker and Anne Lutkus suggest that the *Ditié* should be considered first a political text praising Joan's deeds over those of the dauphin and thus implying a strong criticism of Charles's decisions,[19] Joan's femaleness and virginity play a fundamental part in the poem. As Alan Barr points out, Joan serves as a welcoming *persona* for Christine's desire to locate dignity and respect for women. According to Barr, in the context of the *querelle des femmes*, Joan provides confirmation for that which Christine fought in a large number of her previous works. Barr explains:

> But Joan's timeliness was more than political. If ... Christine de Pisan is effectively at the head of the *querelle*, the advent of La Pucelle was almost inconceivably opportune—as symbol as well as substantial embodiment of all she had been advocating: female virtue, intelligence, strength, and governance.[20]

In an analysis of the transformation of the linguistic reciprocity of the *je* (Christine)-*tu* (Joan), I will show, using Benveniste's terms, the evolution of both the subject of enunciation (Christine) and the addressee (Joan), who is at the same time a subject of the utterance.[21] The Benvenistian notion of the relation between utterer and narrator suggests:

> ... celui qui parle se réfère toujours par le même "je" à lui–même qui parle.... Ainsi, en toute langue et à tout moment, celui qui parle s'approprie "je", ce "je" qui, dans l'inventaire des formes de la langue, n'est qu'une donnée pareille à une autre, mais qui, mis en action dans le discours, y introduit la présence de la personne sans laquelle il n'est pas de langage possible.[22]

> [The one who speaks always refers to himself/herself with the same "I" of the speaker .... Therefore, in every language and at every moment, the person who speaks appropriates the "I" for himself/herself; the "I" that, in the

inventory of linguistic forms, only represents an element similar to others but, in the speech act, introduces the presence of the person without whom language is impossible.][23]

By saying "I," the speaker inscribes his or her own system of reference into the text, within the speaker's own spatiotemporal context. Yet, the "I" of the speaker, by definition, calls upon a "you," the addressee. In stanzas 13–24, 37–47, and 55, Christine openly addresses Charles VII, God, Joan, the soldiers of the French army, the English, the rebels, and the city of Paris and, each time, creates a dialogue situation. The "you," like the "I," is anchored in its own system of reference and is unique, as Benveniste explains: " 'Je' est une personne unique; 'tu' est une personne unique, mais 'il' représente n'importe quel sujet compatible avec ses genre et nombre et peut, répété dans le même énoncé, renvoyer à des sujets différents"[24] ("I" is a unique person; "you" is a unique person, but "he" represents any subject that is compatible with its gender and number and can refer to different subjects when repeated in the same utterance).[25]

According to the Benvenistian paradigm, the utterance opening the poem —"Je, Christine, qui ay plouré/XI ans en abbaye close" (1–2) (I, Christine, who have wept for eleven years in a walled abbey)—explicates the system of reference of the narrator. The autobiographic "I" has just broken out of a time of sadness and solitude, presumably the time Christine spent with her daughter in the abbey of Poissy. We can speculate that she fled there in order to escape the events of the Hundred Years War, since the moment when Christine leaves for Poissy coincides with the beginning of Charles VI's mental illness, which considerably weakened the power of the French crown.

Thanks to the deeds of La Pucelle, the narrator can laugh again and rise above the melancholy expressed at the beginning of the poem: "Par la traïson là enclose,/Ore à prime me prens à rire"(7–8) (I who have lived enclosed there on account of the treachery, now, for the first time, begin to laugh).[26] Leaving the walls of the abbey behind is a kind of renaissance for the narrator, a rebirth that extends from her to the whole nation: "L'an mil CCCCXXIX/Reprint à luire li soleil" (17–18) (In 1429 the sun began to shine again). Christine, in her position as narrator, assumes the role of a speaker for the collective community. In 1429, the sun began to shine not just for her but for everybody, a statement underlined by the use of the first person plural in line 41: "Or faisons feste à nostre roy!" (Now let us greet our king!). The vocative places Christine within the group of loyalists to the French crown.

Yet whoever Christine glorifies, we have to keep in mind that the ultimate force behind Joan of Arc's heroism is God. As Lutkus and Walker write: "Joan [herself] cites God not Charles as the power to whom she is immediately answerable" in the letter she sent to the count of Armagnac on August 22.[27] It is the divine power that wants France saved by a "jeune pucelle." The cause-effect chain between the divine will and a miracle, an integral part of common knowledge in the late Middle Ages, appears as likely:

> Par tel miracle voirement
> Que, se la chose n'yert notoire
> Et evident quoy et comment,
> Il n'est homs qui le peüst croire?
> Chose est bien digne de memoire
> Que Dieu, par une vierge tendre,
> Ait adès voulu (chose est voire!)
> Sur France si grant grace estendre. (81–88)

[... as the result, indeed, of such a miracle that, if the matter were not so well known and crystal-clear in every aspect, nobody would ever believe it? It is a fact well worth remembering that God should nevertheless have wished (and this is the truth!) to bestow such great blessings on France, through a young virgin.]

Christine de Pizan thus employs a laudatory style when she presents La Pucelle as a daughter of God, sent by Him. She constantly underlines and emphasizes the father–daughter relationship between them; the contemporary reader can infer that Joan personifies a rational miracle due to her rapport with divinity.[28] Her relationship to God helps in turn to confirm her credibility as a miracle.

To enhance her credibility, an endeavor crucial to presenting her hero as a woman, Christine situates Joan's achievements in a historical, biblical, and mythological context. Joan's repeated interrogation by the clerics, which historically refers to the exiled French Parlement in Poitiers, where Joan of Arc was interrogated in March–April of 1429, was a well-known fact:

> Et bien esté examinée
> A, ains que l'on l'ait voulu croire,
> Devant clers et sages menée
> Pour ensercher se chose voire
> Disoit, ainçois qu'il fust notoire

Que Dieu l'eust vers le roy tramise. (233–38)

[… and well examined, before people were prepared to believe her; before
it became common knowledge that God had sent her to the King, she
was brought before clerks and wise men so that they could find out if
she was telling the truth.]

The examination by the authorities justifies the acceptance of Joan
as a miracle, as does the mention of Joan accompanying the King:

[Pou plus ou pou mains,]
Par là fu V jours à sejour,

Avecques lui la Pucellette.
En retournant par son païs,
Cité ne chastel ne villete
Ne remaint. Amez ou haÿs
Qu'il soit, ou soient esbaïs
Ou asseurez, les habitans
Se rendent. Pou sont envahis,
Tant sont sa puissance doubtans! (391–400)

[... and he [Charles] stayed there for approximately five days, with the
little Maid. As he returns through his country, neither city nor castle nor
small town can hold out against them. Whether he be loved or hated,
whether they be dismayed or reassured, the inhabitants surrender. Few
are attacked, so fearful are they of his power.]

The voyage of Joan and the king through the French countryside
after the crowning ceremony was an equally well-known fact.

After confirming the historical veracity of Joan's deeds, Christine
places Joan of Arc in a biblical context and thus constructs a system
of belief to support Joan's credibility as a divine miracle:

Hester, Judith et Delbora,
Qui furent dames de grant pris,
Par lesqueles Dieu restora
Son pueple, qui fort estoit pris,
Et d'autres plusers ay apris
Qui furent preuses, n'y ot celle,
Mains miracles en a pourpris.
Plus a fait par ceste Pucelle. (217–24)

[I have heard of Esther, Judith, and Deborah, who were women of great
worth, through whom God delivered His people from oppression, and I
have heard of many other worthy women as well, champions every one,
through them He performed many miracles, but He has accomplished
more through this Maid.]

Joan rises in her courage above the three legendary women who saved their peoples from slavery and, with them, above all other biblical figures.[29] She manifests more strength than the great heroes of antiquity: "Et de noz gens preux et abiles/Elle est principal chevetaine./Tel force n'ot Hector n'Achilles!/Mais tout ce fait Dieu, qui la menne" (285–88) (And she is the supreme captain of our brave and able men. Neither Hector nor Achilles had such strength! This is God's doing: it is He who leads her). The most powerful source of Joan's miraculous persona, however, is her affiliation with the principal actor, God.

Christine's vivid interest in the situation of women and her constant demands on men to change their attitude toward women (as in her *Dit de la rose*),[30] leads her to confirm Joan as a virtuous woman. Her sexual status is openly evoked: "Considerée ta personne,/ Qui es une jeune pucelle" (185–86) (When we take your person into account, you who are a young maiden...). In a context in which virginity is the female virtue par excellence, Christine etches Joan's complete credibility by emphasizing her status as Pucelle.[31]

Three lines farther, however, she invokes a different metaphor: "... et celle/Qui donne à France la mamelle/De paix et doulce norriture,/Et ruer jus la gent rebelle,/Véez bien chose oultre nature!" (188–92) (...who casts the rebels down and feeds France with the sweet, nourishing milk of peace, here indeed is something quite extraordinary!). La Pucelle thus equally symbolizes a mother figure for her country. A virgin, who is at the same time a mother, personifies the Virgin Mary. This evocation of the image of the Madonna, as incarnation of feminine purity on the one hand and of the perfect maternal figure on the other, bestows on Joan the attribute of a miraculous personality.

Yet Joan as virgin and as mother is also represented as a "simple bergiere"(198)(a simple shepherdess) and therefore as a member of the *paysannerie*. In moving from the celestial character of La Pucelle to her status as a woman, and then in emphasizing her low social standing, Christine establishes Joan's affinity to every person, and in particular to every woman.

Christine can now praise Joan as a divine miracle, while at the same time casting her in a terrestrial and human context, in her function as a female hero:

Hee! quel honneur au femenin

Sexe! Que Dieu l'ayme il appert,
Quant tout ce grant pueple chenin,
Par qui tout le regne ert desert,
Par femme est sours et recouvert,
Ce que CV^m hommes [fait] n'eussent,
Et les traictres mis à desert!
A peine devant ne le creussent. (265–72)

[Oh! What honor for the female sex! It is perfectly obvious that God has special regard for it when all these wretched people who destroyed the whole kingdom— now recovered and made safe by a woman, something that five thousand *men* could not have done—and the traitors [have been] exterminated. Before the event, they would scarcely have believed this possible.]

The joyous interjection "Hee!" indicates that readers should focus their attention on the gendered status of the addressee who is the subject of the utterance.

This outcry expresses a sign of liberation from the androgynous armor she wore in such other works as the *Livre de la mutacion de Fortune* and the *Livre de la cité des dames*, where she even finds it necessary to construct a fortress for all virtuous women, in order to protect them from masculine constraints. The renunciation of womanhood in her profession as a writer, as seen in the autobiographical *Mutacion*, and the burden of femininity described in the *Cité des dames*, are thrown aside with the freeing spirit of "Hee! quel honneur au femenin/Sexe!" (265–66) Christine can at last write as a woman and find honor in that status. The evolution of the subject of enunciation advances toward its affirmation as a female "I."

Thanks to the heroic deeds inscribed in history by Joan of Arc, Christine can extend the praise from Joan to all women. The honor for the female sex is thus canonized, becomes part of things "digne de memoire" (54) (worthy of being remembered) which will be included "en mainte cronique et hystoire!" (56) (in many a chronicle and history).

The self-congratulatory verse ending the homage to Joan of Arc, "Explicit ung tresbel Ditié fait par Christine" (489) (Explicit a very beautiful poem composed by Christine), summarizes the triumph of the narrator and the author. The repetition of the date and the year in which the poem was composed underlines again the enunciative system of reference. By establishing an autobiographic link between enunciator and author, the androgynous "I" is metamorphosed into a female subject of enunciation whose authority is derived from the analogy established in the work between the enunciator, "Christine," and the addressee, "Joan." Christine's "I, woman" is revalorized by the narration itself.

Yet the relationship is reciprocal. Not only does Joan bestow authority and dignity on Christine and on women but Christine de Pizan, as the first to record Joan of Arc's heroism, advances and supports the heroine's credibility as a miracle and as a woman. In a larger historical context, Christine marks, with the *Ditié*, the beginning of a long tradition of mythifying Joan of Arc's legendary life, a myth that, for Christine, becomes an emblem of female heroism.

NOTES

1. The three manuscripts of the *Ditié de Jehanne d'Arc* are located in Bern in the Bibliotheca Bonarsiana 205, ff. 62r–68r; in Carpentras, Bibliothèque Inguimbertine 390, ff. 81r–90v; and in Grenoble, Bibliothèque Municipale U. 909. Rés., ff. 98r–102r. The first reedition of the poem dates to 1838; eight editions followed. See Edith Yenal's *Christine de Pizan: A Bibliography* [Metuchen, 1989]. The most recent edition of the poem, published by Angus J. Kennedy and Kenneth Varty (Oxford, 1977), is based on all three manuscripts mentioned above and offers a reliable reproduction of the original poem as well as a solid translation in English. All quotes and their translation refer to this edition unless otherwise stated.

2. Some of Christine's earlier works expressing her concern with these matters are: *Epistre au Dieu d'Amours* (1399), *Dit de la rose* (1401), *Livre de la mutacion de Fortune* (1403), *Livre des trois vertus* (1404/05), *Livre de la cité des dames* (1405).

3. Kevin Brownlee, "Discourses of the Self: Christine de Pizan and the Rose," *Romanic Review* 1 (1988), 199–221.

4. Jacqueline Cerquiglini fittingly entitled her article on that very problem "L'Étrangère," using the term to express Christine's position in relation to the clerics. (*Revue des langues romanes* 2 [1988], 239–51).

5. Maurice Roy, *Oeuvres poétiques*, 3 vols. (Paris, 1886, 1891, 1896), vol. 2, pp. 1–27.

6. Ibid., vol. 2, pp. 1–2, lines 8–16.

7. Thelma S. Fenster and Mary Carpenter Erler, eds. and trans., *Poems of Cupid, God of Love* (New York, 1990), p. 35.

8. For a more detailed study of Christine's effort to attain a position of authority within a male-centered literary system, see Brownlee.

9. Christine de Pizan, *Le livre de la mutacion de Fortune*, 4 vols., ed. Suzanne Solente (Paris, 1959–66).

10. Christine de Pizan, *Mutacion* vol. 1, lines 1391–97.

11. Charity Cannon Willard, *The Writings of Christine de Pizan* (New York, 1994), p. 127.

12. Christine de Pizan, *The Livre de la cité des dames of Christine de Pisan: A Critical Edition*, 2 vols., ed. Maureen Cheney Curnow. Diss., Vanderbilt University, 1975.

13. Lynne Huffer, "Christine de Pisan: Speaking Like a Woman/ Speaking Like a Man," in *New Images of Medieval Women: Essays Towards a Cultural Anthropology*, ed. Edelgard DuBruck (New York, 1989), p. 62.

14. Ibid., p. 70.

15. Marina Warner, *Joan of Arc: The Image of Female Heroism* (New York, 1981), p. 159.

16. Valerie R. Hotchkiss, "Transvestism on Trial: The Case of Joan of Arc." Paper presented to the Symposium on Joan of Arc at the 30th International Congress on Medieval Studies, Western Michigan University, Kalamazoo, 1995.

17. Maureen Quilligan, *The Allegory of Female Authority: Christine de Pizan's Cité des dames* (Ithaca, 1991), p. 280.

18. As Quilligan points out, the self–naming is a practice common in the chronicles. However, the self-naming of the chroniclers is confined to the prologue, whereas Christine repeats the first-person pronoun as well as her name at the end of the *Ditié*. For a detailed study of the matter, see Quilligan, pp. 13–18.

19. See Anne Lutkus and Julia Walker's essay in this volume.

20. Alan Barr, "Christine de Pisan's *Ditié de Jehanne d'Arc*: A Feminist Exemplum for the *Querelle des femmes*," *Fifteenth Century Studies* 14 (1988), 1–12.

21. In "Structures of Authority in Christine de Pizan's *Ditié de Jehanne d'Arc*," in *Discourses of Authority in Medieval and Renaissance Literature*, ed. Kevin Brownlee and Walter Stephens (Hanover, 1989), pp. 131–50, Brownlee looks at Christine's authority as speaking subject, Joan's authority as historical actant, and the relation between the two. I shall conduct a similar analysis by focusing on the scene of enunciation.

22. Emile Benveniste, *Problèmes de linguistique générale*, 2 vols. (Paris, 1966, 1974), vol. 2, pp. 67–68 (La communication). Benveniste points out the specificity of the system of reference: "Or cet acte de discours qui énonce 'je' apparaîtra chaque fois qu' il est reproduit, comme le même acte pour celui qui l' entend, mais pour celui qui l' énonce, c' est chaque fois un acte nouveau" (However, the speech act that utters 'I' appears each time that it is pronounced as the same act for the one who hears it, but for the utterer it is each time a new act). My translation.

23. My translation.

24. Benveniste, 2:202 (*L' homme dans la langue*).

25. This is my translation of Benveniste's quotation.

26. According to her own dating, Christine de Pizan composed the poem only days after the crowning of the dauphin in Reims. Lutkus and Walker's essay in this volume questions the historical veracity of Christine's date of composition by arguing that Christine uses a "probably fictive date to address a factual conflict, perhaps in the hope of affecting the outcome of that conflict or of reinterpreting the significance of that outcome."

27. Lutkus and Walker.

28. Deborah Fraioli stresses Christine's belief that Joan of Arc was France's savior sent by God: "In the *Ditié* the predominant theme of joy and thanksgiving of God derives from Christine's conviction that Joan of Arc is God's divine agent, sent to restore the French monarchy. The Maid is proof that the French are God's elect" ("The Literary Image of Joan of Arc," *Speculum* 56 [1981], 811-830), 826.

29. Esther, Judith and Deborah are part of the *Neuf Preuses*, well-known at the end of the Middle Ages (Warner, p. 205). Once again, Christine relies on common knowledge in her attempt to strengthen her heroine's credibility.

30. Roy, vol. 2, pp. 29–48.

31. Although "pucelle" does not always refer to a young virgin, this is its most common meaning, indicated in A. Tobler and E. Lommatzsch, *Altfranzösisches Wörterbuch*, 11 vols. (Wiesbaden, 1955–93).

PR PAS PC: CHRISTINE DE PIZAN'S PRO-JOAN PROPAGANDA

Anne D. Lutkus and Julia M. Walker

To accept as factual the date of "the last day of July 1429" in the last stanza of Christine de Pizan's Ditié de Jehanne d'Arc *is both to ignore the problem that the poem describes events that took place only two days earlier and to dismiss the political implications of the poet's argument that Joan's expressed desire to take Paris constitutes what is best for France. This essay argues that the poem is political propaganda supporting Joan of Arc rather than Charles VII on the issue of Paris.*

C ritics have spoken of Christine de Pizan's *Ditié de Jehanne d'Arc* as everything from a hymn of thanksgiving to a justification of feminism;[1] we, however, read it as political propaganda presented as poetic prophetic history. In the last stanza of the *Ditié,* the author dates the poem "the last day of July" 1429. The literal acceptance of this date[2] has blinded scholars to the possibilities of viewing the poem as active political propaganda. We question the date as a way of interrogating Christine de Pizan's perception of the relations between Joan and Charles following the coronation at Reims. The historical narrative in the poem mentions the lifting of the siege of Orleans in May, the coronation on July 17, the progress of Joan and Charles toward Paris on July 23, and their arrival at the outskirts of Paris on July 29, only two days before the poem is dated. In their edition of the text, Kennedy and Varty try to explain the apparent speed of composition by suggesting that Christine de Pizan must have begun the poem in May.[3] We disagree, placing our argument at the crux of a twofold question: how soon after the coronation at Reims did Joan herself realize that her goal of taking Paris was at odds with Charles's immediate plans and how soon did her dissent become public knowledge? The answer to the latter question could not possibly be "two days," nor are there any firm grounds on which to argue that this political issue was clearly articulated at any time between the crowning of Charles on July 17 and the expiration of the truce with Burgundy in early August. For Christine de Pizan to see the taking of Paris as a point of contention, her poem must have been written more than two days after July 29. Nor is this argument merely a textual exercise in the dating of a piece of literature. Until now, Christine de Pizan's poem has been read as praising Joan, but not as criticizing Charles. If Christine de Pizan finished this poem only in late August or early September, then what we have is a well-informed and strongly argued piece of propaganda for Joan and implicitly against the king of France on the issue of taking Paris.

Other than that date, itself inscribed within the bounds of the poem, not in the line of prose following the verse, we have no documentation supporting any specific date for the poem. The Bern manuscript, one of the two surviving fifteenth-century manuscripts of the poem, is bound, nonchronologically, with documents dated from 1428 into the 1430s. Willard believes that, after writing the last line, "Christine de Pizan laid down her pen forever, insofar as is known."[4] This may well be true, but it does not follow that she laid that pen to rest on the last day of July 1429. We do not know the date of her death; indeed, this poem has always been used as an argument for her having died before things went seriously wrong for Joan in 1430. The other date cited to define Christine de Pizan's death, however, is late 1431, when her daughter-in-law was granted permission to return from Poissy to Paris. Since there is no reason to believe that Christine de Pizan died long before this, she might have been alive through Joan's trial and execution and the poem could have been written at any time in 1429 or 1430. The poet's inclusion of the date has been read as an unproblematically historical gesture; we suggest that by dating the poem earlier than she wrote it, Christine de Pizan is able to employ the construct of prophetic history all the more effectively because her poem shows a knowledge of acts and situations that did not exist on the last day of July 1429. As an exercise in interdisciplinary studies, this reality is highly ironic, since historians are always accusing poets of playing fast and loose with facts and dates. Here, we argue that a poet uses a fictive date to address a factual conflict, perhaps in the hope of affecting the outcome of that conflict or of reinterpreting the significance of that outcome. We examine the boundary of poetry and history, evaluating Christine de Pizan's poem in relation to the historical events of July, August, and September 1429 and arguing for the poet's power to construct herself as the sybilline voice of past, present, and future French history.[5]

When Charles was crowned, he immediately entered into a treaty with the duke of Burgundy. The terms of the treaty were a two-week truce, after which the duke would cede Paris to the new king. While historical scholars debate the attitude of Charles toward the terms of this truce,[6] we are more concerned with what Joan knew and said about the agreement. Régine Pernoud prefaces her chapter "From Reims to Compiègne" with a letter from Joan herself to the duke of Burgundy asking him to "make a good firm peace" and saying "I beg and require you with clasped hands that you make no battle nor war against us."[7] Pernoud, however, distinguishes the "good firm peace" for which Joan pleads from the two-week truce that actually was negotiated. Indeed, Pernoud makes the point that "Joan was carefully excluded"[8] from any knowledge of this treaty, further stating that the route that Charles took after leaving Reims included "sudden changes of direction which were a torment to Joan and her followers, whose one idea was to make straight for Paris."[9] Making the issue of what Joan knew even more complex, Pernoud cites the testimony of Dunois given at the trial of rehabilitation, and she quotes Joan as saying to the Bishop of Reims while on that supposedly tormenting journey from his city:

> . . . please God, my Maker, that I may now withdraw myself, leave off arms, and go and serve my father and my mother by keeping the sheep with my sister and my brothers who will rejoice so greatly to see me again.[10]

Did Joan know about the truce with the duke of Burgundy? Did she construe it as contrary to the goals behind her own plea that he "make no battle nor war against us" or did she welcome it at face value as a chance to stop fighting? Marina Warner cites a letter from Joan to the people of Reims written during these two weeks:

> My dear and good friends, the good and loyal French people of the city of Reims, Joan the Maid sends you her news and begs you and demands that you entertain no doubts about the just quarrel she is pursuing on behalf of the Blood Royal; and I promise you and assure you that I will never abandon you as long as I live and it is true that the King has made a fifteen-day truce with the Duke of Burgundy

by which he should render him the city of Paris peacefully at the end
of the fortnight. However do not be surprised if I do not enter it as
quickly; for a truce made in this way is so little to my liking, that I
do not know if I shall keep it; but if I keep it, it will only be to
safeguard the honour of the king.[11]

The letter suggests that not only was Joan unhappy with the truce
but that her dissatisfaction was shared by the people of Reims and
that these citizens may have expected some action from the Maid.
Perhaps we can cite with certainty only the judgment of Charles T.
Wood: "Human expectations far exceeded Joan's capacity to deliver."[12]
In a letter to Queen Marie and her mother, Yolande, written while
Charles was in Reims for the coronation, David de Brimeu explicitly
acknowledges the varied agendas of Charles and Joan relative to the
possibility of a treaty with Burgundy. De Brimeu, according to
Pernoud,

> expressed the hope that the king will conclude a 'good treaty' before
> he leaves. The same letter alluded to Joan: 'She leaves no doubt that
> she will put Paris in her power [or make Paris obey].' That was to
> indicate clearly the preoccupations of each one. Joan thought only
> about pursuing an offensive that had been shown as profitable, while
> the king thought only about negotiating and, as to the matter of a
> 'good treaty,' was going to conclude a truce ... of two weeks! After a
> day of triumph at Reims, there is once more total misunderstanding.[13]

Colonel de Liocourt, in his *La mission de Jeanne d'Arc*, states that
Joan actually got Charles to agree to march on Paris, and to that end
"the necessary orders were given" to put an army on the road; on the
next day, however, other forces prevailed on Charles to desist.[14]

No matter how we patch together the contradictory
contemporary documents, one conclusion does emerge: in the two
weeks or fifteen days after the crowning of Charles on July 17, there
is no evidence that Joan was actively trying to take Paris on her own.
There are strong grounds for arguing that she was at least hopeful
that Paris would come into Charles's hands as promised. The
importance of the truce in the context of our argument lies in its
foregrounding of Paris as the specifc issue over which Charles and
Joan would ultimately disagree. Christine de Pizan, living in a convent
where the king's sister was also residing, could have been aware of
the nuances of the truce or the perceptions of the truce by citizens,
such as those of Reims. While she never mentions the truce in her
poem, Christine de Pizan does address the varied interests represented

by the factions among the king's supporters. The mere fact of the existence of the truce on the fictive date of the poem makes the problem of actively taking Paris, which the poet constructs as central, an anachronism.

Whatever Joan may have known or hoped, she did not actively try to capture Paris until September 1429. The letter that she sent to the Count of Armagnac on August 22 makes her priorities plain:

> . . . when you hear that I am in Paris, send me a message and I will tell you in whom you should rightly believe, and what I shall know by the counsel of my just and sovereign Lord, the King of all the world, and as far as I can, what you should do. I commend you to God: May He keep you. Written at Compiègne the 22 day of August.[15]

Here, unlike the letter sent to the people of Reims during the two-week truce, Joan cites God, not Charles, as the power to whom she is immediately answerable. As she attacked the St. Denis and St. Honoré gates of Paris on September 7 and 8, all accounts suggest that she was acting "for Jesus' sake" as the Burgundian Bourgeois of Paris records her words, [16] for St. Denis, "because that is the[war] cry of France," as she said at her trial,[17] and even, as she also said at her trial, "at the request of noblemen at arms who wanted to make a skirmish or some valliance in arms against Paris."[18] Of Charles, she says only that she went "against La Charité at the request of my king."[19] Charles T. Wood makes the point that part of Charles's newly constructed identity as king was that he was to be closely identified with God, indeed "as the regent of God, His lieutenant for the Kingdom."[20] This does not mean that Joan conflated the two in all her discourse; her testimony about the attack on Paris suggests that this undertaking was done *for* Charles, though it may have displeased him at that moment.

The conflict over the taking of Paris is the historical and political paradigm to which Christine de Pizan's poem speaks. Its imperatives would have been meaningless hyperbole if actually composed on the last day of July during the two-week truce when even Joan's rhetoric on the subject of Paris was couched in the subjunctive. Written during late August or early September, the verses would have the force of political immediacy. In that case, the poem draws upon the construct of historical prophecy by being dated in July. Christine de Pizan, like the oracles she cites, constructs herself as knowing what must happen in the future. And again, in either case, she sets herself not on the side of the king but with Joan and Joan's plans for Charles and for Paris.

As Maureen Quilligan points out, in the context of Christine de Pizan's existing work, the "Maid was living, incontrovertible proof of what Christine de Pizan had been arguing all along."[21] In her earlier historical writing, Christine de Pizan "appeals to a humanist ideal more usually associated with masculinist enterprises—historical fame and personal glory," to borrow the words of Quilligan.[22] Here, Christine de Pizan moves away from models of personal fame to images of female saviors, as she invokes Esther, Judith, and Deborah, asserting, as Deborah Fraioli suggests, that "the Maid's accomplishments surpass even the accomplishments of these illustrious women."[23] In a return to her own strategies of sibylline speech, she foregrounds the element of prophecy as she writes of the woman warrior.

Scholars have pointed out[24] that Christine de Pizan first mentions Merlin, the Sybil, and Bede (and thus implicitly the Second Charlemagne Prophecy[25]) in stanza 31, the exact midpoint of the poem:

> for more than 500 years ago, Merlin, the Sybil, and Bede foresaw her coming, entered her in their writings as someone who would put an end to France's troubles, made prophecies about her, saying that she would carry the banner in the French wars and describing all that she would achieve.

Not content to invoke the prophecies of others, Christine de Pizan articulates her own by constructing Joan as the generative force by which these things would be accomplished. In stanzas 42 and 43, she speaks of Joan leading Charles to the Holy Land, where they will both gain glory. As Virgil creates a mythic past for his historical hero, Augustus Caesar, Christine de Pizan creates a mythic future for her hero, Joan of Arc. The voices of Bede, Merlin, and the Sybil speak from the past as the voice of "Je, Christine" speaks of the future. And what of the present? Charles should let, must let, Joan take Paris. "For [the king] will enter Paris, no matter who may grumble about it!—the Maid has given her word that he will," says the voice of "Je, Christine" in stanza 54.

The authority Christine de Pizan invokes at the poem's personal opening is her own—her own and God's. Christine de Pizan identifies herself without the humility topos so common in her other works, identifies the life she has led for the past eleven years, and reminds her readers that Charles VII is the rightful king of France, all in the first stanza of the poem. Beginning "Je Christine," as one would begin a will or a legal testament, Christine de Pizan invokes the authority of no muse or patron saint; she claims her own authority to speak as coming directly from God. Even here, she is a claimant rather than a supplicant, asking God for neither permission nor inspiration but simply for a good memory, speaking of rather than to the Deity:

> But now I wish to relate how God, to whom I pray for guidance lest I omit anything, accomplished all this through His grace. May it be told everywhere, for it is worthy of being remembered, and may it be written down—no matter whom it may displease—in many a chronicle and history-book! (stanza 7)

The restoration of Charles "the rejected child of the rightful King of France" (stanza 5) is what has been accomplished through God's grace; the matter of the poem, which will serve as a model for future chronicles and histories, is as the author describes it in its closing line: "a very beautiful poem composed by Christine."

Before that self-consciously literary line, however, comes the historical device of the date: the last day of July 1429. Christine de Pizan blurs the boundary here, slipping between the historical and the literary in an effort to control the first paradigm within the second. Having inscribed her identity and generative poetic authority at the beginning and end of the poem, she devotes the body of the work to Joan—Joan's effect on Charles, on the French loyal to Charles, on the English, on the French allied with the English, and (most significantly) Joan's effect on the reader. In this version of events, Joan does not derive her authority from having put Charles on the throne; Charles is empowered through Joan. Similarly, Joan herself is empowered by her historian—Je, Christine—just as Aeneas is empowered by the historical voice of the Sybil, who speaks of the Trojan past, the Roman future, and the present-tense warfare.

We can obtain a clearer sense of Christine de Pizan's priorities by calculating the number and types of address within the stanzas of the poem. In eighteen stanzas, the poet emphasizes her own voice by the emphatic use of the first person. In addition to these stanzas, there are twenty-four more in which the je is implicit in the imperative constructions for and questions to those who must heed her voice.[26]

When not employing these most personal strategies, the poet joins herself to the people of France, speaking in the first person plural in seven stanzas. The stanzas of the poem that are unmarked by the constructed personal voice of the poet, although they are framed by such constructions, significantly include both the references to the Second Charlemagne Prophecy and to the historical events of Charles's crowning. These stanzas are set apart by Christine de Pizan as she attempts to differentiate between types of history within her poem.

We are led to this recognition of narrative manipulation by the shifting objects of address within the *Ditié*. The ultimate audience for this poem is the people of France, while the immediate subject is the relationship between Joan and Charles, with the former being figured as the most important. Charles is directly addressed by the voice of the poet in only six stanzas, only once by name; Joan is directly addressed even less frequently: in only four stanzas, also only once by name. On the other hand, the poet never speaks *of* Joan by name, only to her (in stanza 22), while Charles is spoken of by name in four stanzas. By style or title, however, the poet signals her primary subject as she speaks *of* the king in fourteen stanzas and *of* the Maid in twenty-seven.[27] That this is a poem about Joan the Maid, not Charles the king—indeed, about constructing Joan the Maid as both immediately and ultimately more important to France than Charles the king—is borne out by a reading of the passages of prophetic and actual history. Initially and ultimately, Charles is the primary historic figure. But in the historical moment of August or September 1429, the historical moment created within the imaginative boundaries of Christine de Pizan's poem, Joan is the key figure for the fate of France.

Christine de Pizan constructs four paradigms of historical narrative: factual present, factual past, prophetic subjunctive, and prophetic declarative. The factual present is framed by the life of the poet as set forth in the opening stanza of the poem. In the lifetime of "Je, Christine," Charles "the king's son" has "fled in haste from Paris" eleven years before, but now "exactly on the 17th day of July 1429 Charles was, without any doubt, safely crowned at Reims" (stanza 49) and "returns through his country" (stanza 50). Separating these two events, we find the narrative of Joan's early battles in stanzas 33–36: "A little girl of sixteen...drives her enemies out of France, recapturing castles and towns." Interestingly, only Joan's actions are presented in the present tense, even though the coronation at Reims came after the lifting of the siege of Orleans. The agency for present-tense history, then, is Joan.

The factual past is figured first as historical narratives that exist independently of the circumstances of fifteenth-century France. The histories of Moses, Joshua, Gideon, Esther, Judith, Deborah, Achilles, and Hector are mentioned in relation to Joan, but the relationship is not one of causation. The biblical figures may be seen as types of the Maid, but the poet does not claim that they foretold or caused her coming. But this catalogue sets up the paradigm within which the generation of the Second Charlemagne Prophecy can be constructed as the factual rather than the fictive past. Linking the biblical references to the mythic by a reference to divine inspiration in stanzas 29 and 30, Christine de Pizan canonizes the fictive by eliding it with the biblical through the common comparison of Joan herself. Joan is like these historical figures; these figures were divinely inspired; Joan is divinely inspired; Joan is also the fulfillment of historical prophecies; those prophecies are therefore history. As the poet presents it, biblical history and mythic Second Charlemagne Prophecy constitute a seamless whole. The prophecies of Merlin, the Sibyl, and Bede, foregrounded in stanza 31, are "found in history" ("trouvé en historie," l. 239) and are the words of those writers who "made prophecies about her, saying that she would carry the banner in the French wars and describing all that she would achieve" (stanza 31).[28] The past and the present meet in Joan. All that seems to be in question is the future.

Having so carefully erected the construct of prophecy as the key to history, Christine de Pizan is now in a powerful position to locate her words within the protocols of myth, fact, and gender suggested by her ordering of Merlin, the Sibyl, and Bede. Between the mythic Merlin and the factual Bede, she places the feminine Sibyl—a style, not a name, but a style always given to a woman. Within this poem, Christine de Pizan usurps the style of Sibyl to produce two types of prophecy: subjunctive and declarative. The poet narrator speaks to Charles in the former, weaker mode of discourse. In stanza 13, she begins her apostrophe to Charles; in stanza 16, she states that "there will be a king of France called Charles, son of Charles, who will be supreme ruler over all kings," but in stanza 17 she concludes that she can only hope that Charles VII is this "supreme ruler": "I pray to God that you may be the person I have described." By phrasing this identification so tentatively in the subjunctive, Christine de Pizan usurps the power of unconditional historical prophecy for herself; she grants that power unequivocally only to Joan, not to Charles. Charles *may* or *should* be the fulfillment of a prophecy, but Joan *is:* "The beauty of her life *proves* that she has been blessed with God's grace…whatever she does, she always has her eyes fixed on God.…It *is* my belief that no miracle was ever more evident"(stanzas 32–38, emphasis ours).

In stanzas 41–43, the poet sets up a series of statements about Joan's future accomplishments. Joan "will cast down the English for good…will restore harmony in Christendom and the church…will destroy the unbelievers…will destroy the Saracens…will lead Charles" to the Holy Land, which he will conquer. Only here does Charles figure in declarative future history, and again the agency of his participation is Joan. The French construction *par elle* (translated by Kennedy and Varty as the active "she will") places Joan's actions above even her person, although her agency is therefore figured as divinely inspired: these deeds ordained by God for France and for Charles will be accomplished *by* and *through* Joan. These stanzas stress the relation between God's will and Joan's actions; Charles's actions are subordinated within this construction. As this prophetic section of the poem draws to a close, Charles disappears completely.

> Therefore, in preference to all the brave men of times past, this woman must wear the crown, for her deeds show clearly enough already that God bestows more courage upon her than upon all those men about whom people speak. And she has not yet accomplished her whole mission! I believe that God gives her to us here below so that peace may be brought about through her deeds.

> And yet destroying the English race is not her main concern for her aspirations lie more elsewhere, on something higher, that is, ensuring the survival of the Faith. As for the English, whether it be a matter for joy or sorrow, they are done for. In days to come scorn will be heaped upon them. They have been cast down! (stanzas 44–45)

Surely those last lines, if nothing else in the poem, might have been cherished by the chroniclers of the 1450s, had they not been so firmly enmeshed in a narrative that constructs Joan, not Charles, as both a national and virtually apocalyptic leader. Christine de Pizan's strategy of differentiating historical discourse allows her to privilege Joan over Charles by both the formation and the content of her poetry. Without closing the door on the possibility that Charles could participate in this triumph and claim his own place in this prophetic history, as she had always hoped he would, Christine de Pizan makes it clear that he has yet to accomplish as much as had the Maid. The rebels to whom the poet speaks in stanzas 46–48 are defined by their failure to recognize the power of the Maid. While the strong language of these stanzas would not be addressed overtly to the king himself, the warning explicit in these lines speaks just as well to Charles and those of his nobles who made the truce that Joan opposed: "Oh, all you blind people, can't you detect God's hand in this?… Has she not led the King with her own hand to his coronation?"

As we look at the last twelve stanzas of the poem, we return to the argument with which we opened the essay. Christine de Pizan marks these last stanzas with a clear reference to Charles in the historical present, his coronation in stanza 49. But immediately before this, in stanza 48, the poet presents Joan as the agent of that coronation. And after the specific reference to Charles in 49, the coronation stanza, the person of the king begins to fade from the poem. In the following eleven stanzas, the king is represented only by pronoun, by implication, by the words "prince"[29] and "lord" and by that phrase so close to the style that Charles was not quite granted earlier in the poem, "supreme ruler" (stanza 60.)[30] Although Charles does not vanish as completely as he does in the earlier prophetic passage, here we find his presence carefully problematized. Indeed, there is no reference to the king at all in stanza 54, where Kennedy and Varty emend the text to read "for [the king] will enter Paris, no matter who may grumble about it!"[31] Joan, on the other hand, is still the Maid in stanzas 50–54 and 59.

The issue is Paris. On the last day of July 1429, Paris was not actively an issue. The terms of the truce with the duke of Burgundy were still in effect, and there would be no reason for Christine de Pizan to write "I do not know if Paris will hold out" (stanza 53). The next statement—"if it decides to see her as an enemy, I fear that she will subject it to a fierce attack, as she had done elsewhere"—is also more reasonably understood if it was written in mid- to late-August or even September. The poet would have known about the truce, as did the concerned people of Reims whom Joan addresses in her letter. This entire passage about the taking of Paris sits oddly in a poem that is simply one of celebration. Why would a simple poem of celebration conclude as does this one? "But I believe that some people will be displeased by its contents for a person whose head is bowed and whose eyes are heavy cannot look at the light" (stanza 61). These people who will be displeased by this version of history—the same people the poet scorns with the stanza 7 statement that she will write "no matter whom it may displease"—could be only those people who did not see the agenda of Joan as the best plan for France. If these displeased people were merely the defeated minority within the new kingdom of Charles VII, there is no reason for them to be thus privileged at both the beginning and the end of this poem. That the displeased people included not just Burgundians but Charles himself is the logical conclusion. Whether she wrote this poem in August or September 1429 or even later, Christine de Pizan uses the power of prophetic history to place herself clearly on the side of Joan the Maid and against the actions, if not the person, of Charles VII. Nor does she mean this political propaganda to be read as an anonymous act, for she signs every stanza of the document that both begins and ends with her own name. Finally, the tone of the poem suggests that there is still a serious matter to be decided. Whether this is literally the taking of Paris or imprisonment or even the trial of Joan, we cannot know. But whatever the issue, it called forth the strongest rhetorical strategies of a writer known for expressing her personal views. Quite self-consciously, Christine de Pizan built her own structures of authority upon the authority of Joan so that she might argue for the goals of the Maid, thus linking her fate to that of Joan in a self-consuming literary artifact. That her poem must now be resurrected into the canon of her work by the use of many of the same documents employed in the so-called rehabilitation of Joan is surely a "tresbel"[32] example of poetic justice.

NOTES

1. Maureen Quilligan. *The Allegory of Female Authority: Christine de Pizan's Cité des dames* (Ithaca, 1991). Quilligan (p. 280) argues that Joan constitutes a justification for Christine de Pizan's work, contending: "It cannot be entirely an accident then that the unique and singular female writer in late medieval France should so overlap the advent of the unique

and singular female warrior; although it is not possible to prove such things, it does make sense to suppose that Christine de Pizan's arguments, so highly visible to all court members, may have helped prepare them to accept a woman's authority. Her constant retelling of the Amazon myth, arguing for their legitimate domain in the martial realm of their own in text after text, could very well have prepared the culture at court to see a woman warrior as something other than a monster." This, we believe, overstates the case. See Deborah Fraioli's essay in this volume.

2. Charity Cannon Willard, *Christine de Pizan: Her Life and Works* (New York, 1984). Willard concludes her chapter on Joan in Christine de Pizan's biography with the sentimental hope that the writer died before things began going wrong for the Maid. Willard says: "One cannot avoid hoping that she did not survive long enough to learn of the capture of her heroine before the walls of Compiègne in May 1430 or her trial and execution in Rouen the following May"(p. 207).

3. Christine de Pizan, *Ditié de Jehanne d'Arc,* ed. and trans. Angus J. Kennedy and Kenneth Varty (Oxford, 1977), p. 2. Unless otherwise stated, all references to the poem are to this translation.

4. Willard, p. 207.

5. That Christine de Pizan spent most of her professional life writing for royal and noble patrons makes her decision to speak on behalf of Joan, "no matter whom it may displease," all the more telling. That she was nearing the end of her own life adds the weight of final speech to the already empowering strategy of prophecy within the poem. An element of negative evidence that supports this dating and reading of the poem is the fact that, even as he sponsored the rehabilitation of Joan's reputation in the 1450s, neither Charles nor any of the participants produced this document, although its references to the Second Charlemagne Prophecy would seemingly have made it a natural choice for public attention. Charles could hardly have been unaware of a poem by a woman who had written of and for his grandfather, father, mother, and uncles and who, moreover, authored the document while living in the convent of his sister, Marie.

6. See Régine Pernoud, *Joan of Arc: By Herself and Her Witnesses,* trans. Edward Hyams (New York, 1982). Pernoud dismisses the political reality of the truce with the following analysis: "This truce condemned the royal army to inaction; and in exchange the Duke made Charles the fantastic promise that he would hand over Paris to the King. In fact he, and Bedford with him, was simply seeking to gain time: Bedford had called for reinforcements from England immediately after the battle of Patay, and early in July three thousand five hundred knights and archers disembarked at Calais....This army left Calais on July 15th for Paris where it arrived on the 25th" (pp. 128–29).

7. Original in the Archives Départementales du Nord, cited in Pernoud, p. 128.

8. Pernoud, p. 128.

9. Pernoud, p. 130. Paris had always been one of Joan's goals, as her letter to the English on March 22 indicates.

10. Cited in Pernoud, p. 131. In *Jeanne D'Arc* (Paris, 1986), which Pernoud co-authored with Marie-Véronique Clin, Joan's words are analyzed as follows: "This tone of regret, so unusual in her, shows her disarmed before what she now has to combat: incomprehensible treachery that she feels is quite close and that, at every step, precedes her." ("Ce ton de regret, si inhabituel chez elle, la révèle désarmée devant ce qu'il lui faut combattre à présent: la trahison, insaisissable, qu'elle sent toute proche et qui, à chaque pas, la précède") p. 116. Pernoud modifies but does not retract her earlier judgment that Joan knew nothing of the treaty with Burgundy. She and Clin state that Joan "would like to go to Paris, and she does not know that in advance Charles VII had engaged himself to renounce it" ("Elle voudrait se porter sur Paris et elle ne sait pas que d'avance Charles VII s'est engagé à y renoncer").

11. From *Les Lettres de Jeanne d'Arc et la prétendue abjuration de St. Ouen*, le comte C. de Maleissye (Paris, 1911), pp. 6–8, cited in Marina Warner *Joan of Arc: The Image of Female Heroism* (New York, 1981), p. 73. So, if Joan did know of the treaty, was she ready to honor it or was she just waiting for it to fall apart before she marched on Paris? In the face of this letter, it is difficult to believe that Joan knew nothing of the truce, but it is equally difficult to draw conclusions about her intentions—either her intentions regarding Paris or the more immediate intentions raised by this letter.

12. Charles T. Wood. *Joan of Arc and Richard III: Sex, Saints, and Government in the Middle Ages* (New York, 1988), p. 143.

13. Pernoud and Clin, p. 115 : "... s'exprimait l'espoir que le roi concluera «a bon traité» avant qu'il parte. La même lettre faisait allusion à Jeanne: Elle ne fait doute qu'ele ne mette Paris en son obéissance. C'était indiquer clairement les préoccupations de chacun. Jeanne ne pensait qu'à poursuivre une offensive qui s'était révélée si féconde, tandis que le roi ne songeait qu'à négocier et, en fait de bon traité, allait conclure une trêve ... de quinze jours! Ainsi, après une journée triomphale vécue à Reims, on se retrouve en plein malentendu."

14. Colonel de Liocourt, *La mission de Jeanne d'Arc* (Paris 1981), vol. 2, p. 197. "Forte du prestige qu'elle [Jeanne] avait alors, elle obtint facilement l'assentiment du roi. Incontinent, la décision fut prise de partir pour Paris le lendemain 18, et les ordres nécessaires furent donnés pour la mise en route de l'armée." While this initial order may have been Christine de Pizan's source of information, she was even more likely to have heard of the other, more lasting order.

15. From *The Trial of Jeanne d'Arc*. W.P. Barrett, ed. and trans. (London, 1931), p. 180, derived from Wood, p. 128.

16. Cited in Pernoud, p. 135.

17. Cited in Pernoud, p. 139.

18. Cited in Pernoud, p. 134.

19. Cited in Pernoud, p. 134.

20. Wood, p. 150.

21. Quilligan, p. 270.

22. Ibid., p. 250.

23. Deborah Fraioli, "The Literary Image of Joan of Arc: Prior Influences," *Speculum* 56 (1981)811–830. Fraioli stresses that the Deborah image was the most important of these for Christine de Pizan, although unlike Jean Gerson she did not consider the image of a woman warrior unseemly. According to Fraioli: "Christine believed that Joan of Arc's appearance was prophesied five hundred years earlier not only by Bede but also by Merlin and the sibyls. Furthermore, her understanding of the ultimate goal of the Maid's mission comes to her through knowledge of a prophecy popular in France from 1382, called the Second Charlemagne Prophecy"(p. 826).

24. See especially Brownlee's structural analysis in "Structures of Authority in Christine de Pizan's *Ditié de Jehanne d'Arc." Discourses of Authority in Medieval and Renaissance Literature* (Hanover, 1989), 131–150. See also Therese Ballet Lynn's "The *Ditie de Jeanne d'Arc*: Its Political, Feminist and Aesthetic Significance" *Fifteenth Century Studies 1* (1978), 149–56. For a comparison between Christine de Pizan's poem and Martin Le Franc's 1440 verse *De dame Jehanne la Pucelle*, see Harry F. Williams, "Joan of Arc, Christine de Pizan, and Martin Le Franc," *Fifteenth Century Studies* 16 (1990), 233–37.

25. For a discussion of the Second Charlemagne Prophecy, see Marjorie Reeves, *The Influence of Prophecy in the Later Middle Ages: A Study in Joachimism* (Oxford, 1969), pp. 320–31. Reeves dryly remarks that such prophecies "seem to be indestructible. . . [as] the Second Charlemagne survived the madness of Charles VI"(p. 341).

Adding to the power of the Second Charlemagne Prophecy with its insistence upon a king named Charles, was the commonplace axiom of the second and third decades of the fifteenth century: France was lost by a woman (Isabeau) and would be restored by a woman (arguably Joan).

26. In some of these stanzas, the parallel constructions carry on the mode of personal address. For example, in the apostrophe to the English, which begins in stanza 39 "And so, you English ... " continuing through 40 ("You thought ...") into 41 ("And know that she will ..."), the "she will" in 42 and 43 extends the mode of address.

27. The count would be twenty-eight if we included the very last line, with its direct reference to the poem itself, the poem named with Joan's name.

28. "Et leur[s] prophecies en firent, / Disans qu'el pourteriot baniere/ Esguerres françoises, et dirent/De son fait toute la maniere" (ll. 245–48).

29. Stanza 55 is addressed to the citizens of Paris, who acknowledged the English Henry as their offical prince and the duke of Burgundy as their practical overlord. While "your prince" almost certainly does refer to Charles, Christine de Pizan could easily have chosen a less problematic phrase if her only concern was to privilege Charles as the person to whom Paris should yield.

30. Although Kennedy and Varty translate both the stanza 16 title and the stanza 55 style as "supreme ruler," the words in stanza 16 are "Qui sur tous rois sera grant maistre" while the phrase in stanza 55 is "vostre chief greigneur."

31. If anything, the French makes Joan the subject of this phrase: "Car ens entrera, qui qu'en groigne!/—La Pucelle lui a promis."

32. After the sixty-first stanza of the poem appears this line: "Explicit ung tresbel Ditié par Christine."

SPEAKING OF ANGELS:
A FIFTEENTH-CENTURY BISHOP
IN DEFENSE OF JOAN OF ARC'S
MYSTICAL VOICES

Jane Marie Pinzino

In the Rehabilitation Trial of 1456, Bishop Elie de Bourdeilles confronts the Condemnation Trial verdicts and narrates a salvation history of the French people with Joan of Arc as God's protagonist. The truth of this trial testimony lies not in its literal factualness about Joan of Arc but in its vitality as a popular myth of French cultural self-definition.

> Interrogata quale signum ipsa dat, per quod sciatur quod ista sint ex parte Dei, et quod ist sint sancte Katherina et Margareta, Respondet: Ego satis dixi vobis quod sunt sancte Katherina et Margareta. Et: Credatis michi, si velitis.[1]
>
> [Asked what sign she gives whereby it might be known that they come from God, and that they are Saint Catherine and Saint Margaret, she replied: "I have told you often enough that they are Saint Catherine and Saint Margaret. Believe me if you will." [2]]
> —Joan of Arc speaking to officials at her condemnation trial, February 27, 1431.

In 1456, twenty-five years after her public execution at the hands of political enemies, Joan of Arc's conviction was reassessed in an ecclesiastical trial known to us as the nullification, or rehabilitation, trial, an official process that both nullified the condemnation of Joan of Arc as a relapsed heretic and attempted to restore the renown of her memory and surviving family.[3] I examine here the latter aspect of this trial and specifically its effort to rehabilitate Joan of Arc's mystical voices, which the condemnation trial had cast into disrepute. Joan had asserted that angels and saints from heaven commissioned her to liberate France from the English, and it was upon their divine directives that she based the authority of her mission. The condemnation trial had pronounced a damning judgment upon the spirits, naming them as demons and Joan as a deceitful fabricator of divine revelations. In response, the rehabilitation trial undertook to honor the spirits and to defend Joan's mystical experience. The two trials reveal the theological and judicial issues encountered by the late-medieval church in handling a laywoman's claims to divine authority. The trials further shared the growing concern of the fifteenth-century ecclesiastical hierarchy about commerce between women and demonic spirits.

Both trials were politically motivated. Historians have long acknowledged the condemnation as pro-English but have largely overlooked and even denied the pro-French underpinnings of the rehabilitation trial. Régine Pernoud has challenged us to consider the documents of this trial, for she has argued in favor of the factual truthfulness of the rehabilitation trial's testimony and against any suggestion that it may have been politically directed. She takes a firm stand against those who see in it "the beginning of the Joan of Arc 'legend,' by which she is supposed to have been artificially aggrandized and prepared for the admiration of the mob."[4] My interpretation acknowledges both Pernoud's sense of the honesty of the testimony as well as its pro-French sympathies. The two are not incompatible, for the type of truth evident in the rehabilitation trial is a cultural rather than a literal one. I endorse the concept of Joan of Arc as a "legend" not in the sense of a contrived fiction but in the sense of a historical individual cast as protagonist in a people's narrative of cultural self-definition. In the rehabilitation trial, Joan of Arc emerges as a key player in a nationalist drama of political triumph of good over evil. The discussion about her mystical voices concerns not only explicit and doctrinal matters of heresy but also implicit matters of French collective identity and cultural unity, defined as a people chosen by God.

The political backdrop for the fifteenth-century events shows that Joan of Arc was a powerful symbol for both sides of the French-

English conflict. The pro-English (Burgundian) party into whose hands Joan fell in 1430, over a year after her role in the vital French victory at Orleans, worked to defame her self-asserted divine calling and executed her at age nineteen in the marketplace of Rouen in 1431. In the years following, however, political power in France permanently reverted to the pro-French (Armagnac) party of Joan's supporters. Promptly after Normandy and the city of Rouen itself had been restored to the French (1449) and the ecclesiastical archives there were retrieved and opened, the proceedings to nullify Joan of Arc's condemnation were undertaken by her supporters. Conducted during the years 1450–56 first at the request of the French king Charles VII, then under the direction of a papal legate, these proceedings were virtually unprecedented in ecclesiastical judicial history. The original condemnation was declared null and void in 1456, and a lengthy dossier of nine chapters was officially compiled to document the proceedings and argue the nullification.

The rehabilitation trial followed a twofold strategy. First, it sought eyewitness testimony favorable to Joan. Second, it asked eight theologians and jurists to investigate the technical procedures and counter the conclusions of the first trial. These eight treatises implement the scholastic method of using original material (the condemnation trial record) to argue against its own conclusions and then to formulate revised conclusions. I explore here the reflections of one particular rehabilitation trial theologian, Elie de Bourdeilles, whose treatise is the first among the eight treatises in chapter 8 of the rehabilitation trial dossier. Of the eight, this Franciscan bishop of Périgueux (1438–68)[5] demonstrates the keenest interest in the question of Joan's mystical voices and provides for the rehabilitation trial a carefully crafted theological endorsement of her mystical experience and its divine authenticity. Bourdeilles later went on to serve as archbishop of Tours and ultimately as a cardinal.

The treatise of Elie de Bourdeilles offers a theological embrace of Joan of Arc as a legitimate focus of devotion as well as a negative judgment upon the condemnation trial for its method of interpreting Joan in the worst light. Bourdeilles's treatise shows that the trial was indeed directed toward the "rehabilitation" of Joan of Arc. While scholarship since Duparc's critical edition in the 1980s has avoided as historically anachronistic the term "rehabilitation trial" in favor of "nullification trial," I suggest that "rehabilitation" may indeed be the best term we have to capture the prevailing spirit of this trial, especially its careful, explicit, and sustained effort to understand Joan of Arc in the best light, not to mention its validation of her political and spiritual leadership.

In 1431, the assessors in Rouen had directed an aggressive line of questioning toward Joan about the self-proclaimed divine origins of her voices. Contrary to Joan's persistent claims, the Rouen judges found that Joan was a liar, a counterfeiter of divine revelations and apparitions, and that her mystical voices proceeded from diabolical spirits.[6] In the rehabilitation trial, officials did not endeavor to question the numerous eyewitnesses to Joan's life about this issue; rather, they confined their questioning to matters of her outward and public behavior. The matter of Joan's private, mystical experience was considered only in the eight Latin treatises written by theologians and jurists, including Bourdeilles, men who had studied copies of the condemnation trial record and the eyewitness accounts but who had not known Joan personally. Bourdeilles cites scriptural precedent for this priestly function:

> Scriptum est, "Si difficile et ambiguum apud te judicium esse perspexeris et judicum intra portas tuas videris verba variari, venies ad sacerdotes levitici generis queresque ab eis, qui judicabunt tibi judicii veritatem," Deuteronom. XVII, 8.[7]
>
> [It is written: "If there is a judicial case among you uncertain and difficult for you to examine, and a case within your gates in which you see diverse arguments, go to the levitical priests and consult with them, and they will pronounce to you the truth of the judicial case" (Deut. 17:8).][8]

The eight treatises that make up chapter 8 can be collectively summarized as theologically and judicially informed defenses of Joan of Arc. In contrast to the anecdotal and vernacular testimony of the eyewitnesses to Joan's life (chapter 5), these treatises offer a scholarly justification for her moral and religious views. They directly confront the condemnation trial and its judgments. In his effort, Bourdeilles examines the conduct of the original trial in a perspective that consciously assumes "the best" about Joan.[9] The bishop of Périgueux thereby adopts an attitude of deliberate forbearance that he demonstrates is authentic to canon law[10] and the Christian ethical tradition, including scripture itself. Bourdeilles frowns upon the hostile attitude toward Joan evident on the part of condemnation trial officials and cites the teaching of Jesus: "Nolite judicare," ("Do not judge [and you will not be judged]," NRSV, Luke 6:37):[11]

… arguitur per ea que notat venerabilis Beda et alii doctores super verbo "Nolite judicare," quia de incertis et dubiis non debemus sententiam deffinitivam dare sive temere diffinire, neque de occultis judicare, ut docet beatus Augustinus de sermone Domini. [12]

[… it is made clear through what the Venerable Bede and other doctors note upon the statement "Do not judge," that concerning uncertain and doubtful things we ought not to give a definitive judgment nor conclude rashly, nor judge secret things, as the blessed Augustine teaches in *On the Word of the Lord*.]

Whereas the condemnation trial officials had, at least ostensibly, concealed their political sympathies in the official record, the rehabilitation trial officials stated theirs openly. Bourdeilles, for example, assumes an explicitly pro-French theological position and describes God's unique plan for the French people. He describes Joan as the girl sent by God for the consolation of the king of the French and the liberation of his kingdom.[13] In imagery that frequently constructs France as a new Israel and Joan of Arc as a new Moses, Bourdeilles defends Joan's divine vocation to overthrow the oppressive rule of the English in France and to deliver the French from their collective suffering. Writing in the aftermath of final French victory, he narrates a salvation history of the French people with Joan of Arc as God's protagonist. The following captures the essence of his effort:

Missa inquam hec puella ad liberationem et consolationem regis et regni, ad quam liberationem et consolationem non concurrunt angeli mali, ut supra deductum est, et liberavit regnum de manibus dictorum Anglicorum ministerialiter Domino misericorditer cooperante, ut pie credi potest. [14]

[This girl, I say, was sent for the liberation and consolation of the king and the kingdom, to which liberation and consolation evil angels do not agree, as elaborated above, and in service of God she liberated the kingdom from the hands of the said English, with God compassionately cooperating, as one can piously believe.]

Bourdeilles structures his defense of Joan in response to the articles of her original condemnation.[15] He devotes over half of his treatise to the first article alone, one in which Joan is judged to be "primo, revelationum et apparitionum divinarum mendosa confictrix"[16] ("first, a deceitful fabricator of divine revelations and apparitions").

Both the condemnation and rehabilitation trials reflect late-medieval fears about laywomen and their mystical devotion to supernatural spirits of power and authority, but whereas the condemnation trial aggressively accused Joan of the worst in this matter, Bourdeilles argues the best.

Bourdeilles begins his argument on behalf of Joan's mystical voices by demonstrating that heavenly spirits—angels and saints—do exist and visit humans. He makes little practical distinction between "angels" and "saints" and often refers to them collectively as "good" or "holy" spirits. His method is traditionally scholastic, arguing both sides of the issue and substantiating his concluding judgment from textual evidence in traditional Christian sources. He refers to numerous biblical, patristic, and medieval authorities to defend the existence of angels, referring particularly to the biblical books of Daniel and the Apocalypse, as well as to the works of Augustine, Gregory the Great, and Pseudo-Dionysius.

Bourdeilles explains the two basic orders of angels: those who stand near God and sing him praises and those who are sent out to serve on his behalf, guiding and administering the world. He cites the book of Daniel in the Old Testament:

> Millia millium ministrabant ei et decies milles centena millia assistebant ei ... Danielis capitulo VII.[17]

> [A thousand thousands served him and ten thousand times one hundred thousand stood attending him... (Dan. 7).]

Kingdoms, cities, and churches all have guardian angels watching over them, as shown in the Apocalypse. On the point that angels are God's warriors, in addition to citing the archangel Michael in the Apocalypse, Bourdeilles refers to the instruction of Gregory the Great in the *Moralia*:

> Angelicos spiritus Dei milites dicimus, quia decertare eos contra potestates ereas non ignoramus, que tamen certamina non labore sed imperio pugnunt, quia quicquid agendo contra immundos apetunt.[18]

> [We say that angelic spirits are soldiers of God; because we know that they contend against higher powers, though they fight battles not with toil but with authority, for whatever they do, they attack the impure.]

Further, according to Bourdeilles, certain angels are ordained to govern individual persons. Two New Testament texts demonstrate this reality:

> Quidam autem personis, ut inquit Jhesus: "Angeli eorum in celis semper vident faciem mei qui in celis est." (Ev. Math. 18.10), et Actorum, cap. XII (15) "Angelus ejus est."[19]

[Moreover, certain [angels are set] over persons, as Jesus said: "In heaven their angels continually see my face … in heaven" (Matt. 18:10), "It is his angel" (Acts 12:15).]

Bourdeilles explains that both the elect and the reprobate have guardian angels; the Antichrist himself has a guardian angel whom he continually disregards and who will pronounce his judgment on the Last Day. Some angels even preside over other angels.

The fact that angels do not overlook or scorn the weak and the humble is evidenced by the experience of the shepherds to whom the heavenly host appeared in a field the night that Christ was born (Luke 2). Angels appear to women no less than to men, as is known from the experience of the slave and outcast Hagar in Genesis 16, as well as the young Mary in Luke 1. In the analysis of Bourdeilles, neither Joan of Arc's simple and humble origins nor her female sex disqualified her from an angelic visitation. Further, Joan's "frail sex," tender age, and rural upbringing are precisely factors in favor of the divine authenticity of her mystical experience. For, as Bourdeilles puts it, how else is one to account for the young girl's brilliant skill in warfare, her ability to prophesy, and her steady vision of justice?[20]

> Cum enim istam sapientiam non habuerit a natura nec ab arte, oportuit, ut videtur, quod habuerit a gratia, et sic estimari potest quod a Deo, presupposito verumtamen ubique quod contra justitiam non certaret neque humana affectione flecteretur, sed solum zelo justitie ducta….[21]

> [Since she did not have this wisdom by nature or by occupation, it is fitting, as it seems, that she had it from grace, and thus it can be considered that it was from God, with the presupposition, nevertheless, that she never acted against justice, nor was she persuaded by human affection, but led only by zeal for justice….]

An angel's custodial care of human fragility has four aims, according to Bourdeilles: to safeguard the individual from sin, to promote and to instruct the individual in morality, to reveal the divine will, and to preserve virginity and chastity.[22] Concerning this last aim, Joan of Arc herself said at the condemnation trial that she had vowed her virginity to God at age thirteen, when the voices first spoke to her.[23] Bourdeilles presents Joan of Arc as a shining example of an angel's custodial care, for she was universally acknowledged as a steadfast virgin, modest even in her daily life among soldiers in camp. Bourdeilles cites here the thought of Nicholas of Lyra, who identified an angel of the Lord as the preserver of Sarah, wife of Abraham, from sexual pollution in the house of Pharaoh by afflicting the monarch with dreadful plagues (Gen. 12).[24] Further, he cites the blessed Cecilia, of whom it is written that she had an angel of the Lord as a lover, "qui nimio zelo custodiebat corpus suum ut virginitas ejus inviolata conservaretur"[25] ("who with tremendous zeal took care of her body so that her virginity was preserved intact"). Jerome taught that angels can always discern virginity, and according to Cyprian virgins themselves are comparable to angels. Virginity itself is the image of angelic holiness and conforms to the perfection of Christ. Bourdeilles insists that Joan of Arc was honored by all who knew her for her perfect chastity.

In one of the earliest sessions of the condemnation trial, Joan of Arc described her first mystical experience as that of receiving a voice from heaven accompanied by a divine light.[26] Later in the trial, and upon being pressed for more details by the assessors, Joan also described the physical and bodily appearances of the saints Michael, Catherine, and Margaret.[27] Bourdeilles acknowledges that a spirit may speak to an individual in one of two ways, either by voice alone or in bodily form. Importantly, a revelation or apparition is witnessed only by the individual(s) for whom God intends it, with the result that others nearby may be unaware of the event. Bourdeilles discusses the intimate and secret nature of a spiritual visitation, arguing that no one except God has the right to judge such hidden things in the experience of another.

> Sed iste revelationes et apparitiones sunt valde occulte … nullus potuit seu debuit de eis judicare, sed Deo simpliciter judicium relinquere, cui reservantur omnia occulta, prima Corinthiorum, IV.[28]

> [But those revelations and apparitions are deeply secret, (and) no one can or ought to judge them, but simply leave judgment to God, to whom is reserved all secret things (1 Cor. 4).]

Concerning the vocal manifestation of a holy spirit without bodily form, Bourdeilles cites the experiences of Samuel in the temple of the Lord in 1 Samuel 3, as well as Elijah the Tishbite on Mt. Horeb in 1 Kings 19 and John in the Apocalypse 1.[29] Because Joan also described in concrete terms the physical and bodily appearances of Michael, Catherine, and Margaret, Bourdeilles argues that angels and saints, while incorporeal, may indeed appear to human beings in a physical body that has been allotted to them by God. This occurs because human beings must acquire knowledge through the bodily senses, as explained by Augustine in *On the Trinity*.[30] Pseudo-Dionysius teaches that if a holy angel were to appear without the veil of physical form, the divine light would shine too brightly for any person to look upon.[31]

Bourdeilles concedes that the apostle Paul has justly warned that the angel of darkness can transform himself into the outward appearance of an angel of light (2 Cor. 11:14). Therefore, any individual who experiences a supernatural apparition must proceed with caution and pray steadfastly to God for the power of discernment of spirits. Scripture promises that one who prays to God wholeheartedly will not be deceived.[32] Bourdeilles points out that on this matter of prayer, as with her virginity, Joan of Arc was known by all to glow with virtue.[33] Nothing in her life, he argues, existed contrary to the experience of authentic divine revelations and apparitions.

Bourdeilles pushes his defense farther, however. He concludes not only that God worked through Joan but also that he used good rather than evil spirits to do so. This is a key point, for Bourdeilles concedes the spiritual problem that at times God employs evil spirits to accomplish his holy purposes. Joan of Arc could have been the spiritual cohort of the devil, whom God may have nevertheless used for a few good purposes. Bourdeilles cites as an example the story of Exodus 12, in which God sent a bad angel to destroy the firstborn of the Egyptians on the night of the first Passover, thereby using an evil agent to impose his divine will and execute justice. Theoretically, Joan's visions could have been communications from God via the agency of demons; some of her revelations would have therefore been divine, though others demonic. Truth and falsehood would have been perilously intermixed in her revelations and prophecies. In Numbers 22, for example, Balaam was a prophet of demons who sought revelations from demons, but nevertheless some truths were revealed to him by God.[34]

> ... quia facta revelatio a Deo et angelis suis nullam falsitatem continet, sed illa que fit a demonibus frequenter habet admixtam falsitatem, quia, secundum quod dicit Johannes VIII, ipse diabolus mendax est, et pater mendacii.[35]

> [... because a revelation given by God and his angels contains no falsity, but that made by demons often has falsity mixed in, since, according to that which John 8 says, the devil himself is a liar, and the father of lying.]

The devil, Bourdeilles explains further, sometimes reveals certain true things to humans in order to deceive them more effectively, for after many truths revealed by him persons may then be drawn into his falsehoods. [36]

In response to this possibility that Joan's mystical companions were demons, Bourdeilles sets forth the outward features of Joan's devotional life as well as the inward features of her mystical experience. First, he argues that the qualities of Joan's character and faith, including her consistent devotional practice—frequent prayer, confession, hearing of mass, and receiving the eucharist—make it improbable that her spirits were demonic. Further, Joan of Arc embarked on her mission not to acquire worldly honors and riches but to serve God, and she never attributed her victories to herself, but to God alone. It is precisely one of the aims of holy spirits to nurture a moral character of devotion, humility, and discipline, such as that of Joan of Arc. Moreover, whenever Joan herself appealed for spiritual assistance for her work, she did not utter incantations or perform magical arts but rather invoked the Trinity, the Lord Jesus Christ, and the blessed Mary ever virgin. [37] She relied solely upon the king of heaven, not on demonic power. [38]

Second, Bourdeilles considers the private, mystical events themselves, which Joan described in some detail in the condemnation trial. He argues that the spiritual images that Joan saw always appeared in light and brightness, a feature not proper to demonic spirits, who as angels of darkness shun light. Bourdeilles cites the bright light accompanying the holy angels who appeared to the shepherds in a field on the night Christ was born (Luke 2:9). [39] Joan also reported that the first visitations had filled her with fear and trembling, but the spirits in their goodness comforted her and granted her consolation. Bourdeilles states that it is a sign of a good spirit to comfort the fears of the witness, just as Mary was comforted by Gabriel in Luke 1 and the shepherds also by the angels in Luke 2. A diabolical angel, in contrast, seeks always to horrify and to increase fear and trembling rather than alleviate them. The devil seeks precisely to create an agitated and suffering human soul.

Thirdly, on this matter of demons, Joan of Arc's voices always gave her excellent advice, sound and healthful for her faith, which included instructions to confess often, conduct herself well, attend church, and pledge her virginity. All that they taught her aided the salvation of her soul, according to Bourdeilles. [40] Such teachings are wholly repugnant to the devil.

Finally, and of overarching importance in this defense of Joan of Arc's mystical voices, was the spiritual merit of her "causa," her mission to free France. This was the chief divine instruction communicated to her by her angels and saints. Bourdeilles states with firm approval that "nusquam tamen legimus ut malis utatur ad liberationem a malis et exhibitionem misericordie" [41] ("nowhere however do we read that [God] uses bad angels for deliverance from evil and for the granting of compassion"). Bourdeilles explains that while God indeed used a bad angel to punish the Egyptians who had enslaved the Israelites, he used a good angel to lead the Israelites out of Egypt. A holy angel was responsible for conducting the Israelites out of Egypt into the wilderness and on into the promised land, going ahead of them in a column of cloud by day and of fire by night (Exod. 13 and 14).[42] The liberation of the afflicted French people, he argues, must have been the work of good spirits because only good spirits perform God's task of liberation. The fact that Joan of Arc was a simple and artless girl serves only to accentuate the truth that the French victory was granted by the strength of God. Bourdeilles cites here a statement of the biblical warrior Judas Maccabeus:

> ... quoniam non in multitudine exercitus victoria belli, sed de celo fortitudo est," primo Machabeorum III.[43]
>
> ["... or victory in war is not in the size of the army but in the strength of heaven" (1 Macc. 3).]

Bourdeilles therefore resolves respectfully concerning Joan of Arc:

> ...pie credi potest ut angeli sancti Dei custodes venerunt in adjutorium et, per ministerium unius puelle virginis, Domino cooperante ... liberaverunt regnum de tantis quibus subjacebat. [44]
>
> [It can be believed piously that holy guardian angels of God came to assist, and through the service of one virgin girl, with the Lord cooperating. . . they freed the kingdom from the great evils to which it was subjected.]

It is of vital importance for interpretation that while on the one hand Bourdeilles castigates the condemnation trial for endeavoring to judge the secret matters of Joan of Arc's mystical experience, the bishop also does so methodologically in the very same treatise. Bourdeilles undertakes to evaluate both her outward behavior and inward spiritual experience. He himself had argued, however, that the latter aspect was best left to the judgment of God, who alone may judge secret matters. The treatise exhibits a self-contradictory tension between its dual motive to defend Joan's public mission and to protect her private, mystical experience.

Like the condemnation trial, Bourdeilles thereby fosters the principle that the ecclesiastical hierarchy is responsible for knowing the ways and means of both good and evil spirits, as well as for judging the merit of an individual laywoman's mystical experience. His method in this treatise points to the profound clerical ambivalence about the spirituality of laywomen in the late-medieval period. This ambivalence would later lead to an abhorrence of this kind of spirituality so great that it would pull the society into the chilling wave of witchcraft trials in the late fifteenth and sixteenth centuries.

In this treatise of 1456, however, Bourdeilles fully defends Joan as a divine emissary and, crucially for my point here, celebrates the success of her mission. The theological weight of his defense of her mystical voices lies significantly in the realization of her political goals. With the perfect vision that historical hindsight grants, he is able to narrate in the rehabilitation trial a realized salvation history of the French people with Joan of Arc in the leading prophetic role, guiding the French people and struggling in the name of God to fulfill his plan for establishing an independent French people. Accrued merits of previous French Christian kings, according to Bourdeilles, earned favor with God in delivering the French people from their misery and restoring their holy king to the throne.[45] Joan of Arc's role was that of God's chosen, pious, and willing instrument for the granting of divine compassion.

> Ideo pie credendum posse estimo ut Deus excelsus et omnipotens, qui percutit et sanat, humiliat et sublevat, neque derelinquit sperantes in se, meritis precipue beati Ludovici ac predictorum sanctorum regum visitare dignatus sit regnum per unam simplicem puellam, interveniente forsan beato archangelo Michaele et sanctis virginibus prenominatis, ut adscribatur tota liberatio non humane sapientie, industrie, vel potentie, sed tantum divine miserationi et clementie, et meritis precipue ipsorum sanctorum regum precedentium.[46]

[Therefore, I consider that it can be piously believed that God the highest and omnipotent, who strikes down and makes whole, who humbles and raises up, did not abandon those hoping in him, and by the merits chiefly of the blessed Louis and of the aforementioned holy kings, he deigned to visit the kingdom through one simple girl, through the intervention as it happened of the blessed archangel Michael and the holy virgins previously mentioned, such that the whole liberation is not ascribed to human wisdom, industry or power, but to divine compassion and clemency, and to the merits chiefly of its preceding holy kings.]

For Bourdeilles, then, Joan of Arc emerges as a holy woman whom the French people may acclaim and honor as their kingdom's link to the kingdom of heaven. The "truth" of this trial testimony is therefore not factually literal but rather culturally vital. Its truth bespeaks the collective and emotional experience of a people's deliverance from oppression.

NOTES

1. P. Paul Doncoeur, ed., *La minute française des interrogatoires de Jeanne la Pucelle* (Melun, 1952), p. 114.

2. W.S. Scott, ed. and trans., *The Trial of Joan of Arc* (London, 1956), p. 79.

3. For a full discussion on the juridical aspects of the Rehabilitation Trial, see Pierre Duparc, ed., *Procès en nullité de la condamnation de Jeanne d'Arc,* 5 vols. (Paris, 1977–88), vol. 5.

4. Régine Pernoud, *Joan of Arc by Herself and Her Witnesses,* trans. Edward Hyams (New York, 1964), p. 270.

5. Arlette Higournet-Nadal, ed., *Histoire du Périgord* (Toulouse, 1983), p. 148.

6. From the censures of the University of Paris, May 31, 1431 (in Doncoeur, p. 255):

> Toy Jhenne, tu as dit que dez l'aage de XIII ans, tu as eu des revelacions et apparicions d'angelz, de sainctes Katherine et saincte Margueritte, et que les as veues des yeulx corporelz bien souvent; et que ilz ont parlé a toy. Quand a ce premier point les clers de l'Université de Paris ont considéré la maniere desdictes revelacions et apparicions des choses revelees, et la qualité de la personne. Toutes choses considerees qui font a considerer, ont dit et declaré: que toutes les choses dessusdictes sont menteries, faintises, choses seductories et pernicieuse; et que toutes telles revelacions sont supersticieuses, procedantes de maulvaix espritz et dyabolicques.

> [You, Joan, you have said that since the age of thirteen years you have had revelations and apparitions from angels, from St. Catherine and St. Margaret, and that you have seen them quite often with bodily eyes; and that they have talked to you. As to this first point, the clerics of the University of Paris have considered the manner of these said revelations and apparitions, of the things revealed, and the quality of the person. All things considered that are to be considered, they have said and declared: that all these said things are

lies, fantasies, seductive and dangerous things; and that all these revelations are superstitious, proceeding from evil and diabolical spirits.]

7. Duparc, 2.40.

8. Unless otherwise noted, all translations are by the author.

9. "Quia igitur revelationes et apparitiones, quas prefata Johanna se habuisse asseruit, vertuntur in dubium, utrum vere fuerint sive ficte, et sacrosancta romana Ecclesia de eis nihil deffiniverit, nec improbaverit. Ipseque nihil erroris manifesti quod sit contra fidem et bonos mores aut Ecclesie auctoritatem continent, patet quod sunt in meliorem partem interpretande, videlicet quod sunt vere, pie tamen et salva determinatione sacrosancte matris Ecclesie." Duparc, 2.59.

10. See Stephanus Kuttner, "Ecclesia de Occultis Non Iudicat," in *Actis Congressus Iuridici Internationalis* (Rome, 1936), vol. 3: 225–46.

11. Duparc, 2.60.

12. Ibid., 2.56.

13. "... de quadam puella quondam, Johanna nomine, que a Rege celorum sempiterno arbitratur illi directa, in suarum miserationum que a seculo sunt immensa multitudine, ad ipsius regis Francorum consolationem et regni liberationem." Ibid., 2.40.

14. Ibid., 2.54.

15. Certain sources identify twelve articles, while the rehabilitation trial identifies twenty:

> Unde illa sententia lata contra ipsam Johannam continet viginti articulos, in quibus reputatur:
> Primo, revelationum et apparitionum divinarum mendosa confictrix. Secundo perniciosa seductrix. Tertio presumptuosa. Quarto leviter credens. Quinto superstitiosa. Sexto divinatrix. Septimo blasphema in Deum et sanctos et sanctas ipsius Dei in suis sacramentis. Octavo contemptrix legis divine. Nono sacre doctrine et sanctionum ecclesiasticarum prevaricatrix. Decimo seditiosa. Undecimo crudelis. Duodecimo apostatrix. Tredecimo schismatica. Quatuordecimo in fide nostra multipliciter errans. Quintodecimo in Deum et sanctam Ecclesiam multis modis delinquens. Sextodecimo ipsi Ecclesie, domino pape ac generali concilio expresse, indurato animo obstinanter atque pertinaciter sumittere se recusans. Decimo septimo pertinax. Decimo octavo obstinato. Decimo nono excommunicata. Vigesimo heretica.
> (Duparc, 2. 41.)
> [That detailed sentence against the same Joan contains twenty articles, in which it is imputed: First, she is a deceitful fabricator of revelations and apparitions. Second, a destructive seductress. Third, presumptuous. Fourth, a false believer. Fifth, superstitious. Sixth, a diviner. Seventh, a blasphemer against God and the saints and against God's own holy sacraments. Eighth, contemptuous of the divine law. Ninth, a violator of sacred doctrine and ecclesiastical ordinances. Tenth, seditious. Eleventh, cruel. Twelfth, apostate.

Thirteenth, schismatic. Fourteenth, one erring manifoldly in our faith. Fifteenth, one failing in many ways God and the holy church. Sixteenth, one with a hardened soul refusing obstinately and pertinaceously to submit herself expressly to the church itself, the sovereign pope and the general council. Seventeenth, stubborn. Eighteenth, obstinate. Nineteenth, excommunicated. Twentieth, heretic.]

16. Ibid., 2.41.

17. Ibid.

18. Ibid., 2.45.

19. Ibid.,2.42.

20. Ibid., 2.77–80.

21. Ibid.,2.79.

22. Ibid., 2.45–46.

23. Doncoeur, p. 157.

24. "Quarto castitas et virginitatis conservatio, unde angelus Domini conservavit Sarram, uxorem Abraham, ne polluretur in domo Pharaonis flagellando eum plagis maximis secundum Nicholaum de Lira, innitendo dictis Hebreorum, Gen. XII." Duparc, 2.46.

25. Ibid.

26. Doncoeur, p. 91.

27. Ibid., pp. 110, 115, 124, 129, 133.

28. Duparc, 2.56–57.

29. Ibid., 2. 48.

30. Ibid., 2.47.

31. "… et beatus Dyonisius, De angelica Ierarchia, dicat quod non est possibile aliter nobis suportare lucis divinum radium, nisi varietate sanctorum velaminum allegorice circumvelatum, suple de lege communi." Ibid., 2.47.

32. "… in hoc enim casu intelligitur id Jo.xvi [Joh. XVI, 23]: «Si quid petieritis Patrem in nomine meo dabit vobis.»" Ibid., 2.50.

33. "… que virginitate ac devotione et virtutibus rutilabat, saltem humano judicio et ut tenor processus satis videtur innuere et a pluribus fertur, qui eam viderunt." Ibid., 2.63.

34. Ibid., 2.72.

35. Ibid., 2.71.

36. The demonology here draws extensively from Aquinas. See "St. Thomas and the Nature of Evil," in *Witchcraft in Europe 1100–1700: A Documentary History,* ed. Alan Kors and Edward Peters (Philadelphia, 1972), pp. 51–71.

37. "… quia pro liberatione regni et consolatione veniebat, ubi non utebatur incantationibus nec artibus magicis, sed invocatione sancte Trinitatis et Jesu Christi Domini nostri saluteferi nominis et beate Marie semper virginis." Duparc, 2.63.

38. The fourteenth-century inquisitor Nicholas Eymeric wrote a handbook for inquisitors, *Directorium Inquisitorium,* that instructs the following concerning worship of demons: "If, indeed, the means of praying to the Saints which the Church has diligently instituted are considered, it will clearly be seen that these prayers are to be said, not to demons, but only to the Saints and the Blessed. This, then, is the the case of the second category of those who invoke demons. And in this manner the Saracens invoke Mohammed as well as God and the Saints and certain Beghards invoke Petrus Johannis and others condemned by the Church." Translated and quoted by Kors and Peters, p. 86.

39. Duparc, 2.90–91.

40. Ibid., 2.91.

41. Ibid., 2.54.

42. "Unde in percussione Egyptiorum utebatur malis angelis, ut supra dictum est, sed in liberatione populi Israel de manu eorum, utebatur bonis angelis, nam eidem populo dictum est:

«Ecce ego mittam angelum meum qui precedat te et custodiat in via et introducat, etc.», *Exodi* XXIII [20]; nam precedebat angelus in columna nubis per diem et ignis per noctem, *Exodi* XIII et XIV." Ibid., 2.54.

43. Ibid., 2.79.

44. Ibid., 2.53.

45. For a fuller discussion of medieval French political theology, see Joseph R. Strayer, "France: The Holy Land, the Chosen People, and the Most Christian King," in *Medieval Statecraft and the Perspectives of History* (Princeton, 1971), pp. 300–14, as well as Charles T. Wood, *Joan of Arc and Richard III: Sex, Saints, and Government in the Middle Ages* (New York, 1988).

46. Duparc, 2.109.

MARTIN LE FRANC'S COMMENTARY ON
JEAN GERSON'S TREATISE ON
JOAN OF ARC

Gertrude H. Merkle

In the Champion des dames *(1440–1442), Martin Le Franc wrote in defense of his contemporary Joan of Arc. Six of these stanzas, long unknown because they had been excised from the original manuscript, deal with Jean Gerson's "little treatise" about the maid—which is, in Le Franc's words, "much shrewder than we think."*

An important yet little-known contribution to the Joan of Arc literature can be found in six rhymed stanzas (*huitains*) excised from the original *Champion des dames* by Martin Le Franc. They were discovered by Arthur Piaget, appended to the Brussels MS 9466, and published just over a hundred years ago.[1] In these forty-eight lines the poet expresses his opinion about Joan's divinely appointed mission, her male outfit, and *De mirabili victoria*, which Piaget recognized as Jean Gerson's "little treatise."[2] These stanzas (see Appendix) offer a new perspective not only on the notorious lack of success of Le Franc's work but on Gerson's treatise as well.[3]

Martin Le Franc composed the *Champion des dames* between 1440 and 1442, barely twelve years after the tribunal of the Inquisition declared Joan a heretic, condemned her to die, and handed her over to the secular arm to be burned alive on May 30, 1431. A priest as well as a poet, Martin Le Franc became provost of Lausanne cathedral in 1443 and maintained that office for eighteen years until his death. He was also secretary to the duke of Savoy, Amédée VIII, later elected Pope Felix V by the Council of Basel. Le Franc's status and public roles made him particularly knowledgeable about the controversies surrounding Joan of Arc. From the few biographical details gathered from his work, we know that he was born at Aûmale, Normandy;

studied in Paris under Thomas de Courcelles, who took part in Joan's condemnation trial; attended the Council of Basel; was present at Arras at the signing of the peace treaty between France and Burgundy; and remained a papal legate attached to Nicholas V after Felix renounced the tiara.

Until recently, Martin Le Franc was considered "one of the most forgotten writers of the 15th century."[4] His feminist stand and encyclopedic approach, however, have sparked new interest. In championing the cause of women, he found a place in the tradition of the *querelle des femmes*, and his familiarity with the authors of his time has made of him a valued literary critic:

> Le Franc exhibits knowledge of French literature in almost all its forms: Arthurian, beast epic, *chanson de geste*, fabliau, lyric poetry, novelette, religious drama, romances of adventure, the *Roman de la rose*, short tales. Absent are such genres as chronicles, saints' lives, secular drama, pseudo-scientific and travel books—which were not germane to his purpose.[5]

The *Champion des dames* is a 24,000-line poem divided into five books. Written in defense of women and the poor, it rebuts Jean de Meung's *Roman de la rose* and other works by Aristotelian misogynists. Against adversaries who can often be identified, the author celebrates women who confronted historical and mythical adversaries, not only from biblical and classical times but also such contemporaries as Dame Christine de Pizan and Dame Jehanne la Pucelle. Just as Christine did in her *Cité des dames*, Martin Le Franc devoted his book 5 to the blessed Virgin Mary.

De dame Jehanne la Pucelle nouvellement venue en France appears in book 4. The poet devoted forty-five stanzas to Joan. Out of the twenty-eight that tell her story, twenty-two are reproduced by Quicherat;[6] the remaining six are found appended to the Brussels manuscript. Three of these six stanzas deal with the providential choice of Joan and her mission of defeating the English; the others challenge theologian Jean Gerson's comments on Joan's wearing male garments. In the dialogue between the Champion and the Adversary, we find a seminal synopsis of the English and Burgundian bias expressed both in the chronicles of the time and in the accusations against her at her trial.[7] In a voice reminiscent of Alain Chartier's *Quadrilogue invectif,* Le Franc wrote another seventeen stanzas under the title *A l'exemple de la Pucelle le Champion exhorte les nobles cuers de France.* The poet reminds his readers that it was through Joan's courage and suffering that the enemy was defeated and that they must unite in order to bring peace back to France and the Church.

After her victory at Orleans on May 8, 1429, all parties reappraised the Maid's claim to a divine appointment. The defeated Bedford's opinion was simple: he reported to the English crown that his men had been bewitched by a satanic agent in the form of a woman dressed as a man. Her male outfit soon became the focus of controversy. One of the earliest commentaries on Joan's male dress appears in Gerson's *De mirabili victoria.*[8] Its author's status and its comprehensive and analytical nature make it an important document. Dated May 14, 1429, on the vigil of Pentecost—less than a week after Joan's victory—it was written from Lyon, where Gerson, the former chancellor of the University of Paris and Notre-Dame, spent the remainder of his life.

Known as the "most Christian doctor," *doctor christianissimus,* Gerson had worked untiringly with Pierre d'Ailly, his teacher, friend, and predecessor as chancellor, to bring about the end of the Great Schism dividing the Church. Early in his career, Gerson had been called upon to address a king and a pope on their duties. At Constance, he instructed the trial of John Hus, playing an important role until his enemies' wrath forced him to seek refuge at his brother's priory, where he died two months after writing *De mirabili victoria.*

Gerson's ideas were widely influential. In Rome, a cleric, later identified as Jean Dupuy, a French Dominican,[9] had just completed a summary of world history, the *Breviarum historiale.* Upon hearing of the young woman warrior sent to France by God, he added a chapter, then wrote, "As for her male dress...," and stopped, leaving nine blank lines that were more expressive than any treatise.[10] In a series of letters from Bruges between March and November 1429, a young businessman, Pancrazio Giustiniani, wrote his father in Venice about the marvels occurring in France. He quotes Gerson's words, "A Domino factum est istud" (That is the work of the Lord). In his letter of November 20, he writes, "Credere non c'è male, e chi non crede non fa però contra la fede" (It is not wrong to believe but he who does not believe does not offend against the faith),[11] an expanded version of Gerson's French words in the otherwise Latin treatise: "Qui ne le croit, il n'est pas damné" (Who does not believe it is not damned). Since Gerson wrote this remark in the language of the people, it influenced a wider audience.

The belief that the dauphin requested Gerson's opinion on Joan of Arc cannot be substantiated. The *De Mirabile Victoria* however, had a significant impact, because of Gerson's status and expressive prose. Before examining Martin Le Franc's stanzas on the theological essay, let us briefly review the text considered a defense of the Maid.

The 2,000-word Latin treatise can be divided into three parts. In the first, the theologian analyzes the question of faith versus pious belief. Two contradictory opinions can be maintained about faith in the Maid; both can be true, says Gerson. Quoting a contemporary proverb on not trifling with one's faith, reputation, or eyesight, he warns that anyone who would trifle with the truths of faith could be cited before an ecclesiastical tribunal on suspicion of error. The verdict that sent John Hus to the pyre attested to that. The second category of beliefs pertains to pious opinions. It was commonly said that "he who does not believe it is not damned." That remark written in the vernacular defines "the case of the Maid." The author admonishes his readers "not to decide, judge, or openly blame ... these things ... or even approve of them, for judgment and decision must be deferred to the Church, her dignitaries and her doctors."[12]

The second part of the treatise defends the young girl's actions on the basis that hers is "so just an enterprise as the restoration of the king in his kingdom and the very just expulsion and defeat of his obstinate enemies." And that "she does not appear to resort to spells forbidden by the Church, or to disapproved superstitions" and "is not trying to secure her own interest" is evidence that hers is a providential mission. Gerson asks that the abundance of rumors be tolerated and that one should defer to the decisions of higher authorities. Although one of the most eminent theologians of his day, Gerson is careful not to commit himself as spokesman for the Church. Thus the expression "defer to superiors" occurs four times in the text.

The third and final part, written in the form of a legal document, is attached to the previous sections. The triple "truth" governing the Maid's male attire is the subject of Martin Le Franc's recently discovered stanzas. A notice attached to the stanzas indicates that these had orginally been placed between stanzas 2115 and 2116, both of which have remained in the manuscripts. A close reading reveals *De mirabili victoria* to be their source.

In stanza 2115, Le Franc expresses his belief that angels accompanied Joan and helped her. He mentions St. Jerome, who wrote that angels loved chastity and surrounded virgins. He remarks that Joan could not have accomplished what she did had not God and his angels been with her:

> Therefore I believe in good faith
> That angels accompanied her,
> For as we see in St. Jerome
> They love and embrace chastity.
> And I hold for true that they helped her
> To conquer the outer bulwarks
> And, at Patay, blinded the English
> [As they were] hurled backwards.[13]

In Gerson's *De mirabili victoria,* we read about "this Maid, finally surrounded by helpful angels, with whom her virginity forms a link of friendship and relationship, as St. Jerome says, and as is frequently seen in the history of saints."[14] Six stanzas follow, the first of which refers to God, "the author of peace," who never grants long life to those who by word or deed do not encourage it. (One might be tempted to look into the untimely death of Joan of Arc's detractors to justify the poet's line, but that is not our purpose here.) The second stanza recognizes God's will in the mission of the Maid, who as "a little humble creature" was sent "to bring down and confound the resolute English pride." In the third stanza, Martin Le Franc acknowledges that the opinion others hold may be missing the sacred design; however, there are those whose envy keeps them from speaking well of the Maid and who would "put evil interpretation on her person, or simply find fault." He introduces Jean Gerson's "little treatise," which he mockingly rebukes in the next three stanzas:

> People felt it was outrageous
> That she wore the habit of a man,
> For we read in Deuteronomy
> That Moses prohibited it.
> Don't you know what Gerson says on this?
> I mean Master Jean Gerson,
> Who about her a little treatise wrote
> Shrewder than we think.

We have seen earlier how carefully this most eminent theologian avoids committing himself as spokesman for the Church on behalf of Joan of Arc but defers judgment and decisions to higher authorities. In the third part of *De mirabili victoria*, Gerson discusses "three principles" (he calls them "truths," *veritates*) to justify the wearing of men's clothing by the Maid, "elected as she was while following her sheep."[15] Gerson's first theological principle paraphrased by Le Franc in the fifth recovered stanza reads: "The old law (Deut. 22:5) prohibiting woman to dress in man's clothes and man in woman's, in so far as it is judicial, does not obligate in the new law; because according to the truth necessary to our salvation, the old judicial laws were abrogated and do not carry an obligation under the new law." Gerson adds, however, "Such they are, unless it should happen that they be reinstituted or confirmed anew by the superiors."

Martin Le Franc lightheartedly uses peasants' names to illustrate the theologian's point in the fifth stanza:

> The ancient law of Moses,
> To the extent that it is judicial,
> Is not binding on Robin or Jane
> Living the life sacramental,
> If by decree or decretal,
> Such things which formerly were wont
> To serve some specific purpose
> Have not been confirmed anew.

Should, however, these ancient judicial laws be confirmed anew by the superiors of the Church, they would carry an obligation that would drastically change things for the Maid. Indeed, that is what happened: as politics influenced theology, Joan's divinely appointed mission was called into question, and the biblical prohibition of cross dressing, as stated in Deuteronomy 22:5, was used against her. Martin Le Franc does not hesitate to underscore the absurdity of the theologian's logic. In the sixth stanza, he humorously ridicules the old religious law whose prohibitions had long been made obsolete:

> Don't you see that it was forbidden
> That anyone should eat of an animal
> Unless it had a cleft foot
> And chewed its cud?
> To eat of hare no one dared,
> Neither of sow nor of piglet.
> Yet should you now be offered any,
> You would take many a morsel.

Stanza 2116, originally meant to follow the above, offers Martin
Le Franc's argument that supports Joan's wearing male attire. Her
habit, says the poet, was the reason Joan was feared in battle and
looked upon as a proud prince rather than as a simple little
shepherdess.

Martin Le Franc found Gerson's theological essay "shrewder than
we think" (plus soubtil que nous ne penson). It is indeed a clever
defense that permits contradictory theological interpretations. Four
hundred years later, Michelet called it "ce mauvais pamphlet." Others
have doubted altogether that Gerson was its author: Dorothy G.
Wayman termed it a "politically-bent substitution."[16]

Although said to have been written in defense of the Maid, the
treatise is very much a defense of the author. Keenly aware of the
power of ecclesiastical tribunals, he was careful to avoid taking any
personal position. While it is applied to Joan's case, her name is
never mentioned, and the treatise betrays a basic conflict between
the author's belief in divine intervention and his submission to
dogmatic legalism. Gerson's treatise was refuted within the same year
in an *Answer of a Parisian Clerk to Gerson's Apology of the Maid*, also
known as the "Vienna manuscript." It had however already based
the clerical arguments against Joan of Arc on the grounds that she
wore men's clothing. In his comments on the "Vienna manuscript,"
Noël Valois shows how the pro-English Parisian clerk attacked *De
mirabili victoria* and prepared the Maid's indictment: "Il n'en est pas
moins remarquable qu'il ébauche déjà et résume en quelque sorte
tout l'acte d'accusation du 27 mars 1431."[17] Le Franc expresses a similar
thought in his poem. It is important to note that by mocking the
arguments condemning Joan, Le Franc was making light of the
Inquisition, an institution that had lost neither its power nor its
authority.

Its length and content prevented *Le Champion des dames*, dedicated
to Philip the Good, from meeting with success. In a sequel, the
Complainte du livre du Champion des dames à son acteur (The Book
of the Champion des Dames' Lament to Its Author), Le Franc
deplores that his work was received coolly, even with outright hostility.
He writes that "evil tongues" advised the prince that either his work
and its author ought to be burned, or that he should rewrite it:

> Let him be burned alive or fried,
> For his belly is full of poisons,

And thus order him to rewrite it,
Order Martin for several reasons. (ll. 141–44)

Gaston Paris quotes the ill-intentioned critics who said that the Champion "spoke much too freely about everything."[18] It is likely that the stanzas that were removed contained the "poisons" for which the author deserved to be "burned alive or fried." In removing them, he somehow "rewrote" his book.

Consistent with the poem's lack of popularity are the relatively few existing manuscripts. Of the six, only two are dated. The "magnificent manuscript" of Arras, presumably made for the duke of Burgundy himself, is dated 1451; the *Book's Lament* is appended to it. The other is dated 1481, by which time Le Franc had been dead for twenty years and Philip the Good for fourteen. We know that Le Franc was sent to the duke of Burgundy as papal ambassador on March 20, 1447. He could have amended the *Champion* at that time by having the offending stanzas removed from the original, which was then destroyed. As to the excised stanzas, in the light of the ruling at Rouen, they were no doubt considered subversive and deserving of censure, at least for as long as Joan of Arc's condemnation was upheld. They could also be construed as an indictment of the secular leaders' better judgment, once peace was signed at Arras (1435). Of course, these stanzas could have been deemed irrelevant if it had been proved that the treatise was not Gerson's. But then, we may ask, why would anyone endeavor to save these stanzas? They expressed a theological and historical truth that no one could afford to uphold before the annulment of Joan's condemnation. The punishment for a secular court that opposed the decrees of the Inquisition was excommunication on the grounds that it supported heresy.[19] Such excommunication affected both the ruling prince defending the heretic or heresy and the land under his authority. No ruler could afford such a risk. We know that after Joan's condemnation, and well into the seventeenth century, all women wearing men's clothes were condemned by the Church.[20]

In the *Book's Lament*, when Le Franc philosophically concedes that his work cannot please everyone, he consoles himself with the knowledge that at the court of Burgundy there is "a man of wisdom, who will defend the author's honor, his right, and his good name." That man, "as everyone should know," is "le seigneur de Créquy."[21]

Jean de Créqui, seigneur de Canaples, Fressin, et Sains, is the man most likely responsible for saving the six stanzas. He was a close counselor and chamberlain of Philip the Good, one of the first knights of the Golden Fleece. He was badly wounded in the face while fighting at Compiègne against Joan and the French, yet he was a man of integrity, knowledge, and taste. Philip had put him in charge of the dukes of Burgundy's rich collection of manuscripts and library, where for years both he and his wife, Loyse, wielded much authority.[22] The calligrapher and bookbinder David Aubert, an artist in his own right, worked under Jean de Créqui's orders. They easily could have devised an elegant way for safekeeping Le Franc's six censured stanzas, believing that the poet's work, which "like the date-palm tree may take a long time to flourish...will in time yield good and gracious fruit."

NOTES

1. Arthur Piaget, "Huitains inédits de Martin Le Franc sur Jeanne d'Arc," *Le moyen âge* (May 1893).

2. For a discussion on the authorship of this document see Georges Peyronnet, "Gerson, Charles VII et Jeanne d'Arc," *Revue d'histoire ecclésiastique*, 34 (1989), 334–70.

3. Gertrude M. Hunziker Merkle, *Palingénésie de Jeanne d'Arc: étude de thèmes*, Ph.D. diss., Harvard University, (1988), 88–118.

4. Arthur Piaget, *Martin Le Franc, prévôt de Lausanne* (Lausanne, 1888), p. 6.

5. Harry F. Williams, "Martin Le Franc as Literary Critic," *Fifteenth Century Studies*, 12 (1987), 187–92.

6. Jules Quicherat, ed. *Procès de condamnation et de réhabilitation de Jeanne d'Arc dite La Pucelle*, 5 vols. (Paris, 1841–49), vol. 3, pp. 44–50.

7. Merkle, pp. 105–18.

8. Quicherat, vol. 3, pp. 298–306.

9. Peyronnet, 357.

10. J.–B. Ayroles, *La vraie Jeanne d'Arc*, 4 vols. (Paris, 1890–98), vol. 1, p. 55.

11. Ibid., vol. 3, p. 656.

12. H.G. Francq, "Jean Gerson's Theological Treatise and Other Memoirs in Defence of Joan of Arc," *Revue de l'Université d'Ottawa* 41 (1971), 58–80. All subsequent passages from Gerson's text are from H.G. Francq's translation.

13. My translation.

14. Francq, p. 64.

15. Ibid., p. 63.

16. Dorothy G. Wayman, "The Chancellor and Jeanne d'Arc," *Franciscan Studies*, 17 (1957), 273–305.

17. "It is no less remarkable that he somehow already draws up and summarizes the charges brought against her on March 27, 1431" in Noël Valois, "Un nouveau témoignage sur Jeanne d'Arc: réponse d'un clerc parisien à l'apologie de la Pucelle par Gerson, 1429," *Annuaire-bulletin de la Société de l'Histoire de France* (1906), 161–79.

18. Gaston Paris, "Un poème inédit de Martin Le Franc," *Romania* 16: 421.

19. Bernard Gui, *Manuel de l'inquisiteur*, ed. Mallot and Darioux (Paris, 1926), p. liii.

20. Merkle, pp. 119–92.

21. Paris, 437 and 422. I gratefully acknowledge Charity Cannon Willard's suggestion to take a closer look at Jean de Créqui's name.

22. Georges Doutrepont, *La littérature à la cour des ducs de Bourgogne* (Paris, 1909), pp. 38–41.

APPENDIX

Following are the six stanzas found appended to the Brussels MS 9466 of Martin Le Franc's *Champion des dames*, as published by Arthur Piaget in *Le moyen âge*, May 1893, with my translation into English. They are introduced by Stanza 2115 and conclude with Stanza 2116.

Stanza 2115:

Aussy je croy, en bonne foy,	Therefore, I believe in good faith
Que les angles l'accompaignassent,	That angels accompanied her,
Car ilz, comme en Iherosme voy,	For, as we see in St. Jerome,
Chasteté aiment et embrassent	They love and embrace chastity.
Et tien pour vrai qu'ilz lui aidassent	I hold for true that they helped her
A gaaignier les fors bolvers,	To conquer the outer bullwarks
Et a Patay les yeulx crevassent	And at Patay blinded the English
Aux Anglois ruez a l' envers	[As they were] hurled backwards

1. Car nous debvons tous presumer	For we all must presume
Que Dieu qui est aucteur de pais	That God, who is the author of peace,
Permet destruire et consumer	Allows to be destroyed and consumed
Tous ceulx qui ne la veulent, mais	All who reject it, but
Debvons nous dire que jamais	We must be aware that never
Ne laisse il longuement durer	Will he grant long life
Ceulx qui, de parolle ou de fais,	To those who by word or by deed
Ne veulent la paix endurer.	Do not want to endure it.

2. Aussy, comme je conjecture,	Therefore, as I surmise,
Convint que l'orgueul hault posé	It was fitting that pride in high places
Par petite humble creature	By a little humble creature
Fust de son siege deposé.	Should be toppled from its seat.
Par ainsy tout presupposé,	Having thus preordained all
Pour abessier ou desvoyer	To bring down and confound
L'orgueul des Anglois proposé,	The resolute English pride,
Dieu voult la Pucelle envoyer.	God willed to send the Maid.

3. Mille raisons sont en appert	A thousand reasons make evident
Par lesquelles l'oppinion	That the opinion
De moy et des semblables pert	I and others like me hold
De saincte imaginacion,	Is missing the sacred design,
Mais de droicte inclination	Though from righteous inclination
L'envieux ne sçavroit bien dire,	The envious would not know to speak well
Et male interpretacion	And puts evil interpretation
Fait de chose ou n'a que redire.	On the person or only finds fault.

4. Aux gens a semblé estre enorme
Qu' elle vestoit d' omme l'abit
Car on lit en Deuteronome
Que Moyse le deffendit.
Scez tu point que Jarson en dit?
Je te dy maistre Jan Jarson
Qui d'elle ung petit traictié fit,
Plus soubtil que nous ne penson.

People felt it was outrageous
That she wore the habit of a man,
For we read in Deuteronomy
That Moses prohibited it.
Don't you know what Gerson says on this?
I mean Master Jean Gerson,
Who about her a little treatise wrote
Shrewder than we think.

5. La loy de Moyse ancienne,
En tant qu' elle est judiciale,
N'oblige Robin ne Jouenne
Vivans en la sacramentale,
Se, par decret ou decretale,
Telx choses lors accoustumees
Pour quelque fin especiale
Ne sont de nouvel confermees.

The ancient law of Moses,
To the extent it is judicial,
Is not binding on Robin or Jane
Living a sacramental life,
If, by decree or decretal,
Such things that formerly were wont
To serve some specific purpose
Have not been confirmed anew.

6. Ne vois tu pas que deffendu
Estoit que nulluy ne mengast
De beste se l'ongle fendu
N'avoit et qu' elle ruminast?
De lievre mengier on n' osast,
Ne de truye ne de pourceau.
Ores mais qu'on t'en presentast
Tu en prendroyes maint morseau!

Don't you see it was forbidden
That anyone should eat
Of an animal unless it had a cleft foot
And chewed its cud?
To eat of hare no one dared,
Neither of sow nor of piglet.
Yet should you now be offered any,
You would take many a morsel!

Stanza 2116:

Aussy merveille ne te soit,
Combien que chose inusitee
Se la Pucelle se vestoit
De pourpoint et robe escourtee.
Car elle en estoit redoubtee
Trop plus et aperte et legiere,
Et pour ung fier prince contee,
Non pas pour simplette bergiere.

Therefore, marvel not,
Though unusual it may be,
That the Maid wore a doublet
And a short skirt,
For thus she was more dreaded
And capable and nimble,
And looked upon as a proud prince,
Not as simple little shepherdess.

WHY JOAN OF ARC
NEVER BECAME AN AMAZON

Deborah Fraioli

An argument against the widely-held belief that the popularity of the Amazons in late medieval France was a positive influence on the decision of Charles VII's theologians to endorse Joan's mission.

B urgeoning French humanism at the end of the fourteenth century gave the classical Amazons a new popularity. It has been assumed that they had a favorable effect on the reception of Joan of Arc at the court of Charles VII. Late medieval culture was so permeated with examples of the Amazons that educated French society, especially members of the court and clergy, could hardly have escaped knowing them,[1] or remained unaware of the new wave of admiration for the *egregia bellatrix* in art and literature.[2] But the escalating claim in recent scholarship, that Joan was recognized in part because of the endorsement the Amazons afforded her, deserves examination. That the presence of the Amazons in late-medieval culture acted as preparation for the acceptance of a woman's authority in the case of Joan of Arc seems plausible.[3] But the extension of this argument, that the Amazon phenomenon helped induce Charles's authorities to grant official approval to Joan's mission,[4] does not stand up to a detailed examination of the facts. For Joan, who claimed to have been sent by God to save France, glory lay in her weakness rather than a near-virile strength, for by her weakness she proved herself to be the instrument of God. If this is true, then it follows that the Maid was more appropriately validated by the biblical *exempla* of Esther, Judith, and Deborah, who were generally cast in theology and literature as saviors of the people of God, than she was by the godless Amazons. Moreover, the Amazons, whose strength was dependent on training and was therefore of this world, and whose objectives were tailored to masculine standards of glory, offered a less satisfying spiritual and literary heritage for anchoring the role of the *Pucelle de Dieu* in history than did the biblical heroines. In the case of Esther and Judith especially, feminine weakness was valorized by the association with the biblical motif of the weak overcoming the strong (1 Cor. 1:27); one important distinction was that it allowed their femininity to remain intact.

When Charles asked his experts to make a pronouncement on Joan, they avoided identifying the Amazons with Joan's divine mission. Although we have little direct evidence relating to this aspect of the Poitiers investigation, Christine de Pizan, who shows herself conversant in the *Ditié de Jehanne d'Arc* with church opinions related to Poitiers, is also apt to reflect in the same poem other of the prelates' views for which we lack official sources. In the *Ditié,* Christine uses the popular motif of the Nine Worthies, or the *neuf preux* and *neuf preuses,* to endorse the Pauline image of Joan as a weak feminine vessel infused with divine strength, while she implicitly rejects the Amazons' purposeless and empty quest for masculine prowess. Her complete recasting of this secular motif along suitable theological lines directly addresses the inappropriateness of the Amazons as exemplars for Joan. The modifications Christine makes in the composition and function of the Worthies in the *Ditié* instruct us about Joan's negative effect on the fate of this secular motif and perhaps also signal Christine's own contribution to its demise.

To understand the complicated popularity of the warrior woman as exemplified in the topos of the Nine Worthy Women in the late Middle Ages, we need to understand the numerous ways in which adapting the heroic ideal of the Nine Male Worthies to a canon of female exemplars clashed with or contradicted not only conventional behavior for women but also the usual portrayal of women in history. This requires that we first examine the origin of the Nine Male Worthies. The Nine Worthies, who first appeared as an organized canon in the early-fourteenth-century Alexander romance, the *Voeux du paon* (1312), were in effect a showcase of heroes who symbolized for the Middle Ages the pinnacle of masculine military achievement.[5] Divided by religion into three groups of three, this seldom-modified list of names consisted of Hector, Achilles, and Julius Caesar for the pagans; Joshua, David, and Judas Maccabeus for the Jews; and Arthur,

Charlemagne, and the French crusader Godefrey of Bouillon for the Christians. Since the criterion for admission to the topos was military prowess, which represented the masculine ideal in each of the three cultures, there was no dissonance between that ideal and acceptable masculine cultural norms. In late medieval France, the motif may have flourished partly as a blind denial of the increasingly obvious fact that the ideal of engaging in feats of arms to acquire glory and fame was no longer pertinent for a country crushed by the Hundred Years War. But the motif was also a common rhetorical and iconographical mechanism whereby illustrious ancient exemplars were linked to contemporaries as a way of enhancing the latters' reputations, a useful device for court poets seeking to flatter their patrons.[6] The most favorable linkage was the elevation of a contemporary to the rank of tenth *preux*, which is attested, among other examples, in Eustache Deschamps's poems on Bertrand du Guesclin.[7]

It should not surprise us that, despite statements that the formation of the Nine Worthy Women constituted a natural response to a craving for symmetry,[8] no canon of female worthies was immediately created as a pendant to the Nine Male Worthies, nor could it effectively parallel the male canon once it was created. Unlike their male counterparts, for whom vanquishing enemies was the ideal of manhood, women who could defeat men were an unnatural and a humiliating affront to the male ego. A persistent current in ancient literature indicates that warrior women were perceived to be as antagonistic to the notion of male heroism as they were complementary to it. From an anthropological point of view, the Amazons threatened the right order of the universe by refusing the destiny assigned them. As William Blake Tyrrell states: "Amazon customs reverse a polarity whose ideal is the adult male."[9] More than one classical author associates the Amazons' overcoming of feminine weakness as inducing a complementary male effeminacy.[10]

Galleries of women were rarely established along the same lines as those for men. Whereas illustrious biography identified men for inclusion by heroism, catalogues of women were usually organized according to female virtues and vices, as numerous catalogues of good and bad women attest.[11] Women's catalogues employed such categories as reputation for beauty, renown for a single memorable act, resemblance to the Muses, aptitude for peacemaking, or endowment with a sonorous name as the basis for inclusion. The Amazons, although not regular members of any catalogue tradition, were most assimilable in terms of their depiction by male authors to the category of vice. They had experienced an almost seamless reputation for evil, whether in classical literature, the church fathers, or the medieval encyclopedic tradition.[12] So it is at first surprising to learn that when a female canon of worthies finally emerged in Jean Le Fèvre's *Livre de leësce,* more than fifty years after the inception of the male topos,[13] the masculine concept of martial conquest was preserved in the selection of the women by forming a canon of all pagan women warriors: Sinope, Hippolyta, Menalippe, Semiramis, Thamaris, Penthesilea, and Lampedo, from the Amazon tradition, and Deiphyle and Teuca, from Statius and Pliny respectively, or from their medieval literary versions. In inventing the female canon, the triadic division by religion of the males was rejected, probably because citing Hebrew women (of whom Esther and Judith were the most popular exemplars) or Christian saints would have meant abandoning respect for the values of prowess and conquest, which lay at the heart of the topos for the males, in favor of more feminine or more submissive virtues.[14]

To Le Fèvre and many others, the Amazons served a primarily decorative or rhetorical function. One tends to agree with the editor of the *Livre de leësce,* Anton Gérard van Hamel, that the succinct allusion to the female Worthies in Le Fèvre's work probably means that he did not invent the canon himself but drew upon some previous example, which van Hamel believed to be a *mystère mimé* or a procession.[15] But whether he found the Worthies in art (sculpture, tapestry, frieze) or in literature (perhaps as a mere list of names inserted in a French romance), Le Fèvre is likely to have come upon them in some abbreviated form, disengaged from their profoundly negative literary reputation.[16]

There were, however, authors who looked more deeply at the complex notion of feminine heroism than did Le Fèvre.[17] In a series of ballads written in the last decades of the fourteenth century, and thus contemporaneous with Le Fèvre's work, the poet Deschamps varies his lists of famous women, as he considers his options for grouping them, in an apparent attempt to assign women to fixed categories of fame.[18] Deschamps knows the *neuf preuses,* but he constantly modifies the manner in which they are presented, first offering them as an integral group, then interwoven with the *neuf preux*, and finally evoked piecemeal for the sound of their names,[19] as if the act of regrouping were a form of experimentation.[20] Deschamps seems to be experimenting in his ballads with the two conflicting traditions of feminine fame. Should women receive glory for prowess, as men do, or for virtue? As if driven by the idea that a gallery of heroines should consist of more than pagan warriors, he sometimes places a warrior woman alongside Esther or Judith, beside Lucretia or Penelope, St. Anne or the Virgin Mary.[21] But perhaps because he understands the fundamental differences (as we see in his more detailed ballads) among the female Worthies, symbols of prowess and territorial acquisition, the biblical women, types of humility and devotion through whom God avenged his people, and Christian saints, Deschamps remains frozen in the dilemma of female categorization and never recasts the *neuf preuses* in the triadic division-by-religion of the male canon.

At Poitiers, however, one arresting reference to the Amazon image, a sixteen-line poem beginning "Virgo puellares," may suggest that Charles's commissioners held fewer scruples relating to the bad example of the Amazons than did Deschamps.[22] The superficial similarity between the women warriors of antiquity and Joan appears to have been an effective tool for military recruitment, so much so that someone at the Poitiers hearings composed this short Latin poem to bolster military support for the Maid's impending assault on Orleans. In this strikingly secular piece of war propaganda, Joan is portrayed as an Amazon warrior, her male clothing is freely admitted, and she is called "daughter of Mars" instead of the usual "daughter of God" (*fille de Dieu*).

Yet the validation that the new fondness for the female warrior conferred on Joan of Arc, was no more than a superficial legitimization for Joan's mission, ideologically incompatible with its single most important tenet: her claim to have been sent by God. We can be confident that those closely involved with the royalist cause in 1429, who were charged with the task of pronouncing on Joan's claim to a religious mission, knew that the pagan Amazons did not confer serious validation on Joan's Christian mission, despite validating the premise raised by Joan's mission that women could be warriors. The idea was theologically impossible, even given the selective act of memory by which the late fourteenth century had overlooked the Amazons' reputation for ruthlessness, and reincarnated them as symbols of noble heroic valor. The Amazons, even purified in the medieval tradition, were motivated by the sense of their own personal worth, itself the result of their rigorous and systematic military training. In the *Roman de Troie*, Penthesilea proudly announces that the Amazons engage in war for the purpose of acquiring prowess and reputation.[23] This had nothing to do with Joan, who believed that she served a calling of a much higher order. Since she viewed herself as fulfilling a divine mission in the role of divine instrument, she insisted, along with some of the supporters who wrote about her, that no training had prepared her for this mission.[24] Where God provided the strength, there was no need for the physical training typical of the Amazons.

Joan was indeed a member of a new species, the Christian warrior,[25] for whom the Amazons served as a model in nothing but their strength. In order to understand Joan's mission, those theologians whom the dauphin Charles called upon to evaluate Joan's case needed a religious paradigm by which to make sense of her mission. They found it not in pagan literature, or even directly in Christianity, but in Old Testament typology. In Judith and Esther, in particular, they found a model for Joan: these were women who had committed themselves to a religious purpose, to save the people of God. This concept suited the French situation, because certain theologians close to the dauphin had boldly extended the mythology of the French as the "most Christian" nation, especially chosen by God to execute great deeds for the Faith, to the flat assertion that the French were the new people of God.[26] In presumably the first theological treatise ever to discuss Joan's mission, known as *De quadam puella*, the author states: "'People of Israel,' the people of the kingdom of France can, without impropriety, be so called. We know it has always blossomed thanks to the faith in God and to the observance of Christian religion."[27] And the prominent archbishop of Embrun, who may have known this tract, likewise exploits this parallel to prove that God would intervene on behalf of the French as he had previously done for the people of Israel.[28]

To understand Joan as an Esther or Judith meant ignoring their occasional literary depiction as purveyors of feminine wiles, to concentrate exclusively on their biblical function, as saviors of God's elect. The Middle Ages preserved the latter tradition not only in the poetry of Deschamps and Christine de Pizan[29] but elsewhere as well.[30]

Another decisive factor (as old as the book of Judith, but seldom mentioned in France until the Poitiers investigation) distinctly separated Joan's case from the Amazons. In diametrical opposition to the Amazons, the theologians at Charles's court evoked Esther and Judith according to biblical tradition not as topoi of masculine strength but as the embodiments of feminine *weakness*. Esther and Judith gave credence to the concept of the weak overcoming the strong, the triumph of the weak serving to underscore the superiority of divine over human strength.[31]

Christine de Pizan, who was not as isolated at her convent of Poissy as most scholars have imagined,[32] thoroughly understood the habit of thought adopted by Charles's theologians by which Joan could be cast as a new Esther or Judith instead of in the mold of a secular heroine. In her depiction of Joan in the *Ditié de Jehanne d'Arc,* Christine modifies her own previous treatments of Esther and Judith to follow Joan's theologians, whose tracts she apparently knew, in casting Joan as an exemplar of the weak overcoming the strong.[33] Christine adopts the otherwise confusing practice in the *Ditié* of downgrading Joan's heroism at the same time that she should be seeking to promote it and emphasizing through the use of diminutives and other minimizing strategies a distinctly little-girl, nonheroic portrayal of Joan, though never minimizing her miracle.[34] One might have believed in a hero capable of Joan's victories, but not in the tender virgin Christine presents, one who is endowed with grace but not with stature, whose role as mother is belied by the offer of milk from a virgin breast, who is repeatedly upstaged in Christine's poem by the less deserving Charles, and whom Christine all but "forgets" until line 162 of the *Ditié.*[35]

Christine will not venerate martial prowess for its own sake, and thus there is not a single Amazon alluded to in the *Ditié.*[36] To provide a slightly more military prototype for Joan than Esther and Judith, she introduces Deborah, as did Charles's theologians before her, as if she were forcing the all-pagan female Worthies into partial conformity with the males, by offering Esther, Judith, and Deborah as Hebrew counterparts to Joshua, David, and Judas Maccabeus. She knows the belligerent tone of Joan's *Lettre aux Anglais,*[37] but she also knows its claim that all Joan's strength emanates directly from the king of heaven. As Kennedy and Varty rightly point out, in stanza after stanza Christine works in a reminder that the source of all Joan's military accomplishments is God.[38] The very selection for this mission of a woman, the weaker vessel, instead of a man, is a special sign for the French, because it speaks to the greater involvement of God.[39]

Christine takes one final step in the *Ditié* to show that the Jews of the Old Testament, not pagan heroes or heroines, or even Christian saints, provided the central focus for understanding the nature of Joan's mission. Although in stanzas 23–28 of the *Ditié* Christine clearly alludes to the topos of the Nine Worthies through her use of the terms *preux* and *preuses*, she introduces a significant innovation. Reconstructing both the male and female canons in an abbreviated version, she allows only for Hebrew exemplars, substituting Old Testament *miracles* for the feats of prowess normally exalted by the topos. In flagrant disregard for the conventional meaning of the topos—to honor prowess and military conquest—Christine selects Moses, Joshua, and Gideon as male exemplars; Esther, Judith, and Deborah for the women. All pagan female *exempla* are immediately dismissed with a single sweeping comment.[40] These are men and women to whom Joan of Arc is compared, people who performed miracles, infused not with their own power but God's. In this scenario, the Amazons have no place.

Christine de Pizan is no more able than Deschamps to recreate the topos of the *neuf preuses* along the lines of the three religions. In contrast to her earlier treatment of the *exempla* of Esther and Judith, however, where Deborah joins the two premier feminine biblical exempla only as an afterthought,[41] by the time of the *Ditié* she sets Deborah on equal terms with Esther and Judith, as if together the three constituted a revised canon of female Worthies.[42] More important, however, Christine, who knew the literary topos of the *preuses* better than any theologian, allowed herself to be influenced by the theologians' persuasions at Poitiers, that Joan was not a second Penthesilea but a second Esther, Judith, or Deborah, and as one of the terms of that analogy Joan was cast in the role of savior of the new people of God.

What, then, was the aftermath for the Amazons of the appearance of Joan of Arc? The topos of the Nine Worthy Women virtually disappears in France after Joan of Arc. Sébastien Mamerot's *L'histoire des neuf preux et des neuf preuses* of 1461, the only known fifteenth-century French text on the female Worthies written after Joan of Arc, describes a cohort composed solely of Amazons and even celebrates Joan as the tenth *preuse,* opposite du Guesclin as tenth *preux.*[43] But to explain this anomaly we need only realize that Mamerot wrote for Louis de Laval, grandson of du Guesclin himself and sibling of André and Guy, who served in Joan's army. What we have, then, is a case of literature serving family aggrandizement.

In time, the female canon did become symmetrical to the divisions of the male canon, selecting Lucretia, Veturia, and Virginia as the pagans; Esther, Judith, and in a minor deviation, Jael not Deborah, as the Jews; and the saints Helena, Bridget, and Elizabeth as the Christians. This change occurred not in France but in Germany.[44] This new German canon, which draws not on the warrior but the *bonne femme* tradition of female biography, dovetailed with the moral and spiritual image Charles's theologians had tried to project of Joan of Arc's experience, but it does not offer Joan a place, even though its adoption of the three Hebrew women likely derives from France's experience with Joan of Arc. Moreover, despite Joan's probable influence on the softer image of women found in the recast canon that arose in Germany, she may have still been too much an Amazon for inclusion in this new canon.

Joan of Arc seems to have had a negative rather than salutory effect on the survival of the canon of the Nine Worthy Women, which seemed so obviously poised in 1429 to embrace her. Ironically, with the Amazon canon of the *neuf preuses* ready for restructuring along the same religiously divided lines as the *neuf preux,* and with Joan's own history vigorously signaling the names of three Hebrew women perfect for inclusion, events somehow never took their expected course. In all likelihood, the failure to draw the Hebrew women into the canon of Nine Worthy Women is not proof of their unsuitability as Worthies; Christine argues their case cogently by the structural and ideological transformations she imposes on the motif of the Worthies in her *Ditié.* It may mean only that what Charles's theologians did behind closed doors at Poitiers, and what Christine tried to publicize in her sixty-one-stanza poem, never became widely known. Yet in the tight but influential circle surrounding Charles VII the Amazons could hardly have played a part in Joan's being well received by the prelates and counselors of the Poitiers commission.

NOTES

1. Georges Peyronnet argues convincingly that through the influence of humanism Jean Gerson would have known of the Amazons, but it does not necessarily follow that the renowned Gerson would have used the Amazons to justify Joan of Arc, as did a cleric living in Rome who drew an explicit parallel between Joan and Penthesilea (Léopold Delisle, "Un nouveau témoignage relatif à la mission de Jeanne d'Arc," *Bibliothèque de l'Ecole des Chartes* 46 (1885), 649–68. See Peyronnet, "Gerson, Charles VII et Jeanne d'Arc: La propagande au service de la guerre," *Revue d'histoire ecclésiastique* 84 (1989), 334–70.

2. While we can surmise that with the steady popularity of Benoît de Sainte-Maure's twelfth-century *Roman de Troie* (ed. Léopold Constans, 6 vols. [Paris, 1904–12]) Benoît's favorable portrayal of Penthesilea slowly influenced minds in favor of the glory of the woman warrior, the real Amazon impetus came in the mid-fourteenth century from Italian sources. Petrarch's wholehearted admiration for his contemporary Maria de Puzzuoli (see *Letters from Petrarch*, trans. Morris Bishop [Bloomington, 1966], pp. 52–54) and the veritable cult of the Amazons, described by N. Jorga in *Thomas III, marquis de Saluces, étude historique et littéraire* (Paris, 1893), pp. 42–44, manifested in the life of the marquise de Saluces, a self-styled local Amazon, who named her daughter Penthesilea, are but two examples of the renewed interest in the *femme forte* generated by Italian humanism's revival of the classics. In France, a similar enthusiasm is in evidence particularly in the widespread effort to translate the classics started by Charles V. French humanist translators, such as Laurent de Premierfait, to whom we owe an important translation of Boccaccio's *De claris mulieribus*, all had close ties to Italy. Also, the popularity in France of *De claris mulieribus*, perhaps best known through Laurent de Premierfait's translation, *Les cleres et nobles femmes*, created the climate in which Christine de Pizan brought greater visibility to the Amazons by reworking Boccaccio's only superficially feminist biographies in her *Livre de la cité des dames* (1405) (see Liliane Dulac, "Un mythe didactique chez Christine de Pizan: Sémiramis ou la veuve héroïque (du *Mulieribus claris* de Boccace à la *Cité des dames*)," in *Mélanges de philologie romanes offerts à Charles Camproux* (Montpellier, 1978), pp. 315–43; Earl J. Richards, introduction to *The Book of the City of Ladies* (New York, 1982), especially pp. xxviii–xxxviii; and Patricia A. Phillippy, "Establishing Authority: Boccaccio's *De claris mulieribus* and Christine de Pizan's *Le livre de la cité des dames*," *Romanic Review* 77 (1986), 167–93. Finally, there was the widespread popularity of the *neuf preuses*, evident in sculpture at the castle of Coucy, in tapestry, in the *Chevalier errant*, a romance by Thomas III de Saluces, in Jean Le Fèvre's *Livre de leësce* and in many *balades* of Eustache Deschamps. For tapestry, see Louise Roblot-Delondre, "Les sujets antiques dans la tapisserie," *Revue archéologique*, s. 5, 7 (1918), 131–50 ; otherwise, Horst Schroeder, *Der Topos*

der "Nine Worthies" (Göttingen, 1971), pp. 168–203, is the best source for additional information.

3. In my article "The Literary Image of Joan of Arc: Prior Influences," *Speculum* 56 (1981), 811–830, I advanced the idea (815–16), that Christine's willingness to glorify the image of the female warrior in Joan was affected by the poet's knowledge of the Amazons. This is to say that Christine's image of Joan was influenced by the Amazons' late-medieval popularity (some of which Christine herself created). This is different from Maureen Quilligan's implied message in *The Allegory of Female Authority: Christine de Pizan's Cité des dames* (Ithaca, 1991) that Christine was more influential in causing the Amazons' popularity than she was influenced by it.

4. This view is put forth by Charity Cannon Willard in "Early Images of the Female Warrior," *Minerva* 9 (1988), 6, where she notes the superiority of Esther, Judith, and Deborah as exemplars and then adds: "Penthesilea's popularity throughout the fifteenth century also suggests the possibility that it might have been a factor in the acceptance of Joan's mission in the first place, even though it was generally regarded as miraculous." Quilligan singles out Christine's writing as the responsible influence: "[Christine's] constant retelling of the Amazon myth ... could very well have prepared the culture at court to see a woman warrior as something other than a monster. And this preparation would not have hurt Jehanne's chances for being well received by that court," p. 280. Quilligan's crediting Christine has drawn the attention of two reviewers of Quilligan's book. See *French Studies* 47 (1993), 207, and *Speculum* 69 (1994), 237. In a different vein, Marina Warner writes that the Amazon myth "underlies the development of Joan's personality and her gradual rise to prominence," *Joan of Arc: The Image of Female Heroism* (London, 1981), p. 202.

5. Johan Huizinga, *The Waning of the Middle Ages*, trans. F. Hopman (London, 1937), p. 61.

6. R.L. Graeme Ritchie, *The Buik of Alexander or The Buik of the Most Noble and Valiant Conqueror Alexander the Grit, by John Barbour*, vol. 1 (Edinburgh, 1925), p. xli.

7. See Eustache Deschamps, *Oeuvres complètes,* ed. Auguste Queux de Saint-Hilaire and Gaston Raynaud, 11 vols. (Paris, 1878–1903), *Balade* 207, *Balade* 239, *Chanson royale* 362, pp. 101–02. See also Siméon Luce, *La France pendant la guerre de cent ans,* 2nd ed. (Paris, 1890), pp. 231–43. Louis of Orleans made the addition of a statue of du Guesclin, as tenth *preux,* to the great hall of the castle of Coucy: Huizinga, p. 61.

8. Huizinga, p. 61; Schroeder concurs, p. 168. Similarly, Charles Bowie Millican, *Spenser and the Table Round* (Cambridge, Mass., 1932), p. 41, thinks they "sprang up by happy parallel" to the Nine Muses and Nine Worthies; Ann McMillan concurs with Millican in "Men's Weapons, Women's War: The Nine Female Worthies," 1400–1640, *Mediaevalia* 5 (1979), 113. Jules Guiffrey, "Note sur une tapisserie représentant Godefroy

de Bouillon et sur les représentations des preux et des preuses au quinzième siècle," *Mémoires de la société nationale des antiquaires de France* 40, s. 4, 10 (1879), 105, notes the "assiduity" with which the male Worthies were given a female pendant, a view followed by Paul Meyer, "Les neuf preux," *Bulletin de la société des anciens textes français* 9 (1883), 45–46, n. 3.

9. William Blake Tyrrell, *Amazons: A Study in Athenian Mythmaking* (Baltimore, 1984), p. 66.

10. Pierre Samuel, *Amazones, guerrières et gaillardes* (Grenoble, 1975), has gathered together extracts of most of the classical texts on the Amazons, which is useful for tracking various themes. For instance, on role inversion and male humiliation, see citations from Justin and Diodorus, pp. 44–45; Diodorus, p. 53; Strabo, p. 55. For a balanced view of inversion by a modern scholar, see Josine H. Blok, *The Early Amazons: Modern and Ancient Perspectives on a Persistent Myth* (Leiden, 1995), pp. ix–x, who shows that female heroism not only destabilizes but also underscores male heroism.

11. Many but not all important references to the catalogue tradition can be found in Glenda McLeod, *Virtue and Venom: Catalogs of Women from Antiquity to the Renaissance* (Ann Arbor, 1991). A valuable reference for the later catalogue tradition is Marc Angenot, *Les champions des femmes, examen du discours sur la supériorité des femmes 1400–1800* (Montreal, 1977). See also Alcuin Blamires et al., eds. *Woman Defamed and Woman Defended: An Anthology of Medieval Texts* (Oxford, 1992).

12. For the classical period, see Samuel, pp. 43–76, or individual authors. A brief but excellent introduction to the Amazons in the medieval encyclopedic tradition can be found in Michel Salvat, "Amazonia: le royaume de Femmenie," in *La représentation de l'antiquité au moyen âge, actes du colloque des 26, 27 et 28 mars, 1981, Université de Picardie* , (Vienne, 1982), pp. 229–41.

13. See Renata Blumenfeld-Kosinski, "Jean le Fèvre's *Livre de leesce:* Praise or Blame of Women?" *Speculum* 69 (1994), 705.

14. This is not to deny that Judith, for instance, was occasionally praised for her "manly" valor or to overlook the fact that the Hebrew heroines, especially, were sometimes portrayed as ruthless deceivers of men.

15. Anton-Gérard van Hamel, *Les lamentations de Matheolus et le Livre de leësce de Jehan Le Fèvre de Resson,* 2 vols. (Paris, 1892–1905), vol. 2, p. 252. Although the first procession of worthies on record, in Arras in 1339, only mentions the *neuf preux,* Deschamps's *Autre balade* 93 (ca. 1380s) possibly suggests a procession. Whether the original *preuses* were first created for tapestry depends on how long tapestries might be kept before being sold or how long they lasted before needing repair. Four entries in a royal inventory made for Charles VI in 1422 inform us that in 1388 tapestries of the *preux* and *preuses* were sold by Pierre Baumetz to the duke of Burgundy and that in 1396 Jean de Jaudoigne repaired "deux preuse." See Louise

Roblot-Delondre, "Les sujets antiques dans la tapisserie," *Revue archéologique* s.5, 7 (1918), 133–34.

16. The one limitation I find to McMillan's otherwise useful article "Men's Weapons, Women's War" is her failure (despite a brief remark that Amazons "could be admired, but only at a distance," p. 118) adequately to acknowledge that in the Middle Ages honoring "bad women" for their positive traits did not have to entail irony, comedy, or ignorance on the part of the poet of their faults. Contradictory images of female exemplars coexisted quite happily in medieval society. Evidence that the dual nature of *exempla* was entirely tolerable is shown in the selection of reproductions in McMillan's own article, where woodcuts from *De claris mulieribus* depicting lust and ruthless violence on one page contradict the images of courtly Amazons in tapestry on another. For a stronger claim than mine about the dual images of women, see Gabriele Bernhard Jackson, "Topical Ideology: Witches, Amazons, and Shakespeare's Joan of Arc," *Journal of the English Literary Renaissance* 18 (1988), 48.

17. If Le Fèvre's *Livre de leësce* is read as an ironic palinode, then we might assume that he intended the reader to consider the negative side of his *preuses*, but at least in this instance Le Fèvre's brief and casual allusion offers little support for an ironic reference to the *preuses*.

18. McMillan, p. 114.

19. See Deschamps, *Oeuvres, Autre balade* 93, vol. 1, pp. 199–201; *Autre balade* 403, vol. 3, pp. 192–94; *Balade* 482, vol. 3, pp. 303–04; *Autre balade* 546, vol. 3, pp. 89–90.

20. The mistaken notion, corrected by Schroeder, that Deschamps invented the canon of *preuses* may be due to this experimentation.

21. Deschamps, *Balade* 482 or *Autre balade* 546 (see n. 18 above).

22. See Mathieu Thomassin, *Registre dephinal* in Jules Quicherat, *Procès de condamnation et de réhabilitation de Jeanne d'Arc dite la Pucelle*, 5 vols. (Paris, 1841–49), vol. 4, p. 305. See, among other depictions of Joan that echo the Amazons, the letter of Perceval de Boulainvilliers, Quicherat, vol.5. pp. 114-21; Alain Chartier, *Epistola de puella*, in *Oeuvres latines*, ed. Pascale Bourgain-Hemerych (Paris, 1977); and the letter of Guy and André Laval in Quicherat, vol. 5, pp. 105–11.

23. Benoît, *Roman de Troie*: "armes portent por aveir pris" (we bear arms to acquire prowess), l. 23356; see also l. 24100.

24. See trial record for February 22, 1431: "And the said Jeanne answered that she was a poor Maid, knowing nothing of riding or fighting," *The Trial of Jeanne d'Arc*, ed. and trans. W.P. Barrett (1932), p. 44; Pierre Tisset and Yvonne Lanhers, eds. and trans., *Procès de condamnation de Jeanne d'Arc*, 3 vols. (Paris, 1960-71), vol. 2, pp. 47–48.

25. See Kevin Brownlee's discussion of this "radically new category of female heroism" (p. 137) in "Structures of Authority in Christine de Pizan's *Ditié de Jehanne d'Arc*," in ed. Kevin Brownlee and Walter Stephens

Discourses of Authority in Medieval and Renaissance Literature (Hanover, 1989), pp. 131–50; Stephen Nichols, "Prophetic Discourse: St. Augustine to Christine de Pizan," in *The Bible in the Middle Ages: Its Influence on Literature and Art,* ed. Bernard S. Levy (Binghamton, 1992), pp. 51–76, especially p. 69.

26. See Fraioli (n. 3 above) and more recently, Kevin Brownlee, "Cultural Comparison: Crusade as Construct in Late Medieval France," *L'esprit créateur* 32 (1992), 13–24; Nichols, p. 71.

27. H.G. Francq, "Jean Gerson's Theological Treatise and Other Memoirs in Defence of Joan of Arc," *Revue de l'Université d'Ottawa* 41 (1971), 74.

28. Jacques Gélu, *Dissertatio,* in Pierre Lanéry d'Arc, *Mémoires et consultations en faveur de Jeanne d'Arc par les juges du procès de réhabilitation* (Paris, 1889), pp. 575–76.

29. Deschamps, *Oeuvres,* vol. 9, pp. 295–96; Christine de Pizan, *Le livre de la mutacion de fortune,* ed. Suzanne Solente, 4 vols. (Paris, 1959–66), vol. 2, pp. 221–30; 263–71.

30. See Kevin J. Harty, "The Reputation of Queen Esther in the Middle Ages: The Merchant's Tale, IV [E], 1742–45," *Ball State University Forum* 19 (1978), 65–68.

31. Judith 6:19: "O Lord, God of heaven, mark their arrogance; pity our people in their humiliation; show favor this day to those who are thy own"; 9:7: "Thou seest the Assyrians assembled in their strength, proud of their horses and riders, boasting of the power of their infantry, and putting their faith in shield and javelin, bow and sling. They do not know that thou art the Lord who stamps out wars"; 9:10–11: "Shatter their pride by a woman's hand. For thy might lies not in numbers nor thy sovereign power in strong men; but thou art the God of the humble, the help of the poor, the support of the weak"; Cf. 16:6–7. Similarly, 1 Corinthians 1:27–29 states: "Yet, to shame the wise, God has chosen what the world counts folly, and to shame what is strong, God has chosen what the world counts weakness. He has chosen things low and contemptible, mere nothings, to overthrow the existing order. And so there is no place for human pride in the presence of God." References to the topos explicitly or implicitly connected to Poitiers are contained in *De quadam puella,* in Quicherat, vol. 3, pp. 411–21; *De mirabili victoria,* in Quicherat, vol. 3, pp. 298–306; Gélu, pp. 572, 579, 583–84; Florence Gragg, trans. "The Commentaries of Pius II, Book VI," *Smith College Studies in History* 35 (1951), 437–38; a thirteenth-century instance in a Judith *exemplum* can be found in J.L. Grigsby, "Miroir des bonnes femmes (suite)," *Romania* 83 (1962), 44. For a sampling of medieval examples of the topos, including references to Hrotsvitha and Hildegard, see Barbara Newman, *Sister of Wisdom: St. Hildegard's Theology of the Feminine* (Berkeley, 1987), pp. 255–57. See also Nadia Margolis, "Elegant Closures: The Use of the Diminutive in Christine de Pizan and

Jean de Meun," in *Reinterpreting Christine de Pizan,* ed. Earl J. Richards et al. (Athens, 1990), p. 113.

32. For an attempt to dispel this myth, see my article "L'origine des sources écrites et leur fonction pour *Le Ditié de Jehanne d'Arc,* de Christine de Pizan," *Bulletin de l'Association des Amis du Centre Jeanne d'Arc* 17 (1993), 5–17.

33. Christine de Pizan, *Le Ditié de Jehanne d'Arc,* ed. Angus J. Kennedy and Kenneth Varty (Oxford, 1977), ll. 86, 185–88, 198–99, 259–63, 273–74, 283–88, 312.

34. See Margolis's valuable insights in "Elegant Closures," pp. 111–23. Warner apparently does not see that Joan's natural infirmity is a source of honor, for regarding Christine's assertion that the proof of Joan's divine mission lies in her weakness, Warner writes: "It is ironical to find the principle applied by Christine, one of feminism's most outspoken voices" (p. 63).

35. Christine de Pizan, *Ditié*: "vierge tendre," l. 86; "une jeune pucelle," l. 186; "une femme—simple bergiere," l. 198; "qui donne à France la mamelle," l. 189; "avecques lui la Pucellette," l. 393.

36. The reversal this suggests from Christine's long-winded defense of Amazon strength in the *Cité des dames* is explained by the differing nature of the polemics. Christine's defense of the Amazons in the *Cité* is thorough and unflinching (reckless even, in its attempt to wash away the fault of Semiramis's incest [Richards, *Cité,* p. 40]), but it must not be elevated out of proportion to its context, which was to offer a polemical response to Boccaccio based on the feminist argument that if women had written the books they would have been of a different hue. In other words, she makes the point that women's weakness and vice are an artifact of the male misogynist literary tradition. See Christine's *Epistre au dieu d'Amours,* ll. 417–19, in *Poems of Cupid, God of Love, Christine de Pizan's 'Epistre au dieu d'Amours' and 'Dit de la Rose,' Thomas Hoccleve's 'The Letter of Cupid,'* ed. and trans. Thelma S. Fenster and Mary Carpenter Erler (Leiden, 1990), p. 54, and Richards, *Cité,* p. xxxii.

37. Régine Pernoud and Marie-Véronique Clin, *Jeanne d'Arc* (Paris, 1986), pp. 379–80.

38. Christine de Pizan, *Ditié,* p. 12.

39. In the mouth of a writer like Boccaccio, this argument (the weakness of women makes their feats all the more extraordinary) can be interpreted as antifeminist, because it stresses the additional help needed to make women succeed. This is not the case for Christine, who admires Joan inordinately, although her praise of Joan does not rule out a retort directed at Boccaccio.

40. Christine de Pizan, *Ditié*: "and I have heard of many other worthy women as well," ll. 221–22.

41. Richards, *Cité*: "And I do not think that these two ladies [Esther and Judith] are the only ones in the Holy Scriptures through whom God cared to save His people at various times, for there are plenty of others whom I am omitting for the sake of brevity, such as Deborah, whom I spoke of above, who also delivered her people from servitude," p. 147.

42. Christine de Pizan, *Ditié*, l. 217.

43. See Marcel Lecourt, "Notice sur 'L'histoire des neuf preux et des neuf preuses'," *Romania* 37 (1908), 529–37; A. Thomas, "Notes biographiques et bibliographiques sur Sébastien Mamerot," *Romania* 37 (1908), 537–39.

44. See Schroeder, pp. 183–84 and 195–96.

JOAN OF ARC'S LAST TRIAL:
THE ATTACK OF THE DEVIL'S ADVOCATES

Henry Ansgar Kelly

In Joan of Arc's s canonization trial, the Devil's Advocates made serious charges against her modesty, temperance, humility, fortitude, perseverance, and military mission. In spite of fierce rebuttals by the defense team, the jury of Consultors found much merit in the accusations, but the judges (the cardinals and pope) gave her a resounding acquittal.

Joan of Arc has been subjected to many contradictory judgments over the ages, some of which must be characterized by unprejudiced observers (like you and me) as rash, being dictated by political, religious, or ideological biases. But in this paper I will uncover clashing opinions in a forum where we would expect most of the intellectual presuppositions and leanings to be fairly uniform, namely, the papal curia, in Joan's canonization trial. Of course, the accusatory format of the trial guaranteed basic differences of opinion, and the raw material for these opinions derived from the records of similar earlier trials.

Joan was a defendant in six ecclesiastical trials. The first occurred some time after she had made her vow of virginity at the age of thirteen: she was accused in the consistory court of her local bishop of having contracted marriage with a young man and then refusing to acknowledge it.[1] Her second trial was the examination by the dauphin's allies that took place in Poitiers.[2] Then came the trials of condemnation and relapse, and next the rehabilitation or nullification trial, ending in 1456. Finally, the canonization process for Joan began in 1869 and concluded in 1920, a period of over fifty years.[3]

In our consideration of this last trial, we will begin and end *in mediis rebus*, starting with the earliest Roman phase, dealing with Joan's reputation for sanctity, which opened in 1892, and ending with the sessions debating her actual practice of saintly virtues, concluding in 1903. But first a word on the preliminaries. As noted, the formal procedures began in 1869: with a petition to Rome from Felix Dupanloup, bishop of Orleans, on May 8.[4] Far from being inspired by the Franco-Prussian War, the process was in fact delayed by it, and the first local inquisition, held in Orleans, did not open until 1874.[5] The documents that resulted during the course of the process, both in France and in Rome, are remarkable for their lack of any reference to the military and political situations of the day. We must remember that the French garrison that had been preserving Rome from the Italian Republicans for a decade was forced to withdraw on the outbreak of the war in France, leaving Pius IX the "prisoner of the Vatican." His successor, Leo XIII, elected in 1878, continued his political aims of regaining the papal states. After 1887, he tried with mixed results to make an ally of France against the Alliance powers of Germany, Austria, and Italy. Pius X, elected on August 4, 1903, took a sterner line, which led to a break in diplomatic relations with France on July 30, 1904.[6] But the combatants in the spiritual battle over Joan's fate remained above the earthly fray.

The inquisition that opened in Orleans in November 1874 lasted for thirty-three sessions, ending in January 1876. Two further inquisitions were required under Dupanloup's successor, Bishop Coullié, the first in 1885, lasting also for thirty-three sessions (June to November), and the second in 1887–88, comprising twenty-five sessions (December to February),[7] after which the cause was admitted to the tribunal of the Sacred Congregation of Rites.

FIRST DEVIL'S ADVOCATE: AUGUSTINE CAPRARA

In 1892, then, the Devil's Advocate, or, as he was officially known, the Promotor of the Faith, began his assault upon Joan by saying:

> The history of the fifteenth century has consecrated two names especially for praise, for remembrance, and for perennial attention: Christopher Columbus and Joan d'Arc, or Joan Romée, called also the Maid of Orleans. Columbus is famous because of the New World that he sought and found, and Joan because of the recovered fortunes of her native land and its restored freedom and glory. Moreover, just as Columbus did not hesitate to conquer the "dark sea" and to thrust himself into every kind of vicissitude in order to acquire new shores for the Gospel and enter into their possession "in the name of Jesus Christ," so, too, the Virgin of Arc did not fear to take up arms and

commit herself to the perils and hardships of war in order to restore the kingdom of France, at that time almost destroyed, and to consecrate it "through the hands of the dauphin to the king of heaven, who is the king of France."[8]

The Promotor, a priest named Augustine Caprara,[9] elaborates on the problems that Columbus had and the far worse troubles of Joan, who fell into the hands of her enemies and died a relapsed heretic's death at the stake.[10] His final conclusion, however, is that she was no saint and that even her admirable human virtues did not survive her last ordeal: "It seems then that two stages are to be discerned in the life of our Maid. The first was glorious and full of admiration, up to her captivity. . . . But when she was captured and subjected to judicial questions, that greatness of soul gave out, that splendor of divine revelations vanished, and grave faults are seen to have obscured the aforesaid virtues, whatever, finally, they were."[11]

In the beginning of his discourse, the Promotor admits that Joan's execution as a heretic was the result of calumnies, but he refrains at this point from condemning the church authorities who were responsible for it; rather, he gives credit to the church for setting about the process of rehabilitating her: for hardly had Pope Calixtus III ascended the Roman see when, at the request of Joan's parents and kin, he appointed apostolic judges to consider the case anew and to declare what was just. It was entirely right for the church to protect the honor of such a virgin, for, as the present Holy Father, Leo XIII, wisely wrote in his recent letter on Christopher Columbus, the church willingly approves of whatever seems honorable and praiseworthy, and, while keeping its greatest honors for those virtues that pertain to eternal salvation, it does not for this reason disdain the other kind of virtues, "for the signs of divine power also appear in those in whom there shines forth a certain excellent forcefulness of spirit and mind."[12]

Not content with these "rather narrow limits," however, Joan's modern devotees have pressed for even greater honors, those reserved for the most outstanding virtues in the realm of morals. The Promotor says:

> I would not dare to say whether any more outstanding or more difficult case ever existed in previous times. I know, certainly, that in this preliminary seat of judgment it is only a question of the fame, or the "fume," of sanctity; that is, it must be decided whether or not it flourished in the past and still flourishes. But the documents that are submitted seem to prove this very clearly: that no age has been silent

about Joan's *political* virtues, joined certainly to piety and religion, indeed also to a prophetic spirit. But it is only in our own times that one has begun to think about her possession of true and heroic virtues befitting to saints.[13]

He refers to the great work on canonization produced by a Promotor of the Faith from the previous century, Prosper Lambertini, who later became Pope Benedict XIV: he used the example of Joan of Arc to demonstrate that the gift of prophecy could exist apart from sanctity, since in Joan's case there never had been any discussion or judgment concerning her sanctity and heroic virtues.[14]

By speaking of Joan in conjunction with Columbus, and saying that he could hardly think of a more celebrated or more difficult case for canonization than hers, the Promotor was clearly inviting comparison with the recent elaborate attempts to have Columbus considered for sainthood. The formal process had begun in 1873, when Archbishop Donnet of Bordeaux officially requested the admiral's beatification; the petition was declined by the Sacred Congregation of Rites in October 1877, on grounds that the proofs for Columbus's marriage to Beatrice Enríquez de Arana, mother of his son Ferdinand, were insufficient.[15] The effort continued under Giuseppe Baldi, who was named Vice-Postulator of the cause, and he published three volumes of supporting petitions from nearly eight hundred bishops and archbishops, including even a prayer for Columbus's beatification by Pope Leo XIII himself,[16] but the cause never prospered, presumably because the opposition of the Devil's Advocate prevailed.

A similar number of episcopal testimonials had been gathered for Joan, including one from Cardinal Newman[17] (whose own cause for beatification was completed in 1991, except for a requisite miracle).[18] Promotor Caprara makes no reference to these postulatory letters, except indirectly, in alluding to the assertions of her sanctity that had only recently been forthcoming; these assertions, he adds, do not come from "probable causes."[19] That is, they are not based on historical evidence or on acceptable spiritual evidence (for instance, miracles attributed to her intercession).

Caprara proceeds to base his attack on the historical documents that the supporters for her canonization were using, namely, the full records of her trial of condemnation and her later posthumous trial of rehabilitation or nullification. He puts more faith in the records of the trials of condemnation and relapse, without, however, fully adverting to their questionable aspects. Specifically, he wants to establish that the redaction of Joan's responses into seventy articles by the judges' promotor was accurate: that is, that it corresponded truthfully to what Joan actually answered to the questions.[20]

This position was indignantly repudiated by the responding Defender, Hilary Alibrandi, an Advocate of the Congregation of Rites.[21] He rightly demonstrates that the seventy articles were not drawn primarily from her responses but were based largely on the unsubstantiated charges compiled against her before her interrogation began. Moreover, they were addressed not to her but to her judges.[22]

The portions of the records giving the responses that Joan allegedly made to interrogations, both before and after the presentation of the articles, have been generally accepted by historians with cautious confidence as accurately reflecting her words, and Promotor Caprara follows suit; he uses them to cast aspersions on her character. He shows himself critical of the inquisition begun in Orleans in 1874 and transferred to Paris without obtaining jurisdiction from the local archbishop, and he maintains that the deposition received there from De Wallon, the minister of public instruction, was invalid and should be thrown out. But he is less scrupulous about the illegality of the interrogation of Joan of Arc, and, as I have pointed out elsewhere, even Defender Alibrandi and his colleagues were not aware that a church court had no right to interrogate a defendant on anything but public crimes that had been publicly attributed to him or her.[23]

After the Promotor's first chapter, "On Proofs,"[24] he moves to his second major topic, Joan's reputation.[25] He cites Benedict XIV on the need to have a "common opinion" about the solid integrity of life and virtues of a candidate for sainthood, and he goes on to claim that up to the time of her capture she was admired for her military prowess, not for Christian virtue, and that she had no such fame for heroic virtue at the time of her rehabilitation trial.[26]

He wonders what can be considered spiritually heroic in her life. In her youth, she played games with the other little girls, and she loved to ride horses, which made her into a very strong woman. Later on, people took to giving her horses and costly clothes as gifts, and the dauphin ennobled her family. There was nothing wrong about any of this, of course, but it does not constitute heroic or even ordinary virtue.[27] She is to be praised for refusing the superstitious and almost divine honors that the people wished to bestow upon her, which, she protested, can be shown only to saints.[28] Here, Promotor Caprara seems to be admitting a common opinion about her sanctity without realizing it.

He continues: she boasted of her virginity, challenging her interrogators to have her inspected, but she was not always careful of modesty or free of imprudence, because the duc d'Alençon testified that he saw her beautiful breasts at times; nor did she keep herself from the anger that is customary with military persons, unlike holy martial figures like St. Louis and St. Ferdinand.[29]

As for her prophetic powers, and the divine mission they indicated, which her supporters claim as another *probable* indication of her reputation for sanctity, Benedict XIV has already been cited on the point that such charisms do not always go with sanctity, giving Joan as one example and Savonarola as another; furthermore, the Promotor adds, she did not always believe her voices or obey them.[30]

The third element in her holy reputation that her supporters claim for her is that of martyrdom. No one can fail to be moved at hearing of her death, the Promotor says, but the real reason she was killed, on the part of her enemies, was their rage that a woman had defeated them. On Joan's side, an incidental reason was that she had resumed male clothes to protect her modesty; but the principal reason was her constant insistence that she had been divinely sent to rescue France and her affirmation that her revelations and voices were true. Hence, some call her a martyr of modesty and a martyr of faith. But, as Benedict XIV points out, dying for a private revelation cannot be considered martyrdom. Moreover, our Heroine (*Virago nostra*) did not face death like a martyr but suffered it with great anguish and fear.[31] Finally, there is no fame of miracles.[32]

The Promotor's third and final chapter deals with obstacles to the beatification.[33] First of all, the sentence of the rehabilitation trial was not submitted to the pope or confirmed by him; furthermore, the judges did not pronounce her to be *de bono spiritu* but simply repudiated the twelve charges on which she was convicted and nullified her abjuration, without deciding anything about her virtue or sanctity.[34]

Moreover, the Promotor says, when he sees the miserable punishment that was visited upon Joan at Rouen; when he sees a cardinal of the holy church (Beaufort of Winchester), the bishop of

Beauvais (Cauchon), and many other prelates and ecclesiastical and religious men, as well as outstanding jurists and the whole faculty of the University of Paris, traduced as guilty of such a great crime (*tanti criminis reos traduci*); when especially he considers the shameful things the witnesses reported about Father Loyseleur, that he pretended to be St. Catherine and tried to get Joan to say what he wanted, and that he abused the very sanctity of the confessional in order to acquire her secrets and to persuade her to disobey the church, he seriously questions whether they should proceed further with such dishonor to the whole ecclesiastical estate. If the holy see were to add its force to her rehabilitation, what contempt can we imagine is in store for the clergy, what witticisms, especially in these times? For if the perennial enemies of the church reproached it for the ignorant censures of some clerics against Columbus, the imaginary cruelties inflicted on Galileo, and the deserved punishments visited on Bruno, what will they pour forth about the most wicked death by fire inflicted upon an innocent woman by clergymen? This was perhaps one of the reasons why the holy see, after constituting the judges of the posthumous trial of Joan, permanently refrained from passing a definitive sentence.[35]

There is a graver reason for silence. For even though she was declared innocent of the crime of heresy, and even though the judges of the rehabilitation trial admired her outstanding deeds and examples of her virtues, nevertheless, during her captivity she was gravely deficient in ways her defenders cannot excuse. First, there was her leap from the tower at Beaurevoir, which she herself admitted was wrong. She told her judges that she acted out of necessity, and she in no way repented the fault. This savors of heresy, denying free will. She was sorry only that she was injured.[36]

The Promotor will not judge whether Joan was really subject to the bishop of Beauvais's jurisdiction, but let it be admitted that she was not. She should nevertheless have followed Christ's example of submitting to an unjust judge. We need only read her responses to see how far she strayed from the footsteps of her mild Master. She refused to say the *Pater*, unless in confession; she was asked to swear several times and she refused, and when she finally obeyed she protested that she would not reveal everything to the judges. This contempt, joined with arrogance, was typical of her.[37] The Promotor may not have realized that Joan's behavior fell within the rights of a defendant in an inquisitorial trial. But if it had been pointed out to him, he would doubtless have retorted that standing on one's rights is not what one expects of a saint.

Joan did not hesitate to conceal the truth, and she came close to lying, the Promotor continues, quoting Quicherat's judgment that she did so to protect others and that she bent the truth about Charles's "angel," speaking truly only on the morning of her death. Joan's defenders try to interpret these lies as allegories, the Promotor says, but in fact, in confessing herself to be the angel, she called into question all of her revelations. He cites the argument of Theodore de Lellis, that distorting the truth because of pressure from the judges did not constitute perjury, a conclusion that the Promotor rejects.[38]

In her abjuration, she repudiated all of her visions. Her defenders excuse her as motivated by fear, but they do not dare to clear her of all blame. Let us grant that she did not understand the abjuration fully, but that does not excuse her of rashness, for she smiled contemptuously as she signed it.[39] One of the judges of her rehabilitation trial, John Brehal, the Inquisitor of France, compared her abjuration to St. Peter's denial of Christ and his subsequent affirmation of his Lord's divinity, and her modern defenders resort to the same comparison. But the Promotor does not accept their attenuations of her crime. Furthermore, on the day of her death she revoked her revocation of her abjuration. The upshot is that either Joan regarded her visions as true and gravely sinned when she retracted them out of fear; or she considered them to be false and she gravely sinned by affirming them so pertinaciously.[40]

The Promotor then raises what he calls a difficult question, whether Joan humbly submitted—or would submit—her visions and revelations to the church ("Arduam enim vero quaestionem obiici iam nobis video, utrum Ioanna suas visiones ac revelationes Ecclesiae humiliter submiserit"). He clearly believes that Joan had an obligation to submit her revelations to the church (which, of course, she did not), and he does not seem to realize that she had a right at any time to appeal her case to the pope, which the judges would have had to decide on the merits of her appeal, not on the current availability of the pope—and he seems to think that Joan would have known about the pope's difficult situation even before being told about it, since he alleges that she appealed to him only to delay the sentence. He concludes that, in his opinion, this is the main reason why Joan's cause could be prohibited from being heard in this court, since the rationalists maintain that Joan refused to submit to the church, and they hold her up as an example of freethinking. He wishes that the documents were clearer and stronger on the point. It is easier to assert than to prove that she did not understand what was meant by the term "Church Militant." The Promotor goes on to ridicule the three authorities in Joan's nullification trial who maintained that Joan was within her rights to withhold secrets in an ecclesiastical trial: William Bouillé, Robert Ciboule, and John de Montigny; he professes to consider their defense worse than Joan's opposing crime.[41] As I have shown in my essay on the right to silence, even the Defender in his reply shows that he is not aware of individuals' rights and sometimes obligations to confidentiality, which no church tribunal had the right to breach.[42]

As for Joan's boasted visions, how does one tell true from false revelations? The first criterion mentioned by the best authorities is the full and humble submission to the teaching church. The Promotor cites Benedict XIV's example of St. Teresa of Avila as one who constantly consulted with grave and prudent men about the graces and favors God bestowed on her in prayer and raptures (*raptus*). What a contrast with our Joan, who, when asked if she had ever spoken of them with her curate or any other ecclesiastical man, said no![43]

Then, the Promotor pronounces the judgment I cited above, about the two stages in Joan's life, one admirable and the other disappointing.[44] He goes on to admit that in recent times there has been a great surge of favor toward her, and that many persons, outstanding for learning and piety, have pressed for her canonization, almost—to quote her Jesuit champion Father Ayroles—to the point of imperiling the process with their enthusiasm.[45] He concludes:

> Such noble efforts of eminent men, such a universal concern for the Virgin of Arc, moves minds and urges the matter to be weighed more intimately and severely on the balances of the sanctuary, lest perhaps, as Benedict XIV writes in a very similar case, a worthy cause, acceptable to both God and man, should languish altogether neglected —especially if God be heard to invite his friend "to go higher" by means of clear signs and wonders from heaven. Therefore, that person will deserve extremely well not only of France but also of all Christendom who in our own day will bring the cause of the Maid, long suppressed or despised because of many circumstances, some

caused by human malice, some by inactivity or carelessness, into the full light of day, having dispersed the darkness of all difficulties.[46]

In so saying, Caprara seems almost to regret that he has had to bring up the obstacles he has enumerated. We should also note that, far from objecting against Joan as a national heroine, he claims her as a figure of supranational significance.

To the fifty-four pages of animadversions of the Promotor and another forty-seven pages of documents, Defender Alibrandi makes a spirited and highly detailed reply of one hundred and seventy pages; he is often sharp and sarcastic, even indignant, in his reaction to what he takes to be the slurs made by his diabolical colleague against his beloved Maid. But he finds the Promotor's conclusion much to his liking in recognizing the universal desire for her canonization. Since this stage before the tribunal concerns her fame for sanctity, the Defender says, those who urge it must be declared victors. The Judges are also to decide whether there is some evident and insuperable obstacle to her cause, and the Promotor, whom he sometimes calls "Defender of the Faith" (*Vindex Fidei*) but here addresses as "Distinguished Censor" (*Censor Amplissimus*), has confessed that there is no such obstacle, when he intimates that someone could arise to disperse all of the difficulties and bring the cause to the full light of day.[47]

In all parts of the 1893 compilation, Joan is spoken of only as "Servant of God" (*Serva Dei*), but now she has the title of "Venerable Servant of God." She was given this designation somewhat earlier along the way to canonization than was Cardinal Newman, thereafter noted above, because as yet only her fame for sanctity had been established, not her practice of heroic virtue. One might suppose that this was because Newman's cause has proceeded under new rules, for in 1983 the adversarial trial system was eliminated and the Devil's Advocate cashiered—or, rather, the Promotor of the Faith was transformed into the "Prelate Theologian."[48] But the stage at which a candidate was to be declared Venerable remained where it had been specified in the 1917 *Code of Canon Law*, namely, after the establishing of heroic virtues,[49] and, according to Kenneth Woodward, the same thing is stated in Canon Macken's 1910 volume, *The Canonization of Saints*.[50] The *Code* also positively forbids the title of Venerable to be used at the time when the introduction of the cause is accepted.[51] Must we than conclude that Joan was given the title exceptionally early? The answer is no, since Macker's account does not in fact agree with the *Code*. Rather, it matches the description of the beatification process, by Camillus Beccari, published in 1907, when Beccari was the Postulator General of Saints' Causes for the Jesuits, according to which the title of Venerable was juridically given to a Servant of God upon approval of the decree of introduction. The decision is arrived at after discussion and a vote by the Cardinals and the Officials of the Congregation, without vote or participation of Consultors.[52] Beccari's account, which must reflect the procedures in effect when Joan's case was being considered, differs substantially from that of the *Code* in other aspects as well, and I will conform to his outline in what follows.

The title of Venerable is first attributed to Joan in the decree of the Congregation of Rites approving of the introduction of her cause, "after the voice and writing of the Promotor of the Faith, Augustine Caprara, had been heard," a decree dated January 27, 1894, and signed by the pope himself on that day: "Sanctitas Sua rescriptum Sacrae ipsius Congregationis ratum habens, Commissionem Introductionis Causae Ven. Servae Dei Ioannae de Arc, Virginis, propria manu signare dignata est."[53] (This decree, by the way, makes the point that the iniquitous condemnation of Joan for heresy was pronounced by judges who were proponents of the schismatic Council of Basel,[54] which opened some six months after Joan's execution.)

Later in 1894, the Sacred Congregation of Rites published a longish history of Joan of Arc in which no whisper of blame is to be heard. For instance, in the account of the abjuration, we are told that "a small text of abjuration was read to her, according to which she was enjoined not to wear male clothing, not to bear arms, and the like" ("Tunc lecta ei est parva abiurationis schedula, qua ei iniungebatur ne virilem sumeret habitum, ne arma ferret, et alia huius generis"), which compromised her in no way.[55]

SECOND D.A.: JOHN BAPTIST LUGARI

The next records of Joan's process were published in 1901, in two volumes, both titled *Positio super virtutibus*, which I label 1901A and 1901B. The former contains two parts: first the testimony of forty-eight witnesses, dated July 6, 1898, reviewed by Alexander Verde, Subpromotor and Advocate of the Congregation,[56] and second a

Summarium additionale, with data taken from the nullification trial and other documents, mainly published by Quicherat, reviewed by Verde,[57] and a brief *Novum summarium additionale*, containing the formal request of the new Postulator, Xavier Hertzog, the current Procurator General of the Sulpicians, to the new Promotor, John Baptist Lugari, for the "compulsation" (formal authentication and submission) of the rehabilitation trial records. The Promotor first requires the Postulator to take the "oath of calumny," swearing he will act in good faith, and the Subpromotor, Verde, is present to examine all submissions for errors.[58]

In the 1901B *Positio super virtutibus*, there is first a long *Informatio* on the *dubium* in Joan's case, namely: "Is there certainty regarding the theological virtues of faith, hope, and charity toward God and neighbor and also concerning the cardinal virtues of prudence, justice, fortitude, and temperance, and associated virtues, to a heroic degree, in the matter and to the effect that is being investigated?"[59] The account is dated August 8, 1899, and signed by the Advocates John Baptist Minetti and Angel Mariani, and also by Adolph Guidi, and reviewed by Subpromotor Verde.[60] Next comes the *Animadversiones* of Promotor Lugari, dated 15 March 1901,[61] together with a packet of documents,[62] and finally the *Responsio ad Animadversiones*, dated 31 October 1901, signed by Minetti, Mariani, and Guidi.[63] Both the *Informatio* and the *Responsio* are in the first-person singular, and I take it that Minetti is the speaker.

The new Promotor divides his attack in the same way as his predecessor: after a prologue, he speaks first of proofs, then of the main subject under investigation, virtues this time rather than fame, and finally of the obstacles that he sees in the way of a positive response.[64] In the introduction, he willingly admits that Joan was a remarkable person who was moved by divine instinct to bring aid to her king and country. He, too, would rejoice if divine honors could be added to her earthly renown, but, unfortunately, it seems to him that the holy laws of the church stand in the way of such a result, and that for a number of reasons.[65]

In the first chapter, he says that the only valid proofs about the nature of Joan's virtues, so long after her lifetime, can come from historical documents. But the trial of rehabilitation was no less political than the trial of condemnation, except that it was prejudiced in her favor rather than against her. He impugns it in much the same way as his predecessor (though he makes no reference to his account).[66]

In the next chapter, he runs through the texts adduced by her supporters to prove her various virtues, and he finds all of them inadequate to the standard of the saints. Granted, she died a pious death, but, to start with the theological virtues, what was heroic about her faith? As for her possession of the virtue of hope, almost nothing is alleged, and what is said about her love of God and neighbor contains nothing remarkable. The same with the first two cardinal virtues, prudence and justice.[67]

He spends much time on the next cardinal virtue, fortitude. He admits that she suffered much but says that she did not do so willingly. One could, perhaps, speak of her tireless and unbroken fortitude in responding to her judges, but it would be more appropriate to praise her quickness of mind and wonderful memory. Moreover, since fortitude is the chief military virtue, it should be manifested especially in warlike deeds. But in Joan's case there is no testimony in support of such, and much to the contrary. When she received a slight wound, she carried on in a way unbefitting a *bellatrix*. Her fear of imprisonment was different from the attitudes of the saints of history, who positively desired to suffer out of love for God. The Promotor accepts that she was receiving genuine heavenly revelations, but he holds that she misinterpreted what her voices were telling her about being imprisoned and being released from captivity. He concludes that her saints did not speak more openly to her because of her weakness (*imbecillitas*). Therefore, she was far removed from the fortitude of the saints. He ends by telling of her fearful behavior on her death day. "Certainly, I am not one to censure these complaints, these groans of the Maid who was soon to die. For who would not be moved to pity her misery? I maintain only that she did not manifest heroic fortitude."[68]

It is surprising how little testimony there is to her temperance, the fourth cardinal virtue. On the other side, one can find testimony to her lack of the virtue: for instance, her anger toward the promotor of the trial, Estivet. Then, there is her love of luxurious clothing and gifts, much different from what is encountered in the lives of the saints. There are in fact no signs of any ascetic practices in her life. As for her chastity, it is true that she was found to be a virgin, but it was hardly consonant with modesty to boast of it and to offer her body for inspection. Sometimes, it is true, she showed prudent and necessary caution, by sleeping in her clothes when in the field with soldiers. But, Lugari adds, sometimes she acted otherwise. He brings up the duc d'Alençon's testimony again, about seeing her beautiful breasts. This was imprudent of her, and the fact that the duke did not have impure thoughts about her is attributable to the gift of God rather than to her precautions. The same is true of John d'Aulon, who could glimpse her nipples when helping her to arm or her bare legs when tending to her wounds. But the divine gift, if such it was, was not always in evidence. For, not to mention the gross attempts upon her by her captors, there was the case of the tailor who touched her breast and she had to beat him off, and the same with her familiar Raymond Macy when he would try to grope her. Finally, there is little evidence cited as to her humility, and many signs against it, such as, once again, her love of fine things.[69]

The Promotor begins his chapter on the obstacles to Joan's cause by in effect questioning the earlier decision of the Congregation that she had a sufficient reputation for sanctity over the years to be declared Venerable. He repeats Promotor Caprara's citation of Benedict XIV's characterization of Joan,[70] and he addresses Defender Alibrandi's response to it. Alibrandi maintained that Joan's gift of prophecy did in fact prove her sanctity, without considering the possibility that it proved only her divine mission. The Defender next alleged that many men saw in Benedict's words an invitation to submit her cause to the Congregation of Rites, but Lugari replies that this is hardly a probable interpretation of the pontiff's meaning. If he had meant anything of the sort, he would have spoken more clearly, as he did, for example, in the case of the martyrdom of Mary Queen of Scots. He gives Pope Benedict's laudatory history of Mary's life and his conclusion that there seemed nothing lacking in the requirements for a true martyrdom.[71]

Promotor Lugari continues: the principal obstacle to Joan's consideration for sainthood is her reliance on her own judgment in the matter of her revelations.[72] (In his response to this point, Defender Minetti spends a great deal of time showing that Joan consistently attempted to have her case removed from the prejudicial court of the bishop of Beauvais and brought to the pope.)[73] The Promotor's next animadversion is that, even though Joan has been praised for not pursuing her enemies on Sundays or holy days, she often did the contrary. He goes on to say that she was frequently lacking in due reverence toward her judges, even at Poitiers, but more so at Rouen.[74] Furthermore, she not only refused to answer her interrogating judges, she actively misled them with lies.[75] She also showed herself contemptuous of her voices, when she leaped from the tower against their prohibition, and she later admitted her sin. Should not this also stand in the way of her being offered to the faithful as a model of heroic virtue?[76] Finally, in her abjuration, she denied her divine mission. The fearful circumstances that she was in somewhat mitigate her guilt, but they do not entirely remove it. "Therefore, the Maid, in the supreme and gravest time of her life, betrayed the truth, abjuring and renouncing the mandate that she had received from God. Accordingly, even though she was a most noble heroine, even though she freed France from its enemies, even though she was pious and endowed with the most impeccable morals, still her virtues do not seem to be such as to make her worthy of being proposed by a decree of the holy see as an exemplar to be imitated by the Christian faithful."[77]

The above objections of Promotor Lugari and the response of Defender Minetti were prepared for the so-called "antepreparatory congregation," or preliminary meeting, held in the home of the Cardinal Relator, that is, the cardinal from the Congregation of Rites assigned to shepherd the cause through the juridical stages of the process, in this case, Cardinal Parocchi. Only the Consultors of the Congregation were allowed to vote.[78] According to the 1917 *Code*, the "Official Prelates" (whom I take to be the Promotor, Subpromotor, and Secretary) are also present and would seem to have the vote as well as the Consultors. Beccari states that a majority of the Consultors must decide "that the difficulties of the Promotor of the Faith have been satisfactorily solved" before the cause could proceed, whereas according to the *Code* the cause could go forward even with a negative majority, unless it amounted to two-thirds or more of those present, and even then the pope, after being informed by the Cardinal Prefect, might move it to the next stage.[79]

THIRD D.A.: ALEXANDER VERDE

The documents for the next two phases of the beatification process for Joan of Arc, the *congregatio praeparatoria* and the *congregatio generalis*, that is, the preparatory and general meetings, were both published in 1903. The first, which I label 1903A, has the overall title of *Nova positio super virtutibus.* It contains an attack against Joan by the new Promotor of the Faith, Alexander Verde, promoted from Subpromotor. His brief, titled *Novae animadversiones,* is dated April 19, 1902, and is only twenty-four pages long.[80] It is followed by the *Responsio* of the Defender, which fills three hundred and sixty-seven pages.[81] Like the previous response, it is signed by Minetti, Martini, and Guidi and cast in the singular voice, which I take to be Minetti's. Finally, there is an *Expositio virtutum,* unsigned but obviously prepared by the Defenders, of one hundred and ninety-eight pages.[82] Both second and third parts were reviewed by Subpromotor Mariani.

According to the 1917 *Code,* Promotor Verde's assignment in this stage would have been to bring up not only objections of his own but also any objections that he considered valid from the opinions of the Consultors who attended the antepreparatory session.[83] He refers to the Consultors as "P.P. AA.," that is, *Patres Amplissimi,* "Distinguished Fathers," and his short treatise gains force because it is made up largely of their adverse opinions. The Promotor even presumes to be speaking for all of the Consultors, as in his opening statement:

> The Distinguished Fathers think that this is an outstanding and noble cause, but at the same time a most grave and very difficult one, in which they recognize the great absence of proofs, because the instruments for arriving at heroic virtues in the Venerable Servant of God seem to be altogether lacking. For there are neither contemporary witnesses available concerning these virtues nor legitimate and undoubted documents; nor does tradition exist. To begin with, witnesses are lacking. For the juridical inquests are encrusted with the five centuries elapsed since the actions occurred, and therefore the witnesses clearly rely on documents and histories; for which reason they do not even seem to deserve the name of witnesses. Add to this what one of the Distinguished Fathers says: "However upstanding they are as persons, they appear to be virtually in agreement with other defenders of this cause, among whom the celebrated Father Ayroles, S.J., is the most eminent, and to be excessively affected with partiality in favor of the Venerable candidate."[84]

He cites individual Consultors to object that the witnesses at the rehabilitation trial are not pertinent, or give contradictory testimony: for instance, about Joan's resumption of male clothing after her first sentence of condemnation. Contemporary documents stress only her military virtues.[85]

The Promotor himself objects that the Patrons of the cause (referring to the Response of the most recent Defender, Minetti, and his colleagues, which he quotes) rely on newspaper accounts and stage plays to establish her virtues, whereas such sources clearly have no weight.[86] Another Consultor notes that histories show her to be pious but not a saint. Tradition is also lacking, the Promotor adds, at least concerning the deeds of a saintly woman. Of the fifty-four witnesses in one of the Orleans tribunals, nineteen testified only concerning alleged miracles, and of the others the sixteen substantial witnesses drew only on hearsay. They are witnesses only to her general fame, not to specific virtues. After citing other Consultors on the inadequacy of the trial records, the Promotor speaks for all of them: "Nor do the Distinguished Fathers, in weighing the way of life of the Servant of God, judge it to have attained to the highest path of virtue, though they willingly acknowledge her to have been a good and pious adolescent." He proves this general conclusion by citing the words of only one Consultor.[87]

Promotor Verde moves on to the subject of Joan's mission to rescue France from its enemies. Whereas the earlier Devil's Advocates, especially Lugari, willingly admitted the divinely inspired and aided nature of this mission, while denying that it proved her to be a saint, Verde suggests for the first time that perhaps all of her voices were manifestations of hysteria, and he is able to cite a skeptical Consultor to back him up: "I find it surprising," says this Distinguished Father,

> to read that only Gabriel was sent to the Most Holy Virgin to announce the incarnation of the divine Redeemer, whereas two archangels, Gabriel and Michael, appeared to Joan, and in such a way that she really saw, heard, and even touched and adored them. Who knows whether she did not suffer some hallucination and cultivated it as consonant with her own genius. Certainly, she fell short of the "simplicity of a dove" when she concealed the matter from her father and mother, lest she be prevented from her enterprise; and, if indeed she revealed it to her curate, he seemed to have doubted her, and accordingly subjected her to exorcisms.[88]

When the Defender comes to refute these statements, he attributes them, as usual, to the Promotor (or Censor, as he calls him) rather than to the cited Consultor.[89] He has just noted that Leo XIII had already declared the divine nature of her mission in his decree of 1894, and he disposes of the hysteria hypothesis by showing that her case corresponds to none of the clinical descriptions of hysteria; then he takes up Cardinal Bona's signs for the "discernment of spirits," specifically for judging whether or not visions are the vain images of a childish mind.[90] As for the Consultor's remark about Joan's angels, Minetti urges the likelihood that the Virgin Mary was in constant communication with angels, and he goes on to detail the appearance of multiple angels to many holy individuals in history.[91] Regarding those who hold that Joan deliberately refrained from revealing her experiences to her parents in order not to jeopardize her mission, he says that they offer no proof. As for her curate, he distinguishes between her own parish priest in Domrémy, who she knew would hold in confidence all that she told him in confession, and the parish priest of Vaucouleurs, who, doubtless at the suggestion of Robert of Beaudricourt, came to her in surplice and stole and carrying holy water, commanding her to depart if she was evil and to approach if good. She approached, with great humility and devotion.[92] So much for the charge that exorcisms were used against her.

The Promotor goes on to say that her victory at Orleans need not be regarded as divinely assisted, and he balks at comparing her cause to those of Old Testament heroines; for they had the divine mission of preparing for the Messiah, whereas Joan's purpose was merely to liberate France—the country that would later produce Charles VIII, who brought such evils upon Italy; it was also the country from which Francis I emerged, and from which have issued the sophistical and seditious destroyers of all disciplines and good arts, who disturb the peace of almost the entire world. Nothing, therefore, that came before or followed upon her intervention shows her to have been sent from God.[93] This is the closest that any of the opponents of Joan's sainthood come to protesting against her cause on nationalistic grounds.

But if we should wish to grant that her mission was divine, Verde continues, it is nevertheless clear how difficult it is to find virtue in a young female warrior. One of the Consultors is impressed by Benedict XIV's characterization of Joan, cited by Promotor Caprara (and also, as we have seen, by Promotor Lugari), which neither Defender Alibrandi nor the present Defender could refute. In fact, the pope seems to have been gently rebuking those who put Joan's name into private martyrologies. Another Consultor considers her not heretical, indeed, but still not proved a saint. Still another judges her pious but also with some faults of frailty, and yet another finds her sometimes timid, proud, or angry.[94] The Defenders contend that not all eminent virtues need be sought in Joan but only those most appropriate to her life as a Servant of God. It follows, therefore, that she should be outstanding in chastity and employ all means to preserve it. But, as one Consultor says, there are some things in her life not consonant with modesty and insufficiently cautious; another finds it not congruous for her to boast of her virginity and to offer to prove it.[95] Similarly, what should be more proper to a female warrior than fortitude, in which Joan often failed? One Consultor sees weakness in her, especially in her leap from the tower of Beaurevoir. Another finds the Defense unconvincing: her hardships, which were predicted by her voices, were not only not borne joyfully, but not even patiently. He thinks that her constant desire to escape, against the counsel of her voices, completely removes her from the praise of heroic fortitude. She received her sentence of death with great complaining, which takes away from the perfection of her virtue. Add that she frequently made threats against her judges. It will not do to find her of lesser merit than those heroes who think it *dulce et decorum pro patria mori* (as Horace puts it). Still another Consultor finds her strong, not heroic; upright, but not a saint. She suffered, but only because she was forced to, and received word of her condemnation with great lamentation, invoking the divine judge against her human judge. That such human emotions are altogether foreign to the fortitude of saints is passed over in silence by her Defenders.[96]

In his response to this gibe, the Defender deviates from his usual practice and identifies it as coming from one of the Consultors rather than from the Promotor: "But if you listen to the 'other Distinguished Father' telling about the death of the Venerable Maid, you would not know whether he was speaking of a Christian Virgin beloved of God or the Vergilian Sybil" (he cites the mad ravings described in the *Aeneid*). He wonders where the "noble Man" (*Vir egregius*) finds his evidence that the Venerable Maid acted thus. Certainly, the first Promotor (Augustine Caprara) did not see it this way, since he said that even her executioner and bitter enemies were moved to wonder at her fortitude and piety in her last struggles.[97]

Moving on to Joan's lack of humility, the Promotor cites another Consultor, who believes that not enough has been made of the objections about Joan's love of luxurious clothing, her horses, and so on, and the not always humble way in which she dealt with her judges. It all shows an attitude much different from that of the saints. Two other Consultors complain of her lies or dissimulations, especially regarding her sign, and another is disturbed about her repeated refusals to submit to the church.[98]

So there are not only moral failings and a virtual absence of heroic virtue but also definite obstacles standing in the way of a positive decision, and the Consultors are surprised that the demand of the previous Promotor (Lugari) has not been answered, that a systematic list of her heroic virtues be produced. Promotor Verde cites two Consultors to this effect and adds his own view that the Defenders were not able to respond, and that it was presumably for this reason that Father Ayroles tried to make her out to be a martyr, in which case there would be no need to establish heroic virtue. He cites the requests of other Consultors for an organized layout of virtues accompanied with proof-texts, ending with one who speculates that if there had been an inquiry into her life shortly after her death, other obstacles might have come to light. The same Consultor concludes that her divine mission is not relevant, and once it is removed, he does not see what is left.[99]

The Promotor claims that the same is true for "the remaining Distinguished Fathers," who are concerned about the other objections that have been raised, especially her attempt to flee from the tower of Beaurevoir, against the will of her voices. No one can deny that she showed some weakness in thus trying to escape. Her defenders invented reasons, that she wanted to preserve her chastity and to bring aid to the citizens of Compiègne, but they could cite no evidence. Verde gives the words of one Consultor but says that the objections of the others (*reliqui*) are no less grave and severe, and he proceeds to cite the views of another, who finds her action not only one of disobedience but also a tempting of God. If one were to contend that the voices were only offering a counsel rather than making a command, another Consultor says, those especially favored by God cannot disregard heavenly counsels without at least some sin. Still another Consultor finds her rash as well as disobedient.[100]

Finally, the Promotor offers a number of Consultor objections concerning Joan's abjuration. The mildest of the objections is that the circumstances are not entirely clear and more light needs to be thrown on the point, but five other Consultors are more censorious: there is no doubt about the fact that she signed a retraction; true, she did nothing against the Faith, but she failed in heroic fortitude; it was hardly a light matter, since she so bitterly repented of it; after such long resistence, she should not have signed even to save her life; if the early Christians had done so, how could they have been considered martyrs? Repudiating her divine mission because of fear cannot be excused. This failing and her other faults make it impossible to conclude that the virtues of the Venerable Servant of God attained the heroic degree.[101]

The Promotor agrees, and he concludes with the words of two other *Patres Amplissimi*. One says that there still seem to be grave obstacles, and the other, no less gravely, declares:

> I persuade myself that one can never sufficiently condemn the unjust, even impious condemnation of the Venerable Joan of Arc, and, accordingly, one can never rejoice too much over the very thorough trial of rehabilitation that ensued. But from this it follows, in my humble opinion, only that the Venerable Maid can be proclaimed as admirable above measure and endowed with singular gifts, admired as a very chaste virgin and dear to God, and praised to the stars as the liberator of France, with deeds inspired by God Himself. But she cannot, at least not on the basis of evidence thus far adduced, be declared a saint, that is, one who practiced the virtues in a heroic degree.[102]

The fact that Promotor Verde was able to cite a substantial number of the Consultors on the antepreparatory panel with serious objections against Joan's advance to sainthood shows that his exercise was by no means entirely academic and routine. The massive response of Minetti and his colleagues must have done much to defuse these objections, but there was still a requirement for a final volley of doubts.

Minetti's response to Verde's attack of April 19, 1902 is dated February 12, 1903.[103] The preparatory meeting for which it was composed was to be attended by the Cardinals of the Congregation, chaired by the Cardinal Prefect, but, once again, only the Consultors were allowed to vote[104] (in contrast to the 1917 *Code*, according to which only the Cardinals voted, after hearing the new opinions of the Consultors present and any clarifications by the Secretary and Promotor).[105] The cause was clearly approved with dispatch, and a *Novissima positio* had to be prepared for a general meeting of the Congregation, presided over by the pope, with both Cardinals and Consultors voting[106] (according to the 1917 rules, judgment was to be reserved to the pope alone, after an advisory vote of the Cardinals, Official Prelates, and Consultors).[107]

The 1903B volume, *Novissima positio super virtutibus*, contains not only Verde's brief *Novissimae animadversiones*, dated May 9, 1903,[108] and the Minetti-Martini-Guidi *Responsio*, dated June 12, 1903,[109] but, to begin with, a brief *relatio* by the current Relator, Cardinal Ferrata.[110] Ferrata tells us among other things that there had been quite a mortality rate among his predecessors. Cardinal Bilio was first appointed as Relator, or *Ponens*, in 1876, and, on his death, an Englishman, Cardinal Howard, took his place, in January 1886. When Howard "departed from among the living," he was replaced on April 28, 1890 by Cardinal Parocchi. (Actually, Howard had only departed from living among the Italians. He took ill in 1887 and was brought to England in the spring of 1888; he died only in 1892, on September 16.)[111] Cardinal Ferrata was appointed on January 23, 1903, and the preparatory meeting, at which the *Nova positio* was discussed, was held on the following March 17.

Verde begins his *Novissimae animadversiones* by saying that more caution is needed in this sacred forum. He disputes the Defender's characterization of the nature and sufficiency of purely historical documents, adding similar doubts by the Consultors.[112] The last Consultor cited goes on to allege that the winesses to be found in the historical documents concerning Joan stress mainly her military virtues, a theme sounded in the previous exchanges, and another Consultor is cited to similar effect; the latter goes on specifically to question her heroic chastity, disturbed, like others before him, by the duc d'Alençon's report about seeing Joan's beautiful breasts. Moreover, she was *fortis* only when events were favorable, but timid in adversity. What about her flight from the tower, which was contrary to her divine voices, whatever the Defense says? And her abjuration? What of the fear and trembling in her final agony? One should forgive such behavior in a weak woman, but in a heroic woman, no way (*nullo modo*). Another Consultor has doubts about her divine mission; he will believe it only if she is first proved to be a saint.[113]

The Promotor himself disputes the Defender's response about the tower episode. If the articles of the condemnation trial were repudiated at the rehabilitation trial, the sentence of the latter tribunal was never confirmed by the pope; moreover, the facts are established not just from the articles but from Joan's own responses in the body of the trial record. Cauchon could not have so thoroughly tampered with the record as to produce such a consistent falsification. He in fact would have preferred to show her obeying her voices, as coming from the devil. The rehabilitation witnesses do not correct the account of the incident, and their silence confirms it; moreover, all contemporary documents support it, including the Cordeliers Chronicle.[114]

Minetti replies that the only rehabilitation witness who knew about the contents of the condemnation records was Courcelles, who wrote them at Cauchon's direction.[115] Moreover, the Cordeliers Chronicle is the only relevant contemporary document, and it clearly indicates that she did not leap from the tower but rather tried to escape by lowering herself on a rope, which broke and caused her to fall.[116]

As for the abjuration, Verde's predecessor Lugari cited nine witnesses who said that Joan signed some form of recantation. Verde now cites the formula reconstructed by the celebrated Canon Dunand in his *L'abjuration du Cimitière Saint-Ouen*, published at Paris in 1901, which includes the admission that she had committed *lèse-majesté* and seduced the people (p. 152), which in effect was a denial of her divine mission.[117] The Defender replies by showing how tenuous was the basis for that part of Dunand's formula, and by citing another book published by the same author in the following year, *Le problème de l'abjuration de Jeanne d'Arc et les derniers Congrès des Sociétés Savants*, in which he omits these words from the formula.[118]

The Promotor concludes by agreeing with the stong opinion of a Consultor, that at the time of her death Joan receded from the fortitude that she had shown earlier in her life. No one will say that one who behaves in such a way should be proposed as an example for others to imitate, and it is only on such persons that the honors of the altar are to be bestowed in this forum.[119]

The result of the three rounds of debate on the virtues of Joan of Arc was much the same that the Congregation had arrived at in its 1894 synopsis of her life, after dismissing the objections of the first Devil's Advocate. But, as we have seen, it was not without a great deal of soul searching, not only on the part of the two following Devil's Advocates, who had a professional stake in being contrary, but also on the part of the Consultors assigned to the case, who can be thought to have had some genuine concerns. We may not think much of some of these concerns—for instance, their unwillingness to admit of any lapses in persons of genuine holiness or their straitlaced ideals of feminine modesty. But it is gratifying to see that more generous spirits prevailed in the face of persistently repeated objections from functionaries who, it was decided, were living up to their reputation of supporting the devil more than promoting the Faith.

The general meeting of the Sacred Congregation of Rites at which the *Novissima positio* was debated was held on November 15, 1903, presided over by the new pope, Pius X. After the Cardinals and the Consultors voted, Pius postponed making a decision and asked all present to pray for divine light in so difficult a matter. He would make similar statements in subsequent beatification cases,[120] though he seems more concerned in this case than in the others to request prayers from the judges of the tribunal. His decision was formally announced on the Feast of the Epiphany, January 6, 1904, which was also the birthday of Joan of Arc. He summoned to his side Cardinal Cretoni, Prefect of the Congregation, Cardinal Ferrata, the Relator of the Cause, Promotor Verde, and Secretary Panici, and solemnly announced that Joan's practice of all the virtues in a heroic degree was established, and he authorized the move to the next stage, the discussion of four miracles.[121] In the event, three miracles were approved for her beatification, in a meeting held on January 12, 1909, and after another delay for prayerful consideration Pope Pius announced, in the presence of the same four dignitaries, on the following January 24, that she could proceed to beatification.[122] In the actual decree of beatification issued on April 11, 1909, the pope revealed that the vote of the Cardinals and Consultors on January 12 was unanimous.[123] One can only conjecture whether the Devil's Advocate also concurred.

NOTES

1. The marriage seems to have been arranged by her parents; see Pierre Tisset, ed., with Yvonne Lanhers, *Procès de condamnation de Jeanne d'Arc*, 3 vols. (Paris, 1960–71), vol. 1, pp. 123, 127. Joan may have been charged with having given not only future but present consent (i.e., actually

marrying the boy), though actions to enforce mere betrothals seem to have been common in France; see Charles Donahue, "The Canon Law on the Formation of Marriage and Social Practice in the Late Middle Ages," *Journal of Family Practice* 8 (1983), 144–58, esp. 150, 154, contrary to English practice: see R.H. Helmholz, *Marriage Litigation in Medieval England* (Cambridge, 1974), pp. 35–36, especially n. 37.

2. See Charles T. Wood's essay in this volume.

3. A complete set of the beatification and canonization proceedings of Joan of Arc is to be found in Cardinal John Wright's Joan of Arc collection in the Boston Public Library, Bishop Cheverus Room. A copy of the 1893 volume described in n. 8 is also to be found at Harvard.

4. For the French text, see A. Mouchard, *Les fêtes de la béatification de Jeanne d'Arc, Rome-Orléans-la France (1909): souvenirs et documents* (Paris, n.d.), pp. 25–26. Copies of this book are in Cardinal Wright's collection (see previous note) and in the Library of Congress.

5. Ibid., p. 27.

6. A brief account of such matters can be found in J.N.D. Kelly, *The Oxford Dictionary of Popes* (Oxford, 1986), pp. 309–14.

7. Mouchard, p. 29.

8. *Sacra Rituum Congregatione, eminentissimo ac reverendissimo domino Cardinale Lucido Maria Parocchi Relatore: Aurelianen.: Beatificationis et canonizationis Servae Dei Ioannae de Arc, Puellae Aurelianensis nuncupatae, Positio super introductione causae* (Rome: Typis S. C. de Propaganda Fide, 1893) [hereafter referred to as *SRC* (1893)], part 5 (= fifth pagination): *Animadversiones reverendi patris domini Promotoris Fidei super dubio, An sit signanda commissio introductionis causae, in casu et ad effectum de quo agitur?*, pp. 1-2, §1: "Due praecipue nomina ad laudem, ad memoriam, ac perennitatem historia saeculi XV consecravit: Christophori Columbi, et Ioannae d'Arc, seu Romee, quae Aurelianensis puella etiam nuncupatur. Celebris ille namque propter novum ab se quaesitum repertumque Orbem: haec ob restitutas patriae sortes, adsertamque libertatem et gloriam. Accedit: quemadmodum Columbus *tenebrosum mare* conquirere, seseque omnigenis obiicere casibus non dubitavit, ut novas oras Evangelio acquireret, earumque possessionem *in nomine Iesu Christi* iniret; ita Darciensis virgo arma sumere, seseque bellorum periculis laboribusque committere non timuit, ut Galliae regnum tunc prope eversum restitueret, illudque consecraret, *per manus Delphini, caelorum regi, qui est Rex Franciae.*"

The parts of *SRC* (1893) are:

> Part 1: *Informatio super dubio, An sit signanda*, etc., by John Baptist Minetti, 76 pp., reviewed by Subpromotor Gustave Persiani.
>
> Part 2: *Summarium super dubio, An sit signanda*, etc., 212 pp., reviewed by Subpromotor Augustine Caprara. (This must be of an earlier date than part 1, since Persiani succeeded Caprara as Subpromotor when the latter became Promotor.)

Part 3: *Summarium additionale: Excerptum ex processu Aureliae condito anno 1885, super dubio, An sit signanda,* etc., 401 pp., reviewed by Subpromotor Persiani.
Part 4: *Summarium additionale novissimum super dubio, An sit signanda,* etc., 11 pp., reviewed by Subpromotor Persiani.
Part 5: *Animadversiones r. p. d. Promotoris ,* as above, 101 pp.
Part 6: *Responsio ad Animadversiones Promotoris Fidei super dubio, An sit signanda,* etc., 170 pp., signed by Hilary Alibrandi and John Baptist Minetti, reviewed by Subpromotor Persiani.

9. He signs himself as "Augustinus Caprara, S. C. Adv. s. [that is, Advocate of the Sacred Congregation of Rites] Fidei Promotor," 5:54; he signed his review of part 2 as "Augustinus Adv. Caprara S. R. C. Assessor et S. Fidei Sub-Promotor" (p. 212). He appends to his *Animadversiones* a series of longer proof-documents, called *Summarium obiectionale* (pp. 55–101), to which he refers as appropriate in the body of his discourse.

10. Promotor Caprara, *SRC* (1893), 5:2, §2.

11. Ibid., pp. 52–53, § 70: "Duo ergo stadia in puellae nostrae vita secernenda videntur; primum gloriosum, et admiratione plenum, usque ad suam captivitatem. . . . At, ubi capta illa fuit, et iudicialibus quaestionibus subiecta, defecit ea animi magnitudo, splendor ille divinarum revelationum disparuit, ac praegressas virtutes, quaecumque demum eae fuerint, graves culpae obscurasse visae sunt."

12. Ibid., pp. 2–3, §3, quoting Leo XIII's encyclical on the Columbus Quadricentennial, *Quarto abeunte saeculo,* July 16, 1892, *Acta Sanctae Sedis* 25 (1892–93), 3-7.

13. *SCR* (1893), 5:4, §5: "Hisce instructa praesidiis tandem Causa Darciensis Virginis Sacri huius Fori limen attingit: qua utrum anteactis temporibus alia praestantior simul ac diffficilior extiterit affirmare non ausim. Novi quidem in hac praeliminari iudicii Sede nonnisi de Fama, seu de *fumo* sanctitatis agi: utrum scilicet ea nec ne viguerit ac in praesens vigeat disceptandum esse. At documenta ipsa, quae in medium afferuntur, hoc probare apertissime videntur: de Iohannae *politicis* virtutibus, pietati utique ac religioni, immo prophetico etiam spiritui coniunctis, nullam aetatem conticuisse; de veris tamen heroicisque illius virtutibus, prouti Sanctos decet, nonnisi aetate nostra cogitari coeptum esse."

14. Ibid. See *Benedicti XIV, pont. opt. max., olim Prosperi cardinalis de Lambertinis, Opus de servorum Dei beatificatione et beatorum canonizatione* 3.45.9 (Prato, 1839–42, 7 vols.), 3:526: after giving a very favorable account of her life, Lambertini concludes: "Cum tamen de puellae sanctitate et heroicis virtutibus nunquam factus sit sermo, nedum judicium de eis prolatum, hinc inferre licet, prophetiae donum posse a sanctitate esse sejunctum." Caprara cites Lambertini's treatment more fully later, pp. 20–23, §29.

15. See "Colón (Cristóbal)," *Enciclopedia universal ilustrada* (n.d., but published shortly after 1907), vol. 14, pp. 196–243, especially 232.

16. Giuseppe di G.B. Baldi, *La glorificazione del genio cattolico: Sentimenti dell' episcopato ed una postulazione inedita di monsignor Rocco Cocchia, arcivescovo delegato e vicario apostolico a Sua Santità, il sommo pontefice Leone XIII, per la causa di beatificazione dell' incomparabile servo di Dio Cristoforo Colombo* (Genoa, 1879); *Il voto dell' episcopato cattolico per la glorificazione del genio cristiano: Adesioni episcopali alla causa del servo di Dio, Cristoforo Colombo, aggiuntavi una lettera del conte Roselly de Lorgues ed altre testimonianze della cattolica stampa: Seconda raccolta di documenti* (Genoa, 1880); *Cristoforo Colombo glorificato dal voto dell' episcopato cattolico: Terza raccolta di documenti . . . aggiuntovi un articolo del conte Roselly de Lorgues sull' opportunità della causa* (Genoa, 1881). All three of these volumes are in the Library of the University of Michigan. The prayer of Leo XIII is given in the final volume, p. 128. See also Antoine François Félix Roselly de Lorgues, *Histoire posthume de Christophe Colomb* (Paris, 1885), pp. 376-452. Baldi's pamphlet, *Degli avviamenti alla causa di beatificazione di Cristoforo Colombo* (Genoa, 1877; also at the University of Michigan), announces his intention of publishing the results of agitation for Columbus's canonization, in which he gives the place of honor to the sentiments expressed by the celebrated bishop of Orleans, Felix Dupanloup, in a letter written on September 12, 1866 (pp. 12-13).

17. Cardinal Newman, *SRC* (1893), 3:358-59. Only a few of the letters are to be found in the printed file. Newman's letter, like most of the others, is undated, but the dates that are given range from 1879 (p. 357) to 1889 (p. 379).

18. He is therefore entitled to be called "Venerable." See the article by the postulator of his cause, Vincent Ferrer Blehl, "Where Does Cardinal Newman's Cause Stand?" *America* (September 25, 1993), 15-17, and his earlier article, "Prelude to the Making of a Saint," *America* (March 11, 1989). See also Kenneth L. Woodward, *Making Saints: How the Catholic Church Determines Who Becomes a Saint, Who Doesn't, and Why* (New York, 1990), pp. 355-73.

19. Promotor Caprara, *SRC* (1893), 5:4, §5.

20. Ibid., pp.5-7, §§ 7-10.

21. Defender Alibrandi, *SRC* (1893), 6:9-19, §§ 14-30. The Response is "signed" by Hilarius Alibrandi S.C. Adv. and by Iohannes Baptista Minetti, but the first person singular is used throughout (see, e.g., p. 2, §§2-4, and p. 154, § 273), and Alibrandi is repeatedly identified as the author in subsequent exchanges. According to the account of Camillus Beccari, "Beatification and Canonization," in *The Catholic Encyclopedia*, 2(1907), 364-69, each candidate for sainthood has an Advocate of the Cause, whom I take to be Alibrandi, and a Procurator (Proctor) of the Cause, presumably Minetti. Minetti was the author of part 1: *Informatio super dubio, An sit signanda commisio*, etc. As we will see below, Minetti, now an Advocate, is

listed first in the signatures to the Response to the next Promotor (*SRC* [1901B], 4:206), which is also couched in the first person singular.

22. See my account, "The Right to Remain Silent: Before and After Joan of Arc," *Speculum* 68 (1993), 992–1020, especially 1019. Alibrandi was a celebrated professor of ancient Roman law, who had been an advocate for saints' causes since 1863; see E. Volterra, "Alibrandi, Ilario," in *Dizionario biografico degli Italiani* (1960), vol.2, pp. 370–71. He had in fact been appointed by Bishop Dupanloup as Joan's Defender at the end of the first process held in Orleans in 1874–76, but, after Dupanloup's death in 1878, he resigned, exhausted from his labors in what he foresaw would be a strenuous enterprise. His replacement, Lauri, was promoted to the ranks of the opposition, being appointed Devil's Advocate, and his successor as Defender, the poet and artist Tosti, died in the midst of his labors (Mouchard, pp. 27–28), whereupon the task was taken up by Alibrandi once more.

23. Kelly, "Right to Remain Silent," p. 1023.

24. Promotor Caprara, *SRC* (1893), 5, chap. 1, "De probationibus," pp. 5–11, §§6–15.

25. Ibid., chap. 2, "De fama," pp. 12–28, §§16–39.

26. Ibid., pp. 12–14, §§16–19.

27. Ibid., pp. 15–18, §§21–24bis.

28. Ibid., p. 18, §24bis: "Laudanda quidem, quod superstitiosos ac pene divinos sibi a plebe tributos honores declinaret, ac nonnisi Sanctis eos adhiberi posse protestaretur."

29. Ibid., pp. 19–20, §§25–27.

30. Ibid., pp. 20–24, §§28–32.

31. Ibid., pp. 26–27, §§35–37.

32. Ibid., pp. 27–28, §§38–39.

33. Ibid., chap. 3, "De obstaculis," pp. 28–54, §§40–72.

34. Ibid., pp. 28–29, §40.

35. Ibid., p. 30, §42.

36. Ibid., pp. 31–32, §§43–44. The episode of Joan's attempted escape from Beaurevoir will be returned to several times below.

37. Ibid., pp. 32–33, §45.

38. Ibid., pp. 33–35, §§46–49.

39. Ibid., pp. 35–37, §§50–51.

40. Ibid., pp. 37–40, §§51–55.

41. Ibid., pp. 41–46, §§57–63.

42. Kelly, "Right to Remain Silent," pp. 1022–23.

43. Promotor Caprara, *SRC* (1893), 5: 51–52, §68–69.

44. Ibid., pp. 52–53, §70.

45. Ibid., p. 53, §71.

46. Ibid., p. 54, §72: "Tam nobiles praestantium virorum conatus, adeo universale in Darciensem virginem studium, commovent animos, ac

rem intimius ac severius ad sanctuarii lancem perpendere suadent, ne forte, uti persimili in thesi scribit Benedictus XIV, causam Dei et hominum iudicio promoveri dignam iacere omnino et perpetuo derelictam manere contingat; praesertim si claris de caelo signis et prodigiis, Deus amicam suam ut superius ascendat invitare audiatur. Optime itaque non de Gallia tantum, sed universim de re christiana ille merebitur, qui Puellae causam, per tot vicissitudines hominum partim malitia, partim desidia et incuria sive oppressam, sive despectam, aetate demum nostra, disiectis omnino difficultatum tenebris, ad plenam meridiem adducat."

47. *SRC* (1893), 6:170, §307.

48. See Woodward, pp. 90–91.

49. *Codex iuris canonici*, (Rome 1922) canon 2115.

50. Woodward, pp. 77, 83, citing Thomas F. Macken, *The Canonisation of Saints* (Dublin 1910). Woodward recommends Macken's book for those who cannot read the Latin of the *Code*.

51. *Codex iuris canonici*, canon 2084.

52. Camillus Beccari, "Beatification and Canonization" (see n. 28 above), p. 367; Macken, pp. 37, 4–42, 133.

53. "AURELIANEN. Decretum Beatificationis et Canonizationis ven. Servae Dei Ioannae de Arc virginis aurelianensis puellae nuncupatae," *Acta Sanctae Sedis* 26 (1893–94), 500–03. A grammatical note: since *Sanctitas* is feminine, we would have to render the action by saying that "the Holiness of the Pope deigned to sign with *her* own hand," if we wished to follow gender of the original, or "*its* own hand," if we make it neuter. The use of the regal and papal plural in Latin causes similar grammatical awkwardnesses.

54. Ibid., p. 501.

55. "AURELIANEN. Beatificationis et canonizationis Ven. Servae Dei Ioannae de Arco. Synopsis vitae," *Acta Sanctae Sedis* 27 (1894–95), 488–510, especially 504. No date is given; but the document of the Congregation immediately preceeding is dated August 11, 1894, and others before it have the date of September 1, 1894. The document immediately following the "Synopsis vitae" is dated January 29, 1895.

56. *SRC* (1901A), part 1; p. 1 is missing from my copy, but it doubtless carried the title *Summarium super dubio, An constet*, etc. (as below). The introductory letter is signed on p. 2 by the Substitute Secretary, Philip di Fava, and dated July 6, 1898. At the end, p. 527, "Alexander Adv. Verde, S.R.C. Assessor et S. Fidei Subpromotor" indicates that he has reviewed the material.

57. *SRC* (1901A), 2:1–169.

58. *SRC* (1901A), 2:171–75. The original Postulator, appointed by Bishop Dupanloup in 1876, was Albert Jules Captier (Mouchard, p. 27), Hertzog's predecessor as Procurator General of the Sulpician Order.

59. *SRC* (1901B), 1: *Informatio super dubio, An constet de virtutibus theologalibus fide, spe, et caritate in Deum et proximum; nec non de cardinalibus prudentia, iustitia, fortitudine, ac temperantia, earumque adnexis, in gradu heroico, in casu et ad effectum de quo agitur?*

60. Ibid., p. 110.

61. Promotor Lugari, *SRC* (1901B), 2: *Animadversiones r.p.d. Promotoris Fidei super dubio, An constet de virtutibus*, etc., pp. 1–60.

62. Promotor Lugari, *SRC* (1901B), 3: *Summarium obiectionale*, pp. 1–28.

63. Defender Minetti, *SRC* (1901B), 4: *Responsio ad Animadversiones …super dubio, An constet*, etc., pp. 1–206.

64. Promotor Lugari, *SRC* (1901B), 2: *Animadversiones*, chap. 1, "De probationibus," pp. 2–7; chap. 2, "De virtutibus," pp. 7–27; chap. 3, "De obstaculis," pp. 27–60.

65. Ibid., pp. 1–2, §1.

66. Ibid., pp. 2–7, §§2–10.

67. Ibid., pp. 7–15, §§11–24.

68. Ibid., pp. 15–20, §§25–37. The last passage reads: "Profecto non is sum ego, qui has querelas, hos gemitus mox moriturae Puellae exprobrem. Quis enim misellae misericordia non teneatur? Id unum contendo, eam heroicam fortitudinem non ostendisse."

69. Ibid., pp. 20–27, §§38–49.

70. Ibid., pp. 27–30, §§51–54

71. Ibid., pp. 30–32, §§55–57, citing Benedict XIV, *Opus* 3.13.10 (3:119). Benedict also publishes, for the first time, he believes, the letter that Mary wrote to Pius V just before she died, which he discovered in the Castel Sant' Angelo and translated from French into Latin (3:617–19).

72. Promotor Lugari, *SRC* (1901B), 2:33–41, §§59–71.

73. Defender Minetti, *SRC* (1901B), 4:130–47.

74. Promotor Lugari, *SRC* (1901B), 2:41–47, §§72–80.

75. Ibid., pp. 47–53, §§81–86.

76. Ibid., pp. 53–56, §§87–90.

77. Ibid., pp. 56–60, §§91–95. The final passage reads: "Ergo Puella in supremo gravissimoque vitae suae tempore veritatem prodidit, divinitus receptum madatum ejuravit atque abnegavit. Quamvis igitur nobilissima virago ipsa fuerit, quamvis ab hostibus Galliam liberaverit, quamvis pia fuerit atque innocentissimis moribus praedita; attamen eius virtutes tales non fuisse videntur, quibus digna sit quae exemplar christifidelibus imitandum, Apostolicae Sedis decreto, proponatur."

78. Beccari, "Beatification," p. 368.

79. *Codex iuris canonici*, canons 2105–07.

80. Promotor Verde, *SRC* (1903A), 1: *Novae animadversiones r.p.d. Promotoris Fidei super dubio, An constet de virtutibus*, etc.

81. Defender Minetti, *SRC* (1903A), 2: *Responsio ad Novas animadversiones*, etc.

82. Ibid., 3: *Expositio virtutum.* It is preceded by a table of contents.

83. *Codex iuris canonici*, canons 2108-09.

84. Promotor Verde, *SRC* (1903A), 1:1-2, §1: "Conspicuam sane et nobilem causam agi AA. PP. arbitrantur, eamdem vero gravem admodum perarduamque: in qua nempe magnam agnoscunt inopiam probationum, quum instrumenta quibus Ven. Famulae Dei conficiantur heroicae virtutes omnino deesse videantur. Nec enim de his virtutibus aequales testes praesto sunt, nec legitima et comperta documenta, nec traditio. Testes quidem desunt: nam ornatae sunt iuridicae quaestiones quinque saeculis postquam actae res erant, proptereaque testes documentis et historiis plane innituntur: quare ne testium quidem nomine videntur decorandi. Adde quod ipsi, ut quidam e PP. AA. numero ait, 'quamvis spectatissimi sint, apparent et ipsi veluti totidem alii causae huius vindices, quos inter eminet cl. p. Ayroles S. I., et a nimis studio partium abrepti videntur favore Venerabilis.'"

85. Ibid., pp. 2-3, §§2-5.

86. Ibid., pp. 3-4, §6, citing Defender Minetti, *SRC* (1901B), 4:3.

87. Promotor Verde, *SRC* (1903A), 1:4-7, §§7-13. The quoted text reads (pp. 6-7, §13): "Nec vero vivendi rationem Ancillae Dei PP. AA. perpendentes, quamvis eam bonam piamque adolescentem ultro fatentur, censent tamen ad summum virtutum fastigium eamdem prevenisse."

88. Ibid., p. 7, §§14-15; the quoted text reads (§15): "Dicam enim verbis cuiusdam P. A.: 'Miror quod cum pro annuncianda Sanctissimae Virginis Redemptoris divini incarnatione solus Gabriel missus legatur, Ioannae et Gabriel et Michael Archangeli apparuerint, et ita ut eos ipsa realiter viderit, audierit, imo et tetigerit et adoraverit. Quis scit, eam passam non fuisse quandam hallucinationem, talemque coluisse, utpote suo consonam genio? Certe, citra columbae simplicitatem, ne a proposito impediretur, patri et matri rem occultavit, et, si quidem in confessione curato indicavit, ipsi dubitasse videtur, ex quo exorcismis eam subiecit.'"

89. Defender Minetti, *Ad Novas, SRC* (1903A), 2:109.

90. Ibid., pp. 98-109.

91. Ibid., pp. 109-15.

92. Ibid., pp. 116-17.

93. Promotor Verde, *Novae, SRC* (1903A), 1:7-8, §§16-17.

94. Ibid., pp. 8-10, §§18-21.

95. Ibid., pp. 10-11, §22.

96. Ibid., pp. 11-13, §§23-24.

97. Defender Minetti, *Ad Novas, SRC* (1903A), 2:169, citing *Aeneid* 6.45 and Promotor Caprara, *SRC* (1893), 5:26, §35.

98. Promotor Verde, *SRC* (1903A), 1:13-15, §§25-27.

99. Ibid., pp. 15-18, §§28-32.

100. Ibid., pp. 18-20, §§33-36.

101. Ibid, pp. 20–23, §§37–42.

102. Ibid., pp. 23–24, §43: "Nec minus graviter alius P. A.: 'Mihi suadeo,' ait, 'numquam satis reprobandam esse iniustam, imo impiam Ven. Ioannae d'Arc condemnationem; unde nec satis laetandum de ipsius rehabilitationis processu amplissimo. Ex iis tamen tantummodo (meo humili iudicio) sequitur, admirabilem supra modum Ven. Puellam, singularibus ditatam dotibus, praedicari posse: virginem pudicissimam Deoque caram admirari, Galliae liberatricem, operibus ab ipso Deo inspiratis, ad astra laudibus attolli; sanctam vero, idest quae virtutes in gradu heroico exercuerit, saltem ex adductis usque nunc, minime proclamari posse.'"

103. Defender Minetti, *Ad Novas, SRC* (1903A), 2:367.

104. Beccari, "Beatification," p. 168.

105. *Codex iuris canonici*, canons 2108–10.

106. Beccari, loc. cit.

107. *Codex iuris canonici*, canons 2112–14.

108. Promotor Verde, *SRC* (1903B), 2: *Novissimae animadversiones r. p. d. Promotoris Fidei super Dubio, An constet de virtutibus*, etc., 16 pages.

109. Defender Minetti, *SRC* (1903B), 3: *Responsio ad Novissimas animadversiones r. p. d. Promotoris Fidei super Dubio, An constet de virtutibus*, etc., 102 pages.

110. Relator Ferrata, *SRC* (1903B), 1: *Factum concordatum*, pp. 3–7.

111. "Howard, Edward Henry (1829–1892)," in *Dictionary of National Biography*, suppl. vol. 1 (1901), repr. as vol. 22 (Oxford, 1921–22), pp. 874–75; p. 2431 of the *Compact Edition* (Oxford 1975).

112. Promotor Verde, *Novissimae, SRC* (1903B), 2:1–9, §§1–18

113. Ibid., pp. 9–10, §§19–23.

114. Ibid., pp. 10–13, §§24–30.

115. Defender Minetti, *Ad Novissimas, SRC* (1903B), 3:72–74.

116. Ibid., pp. 65, 74–76.

117. Promotor Verde, *Novissimae, SRC* (1903B), 2:15, §§35–36.

118. Defender Minetti, *Ad Novissimas, SRC* (1903B), 3:86–88.

119. Promotor Verde, *Novissimae, SRC* (1903B), 2:16, §37.

120. See, for instance, *Acta Sanctae Sedis* 36 (1903–04), 495, 623, 631, 693, 696.

121. "Decretum Beatificationis et Canonizationis Venerabilis Servae Dei Ioannae D'Arc, Virginis, vulgo dictae puellae Aurelianen.," *Acta Sanctae Sedis* 36 (1903–04), 429-32. He praises her in an allocution delivered the same day, January 6, 1904 (ibid., pp. 464–65).

122. "AURELIENEN. Decretum Beatificationis et Canonizationis Ven. Servae Dei Ioannae de Arc, Virginis, Aurelianensis puellae nuncupatae," *Acta Apostolicae Sedis* 1 (1909), 167–69.

123. "Venerabilis Ioanna de 'Arc' Virgo, Aurelianensis puella nuncupata, renunciatur Beata," ibid., pp. 390–94, especially 393.

JEANNE AU CINÉMA

Kevin J. Harty

For almost a hundred years, filmmakers have been fascinated by Joan of Arc. That fascination has led to a continuing series of films that have cast Joan in a number of different roles: simple peasant girl, wily politician, androgyne, woman, doubting sinner, representative of a nation, and self-assured saint.

The cinematic tradition of the legend of Joan of Arc reflects the complexity of the greater legend of *La Pucelle*.[1] The historical details surrounding the life of the person whom we today call Joan of Arc are fairly well known. What continues to attract us to Joan are not these bare facts but the greater symbolism that has become attached to them. It is this symbolism—or, more properly, this shifting symbolism—that has made Joan such an intriguing figure for filmmakers for almost a century.

Early films about Joan of Arc suffer from the same loss of footage and the same scarcity of records that all early films do, but Joan's story seems first to have taken cinematic form in 1897. In that year, the pioneering Georges Méliès claims to have made a film about Joan in his studio at Montreuil. The film was rereleased several times and eventually ran to fifteen minutes in the form of twelve tableaux as *Jeanne d'Arc*, with a certain Mlle. Calvière, the "première danseuse à ce moment au Trianon-Lyrique de Paris," in the title role supported by a cast of almost five hundred in elaborate costumes, a cast that included Méliès and his wife as the father and mother of Joan.[2] According to catalogue descriptions of the film,[3] *Jeanne d'Arc* presented the following scenes clearly designed to emphasize first Joan's role as national hero and maid of the people and then, in the final tableau, her role as a potential saint of the Catholic church:

1. Village of Domrémy, birthplace of Joan of Arc, in which Joan first appears leading a flock of sheep as a foreshadowing of her later leading the French troops.

2. Forest of Domrémy, where Joan hears her voices and sees her visions of the saints and the archangel Michael.

3. Joan's house at Domrémy, which shows Joan reluctantly leaving her parents as her uncle tries to detain her.

4. Gates of Vaucouleurs, where a sentry first prevents Joan from entering but eventually relents and orders her escorted to the town's governor, Captain de Baudricourt.

5. Castle of Baudricourt, which offers (as the Warwick catalogue says) a "Superb Picture of a Middle Age Interior" and which portrays Baudricourt rather than the dauphin as a wastrel more interested in his venal pleasures than in defeating the enemies of France. Joan eventually convinces him of the seriousness of her cause, and he gives her a sword as she leads French forces into battle.

6. Triumphal entry into Orleans, which includes a "grand" victory procession.

7. Consecration of Charles VII at Reims, which offers shots of the cathedral's "splendid" interior, a magnificent crowd scene, and an elaborate procession.

8. Battle of Compiègne, in which Joan is thrown from her horse and taken prisoner by two Burgundian soldiers. Her followers mount an impressive but unsuccessful attempt to rescue her in a scene that offers "a superb reproduction" of a "Battle of the Middle Ages," with Joan's men storming turrets and blanketing the skies with thousands of arrows as the castle's defenders shower them with projectiles and boiling pitch.

9. Prison, where a clearly exhausted Joan dreams of her village and the visions she had there.

10. Interrogatory, during which Joan's judges try unsuccessfully to get her to sign a retraction of all she has said and condemn her to the stake when she refuses to do so.

11. Execution, the marketplace at Rouen, where Joan is tied to the stake as an inscription is placed above her head accusing her of being a heretic and an apostate. A monk presents her with a cross as Joan breathes her last sigh amid the flames and smoke.

12. Apotheosis, in which the smoke gives way to reveal "golden clouds" in the center of which sit God and the saints awaiting the arrival of the new martyr.[4]

In 1898, another pioneering filmmaker, Georges Hatot, directed a series of short historical films, including one on Joan, *Jeanne d'Arc*. In 1901, the Italian director Mario Caserini made *La béatification de Jeanne d'Arc*, with his wife, Maria Gasperini, in the title role. A second

Italian film based on Schiller's play *Die Jungfrau von Orleans* followed in 1908 or 1909, *Vie de Jeanne d'Arc*, also directed by Caserini and written by Guido Gozzano, with Tina Balli and Aldo Maricci. But little information about these three films survives.[5]

In 1908, Albert Capellani made a French *Jeanne d'Arc* for the Pathé Frères Production Company, for which extensive records survive. The film's release was carefully timed to coincide with Joan's beatification on April 18, 1909. The scenario for the film, by Michel Carré and Capellani, tells a familar story. Joan (Léontine Massart) is first shown as a simple peasant wandering carefree until she hears heavenly voices and St. Michael appears to her telling her to see the king and save her country from the English invaders. Overcoming parental opposition to her mission, she goes to Chinon with Captain de Beaudricourt to see the king, whose place on the throne is taken by a substitute to test Joan's sincerity and legitimacy. Joan recognizes the substitute for what he is. Spying the real king in the background, she kneels before him to request an army. The king, convinced of her sincerity, grants her request. Joan is next shown entering Orleans, attacking Les Tourelles, and routing the enemy. A subsequent shot shows her entering the cathedral at Reims for Charles's coronation. At Compiègne, her enemies succeed in capturing her and condemn her to death for sorcery. In the film's last scene, Joan is burned at the stake in Rouen.

If the film's plot is familar, Capellani's cinematic techniques proved revolutionary for their time. Whereas Méliès relied upon simple tableaux for the several versions of his film, Capellani skillfully balances location and studio shots. Here, Joan is clearly a military leader, and a sequence of long shots halfway through the film presents Joan's soldiers as they attempt to scale the famous towers of Orleans, the wounding of Joan, and her quick recovery to lead her troops again proudly displaying the fleur-de-lis–festooned flag of France. These scenes contrast with the tableaux used later in the film to show Joan's capture in battle at Compiègne. As Richard Abel has pointed out, such contrasts and visual echoes abound in the film.[6]

Capellani's film also nods twice in the direction of contemporary politics. While the film's sympathies clearly lie with the republican view of Joan as a national heroine, Capellani does not totally ignore the more Catholic royalist view that sees her as a saint. In 1904, France and England signed an *entente cordiale* against Germany,

Maria Jacobini as Joan confronts her accusers in Nino Oxilia's film Giovanna d'Arco *(1913).*

because of the occupation of Alsace-Lorraine, the liberation of which has become the new mission of the Maid of Lorraine. The formal split of church and state in France in the following year also tended to widen the divide between those holding royalist and republican views of Joan's place in the national consciousness. In Capellani's film, Joan's enemies are never identified as English troops, and in the final scene depicting her burning the film gives pride of place on the canopied judges' platform to the French bishops rather than to the English soldiers.[7]

In 1913, Nino Oxilia cast the diva Maria Jacobini in the title role of *Giovanna d'Arco,* for the Italian production company Savoia; it was subsequently released the next year in the United States.[8] The film marked the high point of the career of a director who was to die in the trenches of the First World War. In his scenario, Oxilia juggled often conflicting sources to present a balanced portrait of Joan by combining materials from Anatole France's massive two-volume *Vie de Jeanne d'Arc,* first published in 1908, with materials from two works written to counter France's negative portrait of Joan, Andrew Lang's *The Maid of France,* also published in 1908 barely three months after France's attack on Joan, and Gabriel Hanotaux's *Jeanne d'Arc* , which was first serialized in 1910.

Oxilia spent more than two months filming, and he used no fewer than a thousand actors and three hundred horses to create his spectacle. While the film covers familiar ground in telling the story of Joan from her days as a simple girl at home to her death at the stake in Rouen—the film's last title reads, "A saint has passed to her rest"—it also contains two special touches. Throughout her ordeals, Joan is accompanied by Bertrand, identified simply as her companion (no further details about their relationship are given), and in her final captivity, Joan, chained and helpless, is first almost stabbed by the earl of Stafford and then almost tricked by her confessor, Loyseleur. As Joan is taken to her execution, she subsequently pardons Loyseleur, who is shown in his final appearance in the film groveling in the dust begging for that pardon.

Commenting on the American release of the film in 1914, a brief note in *Moving Picture World* opined that the film was a "great production" and

> a two-part subject remarkable for exceptional staging. The number of men involved in the production, the pageantry, the costuming, the great sets, the battles, the use of castles, represent a size and magnificence that might well have justified running the story into many reels.

And while Robin Blaetz indicates that the film "does not appear to have been a success due to the outrageous and inappropriate performance of Maria Jacobini," contemporary reviews of the film were unanimous in their praise for the overall production and for Jacobini's performance in particular.[9]

In 1917, Cecil B. DeMille directed the first cinematic spectacle about Joan, *Joan the Woman*.[10] Jeanie Macpherson's screenplay borrows heavily from Schiller's *Jungfrau von Orleans* in its retelling of the familiar events of Joan's life, although the film omits Schiller's ending, in which Joan escapes the English and the Inquisition. Even more sensitive to contemporary political events than was Capellani's 1908 film, DeMille's film is, among other things, nothing less than a call to arms for the United States to come to the aid of France in the First World War. Joan clearly appears as a symbol of France in need of American assistance, and the film twice shows her silhouetted against a fleur-de-lis that slowly turns into a cross.[11]

The film's prologue finds Eric Trent (Wallace Reid), an English soldier in the trenches in France during World War I, discovering a fragment of a sword he imagines to be Joan's. Armed with the sword, Trent believes he is spiritually and historically connected to Joan as he volunteers to go on a suicide mission against the Germans, France's new invaders. The film's scenario soon establishes that Trent is really a twentieth-century reincarnation of a fifteenth-century knight of the same name who was rescued by and subsequently fell in love with Joan. The medieval Trent's obsession with Joan leads him unwittingly to aid in her undoing. In a moment of genuine pathos, Joan admits that, were things different, she would return his affections. Seeing her burn at the stake, Trent feels his life is over, and in the film's epilogue the modern-day Trent does indeed die on his suicide mission.

Joan the Woman was DeMille's first historical film, and for the title role he cast the opera singer Geraldine Farrar, who was rumored in the press to have had pro-German sympathies.[12] DeMille capitalized on countering these suspicions in an attempt to drive home the film's call to arms. DeMille's reading of the life of Joan is unique on both a personal and a more general political level. The initial titles explain that the film is "founded on the life of Joan of Arc, the Girl Patriot, Who Fought with Men, Was Loved by Men and Killed by Men—Yet withal Retained the Heart of a Woman." In the American version of the film, *Joan the Woman* becomes also a commentary about the battle of the sexes with a possible suffragist context, an interesting response to the life of a woman who was viewed by her accusers as a political, religious, and sexual heretic.

In his recent extensive commentary on *Joan the Woman*, Sumiko Higashi expands upon the film's several political agendas:

> DeMille's epic was in fact part of public discourse enlisting support for an embattled France symbolized by Joan of Arc rather than the modernist aesthetic so alienating to Protestant middle-class sensibility. Patriotic appeals associated with the Maid of Orleans were useful in overcoming American prejudice against Parisian avant-garde movements that contravened sacrosanct notions of genteel culture. An ad, for example, addressed the reader as follows: "Would Joan of Arc Be Burned Today? . . . Is the World Freed of the Arch-Enemies of Truth—Ignorance and Superstition?"[13]

In one of the film's more original and jarring touches, and a scene that stirred protests against the film in Catholic circles, Joan appears before a court of Ku Klux Klan–like white-hooded accusers who

Geraldine Farrar as Joan follows Raymond Hatton as the dauphin in the coronation procession into Reims cathedral in Cecil B. DeMille's Joan the Woman *(1917).*

torment her at Bishop Cauchon's behest. The Klan had reorganized itself in 1915 in what would turn out to be a rising tide of nativism that swept across the country and that DeMille obviously viewed with some alarm.[14]

La passion de Jeanne d'Arc (1927–28), directed by Carl Theodore Dreyer, with Maria Falconetti in her only screen role as the title character, is the greatest film portrayal of Joan. Dreyer treats only the events of Joan's trial after she has been taken prisoner by the English. The screenplay,[15] based upon the ecclesiastical records from Joan's trial, involved a collaboration between Joseph Delteil, whose popular biography of Joan had appeared in 1925, and Dreyer, although parts of the original film were censored in response to criticism from the Catholic Church that the film's depiction of ecclesiastical authorities was too negative.

The film condenses Joan's twenty-nine interrogations into one long tribunal session on the last day of her life. Cauchon convenes the court at Rouen castle, and the settings change quickly from the courtroom to Joan's cell, to the torture chamber, back to Joan's cell, to the cemetery, back again a third time to Joan's cell, and finally to the courtyard of the castle where Joan dies at the stake.

Geraldine Farrar as Joan at the stake in Cecil B. DeMille's Joan the Woman *(1917).*

The film's style was revolutionary in its day. Dreyer simply presents a series of closeups that he felt mirrored the historical records:

> The records give a shattering impression of the ways in which the trial was a conspiracy of judges against the solitary Jeanne, bravely defending herself against men who displayed a devilish cunning to trap her in their net. This conspiracy could be conveyed on the screen only through the huge closeups that exposed, with merciless realism, the callous cynicism of the judges hidden behind hypocritical compassion—and on the other hand there had to be equally huge closeups of Jeanne, whose pure features would reveal that she alone found strength in her faith in God.[16]

The film pays similar attention to set, costume, and language. The film's original negative was destroyed by fire in 1928, but copies of the film have been restored that preserve several versions with only minor differences.[17]

Dreyer's cinematic techniques showed that film could preserve the unities of classical drama and link his Joan with heroines of classical drama as well as with Christ himself, whose passion her own mirrors—a point driven home clearly in the film when, in the second scene shot inside her cell, Joan appears wearing what seems to be a crown of thorns. Despite such lofty links, Dreyer's Joan

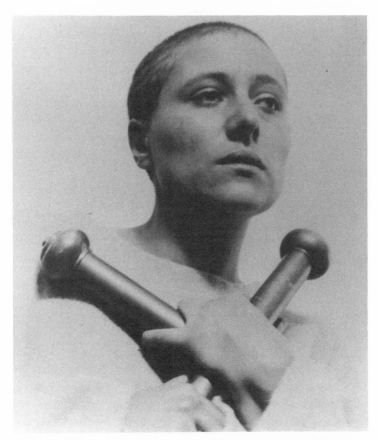

Maria Falconetti as Joan in Carl Theodore Dreyer's 1927-28 film La passion de Jeanne D'Arc. *(Still courtesy of the British Film Institute.)*

remains a three-dimensional human being; the film, with its exclusive reliance on closeups, becomes a study of individual rather than group reactions to the events it presents. In retrospect, as David Bordwell points out, Dreyer's film was crucial

> in changing people's attitudes about cinema, particularly because of its decisive demonstration that film could be an art in its own right. ... The film's unprecedented stylistic rigor, the elevation of its subject, the impeccable credentials of its cast, and its refusal to cater to popular conceptions of entertainment constituted a daring bid for consideration as a full-fledged art work. For better or worse, . . . [Dreyer's film] convinced many viewers that cinema could be intellectually respectable.[18]

La merveilleuse vie de Jeanne d'Arc, directed by Marco De Gastyne in 1928, with the seventeen-year-old Simone Genevois in the title role, has remained a lost cinematic treasure. One of the last great silent films and well received in its day—it was a success in the same year that Dreyer's film was a commercial failure—the film has been overshadowed by Dreyer's *Passion,* with which it shares little more than a central character. The advent of the talkies contributed to the film's limited original distribution within and outside of Europe. The film was all but forgotten thanks to the disappearance of the negative and of most prints until the Cinémathèque Française restored and screened it in 1966 with a new score by Jean Musy.[19]

De Gastyne's film tells a fuller life of Joan than Dreyer's, emphasizing her boyish if not mannish traits. While Falconetti made Joan's suffering poignant, Genevois gives life to her military exploits. The film's bias toward Joan as military leader and national heroine is obvious from the first title:

> Let us always remember that our fatherland was born from the heart of a woman, from her love and her tears, from the blood she spilled for us.[20]

The film's first scenes tell of Joan's childhood and introduce her closest companion, Rémy Loiseau, whom she will later decline to marry— she will instead be the bride of France—and who will eventually follow her into battle, dying at the siege of Compiègne.[21] Joan soon becomes a rallying point for the French, as the film's scenario continues its emphasis on her special role in the history of France:

> And soon, in the heart of the country, another army arises made up of all those who are able to leave their family, their house and their mistress to serve a cause which they sensed was miraculous and which was no other than the birth of France. . . .

> In a few days, Joan turned these rough looters and debauched rovers into disciplined soldiers, giving them a sense of national identity and restoring them to the faith.[22]

While the film does not ignore the interrogations that are the sole focus of Dreyer's film, De Gastyne characterizes the trial as a continuation of Joan's battles with the English on behalf of France. Acknowledged a saint in the film's final title,[23] she is more importantly steadfast in her defense of France's true interest when she is betrayed by French soldiers and clergy into the hands of the English.

The principal battle scenes, which De Gastyne shot before the walls of Carcassonne, included—thanks to the assistance of the French government, which allowed him to use French troops as extras—the proverbial cast of thousands, as did the coronation procession that was shot inside the just-restored cathedral at Reims. The trial scenes differ in technique from those in Dreyer's *Passion*— there is no reliance on closeups here—but effectively convey the turmoil surrounding the legal maneuvering used to engineer Joan's death. De Gastyne's fidelity to location shots is evident even in the trial scenes, which he shot within the abbey of Mont-St.-Michel.[24]

Das Mädchen Johanna, directed in 1935 by Gustav Ucicky, with Angela Salloker in the title role, is a troubling entry in the canon of Joan of Arc cinema. The film bore a Nazi stamp of approval (and perhaps the fingerprints of Goebbels). Judged innocuous in its own time by American and British reviewers, the film can now be viewed in light of events since 1935. The hero of the film is Charles (Gustaf Gründgens), not Joan. The screenplay by Gerhard Menzel offers nothing even approaching the usual outcry against the miscarriage of justice that led to Joan's execution. Instead, the film sees Joan's execution as a brillant strategic move on Charles's part. He clearly knows a dead Joan is more valuable to him than a living rival for national adulation.

In Ucicky's film, Charles is the perfect Machiavellian prince, a man ahead of his time, interested only in the good of his country, a man who can use the navieté of the patriotic but uncomprehending Joan to further the national good. Charles's vision restores France after the humiliating defeats of the Hundred Years War. A present-day Charles, the film less than subtly suggests, lies ready to restore Germany after the humiliating defeats of the First World War.

Such highjacking of history and legend leads to other jaundiced readings of familiar scenes and characters. Much of UFA's publicity for the film stressed its dependence upon historical records—but what records reduce the barons of France to a drunken mob who call for Joan's execution as a witch during the coronation banquet, thus abetting Charles's decision to sacrifice Joan for the greater good of the nation? Though not technically advanced, the film features crowd scenes that overwhelm (though not appropriately or expertly so), and its lighting, scenery, location shots, and costume add richness. Yet the film—at least in the version owned by the Library of

Simone Genevois as Joan rallies her troops in Marco De Gastyne's 1928 film
La merveilleuse vie de Jeanne d'Arc. *(Still courtesy of the British Film Institute.)*

Congress—is an historical muddle, and comments in the American press in 1935, to the effect that the "excellence of a cast makes seeing the film a must," reveal a myopia that today seems unbelievable.[25]

A bland political agenda, a vigorous effort at self-promotion, and an attempt to cash in on the popularity of religious and historical films inform *Joan of Arc*, directed in 1948 by Victor Fleming, with Ingrid Bergman in the title role. The film, with screenplay by Maxwell Anderson and Andrew Solt from Anderson's stageplay *Joan of Lorraine,* is notable more for its use of lavish technicolor than for its message. The script abandons the play-within-a-play format of its source and borrows heavily from the transcripts of Joan's trial for the scenes of Bergman's interrogation.[26] The film's critical reception was mixed, with the majority of positive notices appearing in the religious press. Much was made of the gorgeous sets and costumes— the film's $5-million cost was not for naught, and even covered the cost of a seventy-foot-high figure of Bergman in white plastic armor that was displayed outside the theater for the New York premiere— but characterization is one-dimensional.

Angela Salloker as Joan in chains in Gustav Ucicky's 1935 film Das Mädchen Johanna. *(Still courtesy of the British Film Institute.)*

Both Anderson's original stageplay and his screenplay reveal a consciousness of the fact that the Second World War did not see the defeat of all of America's enemies and that a Cold War was now emerging. Anderson's play opens on a bare theatrical stage, as actors come together for rehearsal of a play about Joan. A young actress, Mary Grey, is hesitant to undertake the role, unsure of how she can give life to Joan's story in light of the ethical and moral compromises it involved. As the play develops, the scene shifts between the contemporary rehearsal and the actual events in Joan's life, with Grey assuming the role of Joan in the play within the play.

In a crucial scene in the play, Joan confronts the dauphin about his decision—premature in her view—to sue for peace. She tells the dauphin:

> Burgundy needs a little peace, my king. But not you. You have all your enemies at your mercy now. . . . You cannot do this, my dauphin. It would mean that you threw away all the advantage we have fought so hard and given so much blood to win.

The action in the play then shifts back to the present with Grey objecting to the fact that Joan seems to be giving "her blessing to corruption." As the scene then shifts again back to Reims and the coronation of the dauphin, Joan kneels in prayer, vowing never again to wear her white armor:

> We are at peace, my king, but not such a peace as we dreamed; no horribly, evilly in armistice, with much of the war to be fought and our enemies preparing while we dwindle here from town to town.

In the film, almost the same confrontation between Joan and the dauphin occurs, but without the interruption of the play within the play and the attempt to frame events that are going on on stage. The film's message is simpler. The end of the war has not brought any lasting security. Enemies, America's enemies and those of the free world, are ready to strike at any moment.

> Your enemies need a little peace, my king, but not you. Let them go to their island and they can have a good and lasting peace. No, we have only to go forward and their last great stronghold is ours.[27]

While the film in some ways launched the Hollywood career of José Ferrer, who played the dauphin, its place in Bergman's own career is more interesting. Hollywood manipulation of the media to create star images is by no means a well-kept secret, but Bergman herself carefully manipulated the media to the same end. Evidently fixated on Joan from childhood, she planned as early as the late 1930s to star in a film about Joan directed by David O. Selznick. The approaching war made it impossible to produce a film in which

Ingrid Bergman as Joan in armor in Victor Fleming's 1948 film Joan of Arc.

English soldiers burned a French national hero at the stake,[28] but the publicity surrounding the announcement established a connection between Joan and Bergman that the actress would continue to encourage. Bergman starred in the first production of Anderson's play, taking the stage in productions in Washington and New York in late 1946 and early 1947. Long indentified with the role of Joan, both on stage and on screen, Bergman with *Joan of Arc* was in part responsible for the most ambitious independent Hollywood film to that date.[29]

Joan of Arc reflects a consciousness in Hollywood of the need for new themes for films. As early as 1943, an article in *Variety*[30] noted that the public was tiring of war films and argued that religious films, especially in light of the success of *The Song of Bernadette*, would enjoy continued popularity. That fact and the attempt to capitalize on the success of a recent historical film, Olivier's *Henry V*, convinced the film's backers to finance the project. *Joan of Arc* presents a story parallel to that of *Henry V*, steeped in a rich history to which all of Hollywood's combined talent could give sumptuous expression. Such a cinematic rendering of the story of Joan (albeit built around Bergman's wooden performance) presented a carefully cultivated popular image of the star that would eventually counter the furor caused by her extramarital liaison with Roberto Rossellini.[31]

Bergman returned to the screen as Joan in 1954 in *Giovanna d'Arco al rogo,* directed by Rossellini and based on Paul Claudel and Arthur Honnegger's 1939 oratorio *Jeanne d'Arc au bûcher.* Rossellini had directed Bergman in a well-received stage production of the oratorio and originally maintained that the film was simply a souvenir for Bergman and him.[32] Throughout the oratorio, Joan appears chained to a stake; she never moves. To solve this difficulty, Rossellini's stylized settings for the film—his first in color—use a combination of static scenes in which a stationary Joan converses with her confessor, Fra Domenico, and flashbacks that present in detail events from Joan's earlier life. What links the two is a book dictated by the angels that Fra Domenico carries, a book designed to free Joan and to let her ascend into heaven in the form of pure light. In a visually fascinating scene, Joan's judges appear wearing the heads of animals. Bishop Cauchon appropriately appears with the head of a pig; the court clerk, with that of a donkey; and the other members of the court, with those of sheep. Rossellini himself, in an interview with François Truffaut and Eric Rohmer, called the film an example of "pure cinema" and characterized its style as "neorealistic."[33]

Giovanna has not been widely shown, and copies of the film are hard to find.[34] Its reception has been mixed. In an exchange published in *Etudes cinématographiques*, Michel Estève argued that the film, like its source, is an unsuccessful and banal attempt to comprehend the supernatural. The film is said to fail because its director is incapable of presenting a convincing meditation on the life of Joan in the way that Dreyer had succeeded in doing in his film.[35] Claude Beylie countered Estève, echoing Rossellini's assertion that the film was "pure cinema" by arguing that it was an example of "pure meditation," its strength lying in the uniqueness of its spiritual dimension. The director's technique, according to Beylie, reduces the spectacle of other films about Joan to a "primitive" examination of the motives and circumstances that led Joan to the stake.[36]

Saint Joan, directed in 1957 by Otto Preminger and starring Jean Seberg and Richard Widmark, with a screenplay by Graham Greene, who in turn followed the outlines of Shaw's play, is a departure from earlier films in its characterization of Joan. Seberg plays a flippant, self-willed Joan who has the annoying habit of referring to the dauphin (Widmark) as "Charlie." The film opens with the king's being visited by Joan's ghost at the time of the rescinding of her sentence. Subsequent events in the film selectively tell the familiar tale: the film jumps, for instance, from the preparations for the siege of Orleans to the coronation in Reims.

In Fleming's *Joan of Arc,* the dauphin betrays Joan when she receives louder cheers than he does at the coronation. In *Saint Joan,* the dauphin, always finicky and impetuous, simply dismisses Joan. In her subsequent trial, the hand of the English, in the person of the earl of Warwick, is everywhere evident as Joan is given more to speechifying than to suffering. The film comes full circle in its conclusion when Joan's ghost is joined at Charlie's bedside by the spirits of Cauchon, Warwick, and a kind English soldier who had fashioned a cross for her to hold at the stake. Condemned to hell for his part in the martydom of a saint, he is nonetheless let out of his torments one day a year because of this good deed.

The film was a critical and a commercial failure, though Preminger, who had long wanted to make a film of Shaw's play and who drummed up enormous publicity for the film in his search for someone to play the title role, always referred to it as his "most distinguished flop."[37] Seberg's Joan remains problematic, wavering between the childlike and the childish. She is no match for the portrait of Joan in Shaw's play, though the film's screenplay borrows

Jean Seberg as Joan in Otto Preminger's 1957 film Saint Joan.

the Shavian epilogue as the source for the framing narrative it uses involving the dead Joan's visit to the dauphin's bedside.

The film goes wrong because Preminger failed to comprehend the essence of Shaw's play. In a 1956 interview with the Canadian Broadcasting Company, Preminger had argued that he understood Shaw:

> I am doing Bernard Shaw's *Saint Joan*, a very successful play in 1923, which I think should be shown as he wrote it. . . . [W]e are strictly adhering to the Shaw dialogue.[38]

In Preminger's view, Joan is right and everyone else is wrong. Shaw, on the other hand, had allowed Joan's accusers their say. In reducing Shaw's text from a play that runs nearly three and a half hours to a scenario that runs less than two, Greene eliminated the complexity that provides a major part of the conflict within Shaw's play and ignored what Ellen Kennedy calls the lines "elucidating her precocious nationalism and incipient protestantism."[39]

Le procès de Jeanne d'Arc, directed in 1962 by Robert Bresson, with Florenz Carrez in the title role, is clearly a reaction to Hollywood's commercialization of the image of Joan at the hands of such directors as Fleming and Preminger. Like Dreyer, Bresson limits his story of Joan to her trial. While Bresson's Joan is unflappable in her convictions and totally believable in her faith, we never fully get to understand why this is. Bresson's camera—unlike Dreyer's with its emotionally manipulating closeups—always remains, like us, at a distance from Joan. Bresson's technique is almost voyeuristic; the film displays a fascination with doorways and peepholes.

Where Dreyer would readily supply pathos, Bresson steps farther and farther back from his subject. In the final scenes of Dreyer's film, a silhouette shot shows Joan's burning body slumping down into the flames as a riot breaks out among the spectators. In Bresson's final shots, Joan's body is gone, and the chains that bound her simply hang from the stake, itself transformed into a symbol of hope. As Bresson has explained:

> Joan's will extended to accepting God's grace even if it meant the end of her earthly life and the beginning of a purely spiritual one. All the desperate machinations of the court have merely fulfilled the promise of Joan's faith.[40]

Florenz Carrez as Joan in Robert Bresson's 1962 film Le procès de Jeanne d'Arc. *(Still courtesy of the British Film Institute.)*

Bresson is not interested in politics or nationalism. The English are almost absent from the film. Bresson commented that he purposely excluded the character of the earl of Warwick—"I didn't want to introduce the psychology of Warwick"—and the English soldier who gives Joan the cross to hold at her burning is invisible except for his helmet: "This detail is so well known to everybody here in France that I only wanted to suggest it by the sight of the helmet."[41] Bresson's film is a personal meditation on the life of a saint.

Eric Rhode's comment that "Bresson is a Romantic conservative yearning for a neo-classical order, an idealized stability, which for him takes a Christian form: the Kingdom of God" is nowhere in his films more true than it is in *Procès*.[42] Bresson's sources are the documents from Joan's trial and rehabilitation, and the film's style is that of an interrogation. *Procès* is in some ways one with the director's

Lancelot du lac, another personal meditation on the nature and possibility of goodness in the world. *Procès* borrows its use of imprisonment as metaphor from Bresson's *Un condamné à mort s'est éschappé* (1956), and like the director's *Le journal d'un curé de campagne* (1951), it addresses complex relationships among faith, divine grace, physical suffering, and spirituality.[43] In the film, Joan achieves grace through her own actions and will. Grace is not a gift, rather it is a goal for the Christian to achieve whether in medieval or modern times.

The most recent cinematic retelling of the legend of Joan, *Jeanne la pucelle*, directed in 1993 by Jacques Rivette, with Sandrine Bonnaire as Joan, has had only limited distribution in the United States. Given the gradual shift to the right in French politics over the past several years, it would not have been inconceivable for a director to produce a new film about Joan with marked political over- or undertones. But as a filmmaker Rivette seems to have no interest in politics. An unrepentant "New Wave" director known for such films as *Out 1—noli me tangere* (1970), which runs almost thirteen hours, Rivette made his film about Joan simply because he wanted a vehicle in which to star Bonnaire.[44]

Rivette's *Jeanne la pucelle* is really two related films, *Les batailles* and *Les prisons,* each running almost three hours. *Jeanne la pucelle* features spare sets and costumes and relies upon an equally lean narrative with references to precise dates and times of day. Witnesses appear at strategic moments in the film to fill narrative gaps by explaining the political and religious forces at work in the events being portrayed on film. Harlan Kennedy's slightly irreverent review of the film captures Rivette's approach to Joan's story:

> Heroic Joan and human Joan get equal weight. Now she strides out to battle, features steeled with fearlessness; now she blubs over an arrow wound or screams at the news of her imminent barbecue. Now, we the audience clamber up wartorn castles, dodging arrows and spears. Now we loll in a castle listening to characters discuss bills or meal menus, or learning how to spit-roast a hare (first catch it, then kill it, then pass it to someone else for skinning and skewering).[45]

Previous films used large casts of extras in battle scenes, but Rivette's underpopulates them with at times less-than-satisfying results. The film also avoids any philosophical, political, or psychological biases; unfortunately, it offers nothing in their place.

Sandrine Bonnaire as Joan in Jacques Rivette's 1994 film Jeanne la pucelle.

Joan here is, as Kennedy points out, partly heroic, partly human—
her last cry of "Jesus" seems one both of anger and of pain. The
European reception of Rivette's film has been respectful, but the
film could use some cutting.

With perhaps uncharacteristic directness, Umberto Eco once
explained the continued fascination that the twentieth century has
with things medieval in this way: "It seems that people like the Middle
Ages."[46] It seems, too, that people like Joan of Arc. No one spirit has
informed film treatments of the legend of Joan, and perhaps such
diversity of treatment is appropriate for a figure about whom history
and legend continue to offer a range of judgments. Brian Stock has
noted that an interest in the Middle Ages can mask religious archaism
and political reaction in any postmedieval period.[47] The same can
be said for the continued interest in Joan. Fifteenth-century France
found her both saint and sinner. She was viewed at best with
respectful curiosity for the next two centuries. A return to an interest
in Joan in the nineteenth century showed France once more
conflicted between views of Joan as a daughter of the church and as
the mother of a nation. Filmmakers have in their turn wrestled with
Joan the simple peasant girl, Joan the wily politician, Joan the
androgyne, Joan the woman, Joan the doubting sinner, Joan the

representative of a nation, and Joan the self-assured saint. The filmmakers and their films have mirrored the continuing revisionism that complicates the story of an ignorant, simple fifteenth-century country girl who managed in the space of less than two years to change the course of European history.[48]

NOTES

1. I am indebted to three earlier discussions of the cinematic treatment of Joan of Arc: a special issue of *Etudes cinématographiques* 18–19 (1962) devoted to "Jeanne d'Arc a l'écran"; Robin Blaetz, "Strategies of Containment: Joan of Arc in Film" (Ph.D. diss., New York University, 1989); and Nadia Margolis, *Joan of Arc in History, Literature, and Film: A Select, Annotated Bibliography* (New York, 1990), pp. 393–406. I indicate any differences I may have with these earlier discussions in subsequent notes.

I do not discuss here documentaries about Joan, made-for-television films, shorter contemporary films, anthology films that include only a segment about Joan (such as Jean Delannoy's *Destinées*), films only tangentially concerned with the historical Joan (*Between Us Girls, Nachalo, The Miracle of the Bells,* and *Joan of Paris*), or films whose only debt to Joan seems to be in their title (*The Mexican Joan of Arc, Joan of Ozark,* and *Johanna d'Arc of Mongolia*). For details on many of these films, see Robin Blaetz, "'*La femme vacante*' or the Rendering of Joan of Arc in Cinema," *Post Script* 12 (Winter 1993), 63–78; Blaetz, passim; and Margolis, pp. 393–406.

2. Both Blaetz, p. 200, and Margolis, p. 399, indicate that the film was made in 1899 and released in 1900, but a letter from Georges Méliès published in 1948 assigns a date of 1897 to at least the first version of the film. See "Le premier 'Jeanne d'Arc' fut tourné en 1897," *Ecran française* 159 (July 13, 1948), 3, 14. In a letter to me dated May 30, 1995, Professor Blaetz points out that the length and the narrative style of the fifteen-minute version preclude its having been made as early as 1897.

3. Blaetz, pp. 38 and 200, records that there is a hand-tinted copy of this film without titles at the Centre Jeanne d'Arc in Orleans, although that copy is only about eight minutes long.

4. I base my synopsis here on the fullest catalogue description of the film, that published by the Warwick Trading Company, Ltd., *The Warwick Film Catalogue* (London, 1901), pp. 69–71. Slightly different details about the film can be found in two other catalogues of early films: *The "Walturdaw" Catalogue of Animated Pictures* (London, 1904), pp. 16–17, and

The Complete Catalogue of Genuine and Original "Star" Films (Moving Pictures) Manufactured by Geo. Méliès of Paris (New York, [1907?]), p. 20.

5. Blaetz, p. 375 notes that only a thirty-second fragment of the Hatot film survives and that the fragment might suggest that the film depicted a Joan hounded by a "malevolent church." The other two films have been lost. For the scarce surviving details about these films, see, in addition to Blaetz, Margolis, pp. 394 and 397, and Maria Adriana Prolo, *Storia del cinema muto italiano* (Milan, 1951), p. 126.

6. Richard Abel, *The Ciné Goes to Town* (Berkeley, 1994), p. 268, although what Abel finds skillful in 1994 an unnamed reviewer for *Moving Picture World* found less than impressive in 1909—see *Moving Picture World* (July 3, 1909), 14. That unnamed reviewer was also critical of Massart's interpretation of the role of Joan. An earlier review of the film in *Moving Picture World* omitted any criticism of this scene or of Massart—see *Moving Picture World* (June 19, 1909), 847—as did reviews in *Kinematograph & Lantern Weekly* (June 17, 1909), 295; *Pathé Frères Weekly Bulletin* 86 (June 21, 1909), [6–7]; and *Bioscope* (October 2, 1913), supplement: xilv.

7. Abel, pp. 268, 518, n. 207.

8. Margolis, pp. 398–400, suggests that the American release in 1914 of Oxilia's film is a separate film from the Eclair Studio. Records at the British Film Institute indicate that Oxilia's film, made for the Italian production company Savoia, was subsequently distributed in England and the United States by several companies, including Eclectic, Eclair, and World Special Films. Both Margolis and Blaetz, pp. 40–41 and 201, cite in passing a 1914 or 1915 Austrian-Italian film, *Jeanne*, about which almost nothing is known but which Margolis associates with Eclectic. It is not impossible that this film might also be a subsequent release of Oxilia's film.

9. See *Moving Picture World* (March 7, 1914), 1215; Robin Blaetz, p. 40. The review by "Mark" in *Variety* (July 17, 1914), 17, is mixed, but the following reviews of the film are unanimous in their high praise for the film and for Jacobini's interpretation of the role of Joan: *Bioscope* (December 18, 1913), 1203; *Picturegoer* (January 17, 1914), 460–65; George Blaisdell, *Moving Picture World* (February 14, 1914), 790; and *Kinematograph Monthly Film Record* 22 (February 1914), 42–43. Aldo Bernardini and Vittorio Martinelli reprint excerpts from two favorable Italian reviews of the film, one from *Vita cinematografica* 21 (November 15, 1913) and one from *Maggese cinematografico* 2 (January 30, 1915), in *Il cinema muto italiano 1913* (Turin, 1994), p. 265.

10. Two versions of the film survive. The original American version is much longer and more diffuse, emphasizing an overly romantic—in several senses of the term—view of Joan. A version in French, based on a recut version of the American original, streamlines the plot substantially to emphasize Joan's mythic role in the French national consciousness. I limit my comments to the American version, a copy of which I viewed at the

Library of Congress. For an extensive comparison of the American and French versions, see Robin Blaetz, "Cecil B. DeMille's *Joan the Woman*," in *Medievalism in North America,* ed. Kathleen Verduin (Cambridge, Eng., 1994), pp. 109–22. Blaetz bases her discussion on the copy of the American version in George Eastman House in Rochester and the copy of the French version in Centre Jeanne d'Arc in Orleans.

11. Joan's role as modern-day savior of France was used in the United States later in the First World War as a popular icon to sell war savings stamps. A Haskell Coffin poster designed for the United States Treasury Department depicts an armored Joan with sword raised aloft standing in front of the French tricolor. The captions above and below the figure of Joan read, "Joan of Arc Saved France. Women of America Save Your Country. *Buy* War Savings Stamps." The poster is reprinted in Anne Llewellyn Barstow, *Joan of Arc: Heretic, Mystic, Shaman* (Lewiston, 1986), plate 8.

12. Farrar had made her operatic debut at the Berlin Royal Opera in 1901, and the popular press had linked her romantically with the Hohenzollern crown prince just before World War I began. See Sumiko Higashi, *Cecil B. DeMille and American Culture: The Silent Era* (Berkeley, 1994), pp. 135–36. Farrar herself countered claims that she was pro-German in comments in an article about the Boston premiere of the film on March 19, 1917, at the Colonial Theater. Farrar attended the premiere with DeMille. See "Boston Premiere of 'Joan' A Notable Affair," *Motion Picture News* (April 7, 1917), 2175. Both Farrar and DeMille faced criticism for her initial casting because she was neither young nor petite enough for the role. For Farrar's response to these criticisms and for her enthusiastic comments about what playing the role of Joan meant to her, see her article, "Joan of Arc, in California," *Vanity Fair* 13 (November 1919), 63, 106.

13. Higashi, p. 140.

14. Ibid., pp. 136–138.

15. Carl Theodor Dreyer, *Four Screenplays* (Bloomington, 1970), pp. 25–76.

16. Quoted by Ib Monty in *The International Dictionary of Films and Filmmakers,* ed. Nicholas Thomas, 2nd ed. (Chicago, 1990), vol. 1, p. 691.

17. See Tony Pipolo, "The Spectre of JOAN OF ARC: Textual Variations in the Key Prints of Carl Dreyer's Film," *Film History* 2 (1988), 301–24.

18. David Bordwell, *Filmguide to La passion de Jeanne d'Arc* (Bloomington, 1973), pp. 60–61.

19. For a review of the first screening of this restoration, see *Variety* (October 1, 1986), 36. The restored version was subsequently shown on French television; see the brief reviews in *Télérama* 2348 (January 11, 1995), 102, and *Le monde radio-télevision* 15–16 (January 1995), 7.

20. Typescript English translation by Ros Schwartz of the scenario for the 1986 restoration and screening by the Cinémathèque Française in the files of the British Film Institute in London, p. 1. The typescript's title is "The Glorious Life of Joan of Arc." The film was first released in Britain in 1931 with the title *Saint Joan the Maid.*

21. Loiseau is present later in the film when his name appears on a series of gravestones marking France's great wars throughout history. The dead Joan's indentification with France's Unknown Soldier and De Gastyne's comment that the script for the film by Jean-José Frappa called for the use of French uniforms from the First World War farther underscore the film's view of Joan as national heroine rather than saint of the church. See Blaetz, "Strategies of Containment," p. 48.

22. Schwartz, "The Glorious Life of Joan of Arc," p. 6.

23. Ibid., p. 12.

24. The file on the film at the British Film Institute contains the "Programme Notes" for a screening of *La merveilleuse vie de Jeanne d'Arc* at the National Film Theatre in 1966. Those notes, also by Ros Schwartz, quote in translation the following comments by De Gastyne, which he originally made in an interview in *Cinemirois* 28 (January 1928): "Directors of historical films are often criticised for not making use of historical remains. After having read all that was possible about Jeanne D'Arc, I went over 3000 miles across France by car, to choose my locations and learn about the possibility of filming in historical places."

25. In his review of the film for the *New York World-Telegram* (October 9, 1935), Gerald Breitigam encourages his readers to see the film, as it may be their only chance to see the work of great actors whom they may never see on the Hollywood screen (p. 35). In raising a red flag about the film, Graham Greene proves an exception to the critical rule in America and Great Britain. In his review for the *Spectator* (October 25, 1935), Greene objected to the tasteless German appropriation of France's national symbol for propagandistic purposes. Greene also notes, with some contempt, the less than subtle parallels in the film between the "burning of the Reichstag and the pyre in Rouen" (p. 663). For a sample of the overwhelmingly positive reviews of the film that appeared in America and Great Britain, see those in *Film Weekly* (October 18, 1935), 33; *Life and Letters Today* 13 (December 1935), 185–86; *New York American* (October 8, 1935), 8; *New York Times* (October 9, 1935), 27; *Sunday Observer* [London] (October 13, 1935), 16; and *Times* [London] (October 9, 1935), 10. The German press defended the film's playing fast and loose with history by citing the precedents of earlier imaginative treatments of the life of Joan by, among others, Shakespeare and Schiller. See "Das Wundermädchen von Domremy," *Filmwelt* (April 28, 1935), [5–6].

26. Paul Doncoeur, S.J., served as adviser to the film. Father Doncoeur, who is best known as the author of one of the standard religious

works on Joan, *Le mystère de la passion de Jeanne d'Arc* (Paris, 1929), then joined the publicity campaign for the film by publishing a series of articles praising its authenticity and its insight into the significance of Joan's life. See "Ingrid Bergman and Joan of Arc," *America* 80 (November 13, 1948), 158–59; "Joan of Arc," *Sign* 28 (November 1948), 26–29, 53; and "Joan of Arc in Fact and Film," *Month* n.s. 1 (May 1949), 313–21.

27. Compare Maxwell Anderson, *Joan of Lorraine* (Washington, D.C., 1947), pp. 92, 98, 101–02, and Maxwell Anderson and Andrew Solt, *Joan of Arc* (New York, 1948), p. 96.

28. See James Damico, "Ingrid Bergman from Lorraine to Stromboli: Analyzing the Public's Perception of a Film Star," *Journal of Popular Film* 4 (1975), 3–19, and Adrienne L. McLean, "The Cinderella Princess and the Instrument of Evil: Surveying the Limits of Female Transgression in Two Postwar Hollywood Scandals," *Cinema Journal* 34 (Spring 1995), 36–56.

29. See Matthew Bernstein, "Hollywood Martyrdoms: *Joan of Arc* and Independent Productions in the Late 1940s," in *Current Research in Film: Audiences, Economics and Law,* volume 4, ed. Bruce A. Austin (Norwood, 1988), pp. 89–113.

30. "Next Cycle to Be Religious, with Interest in War Yarns Receding," *Variety* (March 24, 1943), 1.

31. Bergman was not unique in her attraction to the role of Joan. Shaw was correct in predicting that for women the role would hold the same challenges and attractions that Hamlet holds for men. See Brian Tyson, *The Story of Shaw's Saint Joan* (Montreal, 1982), p. 114. Régine Pernoud has asked rhetorically what actress would not want to play such a role given the range of emotions and the test of mettle it provides. See "Jeanne d'Arc à l'écran," *Cahiers de la cinémathèque* 42–43 (Summer 1985), 41. For an interesting series of insights into what playing the role of Joan has meant for actresses, see Holly Hill, ed., *Playing Joan* (New York, 1987). If recent (1995) rumors in the trade papers are to be believed, even the rock stars Sinead O'Connor and Madonna intend in the near future to try their hands at playing Joan on the screen.

32. Peter Brunette, *Robert Rossellini* (New York, 1987), p. 179.

33. *Cahiers du cinéma* 37 (July 1954), 12.

34. Brunette, p. 180, reports that in 1984 the Cinetaca Nazionale in Turin owned the only print of the film but that it was in such bad condition that it could rarely be shown. Robin Blaetz subsequently found a print of the film at the cinémathèque in Lausanne. See "Strategies of Containment," p. 204.

35. Michel Estève, "Les séductions de l'oratorio filmé ou le merveilleux contre le surnaturel," *Etudes cinématographiques* 18–19 (Fall 1962), 65–71.

36. Claude Beylie, "Défense de *Jeanne au bûcher* ou la sérénité des abîmes," *Etudes cinématographiques* 18–19 (Fall 1962), 72–78.

37. Harry and Michael Medved, *The Hollywood Hall of Shame* (New York, 1984), p. 224.

38. Gerald Pratley, *The Cinema of Otto Preminger* (New York, 1971), pp. 119–20.

39. Ellen C. Kennedy, "Saint Joan," *Films in Review* 8 (June–July 1957), 281.

40. Gaylyn Studlar, "The Trial of Joan of Arc," in *Magill's Survey of Cinema,* ed. Frank N. Magill, Foreign Language Films, vol. 7, TAL–Z (Englewood Cliffs, 1985), p. 3166.

41. Ian Cameron, "Interview with Robert Bresson," *Movie* 7 (1963), 29.

42. Eric Rhode, *Tower of Babel* (London, 1966), pp. 46–47.

43. For further discussion of the links between *Procès* and Bresson's other films, see Studlar, pp. 3162–66.

44. Sandrine Bonnaire, *Le roman d'un tournage: Jeanne la pucelle* (Paris, 1994), p. 11.

45. Harlan Kennedy, "Sam & Jim's Excellent Adventure and Other Side Trips at the 44th Berlin Filmfestspiele," *Film Comment* 30 (May–June 1994), 72–73.

46. Umberto Eco, *Travels in Hyperreality,* trans. William Weaver (New York, 1983), p. 61.

47. Brian Stock, *Listening for the Text* (Baltimore, 1990), p. 73.

48. For their generous assistance in the writing of this essay, I owe a debt of gratitude to Simon Baker at the British Film Institute's National Film and Television Archive; Madeline F. Matz at the Motion Picture, Broadcasting, and Recorded Sound Division of the Library of Congress; Bonnie Wheeler at Southern Methodist University; Charles T. Wood at Dartmouth College; Robin Blaetz at Emory University; and Nadia Margolis, editor of the *Christine de Pizan Newsletter.*

THE "JOAN PHENOMENON" AND THE FRENCH RIGHT

Nadia Margolis

Joan's uniquely powerful appropriation by the French Right finds its origins in the heroine's own time; this affinity is then traced from the French Revolution, through Michelet's history, and the founding of the Action Française to the present. Vichy's image of Joan is illumined by Nazi Germany's idealized woman. This analysis concludes with a plea for vigilance: those seduced by the "Joan phenomenon" sometimes neglect ominous portents of her political reception.

The 1995 electoral gains of Jean-Marie Le Pen and his National Front party invite a retrospective glance at the history of the Right in France. Philosophically more complex than its counterparts in other nations, the French Right has cultivated ideals that in their most laudable form crystallized in the icon of Joan of Arc, simple shepherdess and patriot, by the late nineteenth century. Yet because of its pluralistic nature, this ideology, in its twentieth-century manifestations, suggests disturbing comparisons with that of Nazi Germany.

Throughout French history, the Maid of Orleans has been invoked as an inspirational, indeed validating, symbol. The origins of such appropriation can be traced back to her own time. Indeed, Joan has been more than a symbol or cult: she was a phenomenon. As promulgated by such fin-de-siècle minds as Charles Maurras, Maurice Barrès, and Paul Déroulède, this phenomenon is pluralistic to the point of self-contradiction, risking an ideological confusion with the image of Joan revered by other factions, such as the Left and the Republicans. This Joan is also inconsistent with the woman rehabilitated in 1456. Among the principal formulators of this phenomenon have been intellectuals and scholars: trusted authorities skilled at hiding their biases and *béguins* behind veils of erudition or those who have proceeded in good faith, unaware of their own motives. This essay intends to demonstrate how even the most objective and politically disinterested of these thinkers have contributed to the rebirth of a right-wing Joan.

Although France's Right was founded as early as the Revolution and endowed with a vast polemical literature punctuated by some noteworthy events, it is Nazi Germany, through its efficiency (what the French verbalized the Nazis enacted), that figures in modern memory as the consummate right-wing culture. Such was not the case in the 1930s. Albert Speer, reminiscing about life inside Hitler's Third Reich and the origins of Nazi mythopoesis and aesthetics, repeatedly details the travels to the ruins of Greece, Italy, and medieval, even modern, France for visual and philosophical inspiration, because of what Hitler perceived as Germany's primordial-cultural poverty and resultant self-doubt.[1] Nazi art and ethos borrowed and resystematized the basic elements of order, mystical Catholic piety, militant patriotism (often originating with the more basic variety of border and provincial patriotism), and individual self-sacrifice in formulating the national ideal. But these virtues masked xenophobia, racial hatred, and misogyny: reflexes that arose out of a national desire for revenge in the humiliating aftermath of World War I.

The French Right had no need to borrow from other countries: its national patron saint came ready-made in the figure of Joan of Arc. Like its later German analogue, the French Right pursued an initially noble goal: to restore national identity and pride after defeat by the Prussians and the demolition of the Commune in 1870–71. This goal, however, never freed itself from the petty impulses arising from a disaffected, demoralized population grown impatient with rationalism. Like the Nazis, the French Right clothed such reactions in a panoply of pseudo-scientific evidence propagated by practitioners of ethnography, anthropology, sociology, biology, and history. And while lending credibility to the Right, these mostly fledgling disciplines in turn acquired greater legitimacy for themselves.[2]

A similar situation existed in the early fifteenth century, particularly after the disastrous defeat at Agincourt in 1415.[3] France, or at least the Armagnac party supporting Charles VII against the king of England, suffered from a collective disorientation and psychological depression, from the dauphin on down.[4] The country's most menacing division was no longer among the feudal fiefdoms but between Armagnac and Anglo-Burgundian France. The country's miraculous agent of unification and triumph was Joan the Maid, first during her brief lifetime and more so after her death. Her mortal enemy proved to be the intellectuals; the sly legal scholars of the Sorbonne, eager to regain influence lost after the Council of Constance (also 1415). Yet ever since the deliverance of Orleans from the English on May 8, 1429, the French popular spirit, during any menacing situation, has found solace not in its intellectuals but in the simple girl from Lorraine.

Jean-François Kahn points out that what we now think of as rightist or leftist political tendencies were already operative in Joan's time. Although at the outset one finds royal power behind both Armagnacs and Anglo-Burgundians, it was John, duke of Burgundy, who, by presenting himself as a reformer as well as antimonarchist, won support from the latently insurrectionist urban lower and middle class, especially in Paris—the legacy of Etienne Marcel and later of Simon Caboche. The Burgundians consequently became the first French leftists. The Armagnacs, because they supported the dauphin and his father, Charles VI, before him, end up as the royalists or conservative right wing in this struggle, during which Charles VI was forced to sign the Cabochian ordinance (1413), diminishing his own power, to appease the populace. Kahn points out that one of the authors of the ordinance was Pierre Cauchon, future judge at Joan's condemnation trial.[5]

In such early episodes, we perceive not only the origins of the political polarities and their complexities within France as a burgeoning nation but also the origins of Joan herself as a political icon. The main phases of her brief life would be seized upon by modern political movements as this simplified reconstruction attempts to illustrate. Born of the people (Left) of the purest, Aryan, Gallic race (Right), Joan defends the king (Right) and France (Republican/Right). She reaffirms the dauphin's legitimacy, cast in doubt by his mother's supposed adultery, by her virginity as much as by her military exploits (Royalist/Right). She helps rid France of its worst enemy, the English (all sides, especially Right). A paragon of peasant common sense (Republican/Right), she is also pious to the point of mystical vision and divine designation as savior of France

(Catholic Right) but is duped by officials of church and state (Republican/Left) and is captured and burned as a heretic by the English and their allies at the Sorbonne (Right/Left [Péguy]) and by the very church that had later to canonize her in order to preserve its credibility (Republican/Left). Among the ashes is found her unburned heart, still full of blood (Catholic Right).

The intellectual-historical reality is far more complicated and nuanced, but this sketch hints at the potent images exploitable by the Right. The complete Johannic corpus—the unburned relic of her existence after Rouen in 1431—comprises texts relating to Joan's literary, historical, and political afterlife. It forms a gyrating parade of oscillating but simultaneous strands of interpretation, replete with dialectical fission and fusion, among many diverse groups, subgroups, and individuals, even if we restrict our scope to French reception history, as Michel Winock and Gerd Krumeich have most comprehensively demonstrated.[6] Nevertheless, as Kahn's analysis and our political parsing of the legend reveal, Joan's relationship with God and king presage a more natural affiliation with the Right, while Cauchon's role in the Cabochian uprising and her trial presage the Left's eventual failure to claim her exclusively. Another major facet of the fifteenth-century Joan to be incorporated into modern propaganda, particularly by Vichy, would be Anglophobia.

NOBLER IN THE MIND

Not all intellectuals dealt with Joan as had Cauchon and his magistrates. Many persons and movements selecting Joan as their symbol through the ages have done so with the best intentions. Terms and phrases denoting rescue are frequent in each faction's lexicon.[7] On the other hand, we shall see how her strongest detractors, like Voltaire, enraged the previously dormant literati into feverish activity. Some kind of rational intervention was necessary, since the so-called rehabilitation of 1456 exorcised France's demons while doing little to clear up the mysteries permeating the accusations against Joan. Were her voices truly those of saints or of the devil? Did her mission really mean that France was and would continue to be divinely favored? Was she a daughter of the people or of royal birth? Was she a virgin?

It was, in short, deeply troubling to the God-fearing, humble populace that their savior should have been burned by the very institution whose teachings Joan exemplified and whose prayers she had answered and equally baffling that the king she helped crown should not have rescued her. The burning of this country girl in 1431 left the greatest scar in the national conscience until the decapitation of Louis XVI in 1793,[8] and would eventually surpass even this event, so that by the late nineteenth century she would be compared to Christ as supreme martyr—thus obviating the need for a monarch to ensure France's glorious, divinely ordained destiny. In this way, the scattered christological associations first made by her fifteenth-century apologists, and the device of her banner, "Jesus Maria," would attain fullest development. If Joan-as-Jesus inspired the cult of passive suffering and divine grandeur, what we might call Joan-as-Napoleon coexists out of the need to commemorate earthly, military triumph, as Napoleon himself understood, in reestablishing in 1802 the festivals honoring Joan, suppressed by the Revolution in 1793.[9]

This was the Joan bequeathed to her people by the end of the nineteenth century, when France was again divided deeply from within after defeat from outside, when intellectuals and scholars strove to help rebuild the nation in the eyes of its people. But she had become many Joans, whether Winock's triptych—symbol of Old vs. New France, Catholic-monarchist, democratic-revolutionary— or the quartet newly suggested by Robert Gildea: "Voltairean Joan" (anticlerical); Michelet's Joan (popular, patriotic, spiritual, yet tending toward Republican); Catholic-royalist; and Joan the patron saint of France (nationalist, more patriotic than religious).[10] Officially or personally, the intellectuals rendered a major service by consolidating these Joans as a step toward national unity.

On the level of mass appeal, however, Joan's most flamboyant iconography, verbal and visual, must be credited to the Right. Out of the negativism and paranoia dominating its ideology, she surfaces as the primary positive element promoting the essence of what Maurras and others would term "integral nationalism": an isolationist, racist, repressive form of patriotism. The attempts to integrate the various Joans evolved simultaneously with this search for national unity. As in 1431, the idea of her mission became corrupted in practice: order turned into anachronistic royalism or, worse, repression; piety submitted to the very sort of Church Militant that Joan despised. Patriotism, exemplified in regional and national festivals, succumbed to intolerance and hooliganism; self-sacrifice gave way to a twisted sense of martyrdom on the part of the oppressors when punishing their victims.

The political ritualizing of Joan did not limit itself to her feast-day processions and rites, to which much recent study has been devoted;[11] but just as effectively in the long run, her image and its interpretation turned normally cloistered scholars into crusaders, of various political backgrounds, in the militantly nationalist endeavor to reestablish French identity.[12] Johannic scholarship would galvanize this sense of mission, as when the great Michelet would admonish his pupil Quicherat to convince him of his value as a promising historian in 1852, "au nom de la France, au nom de la vérité, au nom de la grande guerre dont nous sommes les soldats" (in the name of France, in the name of truth, in the name of the great war in which we are the soldiers).[13] French historiography itself had become a battleground, as Michelet's terminology reveals, on which the campaign for Joan promised to be decisive. Largely through the efforts of such men, whether leftists, Republicans, Catholic royalists, or rightists, Joan's status as "national emblem" equals that of Charlemagne and Descartes as the only persons named on a par with the institutions—from *coq gaulois* to the state and kingship—signaling national identity in Pierre Nora's *Lieux de mémoire*.[14]

And yet the factionalism prevailed, as it still does, sometimes violently. How did this come about in the land of Descartes and Rabelais? Where were the voices of reason? Some backtracking is in order. The official birthdate of the Right is September 11, 1789, when, at the Assemblée Nationale, partisans of the king's absolute power first sat to the right of the presider.[15] Joan's evolution as symbol of this party and its factions was already set in motion in reaction to such assaults as Voltaire's mock-epic *La Pucelle* (1730–42): a prerevolutionary, pre-Republican, anticlerical harbinger—and scandalous sex symbol.[16] In a more reverent vein, she would inspire the Republican soldiers of year II, then shift to postrevolutionary opposite to stand for royalism, Catholicism, and order. During the Revolution, Joan, seen as savior of the king rather than of the people, seems to have been supplanted among democratic partisans by the Phrygian-bonneted Marianne. In many ways, the Revolution almost killed Joan off on both secular and religious levels because of her overwhelmingly monarchist affiliation, while the damaging echoes of Voltaire's satire diminished her usefulness for the church.

Enter Germany, on two fronts: romantic literature and scholarship. After the success of Schiller's *Die Jungfrau* in 1801, interest in the heroine rekindled among the literati and also the scholars. When Guido Goerres, son of the German Catholic publicist whom even Napoleon fearfully called "la cinquième puissance,"[17] made plans to edit the trial manuscripts long moldering in Paris, this proved to be too much of a threat to French cultural hegemony. The Société de l'Histoire de France was consequently founded, bids were taken from scholars on the project, and the newly minted *chartiste* Jules Quicherat would edit them and also publish a wealth of literary and historical texts devoted to Joan.[18] His five volumes, completed in 1849,[19] would end up being read by a vast educated public throughout the world, from Mark Twain to Mrs. Oliphant to authors in Meiji Japan.[20]

But it was Quicherat's mentor, Michelet—"no-method Michelet"[21]—who composed the definitive historiographical "hymn" to Joan in 1841.[22] His courses on Joan entranced Quicherat, who by this time was methodically laboring at his edition, which, despite his Republicanism, would constitute the textual relics of the future saint. Michelet's Joan, as inspiring as she was, managed to remain both apolitical and amethodical. She survived the political buffeting of the period better than her creator, whose anticlericalism and anti-Bonapartism in nonhistorical writings cost him his chair.[23]

Michelet's enormously appealing portrait fostered the image of Joan as daughter—but also compassionate mother—of the French people and the land: fulfillment and continued promise of a glorious destiny for the coming Third Republic. Although more modern research has annotated, corrected, and sought to replace the works of Michelet and Quicherat, their influence remains unrivaled in Johannic studies. While Michelet's first approaches to Joan betoken a profound piety, a piety that later became tempered by anticlericalism,[24] both men have come down to us as ardently Republican, anticlerical historians. Yet because of their political restraint, their pioneering work unwittingly fueled the very type of rightist causes and cults they had hoped to abolish by scholarly truth: Quicherat made accessible the primary sources; inadvertently, Michelet accomplished for French right-wing historiography what Leni Reifenstahl would intentionally do for Nazi cinematography.

Charles Maurras founded the Action Française in 1899. A rightist reaction to Gambetta's and, later, Paul Déroulède's Republican, pro-

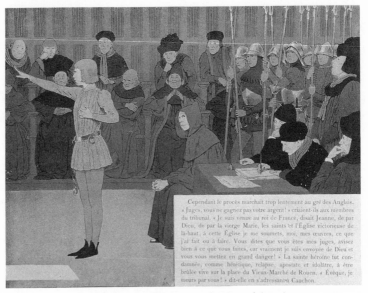

Cependant le procès marchait trop lentement au gré des Anglais. « Juges, vous ne gagnez pas votre argent! » criaient-ils aux membres du tribunal. « Je suis venue au roi de France, disait Jeanne, de par Dieu, de par la vierge Marie, les saints et l'Église victorieuse de là-haut; à cette Église je me soumets, moi, mes œuvres, ce que j'ai fait ou à faire. Vous dites que vous êtes mes juges, avisez bien à ce que vous faites, car vraiment je suis envoyée de Dieu et vous vous mettez en grand danger! » La sainte héroïne fut condamnée, comme hérétique, relapse, apostate et idolâtre, à être brûlée vive sur la place du Vieux-Marché de Rouen. « Évêque, je meurs par vous! » dit-elle en s'adressant à Cauchon.

Figure One: L.-M. Boutet de Monvel (1896)

Dreyfus Ligue des Patriotes (1882)—its first president, Henri Martin, was one of Michelet's students—the AF had arisen out of dissatisfaction with the earlier *Ligue de la Patrie*. While it is beyond the scope of this paper to retrace the pedigree of the Right before and after this moment,[25] we should note that almost every one of its many phases involved possessed its own idea of Joan.

The Action Française not only rewrote history but was able to communicate its doctrines to a wide audience via primary-school textbooks, pamphlets, as well as advanced scholarship, to combat the competing forces of Protestant and Republican anticlerical rationalism.[26] Such Action Française exponents as Maurras, Daudet, and Bernanos devoted much attention to Joan, the aspects of whose icon shifted with the changing moods of the movement during its most dynamic decades (1908–31). Perhaps one of the most jarring assaults on this movement's identity was the Vatican's condemnation of its radicalism in 1926 as destructive to true Catholic beliefs. Not to be deterred, Maurras, Bernanos, and others set about using Joan as a symbol *against* the church, as the figure of martyred innocence now as at her trial in 1430, when she refused to submit to the Church Militant.[27]

Figure Two: M. Albe, ca. 1940–44. Courtesy of EdiMedia, Paris.

Understanding has benefited from recent pictorial surveys of the role of visual and plastic imagery, the most powerful means of conveying Joan's attributes to the public.[28] Three examples represent

Figure Three: O.D.V. Guillonet (1912)

significant phases in the development of Joan from Republican to rightist icon. Louis-Maurice Boutet de Monvel (1851–1913) was the preeminent visual imagemaker of Joan for the later Third Republic in his *Jeanne d'Arc*, a book designed primarily for children. His delicate *jeune fille rangée* watercolors of Joan, whom he portrayed as childlike yet intransigent, often looking to heaven (fig. 1),[29] contrast revealingly with M. Albe's fittingly Germanic woodcut style for Marshal Pétain during the Occupation (1940–44) (fig. 2). If Boutet's Joan is charmingly boyish, even when dressed in armor, as she asserts her graceful, luminous form amid the straight vertical lines and umber-and-black expanses characterizing stolid male officialdom, the Pétainist Joan is mannish: her hair, shorter and without the pageboy effect of Boutet, forms a sort of helmet, while multilayered mail and metal plate cover her thick-necked, muscular frame. The rigidly drawn bouquet she clasps in her left, ungloved hand seems to reinforce this harshness rather than temper it by recalling her gentle peasant-girl origins. Similarly, the wheat ears—spikey, like Joan's spurs (in themselves atypical of a girl who loved animals)—resemble weapons instead of life-giving plants, while we tend to suspect that the daisies in the foreground shadows will soon be trampled under the feet of the masses Joan is leading or plucked by them as territorial trophies, in spite of the artist's intentions. Her gaze points not heavenward but earthward as she glances back protectively at Pétain and his people, her figure framed by the strong-poled (in comparison to the old Marshal's cane), swirling banner invoking and depicting Jesus (as pelican) and Mary. That Vichy's artist underscores her invulnerability and will to conquest more persuasively than he presents any kind of tender nurturing says much about that government's vision and priorities.

From another angle, providing an elegant yet significant intercession between Boutet and Albe, is Octave Guillonnet's magnificent cover illustration for *Jeanne d'Arc,* Funck-Brentano's biography of 1912 (fig. 3), emphasizing through the gilded filigrees a Joan-as-Christ.[30] While Boutet's Joan has just been declared Venerable (1894), Guillonnet represents the further stage as newly beatified Joan (1909): clothed as female *athleta Christi* yet passively suffering on a cross of fleurs-de-lis. She is not nailed and suspended from the cross but rather is standing on the ground—her knees noticeably flexed like Christ's, however—spreading her arms up against it, her eyes tilted upward, as if to signify voluntary assumption of Christ's mission as savior and his martyrdom, not on a cross of wood or gold but on one decorated with and flanked by the royal-dynastic symbol.

There is no blood or violence, no weaponry; neither hand is gloved, as though to confirm Joan's past earthly triumph and present readiness to enter into the higher realm of canonization. Guillonnet's beatified Joan also wears armor yet carries no daisies; despite her Christlike posture and the absence of Vichy Joan's "Jesus Mary" banner, she displays more femininity, more of Mary's qualities, than her Vichy avatar. By the time of Vichy, however, it seems that propagandists no longer bothered with subtle flourishes: fully canonized since 1920, Joan-as-national-saint had now paradoxically become all the more susceptible to exploitation. In this case, Germanic militarism had overtaken her as it had invaded her homeland, and Albe's black-and-white, austere lines reflect intolerance of any nuanced thought about her or Vichy, whether in art, literature, science, or philosophy.[31]

All three images, though different from each other, represent the origins, then fulfillment, of right-wing Joan. Throughout this evolution, we should also remind ourselves that each of the three artists was respected by the artistic and political establishment of his time.[32]

Sculpture flourished at least as impressively, first with the Republicans' monument-building campaign, paid for in part by Joseph Fabre, who lowered the price and donated the profits from his book on Joan in 1883.[33] The most magnificent monument, however, once again comes from the Right: Frémiet's gilded equestrian, fierce-faced Maid standing in the Place des Pyramides, before which Barrès and Déroulède would proudly pose.[34] Another rightist sculptural style of a more serene nature depicts Joan as a solid, protective military-mother figure, as exemplified in the statue by Maxime Réal del Sarte, onetime ardent Action Française activist.[35]

Regardless of such diverse detail among right-wing artists in expressing the heroine's extraordinary presence, none of their depictions was intended to liberate women from their neo-Bismarckian *Kirche, Küche, und Kinder* confinement. The fascist mystique,[36] advocating woman's work only for the state, took care not to intersect deeply with the feminist one, promising women work for their individual well-being, only a portion of which need be patriotic.

Regional patriotism and folklore, especially in the border provinces, were as powerful as learned culture in the nineteenth and early twentieth centuries, just as they had been in Joan's era. As in the fifteenth century, these currents emerged in more fervent and principled form in the provinces, especially at the borders, than in Paris, because of a kind of idealizing distance from centers of official power: such areas as Lorraine were connected enough to feel French (as opposed to German or English) but removed enough to remain unaware of the political corruption of the capital.[37] The patriotic passions of the *vague populaire* burned even among certain intellectuals. Michelet, despite academic training and Parisian birth, was smitten with the image of the simple country girl, untainted by intellectual and urban adulteration, an enthusiasm with which he captivated his students and readers. As Quicherat and others have recalled, Michelet's Joan was more than a work of popularization: it was an emotional experience: "L'épisode de la Pucelle a visiblement attendri tout le monde. Il y avait là des forgerons en blouse qui s'essuyaient les yeux du revers de la main sans se cacher" (The episode about the Maid has visibly touched everyone. Even blacksmiths in overalls were openly wiping their eyes with the backs of their hands).[38]

From among the most significant regional myths arose that of Lorraine: land of Joan, land of Maurice Barrès and other great French politicos. Barrès combined regional mysticism with Boulangist patriotism and nationalism. By 1889, however, Joan "belonged" to the Republicans as well as to the Catholic Right. Nationalist groups planned, during the centenary of the Revolution, a pilgrimage to Joan's birthplace at Domrémy: site, along with the old marketplace at Rouen, of various *jeux de construction* in which episodes of her life were reenacted.[39] Most intriguing about the Lorraine mythopoesis is the reassociation of Joan with sorcery and witchcraft by the early Barrès, Sâr Péladan, and others.[40] As he would also do in the case of Blaise Pascal while visiting ancestral places in the Auvergne, Barrès would conjure up a mystical union with Joan merely by walking meditatively around Domrémy and elsewhere, as he relates in his book *Le Mystère en pleine lumière*: looking to "respirer l'atmosphère où fut préparée Jeanne" (breathe in the atmosphere in which Joan was prepared); in search of her "inexplicable quality." He saw her as a Christian saint more pagan than Catholic, unknowingly motivated by "les vieilles imaginations celtiques" (ancient Celtic imagination), instinctively preferring "saints who shelter fairy fountains behind their utterances."[41] A more occult, marginal cohort of Maurras's crowd and the literary scene was Joséphin Péladan, who called himself "the magus" ("Le Sâr") and claimed, among other things, to have divined Joan's famous secret—instrumental in winning the Dauphin's support at Chinon prior to her mission—by Rosicrucian illuminism.[42] Little matter that such evocations contradicted Joan's own protestations of innocence of such practices before her accusers. In other areas marking Joan's itinerary, it is no coincidence that the most forceful panegyric advocating her canonization was pronounced at Orleans, the city that Joan delivered, by Bishop Dupanloup in 1855.[43]

It is also essential to observe the role of certain political *affaires* in cementing Joan's image for the Right, those of Dreyfus and Thalamas. That of Captain Dreyfus (1896–1906) continues to absorb historians and fanatics. The long-forgotten affair(s) of Thalamas, the Freemason professor who dared teach a rationalist approach to Joan and her time (1904, 1908–09), merits recapitulation.

François-Amédée Thalamas first taught his controversial courses on Joan at the prestigious Lycée Condorcet in Paris. In his efforts to instill in his students a rational, skeptical method of reading history, he recklessly asserted, so it was alleged, that Joan was simply a mascot and, since she probably was raped while in prison, consequently died without her signal attribute, her virginity. As students began reporting such details to their parents, the case went to a closed hearing leading to Thalamas's dismissal.[44] His case, however, aroused enough fervor between nationalists and Republicans to warrant discussion in Parlement, where his cause was defended by the great socialist leader and Dreyfusard Jean Jaurès. Denounced by Barrès and Péguy, Thalamas gained favor with the Republican faction. Four years later, the Sorbonne allowed him to teach a *cours libre* on medieval history. These classes, despite police protection, were frequently disturbed by riots perpetrated by the newly formed young hooligan branch of the Action Française, the Camelots du Roy ("hawkers to the king"), culminating, during their most violent confrontation with his students, the *Thalamistes*, in a public thrashing for the professor (ironically in the amphitheater named for Michelet) by the future sculptor of Joan, Maxime Réal del Sarte, and two other Camelots. Thalamas quickly retaliated by smashing a chair over the face of one of his assailants.[45] The exhilaration of the Thalamas affair made the Action Française more determined in its mission than ever before.

In his study of the slogans and other rhetoric surrounding the Dreyfus and Thalamas affairs, Michel Winock has deftly illustrated the interrelationship of both episodes in a telling analogical chain: Dreyfus: Thalamas: Cauchon: Jews: Freemasons: enemies of France. The Camelots, after harassing and physically attacking Freemasons, like Thalamas, and Jewish professors, would make a point of rallying around Joan monuments throughout Paris, chanting insults at the target of the day.[46] Descriptions of their exploits in the *Action française* and *Libre parole* echo the diction of heroic epics: striking blows, and martyrdom, martyrdom not of their targets but of the attackers themselves, "heroically" wounded in action or imprisoned. Both affairs encompassed the brutal transition between the Catholic right wing and Republican France (although Dreyfus had his Catholic sympathizers, notably Péguy) and, for Thalamas, between the old and new style of history: from mythomania-disguised-as-positivism to empiricism and critique of sources.[47]

To sum up the effects of these and many other developments in Johannic reception history: clearly there existed many political parties in France simultaneously looking to Joan as their guiding image. Even limiting our scope to "nationalists," we find variety and contradiction. The Right, in spite of divisiveness within its ranks— each faction with its own concept of the Maid[48]—succeeded in making her a cult figure, first under the Restoration and then throughout the nineteenth century. Right-wing intellectuals achieved this by exploiting the love of mystery pervading what Georges Goyau has dubbed "the age of Joan of Arc," recreating in their own way the fifteenth-century cult of Joan.[49] In current terms, they were the first to *essentialize* her, just as they did the ideal of Frenchness with which she had become inextricably bound, as patriot, saint, woman—and anti-Semite/xenophobe. Their integration of Joan fared better than their integrated nationalism, in that their Joan became enriched and strengthened rather than dissipated by the conflicts generated by such a mixed persona. Joan would displace the Revolution's Marianne as national patriotic symbol.

MORE INTELLECTUALS, MORE BETRAYAL?[50]

After the initial "birthing period" on which this study has concentrated, the Maid and her legend would survive more major bids by different sides: the Action Française (1929), the extreme-left

Communist party (1936), and further fragmentation under Vichy (1940–44). Under this last regime, she would signify French "moral purification," justifying Anglophobia and anti-Semitism, instead of the customary general xenophobia, so as not to offend the Nazis. Her womanly role and loyalty to her king became translated into total submission to Vichy government and ideology. The Communists then made one more attempt to recapture Joan, in 1942, citing Michelet's model as they had in 1936, with the support of De Gaulle in 1945. But luck was once again with the right wing: VE day took place on May 8, date of Joan's liberation of Orleans. Not even Mitterand's appearance at that city (May 8, 1982) could stem the right-wing Johannic tide.[51] When Le Pen inaugurated his National Front party in 1984, he appealed not only to Catholics, as had earlier right-wing groups, but also to the workers, whom he wooed away from the Left with the latest version of Anglophobia: the resentment of immigrant workers, the scab labor—and thus bane of the unions—of France since the 1960s. Le Pen's Joan stands for this as she does for the French equivalent of "family values," the pristine descendant of Vichy's ideal.

The intellectuals have not been napping through these developments. Obviously, some were hired by the Right and other parties to articulate their respective causes, although given France's long heritage as an indefatigably verbal culture, Le Pen's party emerges as far less literate than that of the nascent Action Française. Though lacking an apologist to equal Barrès or Maurras for rhetorical artistry and intellectual acumen, they have succeeded just the same: no doubt a reflection of a decline of the word, even in France, in the face of television.

Others perturbed by the revival of the Right have sought to warn the public. We might dare to pinpoint the dawn of the great resurgence of interest, whether sympathetic or not, in the French Right by French writers and artists as occurring on and after the years 1969–74: date of "Les evénements" and of the first major screening in Paris of *Le chagrin et la pitié* (1969) by the Swiss filmmaker Marcel Ophuls, respectively.[52] The year 1974 also witnessed Louis Malle's film about a young collaborator, *Lacombe Lucien*.[53] This period inaugurated a boom in national self-scrutiny of the less glorious moments of the Occupation, during which the French forced themselves to confront the fact that they and their parents had not all fought with the Resistance. At the same time, these attempts at exempla elicited the opposite reaction within other groups: a rebirth of rightist sympathy in the face of current threats to the prosperous French—indeed, Western—way of life, rekindling the old tendencies of racism, anti-Semitism, and nationalist isolationism.

One would like to ascribe the current plenitude of publications on the Right to the intelligentsia's desire to incite France and other western countries to consult the mirror of history before repeating the errors of the 1940s. Yet it would seem that political convictions have taken a back seat to an apoliticism different from that of Michelet, who incidentally is enjoying his own revival in recent years.[54] French journalists and scholars often seem to write about rightist and other extremists in the same way that the public seems to read them: in the manner of political-historical "buffs," simply because so many of the Right's proponents were such fascinating and colorful personalities, much more seductive, *because* of their demagoguery, than the political moderates who have saved their country.[55] In so doing, the intellectuals have cultivated a nation of historical hobbyists rather than true students or watchdogs. A valid example of how French scholars inform the general public on the implications of the rising Right might be the "Dossier Jeanne d'Arc" in the popular newsmagazine *Evénement du jeudi* (May 7-13, 1992), a comprehensive, richly illustrated collection of essays by leading French historians far exceeding anything today's American press could provide its readers. The overall message of the "Dossier" is that, even though Le Pen has managed to claim her as his emblem, Joan has been subjected to all manner of appropriation by many factions to the point of disappearance as a real person; Le Pen is just another passing phase. All of this rings true, but it is nevertheless bland in comparison with the more forceful assessments permeating other articles in the same issue of the *Evénement* on U.S. race riots and European political scandals. Appearing slightly earlier, the *Express* ("La France bouleversée," April 3, 1992) registered more alarm over the rising Right amid what it perceived as national complacency, but without the historical depth and insight of the *Evénement* and without any discussion of the FN's appropriation of Joan.

Once again, Joan is at the mercy of the intellectuals; once again, we are confident of making progress. Thanks to a firmer entrenchment of democratic ideals and more scientific methods, conservative, royalist, and other right-wing groups have ceased to dominate historiography, particularly Johannic history, as they did around the turn of the century. If the same base impulses have not disappeared from the right-wing agenda, as attested in the FN's mandate, perhaps this sad fact might inspire historians, whether French, German, or American, to greater vigilance and more effectiveness in informing the public. The "clerks" (to use Benda's medieval-based term) now benefit from a better position in which to function as guardians of free inquiry by virtue of past experience— honed during their forebears' promotion or debunking of Joan of Arc over the first half of this century—and shame, as the heirs of Cauchon, should they commit their own form of "relapse." Perhaps in no other domain these days can medieval studies be so *au courant* and *engagé*.

NOTES

All translations from the French are mine, in both text and notes.

1. Albert Speer, *Inside the Third Reich*, trans. Richard & Clara Winston (New York, 1970), chs. 1–12. passim.

2. See, e.g., Herman Lebovics, *True France: The Wars over Cultural Identity, 1900–1945* (Ithaca, NY, 1992), pp. 8ff.

3. This resemblance was exploited by Pétain and his propagandists in 1942, notably in his speech for the Joan of Arc festival on May 10, reproduced in *Discours aux Français (17 juin 1940–44)* (Paris, 1989), pp. 254–55, also cited in Karen Sullivan, "Jeanne d'Arc sous l'Occupation," unpublished paper given at Cerisy-la-Salle, July 25, 1994. My thanks to Prof. Sullivan for providing me with a copy of her paper. For a concise overview of the period, see H. R. Kedward, *Occupied France: Collaboration and Resistance, 1940–1944* (Oxford, 1985).

4. This sadness and loss of selfhood permeates Christine's opening stanza to her *Ditié de Jeanne d'Arc*, ed. Angus J. Kennedy and Kenneth Varty (Oxford, 1977), p. 28, in which she depicts herself, pre-Joan, as "weeping in a closed abbey for eleven years", on a parallel with Charles' flight and seclusion, after his legitimacy was disputed. For Christine in Vichy, see n. 31, *infra*.

5. "L'Affaire Jeanne d'Arc," *L'Evénement du jeudi* 392 (May 7–13, 1992), p. 63.

6. Michel Winock, "Jeanne d'Arc," in Pierre Nora, ed., *Les Lieux de Mémoire. III: Les France. 3: De l'Archive à l'emblème* (Paris, 1992), pp. 675–733, groups many of these transformations under the terms "une mémoire mobile" and "une mémoire disputée". Winock's essay (hereafter cited as "Winock, *Lieux*") is the most complete and perceptive survey of Johannic appropriation in French cultural history to date. Gerd Krumeich, in *Jeanne d'Arc à travers l'histoire*, trans. Josie Mély, *et al*. Intro. Régine Pernoud (Paris,

1993) [orig.: *Jeanne d'Arc in der Geschichte* (Sigmaringen, 1989)] (hereafter cited as "Krumeich") also expertly traces Joan's evolution in historiography.

7. Even among skeptics like Anatole France, when his assistant reports him as proclaiming, a propos of his projected *Vie de Jeanne d'Arc*: "C'est la course au clocher. Il faut achever notre monument libéral, républicain, avant que les prêtres la juchent sur leurs autels" [This is a race from start to finish. We must finish our Liberal, Republican monument before those priests stick her atop their altars]." In Jean-Jacques Brousson, *Anatole France en pantoufles* (Paris, 1924), p. 23.

8. For the posthumous quasi-canonization of Louis XVI, see Susan Dunn, *The Deaths of Louis XVI: Regicide and the French Political Imagination* (Princeton, NJ, 1995).

9. Winock, *Lieux*, p. 689.

10. Winock, *Lieux*, p. 714. Robert Gildea, *The Past in French History* (New Haven & London, 1994), p. 154.

11. See, e.g.: Charles Rearick, "Festivals in Modern France: The Experience of the Third Republic," *Journal of Contemporary History* 12 (1977), pp. 435–60; Rosemonde Sanson, "La Fête de Jeanne d'Arc en 1894: Controverse et célébration," *Revue d'Histoire moderne et contemporaine* 20 (1973), pp. 444–63.

12. For an analysis of the passionate involvement of the historians in this effort, see Lebovics, *True France*, passim.

13. Cited in Krumeich, p. 97.

14. See the appropriately titled chapters by Robert Morrissey, François Azouvi, and Michel Pastoureau, respectively, in the "Identifications" section in vol. 3 of *Lieux de Mémoire*.

15. Jean-Christian Petitfils, *La Droite en France* (Paris, 1983), p. 7.

16. See Gildea, *The Past*, p. 154. Voltaire's highly embattled, popular poem appeared in 125 eds. from 1755–1835 and 13 more from 1835–1881, as given in Gilbert Zoppi, "Jeanne d'Arc et les républicains," in Jacques Viard, ed., *L'esprit républicain* (Paris, 1972), p. 314.

17. Cited in Georges Goyau, *Jeanne d'Arc devant l'opinion allemande* (Paris, 1907), p. 49.

18. For a chronology of events leading to the publication of Joan's trial records before and after Quicherat, see Pierre Marot's introduction to Pierre Tisset & Yvonne Lanhers, eds., *Procès de condamnation de Jeanne d'Arc*, 3 vols. (Paris, 1960–71). Further background to various phases in Krumeich, passim.

19. *Procès de condamnation et de réhabilitation de Jeanne d'Arc dite la Pucelle*, 5 vols. (Paris, 1841–49).

20. Mark Twain, *Personal Recollections of Joan of Arc…*(New York, 1896); the Victorian novelist, Mrs. Oliphant [Margaret O. Wilson], *Jeanne d'Arc: Her Life and Death* (New York & London, 1896); for Meiji Japan, see Kasuhiko Takayama, "Jeanne d'Arc vue par les Japonais au temps de

Meiji," in *Jeanne d'Arc: Une époque, un rayonnement. Colloque d'histoire médiévale, Orléans, octobre 1979*. Pref. R. Pernoud (Paris, 1982), pp. 279–86.

21. My translation of Lucien Febvre's evocation, "ce Michelet qui n'avait pas la Méthode" in his pre-Vichy assessment of the latter's *Jeanne d'Arc* which, despite its "fadaises patriotiques [patriotic nonsense]," remains "la seule Jeanne intelligible que nous ayons [the only intelligible Joan we have]," in "Entre Benda et Seignobos," *Revue de Synthèse* 5 (1933); repr. in *Combats pour l'histoire* (Paris, 1953), pp. 89–90.

22. Winock's terminology and judgement, *Lieux*, p. 684. Michelet's first lectures on Joan began in 1833; his *Jeanne d'Arc* was first published in his *Histoire de France*, vol. 5 (Paris, 1841) then revised in 1853; the definitive text is by Paul Viallaneix, ed., *Jeanne d'Arc et d'autres textes* (Paris, 1974). His 1839 course notes have been published by Oscar A. Haac, *Revue d'histoire littéraire* 54 (1954) as a monograph supplement.

23. Krumeich, p. 80.

24. For Michelet's shift in faith from orthodoxy to anti-clerical spirituality in his versions of Joan from 1841 to 1853, see Albert Guérard's introduction to his English translation of Michelet, *Joan of Arc* (Ann Arbor, Michigan, 1957). My thanks to Prof. Charles Wood for reminding me of this. Among the many writings on Michelet's historiography since Gustave Rudler's classic *Michelet, historien de Jeanne d'Arc*, 2 vols. (Paris, 1925), see, most recently, Gildea, *The Past*, pp. 154–64.

25. Among the many works on the French Right and those cited *supra*, see Yves Chiron, *Barrès, le Prince de la jeunesse* (Paris, 1986).

26. Stephen Wilson, "A View of the Past: Action Française Historiography and Its Socio-Political Function," *The Historical Journal* 19:1 (1976), pp. 135–61.

27. See Martha Hanna, "Iconology and Ideology: Images of Joan of Arc in the Idiom of the Action Française," *French Historical Studies* 14 (1985), 215–39, although this author deals with exclusively verbal images. Barrès eventually renounced his loyalty to the Action Française, opting for a more Republican mode, but never abandoned Joan (Chiron, *Barrès*, pp. 182–236, 307–11).

28. See examples of painting, posters and sculpture analyzed and reproduced passim in Winock, *Lieux*; Marina Warner, *Joan of Arc: The Image of Female Heroism* (New York, 1981); Claude Ribéra-Pervillé, "Jeanne d'arc au pays des images," *L'Histoire* 15 (Sept. 1979), pp. 60–67; and in "L'Affaire Jeanne d'Arc," *L'Événement du jeudi*.

29. Louis-Maurice Boutet de Monvel, *Jeanne d'Arc* (Paris, 1896).

30. O.D.V. Guillonnet, illustr. in Franz Funck Brentano, *Jeanne d'Arc* (Paris, 1912).

31. This was, after all, the regime that instituted such measures as the Anti-Jewish Statute, resulting in the banishment of Jews, Leftists and

other undesirables from France's universities, among whom the medievalist Gustave Cohen and the Marxist journalist and historian Edith Thomas survive as the most prescient concerning the political exploitability of Joan and her first great apologist, Christine de Pizan, during Vichy's persecution. See Angus J. Kennedy and James Steel, "L'Esprit et l'epée ou la résistance au féminin: Christine de Pizan, Jeanne d'Arc et Edith Thomas," in Liliane Dulac and Bernard Ribémont, eds., *Une Femme de lettres au Moyen Age: Etudes autour de Christine de Pizan* (Orléans, 1995), pp. 495–508. My thanks to Prof. Kennedy for having sent me a copy of his paper, "Gustave Cohen and Christine de Pizan: A Re-Reading of the *Ditié de Jehanne d'Arc* for Occupied France," for the Christine de Pizan Congress at Orléans, July 1995.

32. While Albe's favor with the Pétain régime is obvious, the successes of Boutet and Gullonnet are documented in, e.g., Ulrich Thieme and Frederick Willis, *Allgemeines Lexicon der bildenden Künstler von der Antike bis zur Gegenwart* (Leipzig, 1907–34), 28 vols. Boutet's images of Joan enjoyed particular acclaim in France, Germany and elsewhere: as evidenced in extensive book sales, in his commission to paint three panels on Joan's life for the church at Domrémy, and in well-received exhibits up through at least 1910.

33. *Jeanne d'Arc, libératrice de la France* (Paris, 1883).

34. Often reproduced, these photographs of the July 14, 1912 celebration in Paris, can be found, e.g., in Gildea, *The Past*, p. 157 and Chiron, *Barrès*, betw. pp. 122–23.

35. Reproduction in Warner, *Joan of Arc*, fig. 42, who compares Réal del Sarte's statue to a Mother of Mercy.

36. Term borrowed from Peter Tame, *La Mystique du fascisme dans l'oeuvre de Robert Brasillach* (Paris, 1986).

37. Charles T. Wood, *Joan of Arc & Richard III: Sex, Saints and Government in the Middle Ages* (New York, 1988), p. 130.

38. Letter from Emile Souvestre to Michelet, cited in Krumeich, p. 93.

39. Guy Lobrichon, "Quand l'Eglise brûle, réhabilite et canonise," *L'Evénement du jeudi*, p. 81. For "jeux de construction", Winock, *Lieux*, p. 686.

40. See François Ribadeau Dumas, *Histoire secrète de la Lorraine* (Paris, 1979), ch. 4, "Le Mystère de Domrémy".

41. (Paris, 1926), p. 189. Among many published allusions to Joan, this is Barrès' most complete, cited in Chiron, *Barrès*, p. 309.

42. Joséphin Péladan, *Le Secret de Jeanne d'Arc* (Paris, 1913).

43. For the text of this and other panegyrics, see H. Herluison, *Les Panégyristes de Jeanne d'Arc*, 2nd ed. (Orléans, 1870).

44. Thalamas movingly recounts this episode in the preface to his *Jeanne d'Arc, l'histoire et la légende* (Paris, 1904).

45. Such is the version given in *L'Action française*, Feb. 18, 1909, p. 1, cont'd. Feb. 24, 1909, p.2. The pro-Republican *L'Action* of Feb 18, 1909 relegates the episode to p. 2, declares the "Thalamistes" victorious, and omits the humiliating details, as did other pro-Republican papers.

46. Michel Winock, "Jeanne d'Arc et les Juifs," *H-Histoire* 3 (1979), 227–37, examining such rhetorical strategies as that exhibited by Gaston Méry, "De Cauchon à Thalamas," *La Libre Parole*, 2 Dec. 1904, p. 1.

47. Thalamas's long and curious career would continue to be riddled with conflict, persecution, and disappointment up through the Vichy régime until his death in 1953. See Nadia Margolis, "La Chevauchée solitaire du professeur Thalamas: rationalistes et réactionnaires dans l'historiographie johannique (1904–1945)," *Bulletin de l'Association des Amis du Centre Jeanne d'Arc* 15 (1991), 7–28.

48. Philippe Contamine and others nowadays tend even to refer to *La Droite* in the plural, as in his "Jeanne d'Arc dans la mémoire des droites," in Jean-François Sirinelli, *Histoire des Droites en France* (Paris, 1992), vol. 2.

49. Goyau, a Right-wing polemicist, cited in Winock, *Lieux*, p. 684. For Joan's cult in her own time and thereafter, see Pierre Marot, *Le Culte de Jeanne d'Arc à Domrémy: Son origine et son développement* (Nancy, 1956).

50. This slogan I have derived from Julien Benda's 1927 classic polemic against the role of many French intellectuals, such as Maurras and Barrès, in betraying France and humanity during the Dreyfus Affair: *La Trahison des clercs*.

51. This summary based on Gildea, *The Past*, pp. 162–163.

52. *Le Chagrin et la pitié* was not aired on French television until 1981.

53. *Lacombe Lucien* was recently revived and shown in New York (1995), which may indicate interest in the Right as well as in Malle.

54. The revival of Michelet, and of interest in the politics of historiography in general—perhaps arising out of a need for a moderate voice in the face of extremist progress—is noticeable particularly in Britain and the U.S., whereas historiographical studies in France have appeared at a steadier pace. See, e.g., bibliographies to Lebovics, *True France*; Gildea, *The Past*; William R. Keylor, *Jacques Bainville and the Renaissance of Royalist History in Twentieth-Century France* (Baton Rouge, La. & London, 1979) and Arthur Mitzman, *Michelet, Historian* (New Haven & London, 1990) for evidence of this upsurge since the mid-1970's.

55. With the exception of Eugen Weber's work, especially the classic *Action Française* (Stanford, Ca., 1962) and René Rémond's *La Droite en France* (Paris, 1954), most of the best histories of the Right have only appeared over the past few years, and contain expanded discussions of Joan, e.g., Winock, *Lieux*; Winock, *Nationalisme, antisémitisme et fascisme en France* (Paris, 1990); Chiron, *Barrès*; Contamine, "Jeanne d'Arc dans la mémoire"; Gildea, *The Past*; Sirinelli, *Histoire des Droites*; and Robert

Tombs, ed., *Nationhood and Nationalism in France from Boulangism to the Great War* (New York & London, 1991). Notable exceptions: Marie-Claire Bancquart's ch. "Jeanne d'Arc et les écrivains français de 1870 à 1920," in her *Les Ecrivains et l'histoire d'après Maurice Barrès, Léon Bloy, Anatole France, Charles Péguy* (Paris, 1966) and others; the work of Zeev Sternhell from the 1970's, esp. *La Droite révolutionnaire: Les Origines françaises du fascisme 1885–1914* (Paris, 1978), has been reprinted, no doubt as a response to the current renewed interest in the Right.

EPILOGUE: JOAN OF ARC
OR THE SURVIVAL OF A PEOPLE

Régine Pernoud

We French have trouble realizing the importance of Joan of Arc in our history. Coming in the middle of the Hundred Years War, her epic lasted hardly more than two years, and from that we must deduct an entire year, from May 1430 to May 1431, when Joan was in prison. In March 1429, arriving at Chinon she had predicted, "I will last one year, hardly longer."

The impact of this peasant girl from the Lorraine may have been short and sudden, but the consequences of her character were decisive. She secured the survival of a France that was cut in two both by internal discords, such as the disputes between the Armagnacs and the Burgundians, and by methodical English invasion. France seemed doomed to disintegrate.

This was a threat not just to a geographic entity, the France that we know today, but to the whole of French civilization. In his *Oraisons funèbres*, André Malraux wrote about the stake in Rouen:

> With the first flame came an atrocious cry that would echo, in all Christian hearts, the cry of the Holy Virgin when she saw the Cross looming against the livid sky…. From what was the forest of Broceliande to the cemeteries of the Holy Land, the dead chivalry of old will rise from its tombs: in the silence of the darkest night, unfolding the hands of the reclining stone figures, the valiant knights of the Round Table and the companions of St. Louis, the first soldiers killed during the Fall of Jerusalem and the last loyal followers of the small leprous king. From their shadowed eyes, all the assembly of Christian dreams watched the flames rise that were to burn throughout the centuries, and they saw the motionless form that would become the burned corpse of chivalry.

"The burned corpse of chivalry ...." The French had invented chivalry. About 989, a number of lords and ladies—women as well as men were suzerains —met at Charroux Abbey and took an oath to respect the persons and goods of peasants, clerks, women, and paupers. Henceforth, these groups were protected by what was called the Peace of God. For the first time in history, a distinction between soldiers and the civilian population was established. The Peace of God was soon followed by other measures such as the Truce of God, which prohibited warfare and battles from the first Sunday of Advent (about twenty days before Christmas) until the octave of Epiphany, then from the first Sunday of Lent until the end of Easter week, and, before long, every week from Wednesday evening to Monday morning.

Chivalry itself was born in the twelfth century, when, in a religious ceremony, a knight would solemnly swear to lift his sword only to defend the weak. The ceremony was followed by a program of entertainment and chivalric tournaments. The knight was expected to have, according to the expression of the day, "an able body and a good soul," which meant being both brave and generous. The influence of chivalry on the literary sphere suggests its importance to the society of the day. One early romance, Chrétien de Troyes's *Perceval or the Tale of the Holy Grail*, depicts initiation into the chivalric life.

France in the twelfth and thirteenth centuries was a patchwork of domains, some bigger than and more-or-less independent of the others. One thread, however, runs through them all, and that is the commitment to those institutions of chivalry that permeated manners and inspired courtly poetry.

Chivalry was a demanding ideal. It required the surpassing of oneself; those who possessed strength were expected to put it to the service of the poor. We would be naive to believe that all knights respected this high ideal. Yet the ideal managed to remain vital for at least three centuries. In the thirteenth century, King Louis IX saw himself and was seen as gallant and chivalrous, while his biographer, Joinville, lived as a knight. During this time, no foreign wars were waged other than that to regain the Holy Land. The first venture outside the kingdom was the war waged by Philip III, the son of St. Louis, against Aragon, during which he lost his own life (1285). Except for the Albigensian Crusade and a few short-lived revolts, the lords' supposed continual warfare was confined to insignificant battles for personal ambition, which affected only a small portion of the land and involved few mercenary soldiers. Attention was generally directed to means of defense, rather than offense. In the twelfth century, the crossbow was banned as being too deadly; this ban was respected during a good part of the century. Architects also were preoccupied with defense: their concern resulted in the elaborate system of castles, fortresses, and other fortifications that can still be seen in France today. Offensive strategies were not developed until the early fourteenth century, and even though cannons appeared around 1326, they were rarely used during the remainder of the century. Since defense and fortification were main concerns, this time also marks the arrival of the suit of armor that we now consider typically "medieval": articulated armor plates that transformed the soldier himself into a walking fortress.

Although fourteenth-century warfare as practiced by the Black Prince and du Gueselin had long since ceased to be "chivalrous," the memory of chivalry persisted up to Joan of Arc's age, at least among the common folk. On May 8, 1429, Joan forbade the people to attack parts of the army besieging Orleans, "in honor of Holy Sunday." This use of Sunday Truce in the early fifteenth century—so long after the age of chivalry—is indeed touching.

The early fifteenth century witnessed some irreparable acts, among them the assassination in 1407 of the duke of Orleans by his own cousin, the duke of Burgundy. Such an act would have been considered monstrous in the thirteenth century and did in fact divide the population, causing civil war between Armagnac and Burgundy. This civil war made the English invasion possible. Even the presumed unity of the people of France was shattered. In the past, customs could differ from one domain to the next without undermining the perceived unity of the whole. Henceforth, and chroniclers emphasize the point, merely to refer to someone as an Armagnac when the Burgundians were in power was enough to doom or to ostracize him completely. This marks the first appearance of all those countless ideologies (for or against the Revolution, for or against the nation's invaders) that have so often divided the people of France.

Joan appeared when confusion was at its height. Students and academics deliberately took the side of the power supported by the Burgundians, and Paris was occupied. Normandy was practically reduced to English obedience, and the advance toward Orleans was formidable. The occupying power retained possession of Guyenne as well, and only in the Midi, especially in its "good cities," was the legitimate king favored, not the person who proclaimed himself "king of France and England." Joan of Arc was decisive in ending these all-embracing troubles, by liberating Orleans, and by consecrating in Reims the one king she believed could legitimately claim the crown.

Chivalry in France had declined. The turning point came in the reign of Philip the Fair, when in 1302 he attacked the county of Flanders, whose urban infantry routed his mounted knights at the battle of Courtrai. This disaster became known as the "Day of the Golden Spurs" after the spurs taken from the fallen French that the Flemish used to decorate their Church of Our Lady at Courtrai. The later orders of chivalry celebrated something different from the original chivalric ideal. These orders comprised high aristocracy selected by a lord or the king, and their banquets often degenerated into orgies. Meetings were mostly occasions to wear luxurious cloaks, to reunite the famous, and to organize splendid contests. Chivalric commitment was lost and during this century so charged with natural catastrophes and fratricidal wars French chivalry suffered only defeats, marked by names like Crécy, Calais, and Poitiers.

Joan of Arc seems to have revived chivalric fervor with her mission, such as her victory at Patay on June 18, 1429. This fervor was first evidenced by the sheer number of spontaneous followers ("they found themselves a great many because everyone followed her," noted an eyewitness), and it was confirmed by an enthusiasm for her victory that more than counterbalanced the disaster at Agincourt fourteen years earlier: five to six thousand English enemies killed to only two thousand on the French side. Patay secured the way to Reims, where the legitimate king would be crowned. Even after the death of Joan of Arc, the tide set in motion by her victories continued. Little by little, the conquered provinces freed themselves, with or without the help of Charles VII and his companions such as Dunois or Ambroise de Loré. Normandy became part of France again, freed first by jolts from "the Resistance" and revolt in some of its cities, including Rouen. The participation of an entire people, who had almost lost their independence, would soon invalidate the supposed case for Joan's condemnation. This was so at Orleans and also in the provinces where she originated, along the banks of the Meuse River: this survival of a nearly doomed people was brought about by Joan's extraordinary mission.

A people survived, but not a world, for Joan of Arc also marks the end of the world that had seen the birth of chivalry—and the end of what chivalry once had been, since for some one hundred and fifty years it had been reduced to a shadow, a caricature, of itself. The turning point had come with Philip the Fair, who surrounded himself with jurists and experts in Roman law instead of knights. These advisers brought with them the first ideologies that encouraged the dream of universal monarchy, a dream that led the way toward conquests. In our own century, the French poet Péguy perfectly understood the phenomenon, remarking that Joan thought Charles VII a gallant and chivalrous king when he was actually an administrator concerned with finances. Charles VII was the first to set up a state according to our vision today—his son would bring it to perfection —a state provided with a regular army under royal command and supplied with financial resources. Later, regional particularities disappeared as little by little common rules for all were established. The extraordinary variety of feudal France, where customs varied from one place to the next, would be obliterated. This was a slow process, of course; it would take three centuries of change before this unification would contribute to the Revolution of 1789. Among other things, the notion of private property was imposed, and the main features of this new world became sole authority, general laws, uniform administration throughout the land, and, to complete it all, public school. This is the world we live in today.

JOAN OF ARC AND HER DOCTORS

Marie-Véronique Clin

Joan of Arc's examinations and treatments by doctors and matrons constitute important evidence about both contemporary medical practices and Joan's physical health.

During her brief public life, Joan of Arc was treated by members of several health professions: barbers, surgeons, doctors, and matrons. A study of the situations under which she was examined and treated by these diverse professionals is revealing. Not only does it show early uses of some contemporary medical practices but, more important, it illustrates how the four professions either overlapped or were clearly delineated during this period. Doctors and surgeons, for example, were trained in different schools; their practices and even their social positions were different. Long before Joan of Arc's interaction with them, the roles of these professionals had undergone an intricate evolution.

After the fall of the Roman Empire and the subsequent period of invasions, medical learning in Europe was sustained by monasteries. A monk might be both a doctor and a surgeon. Eventually, the placement of hospitals in the shadows of cathedrals emphasized the canon's role as a doctor. Especially during the earlier Middle Ages, women also played a crucial role in both the practice and the theory of medicine: we might remember that the first hospital was founded in fourth-century Italy by a woman named Fabiola.

Throughout the eleventh and twelfth centuries, physicians were educated and trained in the house of a master and in the hospital. Both men and women could be doctors/surgeons. Because they inspected (*miraient*) urine in a uroscope, a male doctor became known as a *mire*; a female, a *miresse*. In the archives of the Parlement of

Paris, we find women, like men, paying taxes in order to receive authorization to practice their profession. Tax records found in the Taille de Paris in 1313 indicate that an Ameline la miresse had established herself on the rue Porée in Paris.[1] In 1136, another woman, Heluidis, called medica, is recorded as treating the wounds and sores of the poor in the parish of Saint-Martin de Fives in the north of France.[2]

The Third Lateran Council forbade priests and canons to practice surgery, and thus the roles of those who treated the body were separated from that of the men who salved the soul. In addition, and bit by bit, the profession of doctor and surgeon diverged. Jean Pitard, a surgeon of Louis IX (1226–74), established the Brotherhood of St. Cosmas and St. Damian in order to educate surgeons. Two types of surgeons evolved from this, "short-robed surgeons" and "long-robed surgeons." The short-robed surgeon was a barber, limited to treating wounds and bumps. Long-robed surgeons were members of the Brotherhood of St. Cosmas and St. Damian; its strict statutes required initiates to learn Latin and anatomy.[3] Women with a "short-robed" practice were called barbières. In Paris in 1292, Emeline, from the parish of Saint-Pierre, and Emengart, in the parish of Saint-Séverin, were practicing barbières.[4] After the establishment of a faculty of medicine at the University of Paris in 1238, medicine became an accredited discipline, and since women were forbidden to participate in university life the number of women doctors and surgeons swiftly declined. By the thirteenth century, women were subject to lawsuits if they undertook the practice of medicine. Ameline la miresse, who was living in Paris on the rue Guillaume Porée in 1313, was formally prosecuted in 1324–25, as was Agnès Avescot in 1322.[5] It should be noted, however, that in 1479 a cirurgienne, a female surgeon, was chosen to give Louis XI an enema, thus demonstrating that eventually, if rarely, there was some mechanism in place that allowed women to practice surgery.

Long before Joan's time, then, women were confined to certain gynecological and obstetrical roles, especially as midwives and judges of virginity. After the establishment of the medical faculty, women, increasingly limited to domestic roles, were sometimes allowed to work with their husbands, but they were forbidden to practice the intellectual professions independently.

The records of Joan of Arc's three trials—Poitiers, the condemnation, and the nullification—reveal some aspects of contemporary medical practice. The first evidence concerns barbers and surgeons. Joan was injured twice, first between the neck and the shoulder, then in the thigh. Her first injury was sustained during the battle of Orleans. On the battlefield, some soldiers suggested to Joan that through miraculous or magical incantations she could cure herself, but she refused. Her chaplain, Jean Pasquerel, testified during the nullification trial:

> "On May 7, during the assault on Les Tourelles, Joan was wounded by an arrow in the breast, as she had predicted. When she realized that she had been injured, she was afraid and began to cry. But as she told us, she was comforted by her voices. Olive oil and bacon fat were applied to her wound. Then, crying and weeping, she confessed to me."[6]

In other records from this trial, the Bastard of Orleans said "that Joan's injury was between the neck and the shoulder and half a foot deep."[7] The third person who mentioned this first wound was Jean d'Aulon, Joan's squire, who testified: "On that day I heard Joan saying: 'In the name of God, we shall enter the city tonight across the bridge!' and we did so; in the city, I had her treated because she had been wounded."[8] At night, a second medical practitioner, a surgeon, made a proper dressing for the wound in the house of Jacques Boucher, treasurer of the duke of Orleans.

We know, therefore, that a barber dressed Joan's wound with oil and fat. Today, we know that olive oil is good for burns and helps resist gangrene. We know, further, that olive gum guards against fever and that binding wounds with bacon assists healing.

The second wound Joan sustained was in the battle before Paris. She was swiftly restored to full health. In gratitude, she gave to the church of Saint-Denis à la Chapelle a complete set of armor that she had taken from a prisoner.[9] During the condemnation trial, her inquisitors accused her of using mandrake as a healing charm to cure the wound, but she denied it emphatically.[10]

Four licensed doctors saw Joan in Rouen, and we know something of their lives and practices. The first was Guillaume de la Chambre, a licentiate in Medicine (Guillermo de Camera in medicina licenciato),[11] who gave a deposition in the nullification trial. In 1416–17, he matriculated in the faculty of medicine in Paris; he came back ten years later to take his degree and became a "master" in 1436. He served as dean of the faculty from 1448 to 1450. De la Chambre had good relations with the English. In 1436, his name appeared on a list of bourgeois and other inhabitants of Paris who had sworn to abide by the treaty of Troyes. He was among the first of Rouen's English collaborators to greet Charles VII: first in 1448, then in 1450. The University of Paris chose him as its representative at Joan's nullification trial.

Jean Tiphaine received a bachelor's degree in medicine in Paris in 1416 ; he took his license and master's degrees in 1418.[12] The following year, he was named a Regent Master (tenured professor). As a priest, Jean Tiphaine was required to receive special dispensation from the pope in order to teach medicine. He died about 1469. In the 1420s and 1430s, he was on good terms with the invader, so much so that Henry V named him chaplain of the castle of Caen in 1422. In 1432, he served as canon of the cathedral of Rouen. During this period, his successful career culminated in such appointments as that of doctor to the duchess of Somerset, wife of the English governor of Normandy.

Both Guillaume de la Chambre and Jean Tiphaine explained at the nullification trial that they were required, under threat by the English, to assist at the earlier trial. Even then, they took pains to claim that their sole role was the professional one of providing diagnoses of her illnesses.

The third physician, Guillaume des Jardins (Guillermus Gardinis), was born in 1370 in Caudebec-en-Caux.[13] A scholar from the faculty of medicine of Paris, he received his bachelor's degree in 1406 and two years later his license and master's degrees. Named canon of the churches of Bayeux and Rouen by Henry V in 1421, he returned to Normandy, but he died in 1438 before he could give his testimony in the nullification trial.

The last doctor was Roland l'Escripvain (Rollandus Scriptoris).[14] Rector of the University of Paris in 1406, he was appointed Regent Master in 1424. By 1438–39, he had become doctor to the duke of Burgundy. He sat at the condemnation trial on March 3, 1431, but he, too, died before his evidence could be heard at the nullification trial.

CONTEMPORARY MEDICAL PRACTICE

Guillaume de la Chambre, Jean Tiphaine, Guillaume des Jardins, and Roland l'Escripvain were twice asked to examine Joan when she was a prisoner in Rouen. The "venerable Master" Guillaume de la Chambre, then forty-eight years old, tells us that Henry Beaufort, bishop of Thérouanne and the cardinal of England, who was a brother of the earl of Warwick, asked these doctors to attend to Joan and heal her, since he did not want her to die from natural causes. As Warwick declared, he had paid dearly for Joan and he wanted to see to it that she was judged and burned.[15] He urged the doctors to examine her carefully and cure her.

The doctors palpated her and felt her pulse, which was then common technical practice. Guillaume de la Chambre adds that he saw Joan almost naked and could declare according to medical science that she was a virgin and intact; as he palpated her lower abdomen, he found that she was stricta, that is, narrow in the hips.[16] This is a rare record of an instance of a type of medical examination that would subsequently disappear; for several centuries afterward, the diseased body would not be touched. As a result of the examination, the physicians informed Warwick that Joan needed to be bled. Warwick warned them: "Take care; she is sly and could deliberately injure herself to death."

During Joan's second illness at Rouen, the same doctors were summoned. Jean Tiphaine learned that Joan had been vomiting and had a fever. Joan herself told them about her illness, saying that she had eaten a carp sent to her by Cauchon. During that visit, Jean d'Estivet responded to the implication that she had been poisoned by attacking her: "You whore, you have eaten salted fishes and other things you knew were bad for you." She was upset by these accusations and replied that they were not true.[17] Bleeding was recommended on that visit as well.

The last examination was performed by matrons, who twice inspected Joan to see if she was a virgin. She always called herself "Jeanne La Pucelle," "Joan the virgin"; it was crucial to the court to determine whether she was lying. Had she been demonstrated to be nonvirginal, her entire cause would have immediately been discredited. Virginity was essential to Joan and her mission. She said at her trial: "The first time I heard my voices, I promised God that I would remain a virgin."[18] Early in her public life, first at Poitiers in

1429, two matrons examined Joan. Both of them, Jeanne de Preuilly, madame de Gaucourt, and Jeanne de Mortemer, madame de Trèves, (wife of Robert le Maçon, chancellor of France) reported that she was a virgin. During the condemnation trial in Rouen, the English not only alleged that she was not a virgin but also called her a camp-follower, a whore. Joan was so upset by these allegations that she insisted on being officially examined by matrons, both to prove her veracity and to give assurance that she was properly named "Joan the virgin."[19] Jean Marcel recollects: "The duchess of Bedford asked women to examine Joan, and they concluded she was both a virgin and a woman."[20] One of the matrons who determined Joan's virginal status was named Anne Bavon. Jean Monet testified as well to Joan's status, adding that her buttocks had become calloused from riding horses.

We do not know when the examination took place during the condemnation trial, but it must have been during the early days of January, because the duchess of Bedford left Rouen by the end of that month. It is important to emphasize that the duchess was so impressed by Joan and so protective of her virginity that she not only forbade the male guards and soldiers to touch Joan but she also extended that requirement to include men of rank. Even the imperious Cauchon could not forget the advice of the duchess of Bedford, who was, after all, the sister of the duke of Burgundy and the wife of the most important English noble in France, the regent Bedford.

Of all the examinations by the health professionals of her time, the ones that have had the most impact on Joan of Arc's future reputation were those that verified her virginity. On May 29, 1431, when Cauchon found Joan relapsed, he called her "a woman, Joan, named the Pucelle."[21] And yet Cauchon did not incorporate this information about Joan's virginity—information verified by the nullification trial— into the records of the condemnation trial.[22] Apparently, Cauchon felt it was just as politically expedient to keep Joan's virginity intact as it was to suppress the repeatedly obtained medical knowledge of her sexual purity from the official record.

NOTES

1. Ernest Wickersheimer, *Dictionnaire biographique des médecins en France au moyen âge* (Paris, 1979), vol. 1, p. 21.

2. Ibid., vol. 1, p. 273.

3. Edouard Nicaise, *Premiers statuts des chirurgiens de Paris* (Paris, 1893).

4. Wickersheimer, vol. 1, p. 129.

5. Ibid., vol. 1, p. 10.

6. Pierre Duparc, ed., *Procès en nullité de la condamnation de Jeanne d'Arc,* 5 vols.(Paris, 1977–88), vol. 1, p. 395. "In quo insultu et post prandium; ipsa Johanna, sicut predixerat, fuit percussa de una sagitta supra mammam, et dum sensit se vulneratam, timuit et flevit, et fuit consolata, ut dicebat. ... Et apposuerunt eidem vulneri oleum olivarum cum lardo, et post hujusmodi appositionem ipsa Johanna confessa est loquenti, flendo et lamentando."

7. Ibid., vol. 1, p. 320: "... dicta Johanna fuit vulnerata ex una sagitta, que penetravit carnem suam inter collum et spatulas, de quantitate dimidii pedis."

8. Ibid., vol. 1, p. 484: "Et dit il qui parle que ce jour mesme il avoit ouy dire à ladicte Pucelle: "En nom Dé, on entrera ennuyt en la ville par le pont.." Et ce fait, se retrahirent icelle Pucelle et sesdictes gens en ladicte ville d'Orléans, en laquelle il qui parle la fist habiller; car elle avoit esté bleciée d'un traict audit assault."

9. Pierre Tisset with Yvonne Lanhers, eds., *Procès de condamnnation de Jeanne d'Arc*, 3 vols.(Paris, 1960–71), vol. 1, p. 170. Saturday, March 17: "Respondit quod hoc fuit ex devocione, sicut consuetum est apud homines armorum quando sunt lesi; et quia fuerat lesa coram villa Parisiensi, obtulit ea Sancto Dionisio, propter hoc quod est clamor Francie."

10. Ibid., vol. 1, p. 199: "Ad hunc articulum, de mandragora, negat omnino."

11. Wickersheimer, vol. 1, p. 249.

12. Ibid., vol. 2, p. 491.

13. Ibid., vol. 1, p. 239.

14. Ibid., vol. 2, p. 723.

15. Duparc, vol. 1, p. 351. Guillaume de la Chambre: "Et tunc ipse comes de Warwic dixit eisdem quod ipsa Johanna fuerat infirma, ut sibi fuerat relatum, et quod eos mandaverat ut de ea cogitarent, quia pro nullo rex volebat quod sua morte naturali moreretur; rex enim eam habebat caram, et care emerat, nec volebat quod obiret, nisi cum justicia, et quod esset combusta."

16. Ibid., vol. 1, p. 350: "Et scit ipse loquens, prout percipere potuit secundum artem medicine, quod erat incorrupta et virgo, quia eam vidit quasi nudam, cum visitaret eam de quadam infirmitate; eam palpavit in renibus, et erat multum stricta, quantum percipere potuit ex aspectu."

17. Ibid., vol. 1, p. 349: "Que respondit quod sibi fuerat missa quedam carpa per epsicopum Belvacensem, de qua comederat, et dubitabat quod esset causa sue infirmitatis; et tunc ipse de Estiveto ibidem presens redarguit eam, dicendo quod male dicebat; et vocavit eam paillardam, dicendo: 'Tu paillarda, comedisti halleca et alia tibi contraria.' Cui ipsa respondit quod non fecerat; et habuerunt ad invicem ipsa Johanna et Estiveto multa verba injuriosa. Postmodum tamen ipse loquens, peramplius scire volens de ipsius Johanne infirmitate, audivit ab aliquibus ibidem presentibus quod ipsa passa fuerat multum vomitum."

18. Tisset, vol. 1, p. 123. Monday, March 12: "Item dicit quod, prima vice qua audivit vocem suam, ipsa vovit servare virginitatem suam, tamdiu quamdiu (placeret) Deo; et erat in etate XIII annorum vel circiter."

19. Duparc, vol. 1, p. 448. Jean Lefèvre: "sed bene scit quod, quadam vice, cum interrogaretur cur se vocabat Puellam, et si talis esset, respondit: 'Ego possum bene dicere quia talis sum; et, si non credatis, faciatis me visitari per mulieres.' Offerebat se promptam ad visitationem recipiendum, dum tamen fieret per mulieres honestas, ut consuetum est."

20. Duparc, vol 1, p. 379: "Quod audivit dici quod domina de Bethfort eamdem Johannam fecit visitari an esset virgo vel non, et quod inventa fuit virgo."

21. Tisset, vol. 2, p. 354: " Pierre … Pour certaines causes et raisons à exprimer plus amplement, une femme, Jeanne, communément appelée la Pucelle.…"

22. Duparc, vol. 1, p. 455. Andreas Marguerie: "Scit tamen quod, durante processu, reputabatur virgo."

ASPECTS OF MATERIAL CULTURE
IN THE PARIS REGION AT THE TIME
OF JOAN OF ARC

Nicole Meyer Rodrigues

Extensive archeological research in the historical center of Saint-Denis over the past twenty years provides a major corpus of artifact evidence for material culture in the Paris area at the beginning of the fifteenth century.

Since 1973, the historic center of Saint-Denis, a town located nine kilometers north of Paris, has undergone extensive urban redevelopment, providing archeologists with a once-in-a-lifetime opportunity to undertake a major archeological research program. More than a quarter of the old town, an area of approximately thirty-two acres to the north of the royal basilica, has been covered by rescue excavation. In 1982, a permanent Town Archeological Unit was established to deal with archeology within the town as a whole: at present, following completion of the excavation program within the redevelopment area, staff are working primarily on collected data. A series of scientific final reports is planned, the first of which, the "Historical Atlas of Saint-Denis," will be published in 1996.[1] Six hundred of the many artifacts that have been unearthed are already on display in the town museum.

The excavations, performed without interruption for twenty years under the direction of Olivier Meyer, concerned primarily the period covering the sixth century to the sixteenth. The results have provided precious data to increase our knowledge of medieval Saint-Denis in three main areas: historical topography, urban craft industry, and material culture. The area excavated, located to the north of the basilica, constitutes a key site where it is possible to study the simultaneous evolution of the ecclesiastical quarter (abbey, basilica, cemetery, and churches) to the south and the civil district (houses and craft industries) to the north. Archeology has provided direct and indirect evidence for urban craft industries, such as cobblers, furriers, and goldsmiths; the existence of potters' workshops is particularly well documented. The more than thirty thousand small finds form an outstanding corpus of material evidence of everyday life in medieval times.

When using the evidence from these excavations to describe certain aspects of the material culture in the Paris region at the time of Joan of Arc, we have to bear in mind the special status of the site. We are dealing with a city that was closely dependent upon its powerful abbey, frequented by monarchs and other important visitors, and that benefited from the Lendit Fair whose success is linked to the expansion of Paris. It is possible that these two factors led to the gentrification of part of the Saint-Denis population as demonstrated by the many high-quality archeological finds. In 1356, the abbot allowed the inhabitants to build a defensive wall around the town to protect it from the English. An increase in population density within the city walls can be observed during this same period. This phenomenon is no doubt the result of the increased sense of security provided by the fortifications.

The oldest surviving map of Saint-Denis—the 1575 Belleforest Perspective (fig.1)—shows us a town that still has a generally rural appearance: there are many gardens and vineyards, and willow plantations surround the marshy areas. Although written sources seem to indicate that the city remained prosperous during the first half of the Hundred Years War, Saint-Denis suffered twenty-six years of disasters from 1410 until 1436. As with many towns, this was a time of significant demographic, economic, and material decline. The whole region was devastated, but Saint-Denis's situation was particularly dramatic: the town was the theater of violent confrontation as a result of its strategic position commanding the northern access to Paris and the presence of the royal coronation regalia in the abbey treasurehouse.

Archeological evidence for the material culture of those troubled times at the beginning of the fifteenth century comes from two main types of context: first, cellars, cesspits, and other structures used as rubbish dumps, and, second, deposits from the old town river, the

Croult. These wet, oxygen-free environments preserve organic materials and consequently provide a comprehensive sample of objects from everyday life. As is often the case, finds related to eating are best represented, and pottery predominates.

Although pots were still being made in Saint-Denis at the beginning of the fifteenth century, the pottery industry that had been present in the city since the twelfth century was in decline.[2] It is likely that the local pottery, composed of porous sand, was being challenged by stoneware from Beauvais, which was more water-tight and better suited to transporting and storing liquids. Archeological contexts indicate that mugs, jugs, and waterbottles from Beauvais appeared in Saint-Denis during the second half of the fourteenth century. Food was cooked in large single-handle pots called *coquemars* (fig. 2). Examples of *coquemars* from the beginning of the fifteenth century show glazing on both the base and the part of the pot opposite the handle. The glaze was used to protect the pots from the fire and to make them easier to clean. Pottery imitations of metal cauldrons, rarely found in excavations, also existed, while skillets, generally glazed on the inside, seem to have been used more for food preparation than for actual cooking. Handleless jars, called *oules*, were the general-purpose pots during the Middle Ages, but at this late date they seem to be used only for storage, to which function their typical collared rim is well-suited. Crocks, whose capacity can be as much as ten or twelve liters, were used to take drink to the table. This type of pot can sometimes be seen in miniatures in front of the banqueting table. Drinking glasses of this period are also found, their presence indicating urban life of some quality. Glasses with a long stem and ribbed cup, typical at the end of the fourteenth century, are still found,[3] but around the turn of the century glasses with a tulip-shaped cup and ribbed goblets appear (fig. 3). Some glass shards indicate the presence of carafes, and one example of a pewter ewer, with a swan's-neck spout, has been found (fig. 4). Jugs were also used for drinking (fig. 5); at this period, the glaze covers only a small part of the pot and the applied decorative strips are roughly made. A tradition of highly decorated ware still exists, however, represented by multicolored jugs decorated with applied strips forming, for example, flowers, grapes, or wave patterns.

Although tableware also included wide-mouthed vessels, pottery bowls and goblets are uncommon in the archeological record. On the other hand, clear evidence for the use of wooden platters has survived; the owner's mark was sometimes stamped on the base using a red-hot iron (fig. 6). Examples of pewter trenchers and dishes are also rare (fig. 7). Spoons were usually made of wood, typically boxwood, and had turned stems. Examples made from copper alloy are less frequently found but generally have a stem decorated with an acorn knob. Knife handles were made of either wood or bone.

Distinctive lobed cups (fig. 8) appeared at Saint-Denis toward the end of the twelfth century and were still in use in the fifteenth century. It remains unclear whether these "cups" were simply used for drinking or used at table as condiment dishes. The table was sometimes adorned with vessels that were both functional and decorative, as is the case for saltcellars, which are known from at least the fourteenth century. One such example portrays a bagpiper (fig. 9): the bagpipe, a wind instrument carrying connotations of flatulence and its accompanying ribald humor, constitutes a motif well suited to the atmosphere of a medieval banquet.[4]

Archeology has also provided documentation for other groups of domestic objects such as the circular fire-cover or curfew (fig. 10) which was intended to gather together and cover the embers of a central hearth to prevent them from going out and to protect the house against fire. The red-painted flame decoration is to be found on much everyday pottery in the Paris area during the Middle Ages. Pottery lamps generally have a long stem with a small dish to catch oil dripping from the wick.[5] Although no complete item of furniture has been found in excavations, it is possible that parts of furniture, such as chests or dressers, will be identified among the many thousands of pieces of wood that were found in the urban river deposits and which are presently being studied.

Cosmetic accessories are best represented by the double-sided combs made of boxwood or bone, yet objects made from other materials include copper-alloy tweezers or cosmetic sets composed of tweezers, an earscoop, and a toothpick. The archeological documentation also includes ten examples of mirror cases: they were made from wood, ivory, or lead-tin alloy (fig. 11). Of particular interest is an ivory pin or pointer, probably used for parting hair (fig. 12).

Surviving evidence for dress is restricted to various metal accessories such as brooches, beads, buttons, lace-tags, buckles, and strap-ends. Leather straps and belts have been found with copper-alloy decoration—mounts and spangles (fig. 13)—and chain or pendant tags. Thousands of fragments of leather shoes were recovered during excavations of the old town river, which had served as a dump for used shoes and scraps from cobblers' workshops. A study of this corpus of material is in progress and will ultimately enable researchers to draw up a shoe typology for the late Middle Ages. At present, only a few of the more outstanding examples have been restored and resewn (fig. 14). Other leather artifacts include purses and scabbards that are often stamped with floral or heraldic decorations or with motifs taken from the medieval imaginary bestiary. Evidence for trade and exchange comes from coins of different origins and also from tokens, made from a lead-tin alloy and cast in stone molds. A further indication is the presence of ivory, or wooden, writing tablets with their copper-alloy *styli*.

The importance of Saint-Denis as both a shrine and a place of devout worship meant that the town was a major pilgrimage center. Written sources describe the pilgrims' visits but their presence is also reflected through the tiny devotional objects, pilgrims' badges, that they left behind. These thin metal plates, molded in a lead-tin alloy, were sewn or pinned on the hat or cloak: one such example (fig. 15) portrays a crucifixion scene in which we can see St. Denis on the left, the Virgin Mary on the right, and two pilgrims with their staffs below.

The study of these many finds is now in progress. When this phase of the research program is completed, the results will be compared with written sources, in particular the *Livre vert*.[6] This town customary, written in 1411, will provide considerable information concerning economic activity in Saint-Denis at the time of Joan of Arc and complete the contribution that archeology has given to our knowledge of the material culture of this period.[7]

NOTES

1. *Atlas historique de Saint-Denis*, ed. Michaël Wyss, (Documents d'Archéologie Française, 1996).

2. Nicole and Olivier Meyer, "Analyse de la distribution de la céramique dans les stratigraphies d'habitat de Saint-Denis," in *La céramique (Ve–XIXe s.) Fabrication—Commercialisation—Utilisation—Actes du Ier*

Congrès International d'Archéologie Médiévale (Paris, 1985; Société d'Archéologie Médiévale, Caen 1987), pp. 43–53.

3. Nicole Meyer, "La verrerie de Saint-Denis," in *A travers le verre du Moyen Age à la Renaissance, catalogue of the exhibition, Rouen* (Musées et Monuments Départementaux de la Seine-Maritime, Rouen, 1989), pp. 370–81.

4. Catherine Homo-Lechner, "De l'usage de la cornemuse dans les banquets : quelques exemples du XIVe au XVI siècle," *Imago musicae* (1987), 111–19.

5. Annie Lefèvre and Nicole Meyer, "Les lampes en céramique des fouilles urbaines de Saint-Denis," *Archéologie médiévale* 18 (1988), 73–111. Thus far, two hundred lamps or fragments from the Merovingian period to the sixteenth century have been found in Saint-Denis.

6. *Le livre vert de Saint-Denis* (Archives Nationales, LL 1209–11).

7. I would like to thank David Coxall and Evelyn Perry for their advice and their help with the English version of this paper.

FIGURES

Fig. 1 *Pourtraict de la ville de Saint-Denis en France* in 1575. F. de Belleforest. Cosmographie universelle. . . . (Chesneau, Paris, 1575), pp. 280–81.

Fig. 2 *Coquemars*, first half of the fifteenth century. (Document: Unité d'Archéologie de la Ville de Saint-Denis; photograph: E. Jacquot).

Fig. 3 Ribbed goblet, first half of the fifteenth century. (Document: Unité d'Archéologie de la Ville de Saint-Denis; photograph: E. Jacquot).

Fig. 4 Pewter ewer, first half of the fifteenth century. The stamp of a fourteenth-century token bearing the inscription *ave maria gracia plena* is attached to the internal face of the lid. (Document: Unité d'Archéologie de la Ville de Saint-Denis; photograph: E. Jacquot).

Fig. 5 Jug with yellowish lead-based glaze and applied strips, first half of the fifteenth century. (Document: Unité d'Archéologie de la Ville de Saint-Denis; photograph: O. Meyer).

Fig. 6 Wooden platter: turned with an "S" stamped on the base, late fourteenth–early fifteenth century. (Document: Unité d'Archéologie de la Ville de Saint-Denis; photograph: E. Jacquot).

Fig. 7   Pewter dish and trencher with knife blade cuts, first half of the fifteenth century. (Document: Unité d'Archéologie de la Ville de Saint-Denis; photograph: E. Jacquot).

Fig. 8   Lobed cup with yellow lead-base glaze, late fourteenth century–early fifteenth century. (Document: Unité d'Archéologie de la Ville de Saint-Denis; photograph: E. Jacquot).

Fig. 9   Saltcellar with green lead-based glaze portraying a bagpiper, late fourteenth century–early fifteenth century. (Document: Unité d' Archéologie de la Ville de Saint-Denis; photograph: E. Jacquot).

Fig. 10   Circular fire-cover or curfew for a central hearth, late fourteenth century–early fifteenth century. (Document: Unité d'Archéologie de la Ville de Saint-Denis; photograph: O. Meyer).

Fig. 11   Mirror case made from a lead-tin alloy, late fourteenth century–early fifteenth century. (Document: Unité d'Archéologie de la Ville de Saint-Denis; photograph: O. Meyer).

Fig. 12   Ivory pin or pointer, late fourteenth or early fifteenth century. (Document: Unité d'Archéologie de la Ville de Saint-Denis; photograph: E. Jacquot).

Fig. 13   Mounts, spangle, terminal pendants made from copper-alloy, late fourteenth century–early fifteenth century. (Document: Unité d'Archéologie de la Ville de Saint-Denis; photograph: E. Jacquot).

Fig. 14 *Poulaine*. Leather, first half of the fifteenth century. (Document: Unité d'Archéologie de la Ville de Saint-Denis; photograph: E. Jacquot).

Fig. 15   Pilgrim badges portraying the Crucifixion, fourteenth century–early fifteenth century. (Document: Unité d'Archéologie de la Ville de Saint-Denis; photograph: E. Jacquot).

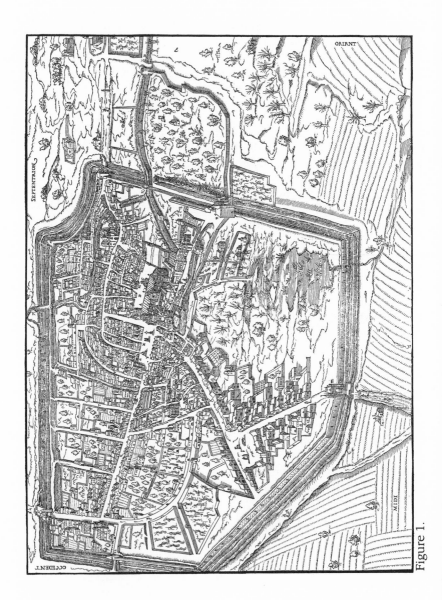

ORIRNT

SEPTENTRION

OCCIDENT

MIDI

Figure 1.

Figure 2.

Figure 3.

Figure 4.

Figure 5.

Figure 6.

Figure 7.

Figure 8.

Figure 9.

Figure 10.

Figure 11.

Figure 12.

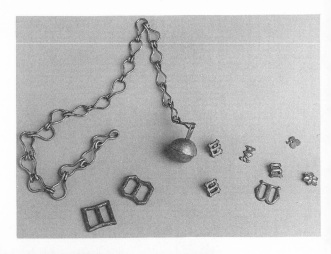

Figure 13.

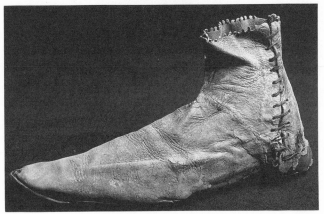

Figure 14.

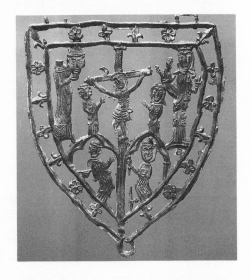

Figure 15.

CONTRIBUTORS

Olivier Bouzy holds a doctorate in medieval history and specializes in eighth- to twelfth-century armament. He has been assistant director of the Centre Jeanne d'Arc in Orléans since 1988 and junior lecturer at the University of Orléans since 1993.

Marie-Véronique Clin is director of the Musée d'Histoire de la Médecine in Paris, and she was formerly associate director of the Centre Jeanne d'Arc in Orléans. She co-authored *Jeanne d'Arc* with Régine Pernoud (Paris, 1986).

Kelly DeVries received his doctorate from the Centre for Medieval Studies at the University of Toronto and is associate professor of history at Loyola College in Maryland. He is the author of *Medieval Military Technology* and the forthcoming *Discipline, Tactics, and Technology: Infantry Warfare in the Early Fourteenth Century.*

Jean Fraikin, editor of *Tradition wallonne*, directs the Department of Ethnology and Regional Languages for the Ministry of Culture in Brussels.

Deborah Fraioli is associate professor of French at Simmons College. She has written about Joan of Arc for *Harvard Magazine*, *Speculum*, CNRS, and the *Bulletin des amis du Centre Jeanne d'Arc*. She has also written about the authenticity controversy in the Abelard-Heloise correspondence in *Falschungen im Mittelalter* (*Monumenta Germaniae Historica*).

Kevin J. Harty is professor of English at La Salle University in Philadelphia. He has previously published essays on Chaucer, Robert Henryson, medieval drama, film treatments of King Arthur, and cinematic responses to the AIDS pandemic. He is co-author with John Keenan of *Writing for Business and Industry* and editor of several works including *Cinema Arthuriana: Essays on Arthurian Film.*

Henry Ansgar Kelly is professor of English at UCLA. He has long been interested in questions of due process in inquisitorial proceedings, having published, among other works, *The Matrimonial Trials of Henry VIII* (1976), "English Kings and the Fear of Sorcery," (*Mediaeval Studies*, 1977), and, most recently, "The Right to Remain Silent: Before and After Joan of Arc" (*Speculum*, 1993).

Anne D. Lutkus, who holds a doctorate in French Literature from Indiana University, is language coordinator in the Department of Modern Languages and Cultures, University of Rochester.

Christine McWebb is a doctoral candidate in French medieval literature who specializes in Christine de Pizan at the University of Western Ontario.

Nadia Margolis received her Ph.D. from Stanford and also trained at the Sorbonne in medieval French literature and language. She is currently writing about Christine de Pizan, whose poetry she has also translated. Her bibliography *Joan of Arc in History, Literature, and Film* was published by Garland Publishing (New York, 1990).

Gertrude H. Merkle received her Ph.D. in Comparative Literature from Harvard (1988) and teaches at the University of Bridgeport. Her essay "Les odes dans *Jeanne d'Arc au bûcher*" appeared in *Paul Claudel: les odes* (Albion Press, 1994).

Nicole Meyer Rodrigues was named director of the Unité d'Archéologie at Saint-Denis in 1994 after twenty years there as head archeologist responsible for objects from urban excavations. She is a member of the Société Nationale des Antiquaires de France.

Régine Pernoud is author of more than forty books on Joan of Arc. She was the founding director of the Centre Jeanne d'Arc in Orléans.

Jane Marie Pinzino is a Ph.D. candidate in Religious Studies at the University of Pennsylvania who is finishing her dissertation on the rehabilitation trial arguments in favor of Joan as mystic, prophet, and warrior.

Susan Schibanoff writes on medieval and early-modern literature, and her recent work focuses on late-medieval European responses to heresy, homosexuality, and the East. She is professor of English and Women's Studies at the University of New Hampshire, where she teaches a course on Joan of Arc in literature, film, art, and music.

Karen Sullivan is assistant professor of Medieval Literature at Bard College. She has recently completed a book on Joan of Arc's trial at Rouen.

Julia M. Walker is associate professor of English at the State University of New York at Geneseo. She is editor of *Milton and the Idea of Women* (University of Illinois Press, 1988) and has published articles on Donne, Spenser, Milton, and Elizabeth I.

Steven Weiskopf is a Ph.D. candidate at Indiana University who has received a Fulbright award and is completing his dissertation on "The Masculine Hysterical Narrative in Late Medieval and Early Modern England."

Bonnie Wheeler is director of the Medieval Studies Program at Southern Methodist University. She writes about late-medieval literature and culture and is the editor of the quarterly *Arthuriana*.

Charles T. Wood is Daniel Webster Professor of History at Dartmouth College and author of, among other studies, *Joan of Arc and Richard III* (New York, 1988).